SUPERVISION OF POLICE PERSONNEL

SUPERVISION OF POLICE PERSONNEL

EIGHTH EDITION

Nathan F. Iannone
Inspector (Ret.)
Los Angeles Police Department
Professor Emeritus
Fullerton College, Fullerton, California

Marvin D. Iannone
Chief of Police (Ret.)
Beverly Hills, California
Assistant Chief of Police (Ret.)
Los Angeles Police Department

Jeff Bernstein
President, Bernstein and Associates
Sergeant (Ret.)
Miami Beach Police Department

PEARSON

Boston   Columbus   Indianapolis   New York   San Francisco   Upper Saddle River   Amsterdam
Cape Town   Dubai   London   Madrid   Milan   Munich   Paris   Montréal   Toronto   Delhi
Mexico City   São Paulo   Sydney   Hong Kong   Seoul   Singapore   Taipei   Tokyo

Vice President and Executive Publisher:
  Vernon Anthony
Senior Acquisitions Editor: Sara Eilert
Editorial Assistant: Lynda Cramer
Media Project Manager: Karen Bretz
Director of Marketing: David Gesell
Marketing Manager: Mary Salzman
Senior Marketing Coordinator: Alicia Wozniak
Production Manager: Fran Russello

Creative Director: Jayne Conte
Cover Design: Karen Salzbach
Cover Illustration/Photo: Fotolia: © ia_64
Full-Service Project Management/Composition:
  Mogana Sundaramurthy/Integra Software
  Services Pvt. Ltd.
Printer/Binder: Edwards Brothers Malloy
Cover Printer: Lehigh Phoenix

Credits and acknowledgments borrowed from other sources and reproduced, with permission, in this textbook appear on the appropriate page within text.

Library of Congress Cataloging-in-Publication Data
Iannone, N. F.
  Supervision of police personnel / Nathan F. Iannone, Inspector (Ret.), Los Angeles Police Department,
  Professor Emeritus, Fullerton College, Fullerton, California,
Marvin D. Iannone,
  Chief of Police (Ret.), Beverly Hills, California, Assistant Chief of Police (Ret.), Los Angeles
  Police Department,
Jeff Bernstein,
  President, Bernstein and Associates, Sergeant (Ret.), Miami Beach Police Department.—Eighth Edition.
    pages cm
Includes bibliographical references and index.
  ISBN-13: 978-0-13-297382-3 (alk. paper)
  ISBN-10: 0-13-297382-0 (alk. paper)
  1. Police—Supervision of—United States.   2. Police administration—United States.   I. Iannone,
  Marvin D.   II. Bernstein, Jeff   III. Title.
  HV7936.S8I2 2014
  363.2'20973—dc23

                                                                                    2012044717

10 9 8 7 6 5 4 3 2 1

PEARSON

ISBN-10:   0-13-297382-0
ISBN-13: 978-0-13-297382-3

brief contents

1

The Supervisor's Role   1

2

The Supervisor's Function in
Organization, Administration, and
Management   13

3

Leadership, Supervision, and
Command Presence   32

4

The Training Function: Problems
and Approaches to the
Instructional Process   69

5

Interpersonal Communications   101

6

Principles of Interviewing   123

7

Some Psychological Aspects of
Supervision   145

8

Special Problems in Counseling
and Remediation   164

9

Employee Dissatisfaction and
Grievances   190

10

Discipline: Principles, Policies,
and Practices   200

11

Personnel Complaint Investigation
Procedures and Techniques   216

12

Personnel Evaluation Systems and
Performance Rating Standards   242

13

Tactical Deployment of Field
Forces   281

contents

Preface   xv
Acknowledgments   xviii

1

The Supervisor's Role   1
Supervisory Position   2
Technical and Supervisory
Competence   4
Organizational Knowledge   4
Basic Supervisory Responsibilities   5
  Planner   5
  Personnel Officer   5
  Trainer   5
  Coach   6
  Counselor   7
  Controller   8
  Decision Maker and
  Communicator   8
  Leader   9
Transition from Officer to Supervisor   9
  Summary   12
  Review   12

2

The Supervisor's Function in Organization, Administration, and Management   13
Administrative Functions   14
  Planning   14
  Organizing   17
  Staffing   17
  Directing   18
  Coordinating   18
Basic Organizational Structures   20
  Line Organization   20
  Functional Organization   21
  Line and Staff Organization   22

Division of Work   23
Unity of Command   24
Span of Control   25
Delegation   25
  Delegation Failures   26
  Delegation Process   27
  Personnel Development by
  Delegation   27
The Exception Principle   28
Delegation of Staff Projects   28
  Researching Projects   29
  Planning Projects   29
  Summary   29
  Review   30

3

Leadership, Supervision, and Command Presence   32
Resistance to Leadership Training   33
Development of Leadership Ability   33
Types of Leaders   35
  Autocratic Leader   35
  Democratic or Participatory Leader   35
  Free Rein or Laissez-Faire Leader   36
Situational Leadership   36
Transformational Leadership
and Empowerment   38
Selection of a Leadership Style   39
Command Presence and Leadership   39
Elements of Leadership   40
  Discipline   40
  Ethics   41
  Common Sense   41
  Psychology   41
Motivation of Employees   41
Situational Analysis and
Self-Appraisal   43
Leadership Characteristics   44

Personality of a Leader   45
Human Relations and Leadership   46
  Manner of the Leader   47
  Language of the Leader   47
  Commendations and Praise by the
  Leader   48
  Criticism and Reprimands by the
  Leader   48
Knowledge of Subordinates   50
Supervision of the Marginal
Employee   50
Order Giving   51
  Direct Commands   51
  Requests   52
  Implied or Suggested Orders   52
  Requests for Volunteers   53
  Method of Communication   53
  Follow-Up   53
Decision Making   54
Drawing of Conclusions   54
Moderation in Supervision   55
Fraternization   56
Example Setting   56
Women Supervisors   57
Supervising a Diverse Workforce   57
Supervising the Multigenerational
Workforce   60
Avoidance of Gender Bias and
Harassment   61
Symptoms of Leadership Failure   62
Leadership Issues in Community
Policing   62
  Summary   65
  Review   67

4

The Training Function: Problems and
   Approaches to the Instructional
   Process   69
Importance of Training   70
  Causes and Effects of Training
  Failure   70

  Remedy for Failure   70
  Instructor's Approach to Teaching   71
Instruction as a Supervisory
Responsibility   72
Need for Training   72
Principles of Learning   74
  Principle of Readiness   74
  Principle of Effect   74
  Principle of Repetition   75
  Principle of Primacy   76
  Principle of Recency   76
  Principle of Intensity   76
Learning Process Variables   76
  Learning Rate   76
  Adult Learner Differences   77
  Motivation   78
  Interest and Learning Effectiveness   78
Learning Patterns   78
Instructional Goals and Specific
Objectives   79
Analysis of Job Tasks and Material
Selection   80
Lesson Plan   80
  Form   81
  Teaching Sequence   81
Learning by Association   83
Five Steps of Teaching   83
  Introduction   84
  Presentation   85
  Review   85
  Application   85
  Test   86
General Problems Affecting
Teaching Method   86
Common Causes of Teacher
Ineffectiveness   87
Teaching Methods   88
  Lectures   88
  Guest Speakers   89
  Role Playing and Field Problems   89
  Stress Management Simulations   89
  Workshops   90
  Demonstrations   90

Group Discussions 91
Panel Discussions 91
Conferences 91
Staff Meetings 92
Planning 92
Follow-Up 92
Use and Misuse of Procedures 92
Use of Questions 93
Use of Teaching Aids 94
Types of Teaching Aids 94
Display Aids 94
Duplicated Aids 95
Projected Aids 95
Three-Dimensional Aids 95
Electronic Media Devices 96
Field Trips 96
Additional Training Resources 96
Summary 97
Review 98

5

Interpersonal Communications 101
Cultural, Environmental, and
Psychological Factors 102
Processes of Communications 102
Barriers to Effective
Communications 103
Failure to Listen 103
Status Differences 103
Psychological Size 104
Noise 104
Language Barriers 104
Fear of Criticism 105
Jumping to Conclusions 105
Filtering 105
Individual Sentiments and Attitudes 106
Intentional Suppression or
Manipulation of Communications 107
Complexity of Communications
Channels 107
Overloading of Communications
Channels 107

Overstructuring of
Communications Channels 108
Overcoming Communication Barriers 108
Determine Objectives 109
Practice Empathy 110
Obtain Feedback 110
Keep Subordinates Informed 110
Be Consistent in Communicating 111
Make Actions Speak Louder Than
Words 112
Listen, Understand, and Be
Understood 112
Characteristics of Communications 113
Autocratic Communications 113
Democratic Communications 113
Free Rein Communications 114
Types of Communicators 114
Written Communications 114
Clarity of Expression 115
Simplicity 115
Accuracy 115
Arrangement 115
Style 116
Summary, Conclusions,
Recommendations, and Plan
of Action 116
Format 116
Email 116
Effectively Managing Your Email 117
The Four Ds for Decision-Making
Model 118
Manuals—Orders 119
Briefing 120
Proofreading and Editing 120
Typical Deficiencies in Writing 121
Summary 121
Review 122

6

Principles of Interviewing 123
Interrogation versus Interview 124
Major Functions of the Interview 124

Preparation for an Interview   124
   Preliminary Planning   124
   Privacy   125
   Types of Questions   125
Conducting an Interview   126
   Interview Opening   126
   Use of Questions   127
   Interviewer Attitude   127
   Employee-Centered Approach   128
   Active Listening   129
Elimination of Bias   130
Confidential Agreements   131
Advice Giving   131
Psychological Reactions in the
Interview   132
Types of Personnel Interviews   132
   Informal Interview   133
   Employment Interview   133
   Progress Interview   135
   Grievance Interview   137
   Problem-Solving Interview   138
   Disciplinary Action Interview   138
   Separation Interview   139
Recording of Results   140
Evaluation of Results   140
Causes of Unsuccessful Interviews   141
   Summary   141
   Review   142

7

Some Psychological Aspects of Supervision   145

Drives, Satisfactions, and Needs   146
   Drives   146
   Satisfactions   146
   Needs   147
Inferiority Complex   147
Catharsis   148
Fixation and Regressive Behavior   148
Supervisory Problem: The Frustrated
Employee   149
Nature of Frustration   150
Barriers Causing Frustration   151

   External Barriers   151
   Internal Barriers   151
Frustration and Performance   151
Some Common Reactions to
Frustration   153
   Aggression   153
   Attitude of Resignation   156
   Escape   156
   Excuses and Rationalizations   157
   Regression   158
   Fixations   159
Frustration Prevention   159
Relief for Frustration: Some
Commonsense Approaches   160
   Summary   162
   Review   162

8

Special Problems in Counseling and Remediation   164

Nature of Problem Drinking   164
Development and Symptoms
of Problem Drinking   166
   Development of the Problem   166
   Symptoms of the Problem   167
Some Options in Treating the
Problem Drinker   169
   Off-the-Job Problem Drinking   170
   Indirect Solicitation for Help   171
   Job-Related Problem Drinking   171
   Drinking and Deteriorating Job
   Performance   172
Counseling for the Problem Drinker   172
   Preliminary Action   173
   Counseling Sessions   173
   Note Taking   175
   Referral   176
   Objective of Professional
   Counseling   176
Emotional and Personal Problems   176
   Psychological Symptoms   177
   Physiological Symptoms   177
   Supervisory Role   177

Counseling for the Emotionally
Troubled Subordinate   178
Management and Remediation
of Emotional Distress   179
   Occupational Stress   179
   Depression   182
   Suicide Awareness and Prevention 183
   Family Discord   184
   Trauma-Producing Incidents   186
   Summary   187
   Review   188

9

**Employee Dissatisfaction and
Grievances**   190
Dissatisfaction with Work Environment   191
Inept Supervisory Practices   191
Misunderstandings of Policies,
Rules, and Procedures   192
Management Failures   192
   Rules of Conduct   192
   Rule Enforcement   193
   Due Process Violations   193
Supervisory Influence on Non–Job-
Related Employee Behavior   195
Recognition of Employee
Dissatisfaction   196
Supervisory Approaches to Employee
Dissatisfaction   196
Employee Grievances   196
   Noncontractual Matters   197
   Contractual Violations and
   Grievances   197
Working with Unions   198
   Summary   198
   Review   199

10

**Discipline: Principles, Policies,
and Practices**   200
Forms of Discipline   201
   Positive Discipline   201
   Negative Discipline   201
Adverse Effects of Punishment   202
Detection of Problem Employee
Behavior   203
Requisites of Punishment   204
   Certainty   204
   Swiftness   205
   Fairness and Impartiality   205
   Consistency   206
   Deterrence for Others   207
Discipline by Example   208
Upward Discipline   209
Interdependency of Discipline,
Morale, and Esprit de Corps   209
Reversals of Administrative
Actions   210
Results of Unsustained Disciplinary
Actions   210
Complaint Investigation Policy   211
   Procedure   211
   Objectives   211
Vicarious Liability   212
Coroner's Transcripts   213
   Summary   214
   Review   214

11

**Personnel Complaint Investigation
Procedures and Techniques**   216
Case Preparation   216
Sources of Complaints   217
   Internal Complaints   217
   External Complaints   217
   Anonymous Complaints   217
Non–Job-Related Misconduct   218
Observed Infractions   218
   Discuss in Private   218
   Record Results   219
   Follow Up   219
Complaint Types   220
   Primary Complaints   220
   Anonymous Complaints   221

Complaints from Intoxicated
Persons   221
Second-Party Complaints   222
Recording of Complaints   222
Complaint Investigation   223
Avoidance of Premature
Conclusions   223
Prevention of Additional Harm   224
Arrest and Booking of an
Employee   224
Promptness of Investigation   225
Collection of Negative
Information   225
Personnel Record Check   225
Interview of the Accused
Employee   226
Legal Counsel   227
Written Statements   228
Avoidance of Face-to-Face
Encounters   229
Searches   229
Lineups   230
Investigative Aids   231
Physical Tests   232
Procedural Due Process
Requirements   233
Charges and Specifications   234
Balancing Test   234
Protective Rules for Employees   234
Reporting Procedures   234
Investigative Report   234
Pagination and Cross-References   236
Avoidance of Offensive
Terminology   236
Classification of Complaint
Investigations   237
Discipline and the News
Media   237
Disposition of Complaints   238
Notification to the Complainant   238
Notification to the Accused
Employee   238
Imposition of a Penalty   238

Disciplinary Failures   239
Summary   239
Review   240

12

Personnel Evaluation Systems and Performance Rating Standards   242

Objectives of Evaluation Systems   243
A Case for Evaluation Systems   243
Causes of Evaluation System Failures   245
Indifference   245
Employee Pressures   245
Failure to Train Raters   246
Rating Abuses   246
Slipshod Procedures   247
Rating Shortcuts   247
Gathering and Recording of
Performance Data   247
Recording Methods   247
Critical Incident Technique   248
Rating Traits   248
Performance Standards   256
Rating Criteria   256
Patrol and Traffic Personnel   257
Investigative Personnel   258
Staff and Auxiliary Personnel   259
Rating Standards   259
Employee Ranking   259
Representative Employee
Standard   260
Ideal Employee Standard   260
Numerical Standard   260
Forced-Choice Standard   261
Rater Characteristics   268
Common Rating Errors   269
Leniency   270
Personal Bias   271
Central Tendency   271
Halo Effect   272
Related Traits   272
Overweighting or Recency   272
Subjectivity   272

Validity and Reliability of Ratings 273
  Validity 273
  Reliability 274
Evaluation Period 274
Rating Methods 275
  Composite Ratings 275
  Group Ratings 275
  Individual Trait Ratings 276
Discussion of Rating with Employee 276
  Interview 277
  Acknowledgment of Rating 277
  Follow-Up 277
  Written Notification of Rating 277
  Summary 278
  Review 279

13

Tactical Deployment of Field Forces 281

Supervisory Responsibilities in Unusual Occurrences 281
Basic Procedures for Unusual Occurrences 282
  Communication of Field Intelligence 283
  Establishment of a Command Post 284
  Incident Command System (ICS) 284
  Reconnaissance 285
  Logistics Aide and Press Relations Officer 286
Operational Guidelines for Unusual Occurrences 287
Barricaded Persons 287
  Hostages 287
  Direction of Assault 288
Operating Procedures in Hostage and Barricaded Suspect Cases 289
  Preliminary Operations 289
  General Considerations 290
  Rational Suspect 291
  Emotionally Troubled Suspect 291
  Assault Tactics 292
  Response to the Active Shooter 294
Search for Other Suspects 294
Arrest of Suspect 294
Civil Disorder: Minor Unlawful Assemblies 295
Civil Disorder: Major Disturbances 296
  Communications 297
  Field Tactics 297
  Use of Force 299
  Arrests 299
  Use of Chemical Agents 299
  Hostile Sniper Fire 299
  Limited Withdrawal 300
  Follow-Up Action 300
Labor Disputes 300
  Maintenance of Impersonal Attitude 301
  Avoidance of Fraternizing 301
  Display of Weapons 301
  Meeting with Labor and Management Representatives 301
  Control Tactics 301
  Strike Scene Arrests 302
Disaster Control 302
  Basic Operational Procedures 303
  Evacuation 303
  Rescue 303
Chemical, Biological, or Radiological Attack 304
  Indicators of a Chemical Attack 304
  On-Scene Indicators 304
  Indicators of a Biological Attack 305
  Indicators of a Radiological Attack 305
  Response Actions 306
Aircraft Crashes 310
  Precautions in Rendering Aid 310
  Security of Military Aircraft 310
Bomb Threats 310
  Evacuation Procedures 311
  Search of Premises 312
  Bomb Precautions 312
Major Fires 313
  Evacuation of Fire Area 315
  Antilooting Patrols 315

Area Searches 316
Missing Children 316
Broadcasting Procedures 316
Initial Search 317
Operating Procedures for
Widespread Search 317
Search Teams 317
Residential Search Patterns 317
Open-Area Search 318
Wanted Persons 318

On-Scene Procedures 318
Search Strategies 319
Business District Searches 320
Building Searches 320
Department of Homeland Security
Initiatives 321
Summary 323
Review 325

Index 327

Preface

Welcome to the eighth edition of *Supervision of Police Personnel*. Known as the "Bible of Police Supervision," this edition has been updated and streamlined. The result has been a good blend of theory and practice.

We know most of you reading this book are either studying for a promotional exam or college class, or have already been promoted and are using this book for guidance and direction. Those of you who are familiar with the book will note that some chapters have been removed or consolidated. This is all based on user feedback. Additionally, pictures have also been added for the first time.

The primary aim of this book is to help you to understand the principles and practices of police supervision. Our goal as authors is to help you become successful and effective supervisors. Today's work environment places strong demands on the effective police supervisor. Many challenges await. We have found that the best supervisors always show concern for their agency, employees, and the public. They also have excellent inter-personal and communication skills.

If you study the book thoroughly, it will help you to become the best supervisor you can be. The information in it has been tested over time. The original text was written by Professor Nathan Iannone. He is considered by many to be a true visionary in the field of police supervision. The sixth edition of the book was later updated by his brother, Marvin Iannone. Like his brother Nathan, Marvin also rose through the ranks of the Los Angeles Police Department.

Finally, the seventh and eighth editions were updated by Dr. Jeff Bernstein. You should know that he did not start off as Dr. Bernstein. He first worked as a police officer, detective, and police sergeant with the City of Miami Beach. As a Doctor of Psychology, he is considered one of the leading experts in police promotional exam preparation. He has prepared thousands of police officers for promotional exams. Since most of you are reading this text for your promotional exam, we have prepared the following guidance for you.

Promotional Exams: How to Get Started with Your Preparation

Preparing for promotion is an important career decision. This is particularly true today as the competition for supervisory and command positions in law enforcement agencies is fierce. The challenge for those who are serious about promotion is that they must be more prepared today than ever before. The road to promotion is one of hard work and personal commitment. The key to success will be determined by how well you prepare.

When a promotional exam is announced, just starting your preparation is one of the hardest things to do. We firmly believe the early bird does get the worm. Here are five things you can do to begin your preparation:

1. DEVELOP A PLAN

Start thinking about exactly what you're going to do. Make the commitment: When am I going to study? Where am I going to study? Who am I going to study with? And so on.

Speak with successful supervisors and managers in the workplace. Ask them about their study techniques.

Before you begin studying, make an appointment to have your eyes checked, especially if eye fatigue is occurring more frequently than normal.

2. GATHER UP ALL THE MATERIALS

Keep your study materials updated—for example, law books, guidelines, textbooks, test prep guides. Once you obtain all the materials, put them away. Then, just take out one item at a time to study. This way you won't feel overwhelmed.

3. ESTABLISH THE PROPER MIND-SET

If you're taking a test to become a boss, you have to start thinking like one. This is especially true while you're working. When you hear calls on the radio for a supervisor, think about what you would do with respect to proper supervisorial principles. Critical incidents, complaints, performance issues—how would you handle them?

4. BE POSITIVE!

How much time do we spend complaining every day at work? A lot, right? Well, when it's exam time, avoid the whiners and complainers. Complaining is a time waster that distracts you from studying. Stay with the positive people who are focused on studying.

5. BEGIN YOUR STUDY

If you sign up for a study group, it should be in addition to your individual study. Think of the total study time in small increments. Study at least two to three hours per day, five days a week. Choose a quiet place and select a time when your energy level is highest.

Log your study time and chart your readings on a calendar. Set goals and deadlines and follow them. Make adjustments as needed.

Periodically reward yourself and your family for your hard work.

Don't take on major responsibilities or projects while you're studying for the exam.

For more information on preparation for promotional exams, go to www.bernsteintestprep.com. It's up to you to get your plan into motion. If you don't put the time and effort in, somebody else will. Best of luck in the promotional exam process.

New to the Eighth Edition

Photographs are utilized throughout the text

Preface

Valuable Tips for Promotional Exam Preparation

Chapter 1

Making an Effective Transition from Officer to Supervisor

Chapter 3

Transformational Leadership and Empowerment
Ways to Increase Command Presence
Supervising a Diverse Workforce
Suggestions for Supervising the Multigenerational Workforce

Chapter 5

Strategies for Effectively Managing Your Email

Chapter 8

Suicide Awareness and Prevention Tips

Chapter 9

Working with Union Representatives

Chapter 13

New Bomb Threat Stand-Off Guidelines

Supplements

To access supplementary materials online, instructors need to request an instructor access code. Go to www.pearsonhighered.com/irc, where you can register for an instructor access code. Within forty-eight hours after registering, you will receive a confirming email, including an instructor access code. Once you have received your code, go to the site and log on for full instructions on downloading the materials you wish to use.

This text is accompanied by the following supplements:

- *Prentice Hall's Test Prep Guide to Accompany Supervision of Police Personnel*, eighth edition (includes Multiple Choice and True/False Practice Questions)

  (This may be ordered at www.bernsteintestprep.com)

- Online Instructor's Manual with Test Bank
- Online MyTest Testbank
- Online PowerPoint Presentations
- CourseSmart e-Textbook (http://www.coursesmart.com)

Acknowledgments

The eighth edition of *Supervision of Police Personnel* would not be possible without the advice and assistance of many people. The authors wish to thank the following contributors, reviewers, and support staff.

Contributors

Lt. Herbert Williams, Woodbridge Police Department
Captain Michael Bartuccio, Winslow Township Police Department
Michael Markowicz, Bernstein & Associates

Reviewers

Vanessa Dixon, Middlesex Community College
Richard Martin, Mercer University
Gerald Zeborowski, Joliet Jr. College
Xavier Jorge, United States Marshalls Service

Support Staff

Melvin Olmedilla, Bernstein & Associates
Vincent Sonalan, Bernstein & Associates
Sara Eilert, Senior Acquisition Editor, Prentice Hall
Elisa Rogers, 4-development
Daniel Richcreek, 4-development
Jessica Sykes, Pearson Prentice Hall
Tiffany Bitzel, Pearson Prentice Hall
Mogana Sundaramurthy, Integra-PDY, IN
The assistance of all those involved is much appreciated.

Dedication

Our special thanks to Clara, Patricia, and Edna for their never-ending support and patience.

1

The Supervisor's Role

Chapter Objectives

This chapter will enable you:

- To become acquainted with the supervisor's role
- To gain an understanding of the basic responsibilities of the supervisor
- To become familiar with the supervisor's objectives

In modern administrative terminology, *management* denotes the process of directing and controlling people and things so that organizational objectives can be accomplished. *Supervision,* as part of the management process, refers to the act of overseeing people. It is an activity that takes place at all levels in the organization except at the work level, although many of the tenets of good supervision apply to the nonsupervisory officer in his daily dealings with the public.

Nowhere is the application of management and supervisory principles more important than at the first level where the productive capacity of the enterprise is directly controlled. The worker's performance and morale are more strongly influenced here by his immediate superior than by any other factor in his environment. This is true not only because the supervisor and employee have a close relationship but also because the superior exercises such a strong influence on the subordinate's physical and social environment. It is for these reasons that the first-level supervisor's job is a key position in any organization. The precepts presented in this text, with few exceptions, are especially directed to these supervisors. These precepts have been tested and proven highly effective, not only in the law enforcement community and closely allied agencies but also at all levels of the hierarchy in any organization where supervisory relationships exist.

In the law enforcement agency, first-level supervisors are of special importance because of the great need for teamwork. On them rests most of the responsibility for providing the cohesive force that welds the workforce into a well-functioning, smoothly operating unit.

Leadership expert John C. Maxwell has said, "if you lead people well and help members of your team to become effective leaders, a successful career path is almost guaranteed."[1]

---

[1] John C. Maxwell, *The Five Levels of Leadership* (New York: Hachette Book Group, 2011), p. 5.

Supervisory Position

People are responsible for production. The supervisor is responsible for people. He accomplishes the objectives of the organization by getting things done through them. He must be an expert in handling them to be a successful leader. To this end, he must develop the art of influencing others, coordinating their efforts, and directing them to proper goals in such a way as to obtain their obedience, confidence, respect, and loyal cooperation.

People like to be led by those whom they respect and in whom they have confidence. The first step in gaining this confidence and respect is taken when the supervisor exemplifies by his personal conduct that which he demands from his subordinates. If he then provides them proper leadership, they will respond with the highest performance, with a minimum of conflict and a maximum of satisfaction.

The supervisory officer must be adept at applying the principles of wholesome human relations with common sense so that he can best integrate the needs of employees with the goals of management. He should allow them to participate in decisions that affect them, but he must avoid crippling himself as a supervisor by carrying democratic leadership so far that his subordinates will expect him to "take a vote" before making every decision. Undoubtedly, when those affected by a nonemergent decision are consulted before it is made, the process will take longer but implementation will be much swifter.

To many supervisors, advancement into a position of authority involves a considerable change in lifestyle from being a follower to being a leader and requires a radical change in philosophy and thought processes, especially in the area of human relations. As the supervisor gains experience, he will increasingly appreciate how his actions affect the economic security, advancement, and emotions of his subordinates. He will appreciate the effects of his activities on their general welfare and morale. He will not become lulled into believing that because his morale is high, the morale of his subordinates is also high; he will recognize symptoms indicating that it is low and take corrective action promptly whenever his position permits. He will realize, as David Lieberman explains, that morale cannot be achieved through incentive or policy.[2] He can influence it, however, if he remembers that people are interested in themselves and in the things that affect them. He should provide them with performance feedback that will give them a sense of their worth within the organization.[3] One of their basic needs is a feeling of stability and security in their work. This should be provided for them insofar as possible because people do not perform well when they are exposed to conditions that cause tension and anxiety.

Any leader must accept the fact that his subordinates are all different. They will react in different ways at different times. They will often resist his efforts to do what they know he has to do to make the organization a better place to work. Now and then, some will become incensed at what they consider a trivial criticism if it is not given with

---

[2] David J. Lieberman, Ph.D, *Executive Power: Use the Greatest Collection of Psychological Strategies to Create an Automatic Advantage in Any Business Situation* (Hoboken, N.J.: John Wiley & Sons, Inc., 2009), p. 34.

[3] Paul Levy, *Industrial Organizational Psychology: Understanding the Workplace* (New York: Worth Publishers, 2011), p. 116.

the utmost tact and diplomacy. They will sometimes resist changes in their duties or assignments, and some will quit if they see greener pastures elsewhere. He can expect disloyalty from some and intense loyalty from others in his complex job of managing people.

The supervisor must be able to help his subordinates establish and achieve reasonable goals. He must be able to provide answers to their many job problems and to give them wise counsel and assurance in their personal and professional lives when the need arises, recognizing that they will not all react the same when he tries to help them. At times, they will misinterpret his motives and accuse him of meddling in their affairs, yet their affairs are his when their performance is affected.

The supervisor is selected by management. He derives his official authority from that source, but his real authority stems from the spirit of cooperation, respect, and confidence that he is able to gain from his subordinates. He is expected to represent management's interests to the workers and their interests to management. He is a buffer between workers and higher authority. He absorbs heat from above without passing it along to them. To his subordinates, he is the department. His virtues personify those of the department. If he is fair in his dealings with them, if he is considerate of their welfare, and if he is stimulating, they attribute these characteristics to the organization. If he is unjust, inconsistent, and unfriendly, they are likely to think the organization is also because he reflects, to them, what it is.

In the long run, the interests of management and the worker are identical. The small differences between the two can ordinarily be resolved by the effective supervisor if he avoids prejudice, develops a judicial attitude by basing decisions only on the facts, knows the rules under which he and his subordinates must work and appreciates the intent of such rules, studies his subordinates to gain an understanding of them, leads them in a joint effort instead of driving them, and practices loyalty to his organization and to those with whom he works.

He is responsible for keeping his superiors informed through oral and written reports. This requires that he keep himself informed through records, research, and inspection. He is obliged to keep his subordinates apprised about matters affecting them. In doing so, he must communicate clearly by learning to avoid the barriers that hinder effective communications. He conveys official policy downward and tries to sell it to subordinates even though he sometimes does not agree with it and knows it will be resisted.

The supervisor should avoid filtering intelligence to his subordinates or superiors. He must not tell them only what he thinks will make them happy nor keep from them news he thinks will make them unhappy. He must always keep his superiors informed so that their decisions may be made on unexpurgated information, not on partial data that have been taken out of context. When he is in doubt as to how much detail he should pass on to them, he should resolve the doubt in favor of conveying too much rather than too little. In doing so, however, his discretion must be impeccable lest his motives be misconstrued. He should be aware of the fact that the communication may breed rumors.

The supervisor often finds it difficult to reconcile the goals of management with the goals of the employees and the sentiments of their social group. He is often torn between the loyalties he owes both, but he must realize that the best interests of the organization must prevail.

Technical and Supervisory Competence

Supervisors need not become highly skilled in every technical aspect of the job they supervise to be effective—to do so would impose an impossible burden on them—but they should have a good working knowledge of the principal aspects of the job for which they are responsible. They must have a basic understanding of the other scientific disciplines that have contributed to the science of leadership. The psychologist has contributed to an understanding of human behavior. The sociologist has attempted to explain ethnic cultures and group relationships. The anthropologist has tried to explain the developmental aspects of society. The physical scientist has given law enforcement a vast source of technical data that have contributed to the advancement of scientific criminal investigation, just as have many other disciplines.

Every supervisor should keep himself abreast of fundamental changes in practices, techniques, and procedures in order to be equipped to carry to his subordinates the information they need to perform their jobs properly. He should prepare himself for this position by gaining a good working knowledge of the principles of organization, administration, and management; he should know and understand the principles of performance evaluation. He should become an expert in directing the efforts of his subordinates into the most productive channels. He should know how to make assignments, through the process of delegation, of many tasks that others below him are capable of performing as well as or better than he can. In delegating routine tasks to subordinates, the expert supervisor will give them sufficient authority to match the responsibility he has imposed on them. He will then hold them accountable for the job, but he will realize that *final* responsibility for the job is his, because he cannot shed his responsibility for a task merely by delegating it to someone else. If he delegates well, he will conserve his time for carrying out his prime duty of supervising rather than performing routine operational activities.

Organizational Knowledge

The supervisor should prepare himself for his position by gaining knowledge and understanding of the policies, rules, procedures, practices, functions, and objectives of his organization. He should be thoroughly versed in the functions and operations of his local subdivision of government and should have an understanding of its relationships with other units of government. He should be fully acquainted with those agencies that work in conjunction with his own. Their facilities for providing rescue work, ambulance services, welfare activities, or other services should be well known to him. He should be thoroughly familiar with the local political atmosphere, although he should scrupulously avoid political entanglements and alliances that might hinder the accomplishment of his official duties.

The successful supervisor will understand the legal ramifications of his office; his obligations, liabilities, and responsibilities for the acts of his subordinates under the law; and the restrictions under which he operates. He will keep himself informed of the functions, jurisdiction, and authority of persons occupying the diverse positions in his and related organizations so that he can best carry out his coordinating activities. At the same time, a supervisor must understand the importance of the informal organization within the police department. The Volcker Commission emphasized the importance of understanding informal organizations in "The Report of the National Commission on the Public

Service."[4] Within most police departments, there are groups that operate without official authorization. The effective supervisor should be familiar with these groups as well as their leaders because these groups have influence in the department. A successful supervisor is able to deal effectively with both the formal and the informal organization.

In order that he may provide appropriate guidance and counsel to his subordinates, he must be familiar with the personnel rules, policies, and practices governing such aspects of the job as selection of personnel, promotional systems, assignment policies, termination procedures, sickness benefits, retirement plans, disciplinary procedures, merit ratings, leaves of absence, contractual agreements between employees and management, and vacation policies.

Basic Supervisory Responsibilities

The common elements of supervision can be grouped under those activities that relate to the direction of people and all it implies (their control and development) and to the multitude of interpersonal relationships between them and their supervisor. In his day-to-day relationships with people, the supervisor is expected to function in the following ways.

Planner

He must be an expert in planning operational activities and using different methods. He must be capable of inspecting work systems, conducting studies, analyzing data, and developing mature recommendations for constructive changes in organization and operation when necessary. If he is to best perform his duties, he must be able to forecast future needs of his organization as part of his planning activities, anticipate problems, and make decisions ahead of time to solve them. He should familiarize himself with work simplification practices to bring about greater efficiency in his organization through the streamlining of procedures, reduction of paperwork, and effective use of personnel resources.

Personnel Officer

The supervisory officer should strive to assign his subordinates as scientifically as possible to the positions for which they are best suited and to the places and at the times where they are most needed. He will place "round plugs in round holes" wherever possible because happy workers are usually productive ones.

Studies have revealed that there is a marked relationship between productivity of an individual, his job satisfaction, and the type of supervision he has received. Employee-centered supervisors obtain better results than production-centered ones.[5]

Trainer

The best supervisors develop their abilities to train their employees to be efficient, effective producers who gain satisfaction from their work. When the supervisor neglects to

---

[4] "The Report of the National Commission on the Public Service," in *Leadership for America: Rebuilding the Public Service* (Lexington, Mass.: Lexington Books, 1990).

[5] Neal M. Ashkanasy, Celeste Wilderom, and Mark F. Peterson, *Handbook of Organizational Culture and Climate* (Thousand Oaks, Calif.: Sage Publications, 2000).

Crime Scene
Investigation
(© Loren Rodgers/
Fotolia)

develop his capacity for the role of teacher, he deprives himself of a means of upgrading the service and ensuring that the standards of performance in the organization are maintained through the training process.

He must carry out his training function in all types of settings. If he is to be an effective teacher, he must gain knowledge and understanding of the learning process, the effects of individual differences on learning, and the psychological factors involved in teaching. He will become proficient in the use of a variety of techniques that will make his training activities most meaningful. He will be able to do some training at the scene of a crime or while making a routine contact with a subordinate much as he does in a formal classroom setting.

Coach

Coaching is an integral part of the supervisor's responsibilities. The supervisor shares his knowledge and expertise, and lets the employee know how he can improve performance. The skill of coaching refers to the practice of confronting an employee with his or her job performance record with the objective of finding ways to overcome deficiencies and improve job performance. Properly used, it can be an excellent motivational tool that stimulates employees to achieve peak job performance.[6] Through the coaching process, knowledge, skills, and abilities are enhanced. It's a process of providing guidance and direction to officers in a way that allows learning and development to occur. When this happens, performance is improved.

---

[6] Jeff Bernstein, *Situational Management for Chicago Police Sergeants* (Davie, Fla.: Bernstein & Associates, 2013).

Coaching Session
Lieutenant Herb
Williams coaching
Sergeant Sharonda
Morris.

More and Miller state that "Supervisors who work with employees as coaches create a working environment that increases employee competence, provides for greater fulfillment, allows for a greater contribution to the organization, and exposes officers to what can really be meaningful work." Officers who are coached accept responsibility more readily, are clear about performance expectations, and are committed to the organization. They become oriented to the mission and goals of the department, follow the vision of the organization, and have an opportunity to attain individual goals.[7]

While in the field, supervisors are in a great position to observe skill deficiencies in their employees. One important area in the field is "street survival tactics." Supervisors should be aware that coaching opportunities present themselves every day. A good coach will take advantage of these situations to help develop his employees.

Counselor

Supervisorial counseling typically involves a meeting between the supervisor and the employee. Counseling relates to the supervisory practice of actively listening and responding to employees' complaints, grievances, and problems. Employees can use these communication practices to express matters of concern to their superiors. The purpose of the counseling session could be any number of things. For counseling to be effective, the supervisor should have a good working relationship with his subordinates. The focus of the meeting may be to help an employee with a work-related concern, or an employee's personal problem. It can take place in the office, or out in the field. If the supervisor gets to know employees as individuals and demonstrates concern for their welfare, the counseling process will be enhanced. A supervisor is required to address work-related performance deficiencies. The counseling goal here is to improve performance.

---

[7] Harry W. More and Larry S. Miller, *Effective Police Supervision* (Burlington, Mass.: Anderson Publishing, 2011), p. 297.

Another instance where counseling is appropriate is when the employee requests the supervisor's help with a personal problem. Everyone experiences personal problems in their life. The employee may have just experienced a death in the family. The supervisor can help the subordinate just by listening or providing some assistance. Thus, counseling is an important skill that all supervisors must develop.

Controller

Every supervisor worthy of the name must learn how to control his subordinates properly. He must make proper follow-ups to determine that rules and regulations have been followed and orders properly executed. When necessary, he must take disciplinary action either positively through the process of training or negatively through punitive action. He must never obstruct corrective action when it is justified merely because of personal motives, but he must do everything proper, honorable, and legal to protect his subordinates from unjust punishment. At the time of recruitment, when facts are in conflict, doubts should be resolved in favor of the organization because questionable persons cannot justifiably be recruited into the police service. However, in disciplinary matters involving an employee, the organization is bound by a policy of fairness and cannot honorably punish an employee on the basis of unfounded or unproved charges, slander, gossip, or malicious innuendos. An employee must never be punished merely because of an unproved outcry by the news media or vocal special-interest groups or individuals.

The supervisor must expect some mistakes from even the most able of his subordinates. Errors are bound to occur, especially with inexperienced employees. When they do, they should be treated as constructively as possible. When mistakes "of the head" are made, often the training value exceeds the harm done; if the mistake is "of the heart," negative corrective action may be indicated to prevent a recurrence. When punishment is necessary, it should be administered promptly, without hostility or anger and never in a spirit of retribution or revenge.

Perfection should not be expected of workers, since demanding this degree of excellence in performance will usually result in wasted time, frayed nerves, and frustration. Seldom will employees be equipped with the physical or mental resources to render the level of performance that even approximates the perfectionist's expectations. This type of person is a wearisome individual; he is seldom satisfied with the performance he receives from others and only causes them anxiety and frustration.

Decision Maker and Communicator

One of the primary functions of the supervisor is decision making. When he makes decisions, he often helps shape policy for the organization. If a decision is indicated, he must not vacillate. A bad decision is sometimes better than none at all. When it affects others, it should be communicated to them clearly and simply to prevent misunderstandings and resistance. When change results from decisions, those affected will often resist because the change is interpreted as a threat to their security and they are forced to make adjustments. The resistance will usually be reduced if the need for the change is explained. However, the supervisor need not justify all changes and should not apologize for them. To do so might be interpreted as a mark of weakness in carrying out management objectives. Worse, he is likely to be accused of being disloyal or of trying to escape responsibility for an unpopular change by blaming someone else for it.

Timing of a communication that affects employees and selection of the location where it takes place are important if the change is to have the greatest acceptance. Sometimes the sowing of a seed that a change is about to take place will allow the idea to take root in the minds of employees, with a resultant lessening of their resistance to the change. The manner in which the superior officer communicates with his subordinates has a vital bearing on their interpersonal relations. Subordinates often resent a supervisor's bad manner in giving an order more than the bad order itself.

Leader

A major responsibility of every supervisor is to provide leadership for the employees under him. To become a good leader, he must possess the traits of honorableness, courageousness, and vitality. He must be reasonably intelligent, must have good common sense, and must be persuasive and flexible. He is not born with these characteristics, but he can develop his leadership ability by adopting the desirable traits he has observed in good leaders or, at least, trying to adapt those traits to his own style.

Every supervisor has an inherent responsibility to motivate his subordinates by giving them positive incentives that will encourage them to achieve and maintain a high level of efficiency. He must provide them an opportunity for personal and professional growth. They need to feel that they are progressing toward achievable goals. He can help them by providing enlightened leadership. He will strive to overcome the inertia and dogma that impede the professionalization of law enforcement. If he is firmly committed to the tenets of his profession, he will give a full measure of effort and careful attention to his duties whether he likes or dislikes his employees and whether his efforts are appreciated or not. He must stand by his convictions in spite of adversity and must adhere to those high moral standards of his profession regardless of a departure from them by others. He should adopt new principles when the need for higher or better ones becomes evident.

Transition from Officer to Supervisor

Making the transition from line officer to supervisor is a challenging time. As a supervisor, you are now part of the management team. Instead of going from call to call or conducting investigations, you are now the overseer. You are responsible for the actions of those who work for you.

You are expected to counsel, train, and discipline subordinates. You are considered a key player in ensuring the goals of the agency are accomplished. It's a unique position. You represent management's position to your employees, and take employee issues and concerns to management. You need to support your employees when they're right, and discipline them when they're wrong. That may include an officer with whom you recently worked. It could be someone on the same squad, shift, or division. Except now he works for you.

Investigating citizen complaints is another of your supervisory responsibilities. When you get that complaint on one of the officers you used to work with, it must be investigated. Your mind-set is very important. You're not on the squad as an officer

anymore. Let's say you're the supervisor, and the complaint from the citizen involved verbal discourtesy on a traffic stop. You sustain the complaint after talking with the citizen, talking with the officer, and viewing the in-car video. Now it's time for discipline. It's the second offense. You decide to write a formal letter of counseling. You present it to the officer during the counseling session. He looks at you with surprise and says, "WTF, you know this lady, you know this is bullshit." Okay, I did say it would be challenging! Personal adjustments need to be made. Again, you are the supervisor now. Establish the right mind-set.

The most effective supervisors show concern for employees, as well as concern for their organization. Supervisors should be there to assist when employees ask for help, and when performance is substandard. They should try to balance both employee and organizational needs. However, when these needs conflict, organizational needs must come first.

Guidelines for Successfully Making the Transition from Officer to Supervisor

1. *Educate yourself for your new position*—Take a look at the job description. Find out what your boss expects, and what performance evaluation factors you're being evaluated on. Learn the skills to be an effective supervisor.
2. *Look, listen, and learn about your new work environment*—Review the personnel files of all employees assigned to you. Take a look at productivity, morale, and your team. Get to know your fellow supervisors.
3. *Show a genuine interest in and concern for your employees*—Meet with them and get to know them. Let them know what you expect. Listen to their grievances, and do your best to resolve them. Get their input and involve them in problem solving.

4. *Communicate regularly with your employees*—Keep them informed and updated on the issues that affect them. Meet with your employees individually at least twice a month. Review positive and negative performance issues.

5. *Lead by example*—Be a positive role model. Employees will judge you on what you do, not what you say. Take charge when necessary.

6. *Support management's policies and decisions*—You are part of the management team and must support it. Blaming higher management for new or unpopular policies is inappropriate. You can still take employee suggestions for improvement to higher-level management.

7. *Ask for guidance and direction when you need it*—As a new supervisor you're not expected to know everything. Ask your boss or fellow supervisors for help when necessary.

8. *Treat people fairly and with respect*—This is how you would like to be treated. Don't abuse your authority. Use it as necessary.

9. *Do the right thing*—Be honest, ethical, and moral in your dealings with others. Don't play favorites or be overly familiar with your employees. Don't oversupervise, and let your employees do their jobs. Demand excellence and praise frequently.

10. *Enjoy the benefits the position brings*—Enjoy the challenge, prestige, different assignments, and the monetary rewards. Have fun. Take pride in what you have accomplished. Develop and mentor others.

The objectives and responsibilities of the supervisor are outlined in the chapters that follow. Let's examine the principles, practices, and techniques that can be used in achieving these objectives and fulfilling these responsibilities.

Pittsburgh Police Sgt. Shawn Malloy is sworn in as a new lieutenant. (© ZUMA Press/ Newscom)

SUMMARY

The first-line supervisor occupies a key position in any organization because of his direct influence on the conduct and performance of those who do the work. Coordination of people and units within the organization so that it will operate effectively is a vital function of his position. If he fulfills his responsibilities improperly, coordination is likely to be poor.

Advancement to a position of authority requires a considerable change in philosophy and lifestyle of the supervisor because it involves leading rather than following others. In his leadership role, the supervisor will find that each of his subordinates is different. He can expect different reactions from them when he tries to help them in establishing and achieving their goals.

Although the long-run interests of the organization are identical to those of the workers, the supervisor's position places on him the obligation of resolving the minor differences that sometimes arise. It is his responsibility to provide representation between them. He must keep both groups accurately informed in matters affecting their mutual interests if he is to perform his role most effectively.

Although supervisors need not be highly skilled in all the technical aspects of the jobs they supervise, they should have a good working knowledge of the principal aspects of such jobs. They must acquire an understanding of the basic principles of leadership and the tenets of organization and management if they are to perform their complex tasks efficiently and effectively.

The difficulty of making the transition from officer to supervisor is reduced when you fully understand your new role. The information in this book will help you to effectively deal with the challenges a new supervisor will face. If you make the commitment to be an effective supervisor and work hard to be the best you can be, you will be successful.

REVIEW

Questions

1. Define the term *management.*
2. Distinguish between management and supervision.
3. Discuss the types of institutional knowledge a supervisor must possess.
4. What are the basic supervisory responsibilities? Discuss how they affect the supervisor in obtaining the best performance from his subordinates.

Exercises

1. Discuss the basic responsibilities of the supervisor, and describe two or three practical ways he can carry out each of them.
2. Give examples of how supervisors you have known have failed to carry out their responsibilities. What could they have done better?

2

The Supervisor's Function in Organization, Administration, and Management

Chapter Objectives

This chapter will enable you:

- To gain an understanding of the types of organizational structures and how they can be used to aid in the management process

- To become familiar with the supervisor's administrative functions

- To become acquainted with the fundamental principles of organization, administration, and management

- To gain an appreciation of how the tenets of administration and management affect the supervisor

An organization is a structure through which people work as a group. Whenever two or more persons are associated in doing something, there is some sort of organization. It presupposes an orderly arrangement between individuals and groups, but a mechanical structure alone will not ensure the effective accomplishment of organizational objectives. Direction and control must be provided so that the necessary coordination of human effort can be achieved. Paul Hersey and Kenneth Blanchard state that "the focus of [an organization's] administrative subsystem is on authority, structure, and responsibility within the organization: who does what for whom and who tells whom to do what, how, when and why."[1] Such direction is the essence of the supervisory function.

The major portion of the supervisor's job may be categorized into three broad areas: leading, directing, and controlling individuals and groups that are formally or informally arranged. The formally structured and recognized relationships within the organization will have superimposed on them the informal groups,

---

[1] Paul Hersey, Kenneth H. Blanchard, and Dewey E. Johnson, *Management of Organizational Behavior: Leading Human Resources* (Upper Saddle River, N.J.: Pearson Education, 2008), p. 10.

with their own leader or leaders, unrecognized on the organizational charts. Through these natural leaders, often without bars or stripes, the wise supervisor will accomplish many of his objectives.

Although his job deals primarily with the directing of subordinates, the supervisor also must concern himself with the internal conditions of the organization involving both concrete matters, such as environmental working conditions and the provision of equipment, and more abstract factors, such as morale and esprit de corps. These factors cannot be separated from his typical administrative functions.

Administrative Functions

The major duties of supervisory personnel in an establishment differ only in degree from those of the chief executive, as described in Gulick's POSDCORB. The acronym POSDCORB represents a concept that is designed to call attention to the various functional elements of the work of the chief executive, developed because words like *administration* and *management* have been overused to the point they have lost all specific content.

POSDCORB is made up of the initials and stands for the following activities:[2]

Planning, that is working out in broad outline the things that need to be done and the methods for doing them to accomplish the purpose set for the enterprise;

Organizing, that is the establishment of the formal structure of authority through which work subdivisions are arranged, defined, and coordinated for the defined objective;

Staffing, that is the whole personnel function of bringing in and training the staff and maintaining favorable conditions of work;

Directing, that is the continuous task of making decisions and embodying them in specific and general orders and instructions and serving as the leader of the enterprise;

Coordinating, that is the all-important duty of interrelating the various parts of the work;

Reporting, keeping those who the executive is responsible for informed as to what is going on, which includes keeping himself and his subordinates informed through records, research, and inspection;

Budgeting, all that goes with budgeting in the form of fiscal planning, accounting, and control.

Many of these executive functions are passed on to subordinates at all levels of the hierarchy through the process of delegation.

Planning

In his planning function, the supervisor must forecast needs and problems and prepare plans to meet them. Those plans that are guides to the daily performance of operating personnel at the lower level of the hierarchy must be more detailed and meticulous than those for personnel at or near the top of the organization.

Sound organization directly relates work to be done to objectives to be achieved. Good planning is at the hub, since it provides the framework for organization by specifying what should be done to meet objectives, who should do the work, and how their

---

[2] Tony J. Watson, *In Search of Management: Culture, Chaos and Control in Managerial Work* (London: Thomson Learning, 2001), p. 35.

efforts can be coordinated. It is essential in the delegation process because when work responsibility is defined, the supervisor is able to delegate at least part of his work to others. Communicating what the organization's goals are and defining the means for achieving them are also means of motivating employees.[3]

Plans enable the supervisor to make decisions in advance, but they are useless if they are not effectively communicated to personnel who are expected to follow them. Whether they are communicated by a manual, written orders, or verbal commands, they should be explicit and clear. It is a fundamental fact of life that if such communications can be misinterpreted, they will be. Accordingly, standing orders and those that are complicated should be written to reduce confusion and misinterpretation.[4] Policies, orders, and plans should be concise and clear while being flexible enough to allow adjustment as conditions dictate. "The police role is much too ambiguous to become totally standardized, but it is also much too serious and important to be left completely to the total discretion of the officer."[5]

Plans may be classified into several types according to the purposes they serve. Procedural plans relating to standard operating procedures (SOPs) are useful as guides to personnel in such activities as serving and processing arrest warrants, recording and processing crime or incident reports, and processing traffic citations. Each supervisor should constantly review these day-to-day procedures and make recommendations for changes as needs arise to increase operational efficiency.

Tactical plans are those that are prepared to meet exigencies encountered by police, such as widespread civil disorders, unusual crime problems, civil defense needs, or major disasters. These plans are usually developed considerably in advance of expected incidents and are largely based on field intelligence supplied by supervisory personnel and the expertise they are able to provide in assessing future needs. The plans are designed to guide personnel in controlling unusual happenings and restoring order as quickly and as efficiently as possible. The methods of control are substantially the same as in ordinary police operations but must be expanded to meet the requirements of each occurrence. Therefore, it is necessary that such plans be basic, flexible in nature, and adaptable to modification as the need arises.[6]

Sometimes the basic framework for tactical plans is incorporated into a tactical manual. Such principles are guideposts to tactical operations of all kinds.

Operational plans are those designed to give guidance and direction to personnel in the performance of normal police activities. These are the plans that are guides to personnel in activities such as the deployment and distribution of personnel or the search for suspects or lost persons.

Auxiliary services plans are those that implement normal operations, such as in the recruitment of personnel or public and community relations activities.

---

[3] Richard L. Daft and Dorothy Marcic, *Understanding Management* (Mason, Ohio: South-Western, 2011), p. 142.

[4] The techniques of communicating plans to personnel are described in detail in Chapter 5.

[5] Kenneth Peak, Larry K. Gaines, and Ronald W. Glensor, *Police Supervision and Management in an Era of Community Policing,* 3rd ed. (Upper Saddle River, N.J.: Pearson Prentice Hall, 2010), p. 12.

[6] Los Angeles Police Department, Los Angeles, Calif., *Tactical Manual,* 1992.

Deputy Chief
Vincent Quatrone,
Community Relations
Captain John
Scimeca, Patrol
Division Captain
Richard Policastro
engage in a tactical
planning operation.

Fiscal plans relate to such matters as budget preparation and the use and control of funds allotted for personnel, equipment, and supplies. The supervisor should adopt the practice of recording justifications for such personnel, equipment, and supplies as the need arises. Many find a perpetual budget file useful for such a purpose. They record specific data throughout the year concerning budgetary needs. When the budget period arrives, a cumulative file is available to aid them in their fiscal planning.

Policies are plans consisting of a set of broad principles that guide personnel in the accomplishment of general organizational objectives. These are generally established by top management, although supervisors and unit commanders often establish policies for operation of their particular units.

Policies should be written whenever practicable, but often they are not. They evolve from the experiences of the organization; from the established, traditional customs and standards essential to its welfare; and from legal and social constraints imposed on its activities.

A policy manual is worthwhile as a guide for personnel to apply to all facets of police operations. For example, the N.J. Attorney General's Office mandates that all police agencies in the state implement a policy management system to help officers be aware of the many policies, rules, orders, and plans they are responsible to follow. "Employees must understand what management wants to accomplish and what behavior is expected. Each category of documents in the policy management system should be issued in a distinctive, readily identifiable format."[7] Indeed, as the movement toward

---

[7] *Internal Affairs Policy and Procedures* (Trenton, N.J.: N.J. State Attorney General's Office, Division of Law and Public Safety, 2011), pp. 11–18.

professional accreditation grows, the need for a ready reference of regulations is more important than ever; the Commission on Accreditation for Law Enforcement Agencies (CALEA) now requires its members to adopt 38 chapters comprising 480 individual standards.[8] Such manuals are being developed more frequently in recent years than in the past as a means of communicating to employees organizational objectives.

Policies—such as those mandating that personnel cooperate with the news media, prescribing that personnel enforce the law fairly and justly, or requiring that personnel be prepared to take appropriate action at all times when the need arises—are stable and change slowly because they are based on broad organizational objectives that change little.

Every supervisor should be alert for confusion in the interpretation of policy by his subordinates—especially at times when policy is changed or when subordinates join his unit from another where it is interpreted differently. When such confusion is revealed through feedback, he should promptly take whatever steps may be required to clarify conflicts and ensure uniformity in application.

Rules and regulations are plans providing specific guides to conduct and performance. They are parameters for acceptable conduct provided by management. As principles of action and conduct, they are a means by which deviations from policy may be prevented. In content, they control explicit behavior; therefore, they are subject to more rapid change than are policies.

In order for them to be effective, rules and regulations must be current, reasonable, and clear. Above all, they must not be arbitrary, reflecting only the views of management. Rules may be made at any supervisory level of the organization to implement policy. Whether they are made by the first-line supervisor to aid him in carrying out the functions of his unit or by a higher authority, the supervisor should constantly be alert to a need for modifications so that he will be able to make appropriate, timely changes or recommendations for changes that may be indicated.

Organizing

Like planning, this function is a perpetual one. The supervisor must continuously analyze the organizational structure within his sphere of operations to facilitate communication between the elements of the hierarchy and provide clear-cut downward lines of authority and responsibility and upward lines of accountability. Even minor organizational changes in his unit might bring about substantial improvements in operations.

However, there are times where organizational change may create problems of coordination and cooperative effort. It is the supervisor's responsibility to ameliorate these problems when they arise.

Staffing

Recruitment, training, and placement are proper and necessary staffing functions of each supervisor. Recruitment, while generally thought of as primarily a responsibility of top management, is a vital function of personnel at all levels. In reality, informal recruitment by members through personal contacts is often the best means of staffing departments.

---

[8] CALEA, from http://www.calea.org, accessed April 26, 2012.

Members can persuade recruits that the department is a good place to work, and this is generally the most effective and consistently productive method available to meet staffing needs. Indeed, it should be encouraged at every opportunity by all supervisors.

The supervisor's training function, as previously discussed, is closely allied to his responsibility for the proper placement of his subordinates. Although every employee cannot be assigned to precisely the task he prefers, every effort should be made to place him in the niche for which he is best suited. The net result to the organization is improved performance, since an employee who likes to work at a particular task is likely to be more productive than one who is discontented or bored with it. Far more effective results will be realized from placing a subordinate in a position that will challenge him than from placing him in one that requires something less than total effort. Boredom and monotony are most destructive of initiative and industry in an employee. The wisdom of placing round pegs in round holes has been amply demonstrated.

Directing

The function of providing direction to subordinates and control of their activities is one that consumes much of the supervisor's time. His position embodies the decision-making process in which he is constantly engaged. He not only must collect the necessary information and evaluate it before deciding issues but also must communicate his decisions to subordinates through orders, instructions, and all other means available to him. He must serve as a leader in the enterprise—not to drive but to lead, direct, and control personnel. He accomplishes this by securing effective action through the judicious use of his authority and by the application of common sense and practical psychology. Whenever possible, he uses positive methods by creating realistic inducements for proper performance rather than the negative method of penalizing for improper performance.

The supervisor must let his subordinates know what he expects from them. They will soon learn what they can expect from him. If his expectations are high, their production is likely to be high also; if he expects little from them, their performance will probably be poor.

The directing function involves not only putting a prepared plan into operation but also following through with observation and inspection to determine that the work ordered was actually and properly done. A follow-up or control system[9] is a must for organizations and leaders. Without it, authority is weakened, delegation is impaired, and the whole process of direction becomes more difficult. A supervisor who gives an order or makes an assignment and then fails to follow up to see that it is carried out as directed will soon abrogate his supervisory authority.

Coordinating

Perhaps no function of management is more important than that of coordination of human effort to ensure unity of action not only between individuals but also between organizational units. This activity must occur at all levels to prevent disharmony. As organizations increase in size and complexity, the need for coordination becomes greater. The degree of

---

[9] John C. Maxwell, *Developing the Leader Within You* (Nashville, Tenn.: Thomas Nelson, 1993), p. 181.

specialization, the area covered, the distance between elements that must work together, the skill of persons doing the work, and the dissimilarity of functions involved in the enterprise determine the need for coordination. Channels of communication and lines of authority become more indistinct as the nature of the organization increases in complexity, and often its prime mission becomes clouded in the minds of individuals who comprise it. Organizational objectives may give way to personal objectives, which will soon permeate the group and destroy its esprit de corps.

The essential activity of coordination can best be accomplished through direct communication. It can seldom be accomplished by mandate. Coordination of effort is difficult, even almost impossible in any effective degree, if the common objectives of the organization are not accepted by those who are expected to act in unison.

The wise supervisor will take it upon himself to develop friendly rapport with supervisors of related units allied in common purposes within and outside the organization. He will accomplish this through informal meetings, formal associations, and maintenance of friendly relations. The interchange of personnel on a training basis for short periods of time, perhaps a month or two, will increase employees' understanding of each other's jobs and will tend to foster coordination. The first-line patrol supervisor assigned to the investigation division for a short training period, for example, will invariably bring to his subordinates on his return to his regularly assigned patrol post an improved (or at least a broader) insight into the problems of the investigator and his job, thus contributing materially to improved relationships between two units that have traditionally experienced friction. This increased understanding of each other's responsibilities is a paramount factor in the process of bringing about better relationships between two such

Police officers receive assignments at the beginning of their shift in Brooklyn, New York
© Marmaduke St. John/ Alamy

units where friction occurs primarily because the people in one do not appreciate the problems of the other. Such a program, properly administered for training, has proved to bring about a healthy cross-fertilization of understanding between participants and should well become a matter of departmental policy.

By his attitude, the supervisor can establish a climate in which the spirit of cooperation will thrive among his subordinates. Hostile, suspicious, or unfriendly relations between supervisors of allied units will invariably be reflected by misunderstandings, rivalries, and ill will between their respective subordinates. This is because the supervisors' attitudes will often quickly permeate their whole units. Smooth operations will be hampered by these barriers to effective cooperation.

The degree of coordination achieved in any organization will directly approximate the level of willing cooperation between individuals in the various units that must work in harmony to accomplish the mission of the enterprise. If the organizational structure clearly provides for a system of authority so that those in charge can interrelate the various elements of the establishment and create a unity of purpose in the minds of the employees, coordination will follow.

Basic Organizational Structures

An organizational structure is a mechanical means of depicting, by an arrangement of symbols, the relationships that exist among individuals, groups, and functions within the organization. Lines of authority and responsibility and functional relationships between groups and individuals are shown in graphic form. Even the most innovative of modern organizational structures are but modifications or conglomerates of one or more of the basic types of organizations.

Line Organization

The straight-line organization, often called the individual, military, or departmental type, is the simplest and perhaps oldest form and is seldom encountered in its true form in any but the smallest of organizations. The channels of authority and responsibility extend in a direct line from top to bottom within the structure. Authority is definite and absolute (see Figure 2–1).

While the line-type organization has many advantages, it also has some inherent weaknesses, which sometimes make its use impractical. Perhaps its greatest advantage is that it is utterly simple. It involves a division of the work into units with a person in charge who has complete control and who can be held directly accountable for results, or lack of them.

Quick decisions can be made in the line organization because of the direct lines of authority, and because of these direct lines, each member in the chain of command knows to whom he is accountable and who is accountable to him. Because responsibility is clearly fixed, discipline is easily administered, responsibility for making decisions is well identified, and singleness of purpose is fostered. Coordination of effort is relatively easy to achieve because functional overlapping between units, a prime cause of friction in any organization, can be minimized.

One disadvantage inherent in the line-type organization is that supervisory personnel are too often required to perform the duties of specialists because little use is made of

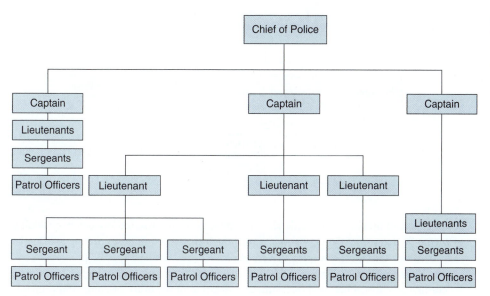

Figure 2–1
*Line- or
Military-Type
Organization.*

the latter for giving advice and counsel to line units. It is also often difficult to establish functional definition at the outset, but once it has been achieved, duplication of effort can be reduced. If jealousies exist between managers of the various units, each unit will tend to become "departmentalized," with the result that harmony of operation will be reduced and internal frictions will arise.

Functional Organization

The functional organization in its pure form is rarely found in present-day organizations except at or near the top level. Unlike the line-type structure, establishments organized on a functional basis violate the prime rule that workers perform best when they have but one supervisor. The functional organization divides responsibility and authority among several specialists, such as the person responsible for all training, the employee directing the community relations activities of all units within the department, or the officer having line authority over any employee handling a case involving a juvenile. The functional responsibility of each "functional manager" is limited to the particular activity over which he has control, regardless of who performs the function (see Figure 2–2).

Coordination of effort in this type of organization becomes difficult, since the employees responsible for results may be subject to the functional direction of several persons. Discipline is difficult to administer because of this multiheaded leadership. There may be considerable conflict among the functional administrators, resulting in much confusion among line personnel. Lines of authority and responsibility are fragmented into many functional channels, making each supervisor responsible to several superiors based on the function he happens to be performing.

One format in which the functional organization has been very successful is the task force. Every state now has a joint terrorism task force, which is a collaboration of federal, state, and local law enforcement agencies. Many smaller state task forces exist for varied purposes such as narcotics enforcement and auto theft investigations. In the early 1980s,

Figure 2–2
*Functional-Type
Organization.*

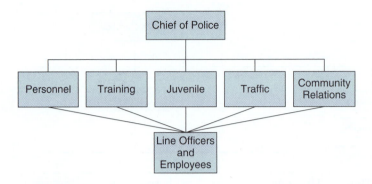

a task force of more than 300 federal, state, and local agents arrested suspected serial killer Wayne Williams in Atlanta, Georgia.[10] Although the structure poses unique managerial challenges, a task force can often be very effective in addressing a specific problem.

One reason task forces can be very effective is because they are highly focused on coordinated effort. However, their inherent violation of the unity-of-command principle causes them to get bogged down over time. Agencies have primary authority for their respective jurisdictions, but an investigation crossing borders may be taken over by state or federal authorities. Long-term task forces may have different supervisors for field operations, budgeting, scheduling, and training. Incompatible databases and politics are among the most glaring difficulties faced by task forces.[11] Research on the D.C. Sniper Task Force emphasized the importance of having just one executive in charge, with excellent communications among all members.[12]

Line and Staff Organization

The line- and staff-type organization is a combination of the line and functional types and is found in almost all but the very smallest police agencies today. It combines staff specialists or units with line organization so that the service of knowledge can be provided to line personnel by specialists such as the criminalist, the training officer, the research and development specialist, the public relations officer, and the intelligence specialist. Channels of responsibility and authority are thus left intact, since the specialist's responsibility is to "think and provide expertise" for the line units, which are then responsible for "doing." The line supervisor must remember that he obtains advice, not commands, from the staff specialist (see Figure 2–3).

In normal operations, the staff supervisor has line command only of those subordinates in his particular unit. If he and the line supervisor recognize this limitation,

[10] Charles R. Swanson, Leonard Territo, and Robert W. Taylor, *Police Administration, Structures, Processes, and Behavior*, 8th ed. (Upper Saddle River, N.J.: Pearson Prentice Hall, 2011), p. 236.
[11] E. R. Gehl, "MultiAgency Teams: A Leadership Challenge," *The Police Chief* (October 2004), 150.
[12] Gerald Murphy and Chuck Wexler, *Managing a Multi-Jurisdictional Case: Identifying the Lessons Learned from the Sniper Investigation* (Washington, D.C.: Police Executive Research Forum, October 2004).

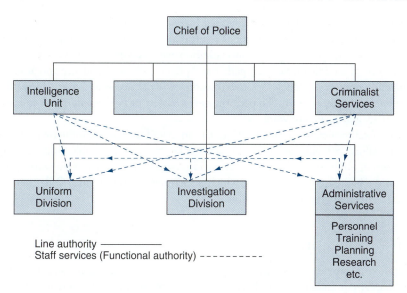

Figure 2–3
*Line- and Staff-Type
Organization.*

coordination between line and staff personnel can be achieved without undue friction. Failure to recognize these line and staff relationships is the greatest and most frequent cause of friction in an organization and one of the most prominent barriers to effective coordination.

Division of Work

Organizational structures are established to designate how work is to be divided among the various components of the establishment. Regardless of what basis is used for this division—whether work is apportioned according to function performed, as in the laboratory; by area, as in a system of precincts, geographic divisions, or beats; by clientele handled, as in youth activities or juvenile offenses; or by purpose, as in public relations activities, traffic control, and the like—the division must be logical and practicable.

Usually organizations are structured according to a combination of these bases. But regardless of the way the division of work is made, if it does not result in improved operations, economies to the organization, or convenience to those served, the division should be avoided. Changes in structure should never be made for the mere sake of change.

Insofar as practicable, homogeneous work should be apportioned to the same unit. Work that involves divergent functions or purposes will eventually cause friction and inefficiency if placed within one unit under the control of one supervisor.

The division of work involves not only the breaking down of a particular job into its component parts but also the recombining of these parts (synthesis) into a completed unit of work. The combining requires coordination if it is to be accomplished effectively.

The process of dividing work involves both analysis and synthesis. A function of prime importance for the supervisor is constant analysis of the nature of the work performed in his unit for the purpose of determining if it is effectively divided between the various units and individuals of the organization. Too frequently, tasks that should be combined into one function are fragmented into several, which breeds inefficiency. For example, considerable inefficiency might result if a patrol officer in an organization large enough to permit some degree of specialization were required to make a preliminary investigation of a crime on his beat, gather and preserve physical evidence and attempt to evaluate it, conduct the follow-up investigation, type the necessary reports himself, and then present his case in court. To perform such a variety of tasks would result in lowered productivity and quality of work.

For best results, the principle of specialization and the law of productivity, as stated by Leon Alford,[13] require assigning to each worker the fewest possible kinds of tasks or operations in order to improve the quality and increase the quantity of his work and giving him the highest class of work for which his natural abilities fit him. Only then is the greatest individual productivity possible.

Unity of Command

In addition to providing a logical arrangement of work, organizational structure should provide clear-cut channels of authority. The principle of unity of command should be practiced in every organization. This principle requires that every employee be under the direct command of but one superior.[14] Thus each worker should be accountable directly to only one supervisor in normal operations. It is recognized that the principle occasionally is violated in organizations that function exceptionally well despite what is classically considered almost a fatal breach of an inviolate principle. Close analysis will probably reveal, however, that such organizations operate effectively because of exceptional leadership. Management folklore has numerous accounts of such occurrences—just as in the folklore of engineering, the bumblebee is said not to have the physical capacity to fly.

The principle of unity of command applies to those who are commanded, not to those who command. It does not relieve the supervisor from the responsibility for taking action in emergency situations that require immediate supervisory attention, decision, or disciplinary action (even against a subordinate assigned to another unit). This exception does not justify the specialist assuming command over line personnel in normal operations, although the practice is occasionally permitted if only by implication. Neither does the exception make more acceptable the routine practice of some superior officers of dealing directly with operating personnel instead of through their immediate supervisors. Such practices will cause friction and tend to undermine the supervisor's authority over his own subordinates. It will invariably cause confusion, insecurity, and a lowering of confidence of workers subjected to such habitual breaches of the principle in normal operations.

The Department of the Army stresses that "unity of command assures unity of effort by the coordinate action of all forces toward the common goal.... Where unity of command cannot be realized [because of legal sanctions involving agencies from several

---

[13] Leon Pratt Alford, *Laws of Management Applied to Manufacturing* (Easton, Pa.: Hive, 1981), p. 82.

[14] Donald Mosley Jr., Donald Mosley Sr., and Paul Pietri, *Supervisory Management* (Mason, Ohio: South-Western, 2011), p. 108.

levels of government, as in joint efforts to control civil disorder or provide mutual aid] at least unity of effort should be realized. The establishment of joint operations centers; the recognition of each other's capabilities and limitations; and a positive attitude will contribute to unity of effort."[15]

Span of Control

This principle has been applied to the police, military, and administrative organizations. The span of control relates to the number of subordinates who can be supervised effectively by one supervisor. This limit is small, from three to five at the top level of the organization, and broadens at the lower levels. It is dependent on such factors as the capacities of the supervisor and those supervised, the types of work being performed, and the complexity of the work. Other determining factors include the area covered by it, the distances between elements, the time needed to perform the tasks, the homogeneity of operations, the types of persons served, and the effectiveness of managers.

The tendency in modern police operations is to exceed the bounds of effective control. Chiefs of police and other high administrative officers too frequently attempt to exert direct control over too many subordinates. Field supervisors at the operational level are expected to do likewise. The results are delay and confusion because of the bottlenecks the practice causes. Rather than delegate some of his functions to subordinates, the top administrator too often attempts to retain close contact with every phase of the operation and will not relinquish his control until he comes to realize the limits of his capabilities; until then, the total organization suffers. Superior officers should make every attempt to avoid requiring their supervisors to spread themselves so thin that they find it necessary to neglect their primary job of supervising because of the excessive number of details associated with the job they are given to oversee.

The supervisor can effectively reduce his span of control by delegating work (as discussed next), but in doing so, he must clearly define tasks for those who are to perform them, properly communicate necessary instructions to them, and require that they do completed staff work. Then, if employees receive proper training so that they require less supervision and control and are given sufficient authority to perform requisite tasks, the supervisor will be able to devote more of his efforts to those exceptional matters requiring his personal attention.

Delegation

The principle of delegation relates to the process of committing an activity to another's care. It is closely related to the principle of span of control in that even though the span is excessive, the harm from it can be reduced by the delegation of much detail to subordinates. Those supervisors who refuse to allow anything to be done except under their

---

[15] U.S. Department of the Army, *Field Manual 19-15, Civil Disturbances Operations* (Washington, D.C.: U.S. Government Printing Office, 2005), from http://www.fas.org/irp/doddir/army/fm3-19-15.pdf, accessed on April 25, 2012.

direct control are the primary causes of the crippling bottlenecks that slow or stop effective operations.

Proper delegation frees the supervisor from many routine tasks and enables him to devote more of his time to broader planning activities. In addition, it provides other worthwhile benefits to employees to whom jobs are delegated. It gives them an opportunity to increase their job knowledge by performing new tasks that are not ordinarily their responsibility. It is an excellent tool for developing personnel for positions of greater responsibility and for increasing their initiative in accomplishing new tasks. Without such opportunities, workers often develop feelings of insecurity and frustration. They often begin to wonder if the supervisor has confidence in them, or they feel that there are no avenues open to them for developing their capacity for higher positions.

If results only are to be evaluated, the astute supervisor will delegate to the most competent people who will make him look best; however, he must weigh the benefits to others of the training they are likely to derive from performing the delegated task against his own self-interests.

Although many activities can be passed down to others through the process of delegation, the supervisor cannot avoid the responsibility for such activities. Many supervisors have suffered dire consequences by assuming that a job entrusted to a subordinate relieved them of their responsibility for completing the job. They should be encouraged to delegate all possible tasks to the lowest possible level in the organization *where the necessary ability to perform them exists*, but in so doing, they do not shed their responsibility for the completion of the task and their accountability for the results.

Experience has shown that the average employee can and will accept greater responsibilities beyond his ordinary duties and will perform surprisingly well when he is delegated a task and given credit for its accomplishment, but the supervisor must avoid delegating tasks beyond the capacity of his subordinates to perform them. He should refrain from delegating only distasteful or onerous tasks and should not attempt to "delegate away" his responsibility for certain basic duties that only he should perform. Stephen Covey recommends a radical increase in the empowerment of employees when delegating. Covey uses "win/win performance agreements," essentially negotiated documents describing the goals of the task, the management support promised, and the rewards and penalties to be expected. Used properly, the effective supervisor "can greatly increase his span of control. Entire levels of administration can be eliminated. Instead of supervising six or eight, such a manager can supervise twenty, thirty, fifty, or more."[16] Although such numbers are well beyond the commonly accepted spans of control in policing, the potential benefits of this delegation style must not be ignored.

Delegation Failures

Delegation is done poorly when the supervisor allows his subordinates to delegate upward more quickly than he learns to delegate downward.[17] If he does not delegate, then he has not learned how, he has never really appreciated the training value of delegating or the need for avoiding routinized tasks that others can do better (and sometimes more

---

[16] Stephen R. Covey, *The 7 Habits of Highly Effective People* (New York: Simon & Schuster, 2005).

[17] John C. Maxwell, *Developing the Leaders Around You* (Nashville, Tenn.: Thomas Nelson, 1995), p. 161.

economically), he has an overabundance of confidence in his own capacity for detail, or he does not have confidence in his subordinates.

Delegation Process

When a task is delegated to an employee who is competent to perform it, enough authority to complete it must also be delegated, but the process must be consistent. Subordinates will be confused by a grant of total authority at one time and a total absence of it at another. Once authority has been granted, the supervisor must consistently refuse to take back what he has delegated simply because the subordinate thinks the task is too difficult or is reluctant to make a decision he is perfectly capable of making. In either case, the subordinate needs further training in how to do the task, or he needs to be given assurance that he has the necessary decision-making authority:

> The primary function of the manager is to preside over the process of delegation. This requires all of his judgment and much of his time. He is constantly attempting to provide, through the means of delegation, the opportunities of growth which the people under him demand. The strength of any organization increases with the ability of people at all levels to accept responsibility. The assignment of responsibility should never be static as implied by organization charts but should be changed with the situation and with the increasing capacity of people who are receiving proper management attention. As a responsible manager delegates responsibility to the people below him and devotes attention to qualifying them to discharge this responsibility well, he is developing himself as well as increasing the satisfaction and caliber of his subordinates.[18]

Delegation may be accomplished by a specific or general directive given either in writing or orally. A simple task may be delegated in a simple manner. A complex delegation should be supported by a comprehensive written directive clearly identifying the problem and the procedures to be followed if necessary. It is imperative that instructions are complete and clear lest the assignment be misconstrued, in which case the subordinate assigned the task could not be held responsible for it. If a subordinate is given an assignment to provide an answer to some vague problem but does not understand what the problem really is, his job will be unproductive, wasteful, and frustrating.

Once a job has been delegated, its importance has been explained, and necessary instructions have been clearly given for its accomplishment, the supervisor should discreetly follow up as needed to ensure that the employee is progressing satisfactorily. Assistance should be given to overcome obstacles the employee is not equipped to handle, but care should be exercised that he is not given so much help that his initiative is taken away. The process of delegation loses its value as a supervisory tool if follow-up inspections are not made to ensure that objectives are accomplished and deadlines are met.

Personnel Development by Delegation

The practice of delegation contributes to the development of subordinates to perform the supervisor's job when he is absent or unable to act. A program of this nature is variously denominated "executive" or "supervisory development" or simply "personnel

---

[18] U.S. Army Logistics Management Center, *Principles of Management: Special Text 38-1* (Washington, D.C.: U.S. Government Printing Office, n.d.), p. 15.

development," which is a more all-inclusive program of training subordinates at all levels of the hierarchy to "take over" when necessary.

Some supervisors are reluctant to develop subordinates because of the fear that they will become competitors. However, if the supervisor's job is performed well in his absence by others who have been trained to do it, he will eventually receive credit for his efforts.

A watch commander should train each of his sergeants to take over while he is absent on vacation, has days off, or is on sick leave. The practice of training only the senior sergeant for this duty decreases flexibility and deprives younger supervisory officers of training they may badly need in some emergency when the responsibility of a higher position is thrust on them. It is better that errors be committed at a time when they can be corrected constructively under the watchful eye of an experienced supervisor than when they occur under emergency conditions and an error might be critical. Often it is argued that the senior supervisor should never be required to operate under the direction of one of junior standing because of the adverse effect such an arrangement might have on the morale of the senior; however, such argument is tenuous, and such adverse effects (if they exist) can be avoided by adopting the executive development principle as a policy program within the agency.

The development of subordinates is essentially a problem of training wherein the subordinate's skill and efficiency are increased. This increase in his ability to render a service requiring a higher degree of responsibility enhances his confidence, gives him satisfaction, and provides him an incentive of new goals toward which he can strive. His superior gains an increased freedom from details of his operation, which enables him to devote more time to making policy, supervising, and planning.

The Exception Principle

Developing subordinates to take over in the boss's absence involves training, just as does the exception principle, which specifies that the head of an organization or unit within it should not find it necessary to act personally on each matter coming under his general jurisdiction. Rather, he should have to act only on those exceptional matters that require his personal attention.

The exception principle is inseparable from the principle of delegation. It prevails at all levels of the organizational hierarchy and is dependent on the effective application of the delegation function, which will free the superior from a mass of routine detail that might be better handled by others below him. Training is the key to the successful application of the principle. Superior officers should pass on all possible work to subordinates except that which is appropriate to the particular level that the superior occupies. He should reserve for himself only those decisions his subordinates are not equipped to make. He should avoid becoming bogged down with detail so that he can be free to integrate the work being performed within his sphere of operation into that of the entire organization.

Delegation of Staff Projects

The principle of completed staff projects requires that the person to whom work has been assigned through the delegation process complete it so that the only thing left to be done by the person who delegated it is to approve it. If he disapproves it, the delegation of work was not successful, since the principle requires that everything must be done that the person making the assignment would have done had he had the time to do the work himself.

Researching Projects

Usually the task assigned can be completed without an in-depth investigation and study. On occasion, however, a project requires considerable inquiry preliminary to the submission of a formal report. In such cases, the person to whom the work has been assigned must work out all details completely. All the legwork of gathering pertinent data must be performed after the approach to the problem has been carefully planned and a line of procedure decided. What data are needed? Where can they be obtained? What are the views of interested persons and those affected by the project? Consultation with specialists and a review of the related literature on the subject may furnish the answers to these questions.

Planning Projects

Once data required for the project have been accumulated, they should be studied carefully, refined, and organized into a logical draft if a written report is required. Usually restudy and rewriting are required to refine the product to a point where it is suitable for presentation. The more difficult and complex the problem is, the more tempting it is to present it in piecemeal fashion.

If a plan of action is proposed, it should be well coordinated, unequivocal, and supported by factual data. Accuracy of supporting material should be unimpeachable, since the superior may refer to the material as supportive of his contention or request. Should he commit himself to a course of action only to find that the basis for his commitment is spurious or inaccurate, he risks embarrassment and damage to his reputation.

Ordinarily, a summary report—concise, brief, and to the point—should be included. Often it should be placed at the beginning so that the superior can conserve time reviewing details of the project. Such a summary should be supplemented by a more detailed section suitably referenced to appropriate addenda, which may provide further particulars as might be desired.

Finally, the person preparing the report should place himself in the position of the superior to whom it is to be submitted. Would he sign it, thereby staking his professional reputation on the contents? Would he approve it as written? If the answer to either of these questions is no, complete staff work has not been done. The report should be restudied and rewritten with the objective of protecting the boss from half-baked ideas, endless memoranda to digest, or immature proposals.

SUMMARY

Organization is a medium through which work is accomplished by individuals or groups associated with each other in doing something. Organization involves not only physical matters but psychological ones as well, since it involves individual and group relationships welded together through the coordinating activities and leadership of managers.

The supervisor's main administrative activities are described by Gulick's concept of POSDCORB. The planning activities of the supervisor are a constant process. Well-made plans in effect enable him to make decisions in advance to aid him in accomplishing the objectives of the organization. His organizing function, which is closely related to the planning function, requires that structural changes be made as the need arises to provide a more effective medium through which work can be distributed and performed. His staffing responsibilities involve the placement of subordinates into positions for which their capabilities best fit them. Perhaps one of the supervisor's most important functions is the training of employees so that they will perform their tasks effectively, efficiently, and safely. Much of the supervisor's time is consumed by his control activities embodied in the direction function, which is accomplished by observation, inspection, and follow-up.

The coordination of human effort is the function of the leaders of an enterprise that determines how effectively the elements of the organization perform in conjunction with each other. Cooperative effort is the essence of coordination. The reporting function involves the process of communicating down with subordinates, up with superiors, and across organizational channels with other units. It dovetails with the process of coordination of efforts.

The supervisor is responsible for the constant and never-ending process of analyzing how work is apportioned so that the individual and group elements within the organization will be performing similar amounts of work per employee. Changing organizational responsibilities will necessitate realignment of workloads so that a logical and practical division of work may be realized. Such realignments will also require that attention be given to the number of subordinates and the amount of detail over which the supervisor exercises control. His span of control and the amount of attention he is capable of giving to his responsibilities are limited by the nature of the job and the capacity of his personnel.

The ability of the supervisor to perform his complex duties efficiently and well will depend to a large degree on how skillfully he is able to delegate routine tasks to others and to retain for his personal attention only those exceptional matters he should handle himself. The more effective this delegation process is, the fewer bottlenecks he will create in the operations of his unit. In addition, he will be freed to engage in the broader context of planning, creative thinking, and essential external relationships. The effectiveness of this process of delegation is largely dependent on how well subordinates have been trained both to assume responsibility for routine acts and decisions for which they are equipped and to engage in completed staff work.

REVIEW

Questions

1. List the various elements of the chief executive's activities as described by Gulick, and discuss how each applies to the first-line supervisor.

2. What is meant by the word *organization*?

3. How may a supervisor best utilize the talents of the natural leaders in the organization even though they are not officially designated as such? What are these natural leaders called?

4. What are the four main bases for dividing work in the police service? Give two examples of each.

5. What is the principle of specialization?

6. What is the law of productivity?

7. Define unity of command, and discuss the factors that affect its application.

8. What is meant by "span of control"? How is it affected by organizational structure? What other factors affect span of control?

9. Discuss how failure to delegate causes bottlenecks in an organization. Give examples.

10. Why can ultimate responsibility *not* be delegated?

11. Discuss the benefits the supervisor can derive from effective delegation.

12. What is the exception principle?

13. Define the essential nature of completed staff work.

14. How do delegation, the exception principle, and the principle of completed staff work inter-relate?

Exercises

1. Prepare a simple chart of your organization or of another one. Identify the type of organization, the advantages and disadvantages of such a structure, and some possible means of eliminating its disadvantages or of increasing its advantages.

2. Prepare a simple organizational chart of at least two other types of organizations. Discuss the advantages and disadvantages of each.

3. Draw a chart of an organization you would consider "ideal" in a police organization of 50 sworn and civilian employees, and then two more charts for organizations with 100 and 300 employees. Justify the appropriateness of each structure.

3

Leadership, Supervision, and Command Presence

Chapter Objectives

This chapter will enable you:

- To become acquainted with the principles of leadership development
- To become familiar with the types of leaders and the characteristics of each
- To gain an understanding of the techniques of supervising marginal employees
- To gain an appreciation of the need for applying good human relations in supervising employees
- To become acquainted with the basic criteria for decision making

Leadership may be defined as the art of influencing, directing, guiding, and controlling others in such a way as to obtain their willing obedience, confidence, respect, and loyal cooperation in the accomplishment of an objective. It is the human factor that binds a group together and motivates it toward goals. Leadership is truly an art. It embodies a set of basic principles, the application of which facilitates human endeavor. It involves more than just a grant of authority. A distinction can be seen in the following:

> When men obey another because of fear, they are *yielding*. Their obedience is given grudgingly. There is little loyalty or teamwork, and no desire to give their all for a common cause. But when men *follow*, they do so willingly—because they *want to do* what a leader wishes. Herein lies the distinction between being an authority and being a leader. The leader stimulates, motivates, and inspires the group to follow willingly, even eagerly. The authority pushes and drives his men who yield and obey because they fear the consequences of disobedience.[1]

There are as many levels of leadership proficiency as there are leaders. At different times and for different tasks, the degree of supervisory skills called for will vary. Yet there is a close positive correlation

---

[1] John A. Eterno, Eli B. Silverman, and Hugh Orde, *The Crime Numbers Game: Management by Manipulation* (Boca Raton, Fla.: CRC Press, 2012).

between organizational effectiveness and the abilities of supervisors to skillfully apply those proven principles of leadership that have evolved from the experiences of industry and the military, from the social sciences, and from other disciplines. The supervisor who has managed to learn and apply these principles will find his job easier and the productivity of his subordinates greater. The subordinates' apprehension of authority will be lessened, and their respect for their leaders will increase. The result will be better understanding and fewer conflicts of purpose between those who direct and control and those who constitute the workforce of the organization.

Resistance to Leadership Training

That considerable resistance to leadership training exists cannot be denied. This resistance is usually the result of the inability of some supervisors to adopt and apply realistically the principles of leadership to their own particular assignments. They perform their leadership tasks in the traditional stereotyped fashion. They look back at the brand of supervision they have received and reflect, "If it was good enough for me, it should be good enough for my subordinates." They are apt to supervise as they have been supervised. They find this attitude difficult to change. Often, those who most need to change are those who resist change most because they believe they are already good leaders and cannot recognize the symptoms showing they are not.

Some supervisors resist adopting more refined supervisory practices because many of these are intangible and require more effort than those to which they have been accustomed. They may resist because of the military connotation supervision implies in the quasi-military law enforcement, that is, I lead and you follow.

The application of many proven principles and scientific methods of supervision may initially require more energy than do some of the hard-driving tactics to which supervisors have become accustomed, but over time they usually become easier than the old unscientific approach. In addition, more often than not, the new principles are more effective in the long run and produce better results. Becoming skillful in applying sound leadership techniques requires diligence, but every supervisor worthy of the name must recognize the need for performing his tasks in such a way as to sustain a high organizational spirit and, at the same time, achieve maximum productivity.

Development of Leadership Ability

Leadership ability is not inherited. There are no born leaders. Undoubtedly there are some natural endowments that affect the relative abilities of individuals to become good leaders. Some physical traits, aptitudes, types of intelligence, and temperament characteristics are examples.

Any reasonably intelligent person with enough forcefulness to develop his ability to inspire others to follow him can earn leadership status. He may never be recognized on the organizational charts, and he may never be awarded stripes or bars, but he nevertheless is a leader if others are desirous of following him. The true leader—the ideal for the organization—is the leader recognized as such formally *and* granted leadership authority not only by his organization but also by his subordinates. The grant of authority by the latter is the only *real* source of authority.

The granting of formal authority does not ipso facto make a person a leader. Leadership status must be earned. The necessary qualities may be developed by training and self-discipline. When necessary, habits can be changed and emotions controlled. Mannerisms, speech, manual and mental skills, and attitudes can be altered by training calculated to develop or improve leadership ability, but this requires diligent effort. If leadership ability is learned slowly through trial and error, morale and performance are likely to suffer in the process because of the errors that are bound to creep into the supervisor's underdeveloped judgment.

There are numerous programs to help supervisors develop their leadership skills. Outstanding training is offered by the Southern Police Leadership Institute (http://www.louisville.edu/a-s/ja/spi), the West Point Command and Leadership Program (http://www.njsacop.org/), and the FBI's National Academy (http://www.fbi.gov/hq/td/academy/na/na.htm).

The best leaders make their jobs appear easy because they have the fewest problems. They learn to recognize symptoms that problems are developing and have the fortitude to take timely preventive action before the problems become unmanageable. Those who avoid problems by sidestepping issues that should be treated forthrightly may continue to hold their positions but are bound to fail as leaders.

250th Session—Students in session 250 at the FBI National Academy in Quantico, Virginia.

Types of Leaders

Many types of people make good leaders. There is no single leader type. Most leaders can be classified according to their individual approach to leadership under one of the following categories.

Autocratic Leader

The autocratic leader is highly authoritative. He makes decisions without allowing subordinates to participate. They are often made to feel that they are not part of the team because they are not allowed a voice in the decision-making process. They do, however, know where they stand because he goes by the book. He is the martinet who directs, commands, and controls his subordinates in such a manner that no one ever forgets who is the boss. He rules through fear, intimidation, and threat. He is a driver who uses his authority lavishly, demanding complete and unquestioning obedience from his employees. He is often thought of as the tyrant among supervisors. He is primarily leader centered, having little concern for others and considerable interest in his own supervisory status, but this approach does not work well for long. Employees will start to resist. They will sabotage the work effort in many ways to show their displeasure.

Many years ago leadership experts determined that when conditions are unstable during periods of stress or emergency, when initiative and decisiveness are needed, when there is usually no time for permissive leadership and no time for discussion with subordinates before each decision is made, and when bold, rapid action is indicated, the autocratic leader is most likely to succeed,[2] provided he has the capacity to make sound, workable decisions. If he is unable to do that, style alone will not help him to obtain good results for long.

Democratic or Participatory Leader

The supervisor who leads democratically, seeking ideas and suggestions from his subordinates and allowing them to participate in decision making that affects them, by and large secures the best results as a leader.[3] He uses little authority because he encourages his employees to participate with him in getting the job done. He treats them as associates in a joint venture and thereby increases their feelings of responsibility and their sense of achievement, recognition, and personal growth, but most important, he increases their commitment to the goals of the organization. This is the essence of participative management, which works well when circumstances permit employees to participate in the decision-making process.

At times, however, such as in emergent or unusual situations, purely democratic leadership will work poorly. In these cases, the most effective leaders will blend into their style more forceful measures that will produce the quick, decisive action needed. In such situations, the stronger leaders make it understood that participative management means "I manage and you participate."

---

[2] Bernard M. Bass, *Leadership, Psychology, and Organizational Behavior* (Westport, Conn.: Greenwood Press, 1973), pp. 438–40.

[3] Keith Davis, *Human Relations at Work*, 6th ed. (New York: McGraw-Hill, 1981), p. 157; Rosabeth Moss Kanter, *The Change Masters* (New York: Simon & Schuster, 1984), pp. 242–43.

The democratic leader is keenly aware of the human factor in managing others. As an employee-oriented leader, he secures better performance from his subordinates, motivates them better, and enables them to derive greater satisfaction from their efforts. Most probably, he not only will be a popular leader but will also be respected by his group. Popularity and respect need not be mutually exclusive.

Free Rein or Laissez-Faire Leader

The leader who plays down his role as such, and exercises minimum control, seldom gives his subordinates the attention or help they need. He does not interfere with them but permits a laissez-faire or leaderless operation. His failure to maintain contact is often as harmful as an excessive amount of supervision.

This type of supervision does not work well. It is an easy course for the supervisor to follow—especially when he is more concerned about being liked by his subordinates than being respected by them, but this invariably produces a climate of permissiveness. Feelings of insecurity develop among workers because they are left without the positive direction and guidance they look for and expect from their leader. As a result, morale, discipline, efficiency, and production begin to deteriorate, and the leader loses control.

Situational Leadership

The responsibility of supervising and managing others is not simple. Situations can be complex, and people are much more so. No one management style can work in every situation: A crisis, such as a hazardous materials spill, may require a direct management approach; supervising highly trained crime scene or accident investigators can be much more hands-off; developing a strategy for a patrol unit to address a neighborhood disorder problem could require a more collaborative management style. One supervisor can be highly effective in each situation as long as he can adapt his style to the needs of that situation. This is the essence of situational leadership.

Hersey and Blanchard developed situational leadership to help supervisors understand how to diagnose situations and then apply the correct management style for maximum results. The leader's style is a combination of task behavior (giving specific instructions) and relationship behavior (convincing workers to exert effort). The style the leader uses in a situation is dependent on the workers' readiness, which is a combination of ability and willingness.

> *Readiness Style 1.* When the workers are both unable to do the job and unwilling to try, the leader uses Leadership Style 1 (telling), which is high in task behavior but low in relationship behavior. For example, a new officer has limited training in first aid and is insecure about attempting to perform CPR (willingness is therefore low). The sergeant gives specific instructions: "Check for a pulse. Ok, no pulse? Measure off the xyphoid process, and get your hands in position. He's not breathing. I'll bag him and you do the compressions. Go deeper. Go faster. Good."
>
> *Readiness Style 2.* When the workers are unable to do the job but are willing or confident, the leader uses Leadership Style 2 (selling), which is high in task behavior and high in relationship behavior. For example, new officers are eager to go out and write a lot of traffic tickets, but the sergeant wants to teach them how to be more effective in

Topeka, Kansas Police Officer investigating a car accident.
(Corey Jones/the Capital-Journal)

traffic enforcement by adding some new behaviors to their limited skill sets: "I know I don't have to twist arms to get you guys to write tickets! But I want to show you how to handle violators so that they'll accept a ticket without calling internal affairs about your attitude. Is that something you'd be interested in knowing? I'll show you how; then you try it the same way."

Readiness Style 3. When the workers are very capable but are unwilling or insecure, the leader uses Leadership Style 3 (participating), which is low in task behavior and high in relationship behavior. For example, a squad of experienced officers is very capable but strongly disagrees with a new directive requiring that they document every activity they perform while on duty. The sergeant says: "Guys, I'm in this with you, and I'm going to keep a log of everything I do, too. But I can't go back to the administration and represent your position if you don't give the new policy a fair shot. So I need for you to follow through on this and record all your activities on your daily log, and I'll be checking them periodically throughout the shift. Look, when we capture just how much we really do, we'll be in a much stronger position to argue that we really are short-handed out here."

Readiness Style 4. When the workers are very capable and very willing, the leader uses Leadership Style 4 (delegating), which is low in task behavior and low in relationship behavior. For example, a detective squad is typically closer to Readiness Style 4 because it is mainly comprised of experienced officers who want to be there and who in fact may be sent back to patrol if their work is not up to par. The sergeant says: "Burglaries are up quite a bit in Area 3-A. I want you guys to review the reports, come up with a plan to address this problem, and submit it for my approval by 3:00 P.M. today. I know I can count on you to settle this."

"Situational leadership is based on an interplay among (1) the amount of guidance and direction (task behavior) a leader gives; (2) the amount of socio-emotional support (relationship behavior) a leader provides; and (3) the readiness ('maturity') level that followers exhibit in performing a specific task, function, or objective."[4] It was developed to help leaders be more effective in their dealings with subordinates.

Transformational Leadership and Empowerment

As a society we are rapidly changing. These changes present constant challenges to the supervisor. Successful and effective supervisors adapt. They motivate their workers to utilize creative problem solving. They reinforce the department's vision and desired culture.

James MacGregor characterized leaders as transactional (when one person takes the initiative, making contact with others for the purpose of the exchange of valued things) or transformational (when one or more persons engage with others in a way in which the leader and nonleader raise one another to higher levels of motivation and morality).[5] According to the Center for Leadership Studies (CLS), "Transformational leaders set high standards of conduct and become role models, gaining trust, respect and confidence from others; articulate the future desired state and a plan to achieve it; question the status quo and [are] continuously innovative, even at the peak of success; and energize people to achieve their full potential and performance."[6]

Bass suggested that transformational leadership motivates followers to produce more than expected by raising follower consciousness about the importance and value of certain goals, encouraging followers to transcend self-interest for the sake of the group or organization, and motivating followers to address higher needs.[7] The transformational leader empowers his employees to make decisions and handle situations.

By opening up the decision-making process, power is shared with the workers. This results in a number of benefits for the workers, supervisor, the agency, and the public. According to Seiter, in its pure sense, empowerment is an approach that is broader than supervising or delegating. It is more concerned about the overall culture of an organization. It is more than asking employees their opinions about policies and procedures. It extends beyond involving employees in creating solutions to problems. Empowerment involves pushing decision making down to the lowest possible level and letting employees manage themselves and make decisions. Empowerment involves giving employees the authority to create new approaches when they believe a new way improves the old. Empowerment involves providing employees with the principles and values of the organization, along with the desired outcomes (vision and mission), and encouraging them to make

---

[4] Paul Hersey, Kenneth H. Blanchard, and Dewey E. Johnson, *Management of Organizational Behavior*, 9th ed. (Upper Saddle River, N.J.: Prentice Hall, 2008), pp. 142–48.

[5] James MacGregor Burns, *Leadership,* 1st ed. (New York: Harper Perennial, 1978).

[6] Karen Matison Hess and Christine Hess Orthmann, *Management and Supervision in Law Enforcement*, 6th ed. (Clifton Park, N.Y.: Delmar-Cengage Learning, 2012), p. 17.

[7] Bernard M. Bass, *Leadership and Performance Beyond Expectations* (New York: Free Press, 1985).

decisions and respond to situations in ways that are consistent with accepted principles and values, while moving the organization toward its desired outcomes.[8]

Seiter contends that the end result of leadership in an organization is to empower employees to make decisions and respond to situations in a manner consistent with the culture, principles, ethics, and values desirable within an agency. When the leaders of all levels successfully carry out their activities already described, employees will adapt their behavior to conform to the culture, organizational direction, and professional approach desired. By creating the proper empowering environment and ensuring employees understand the vision and direction of the agency, employees are better prepared to make appropriate decisions and function in a professional manner.[9]

Selection of a Leadership Style

There is no set of hard-and-fast rules for supervising in every work situation. Each supervisor must determine which style of leadership he thinks is best for his particular working environment. This determination must, of necessity, be based on his own personality, the personalities of his subordinates, and his goals and theirs, yet he must avoid becoming bogged down in his supervisory style. If he does, he is likely to fail to capitalize on the inherent capabilities of his subordinates and their desire to perform well.

All types of leadership will work with varying degrees of success if the conditions are favorable and the situation permits a particular approach. The selection of the right approach for the right situation is the key to skillful leadership.[10]

Command Presence and Leadership

Command presence to some denotes a military bearing, and some think it means a distinctive type of appearance and conduct; others believe that command presence is comprised of the same ingredients as leadership. In reality, it is a composite of all those traits. It is the natural manner of an individual indicating a complete command of his mental and physical faculties and emotions. It encompasses the qualities of dignity, self-assurance, and poise. It is that outward appearance that denotes that the person has the ability and qualifications to take command of any situation. When the leader has command presence, he remains cool, calm, and collected in the face of conflict and exerts a confidence and self-control while handling a crisis.[11] It is often said that command presence is best reflected by the leader who looks calmer and calmer as things get worse and worse. The leader's attitude quickly permeates a group. If he displays anxiety, the group members will develop it and will not perform well in this atmosphere of anxiety and tension.

---

[8] Richard P. Seiter, *Correctional Administration,* 2nd ed. (Upper Saddle River, N.J.: Pearson Prentice Hall, 2012), p. 223.

[9] *Ibid.*, p. 227.

[10] O. Jeff Harris and Sandra J. Hartman, *Organizational Behavior* (Binghamton, N.Y.: Haworth Press, 2002), p. 247.

[11] Craig E. Runde and Tim A. Flanagan, *Becoming a Conflict Competent Leader: How You and Your Organization Can Manage Conflict Effectively* (San Francisco, Calif.: Jossey-Bass, 2007).

Chicago Police Superintendent Garry McCarthy, center, directs his officers as protestors march outside of NATO Summit in Chicago. Approximately 20,000 protestors marched on NATO's biannual summit before a small group began clashes with officers. (© UPI/Mark Cowan/Newscom)

Lt. Chris Cole offers some tips for improving a supervisor's command presence:[12]

Look Sharp—Present a positive image to the public. Be well groomed with a clean-pressed uniform. Ensure your badge, brass, and shoes are polished.

Act Sharp—Carry yourself with professionalism and authority. Know your job. Walk tall, speak clearly, and stand up straight. Doing so will help project your command presence and authority.

Be Sharp—Keep yourself well rested and exercise regularly. Be honorable, have integrity, display teamwork. Build trust with your community and with your subordinates. Remember the importance of making a positive first impression, as that is how others will perceive you.

Elements of Leadership

It is impossible to draw a clear-cut line between personal qualities of leadership and the external expressions of those qualities through action. The characteristics of the leader are too closely interrelated, too interlocking, to permit complete isolation of one from another.

Discipline

A high level of discipline in its broadest sense in an organization is perhaps the best mark of good leadership. Ordinarily, if it is present, a high level of esprit de corps and morale will result together with increased efficiency.[13]

---

[12] Lt. Chris Cole, *Improving Your Command Presence,* from http://www.lawofficer.com, accessed on April 28, 2012.

[13] See Chapter 10 for a discussion of the relationship between discipline, morale, and esprit de corps.

Ethics

The position of true leadership places on the leader a moral obligation to adhere strictly to the high standards of honor and integrity he expects of his subordinates—and which they and his superiors have the right to expect from him. His moral code must be beyond reproach. He not only must avoid all evil but also must avoid all appearances of evil. His conduct is appraised in three frames of reference: what it actually is, what he thinks it is, and what it appears to be to others.

Common Sense

Common sense is one of the most valued characteristics of a leader and is the hallmark of true leadership. Excellent leaders are guided by proper regulations and procedures, but they use good judgment when applying them. "Common sense always represents the action that gets the best results, with the least cost or side effects."[14]

Psychology

The maintenance of a high level of discipline and morale requires some practical knowledge of the psychological factors that affect human behavior.[15] Few supervisors have an instinctive or intuitive knowledge of these factors. That comes only with training and experience.

   To gain the willing support and cooperation of subordinates, the supervisor must learn those principles and techniques of leading them by sound logic and clear thinking rather than by driving them by arbitrary methods. He must recognize that few of them will respond consistently in the desired manner to the autocratic, dictatorial supervisory approach and that if he uses good common sense in applying the basic principles, he will seldom be required to get things done by displaying his authority. He will find that best results will be obtained if he uses his authority sparingly and rarely displays it. If he demonstrates that he *is* a leader, his subordinates will recognize him as such. Since he accomplishes his objectives through the efforts of people, he must develop at least a rudimentary understanding of the things that motivate them.

Motivation of Employees

All the leadership skills the supervisor manages to develop can be applied in one way or another to the motivation of his subordinates. Motivation involves the application of incentives, which encourages a certain positive pattern of behavior and attitude and contributes to the accomplishment of organizational objectives. Unless the employee agrees with these objectives and believes they are attainable, he will not be able to commit himself to them. If he can't, he won't be motivated.

   The effective supervisor will recognize the difference between giving employees a desire to produce well because of high job satisfaction and trying to force them to do so—deviously or otherwise. This is motivation versus manipulation.

---

[14] William S. Cottringer, "Common Sense Leadership," *Law and Order*, 52, No. 9 (September 2004), 110.

[15] See Chapter 7 for a further discussion of the psychology of behavior.

Employees are stimulated to produce best when they are provided with positive incentives that satisfy individual needs. This satisfaction leads to pleasurable experiences. Incentives such as recognition by supervisors and peers, praise, opportunity for development, an interesting and challenging job, increased responsibility, advancement, and fair treatment by supervisors are strong forces in motivating people and can usually be directly controlled by supervisors. When incentives are properly applied, they result in satisfaction and pleasure. People tend to repeat behavior that produces these sensations and discontinue behavior that does not.

Supervisors should be constantly aware that what motivates one person may fail entirely to motivate another because of individual differences. What might be a strong motivator at one time may lose its effect after a while.

Money and other material incentives are vastly overrated as positive motivational influences because they become weaker and weaker as physical human needs are progressively satisfied. The employee hungry for the satisfaction derived from such motivators as praise and recognition is usually a good producer, but when he becomes disinterested in his job and the satisfactions available from it, he sometimes loses his drive to produce. Motivation through the process of inspiration is unquestionably the most difficult yet the most powerful and lasting force in forming attitudes that will induce workers to make fuller use of their potential.[16]

Recognition is a strong motivating force in people. The supervisor can make good use of this force by giving employees credit for their accomplishments as a means of satisfying their drive for recognition. People obtain satisfaction from doing a job well and knowing that others—especially their superiors—have noticed their efforts. The supervisor can give this recognition if he understands the principles of objective personnel evaluations and applies them. In addition to providing recognition for deserving personnel, merit ratings will force him to appraise his subordinates periodically in relation to each other and rate them according to their value to the organization.

The supervisor should utilize every positive motivator at his disposal to stimulate his subordinates toward the highest productivity their capabilities will permit. He can assist them by establishing an atmosphere of cooperation in which each member of the organization strives of his own volition to assist others in achieving organizational objectives. He can push his subordinates, or he can motivate them so that they will react favorably on their own to achieve these goals.

The supervisor can keep the productivity of his subordinates at a high level if he lets them know just what he expects of them and then provides positive incentives for excellence of performance. His subordinates will ordinarily strive to do a good job. He can make it easier for them to do so by providing recognition for their efforts and by helping them to correct their mistakes by training or positive discipline. By avoiding inconsistent and arbitrary supervisory practices, he can gain their confidence and respect, which are vital in the process of motivation.[17]

Negative motivators such as fear, coercion, intimidation, and punishment should be avoided except when more constructive, positive means have been tried and have

---

[16] Kenneth W. Thomas, *Intrinsic Motivation at Work: What Really Drives Employee Engagement* (San Francisco, Calif.: Berret-Koehler, 2009), p. 24.

[17] Brette McWhorter Sember and Terrence J. Sember, *The Essential Supervisor's Handbook* (Franklin Lakes, N.J.: Career Press, 2007), pp. 72–73.

failed. Negative motivators tend to cause employees to develop rather sophisticated and undesirable avoidance techniques; they soon learn how to avoid being discovered when they commit acts that may lead to unpleasant responses by their superiors.

Fear, as a negative motivator, involves threat, direct or implied, and a degree of intimidation; but because human beings can shield themselves by developing a tolerance of stress, fear soon loses its value as a motivating force. The employee will soon become hostile, or the organization will lose him.[18] Although the proper use of punishment as a negative motivator has withstood the test of time, it must be used reasonably, fairly, and consistently or it will produce resentment, frustration, hostility, bitterness, and marginal performance, with the low morale that accompanies these reactions.

The supervisor cannot hope to eliminate *all* practices that act as motivation barriers, but he can concentrate his efforts on eliminating many of them. He can avoid those heavy-handed practices that impose unfair or unreasonable demands on his subordinates. He can improve his communications with them so that they will clearly understand his directives, his goals, and the objectives of the organization. He can make an effort to increase the esprit de corps in his unit to help improve the morale of his subordinates. He will avoid those courses of action that cause strife, confusion, anxiety, insecurity, or mistrust within the organization. He will engender in employees a feeling of trust, knowing that he will support them whenever just need arises. He will foster and encourage initiative among employees and reward them for their excellence of performance. He will provide training that will help them develop the competence required for their jobs. He will not just fill the position of a leader but will be one.

Material factors in the job, such as fringe benefits, physical working conditions, and pay, do not necessarily guarantee improvements in performance and attitudes. However, often they do, and they also tend to prevent morale and effective performance from deteriorating. Although the supervisor at the lower levels of the hierarchy often has no direct control over such aspects of a job, he should be aware that they may affect employee efficiency adversely. When they do, he should make timely recommendations for whatever corrective action is indicated.

Situational Analysis and Self-Appraisal

The supervisor should constantly evaluate his leadership qualities in an objective manner so that he might gain some insight into his strengths and weaknesses. Does he consistently act as a leader should? How has he reacted to stressful problems? Has his behavior resulted in the most productive solution?

Honest self-appraisal is difficult because someone often interprets what he does in accord with his own motives and not in accord with others' interpretations of what was done. When the supervisor recognizes his own deficiencies, he can usually correct them by systematically setting out to learn all he can about supervisory skills. The biggest problem is in honestly admitting to himself that his techniques might be wrong from time to time.

Supervisory incidents might well be reconstructed to determine if sound leadership principles were followed, if proven techniques were utilized, and if the supervisory

---

[18] Charles A. Hanson and Donna K. Hanson, "Motivation: Are the Old Theories Still True?" *Supervisory Management*, 23, No. 6 (June 1978), 11.

action taken was objective, without the interference of emotion or prejudice. This does not suggest, however, that blind adherence to a mechanistic approach should be followed. Reliance on such an approach may cause supervisors to concentrate on the more superficial aspects of their relationships with employees rather than to try to gain a genuine understanding of them. Thinking, feeling people—unlike things—cannot be treated as figures in a formula. Mechanistic supervision will quickly be recognized and may become the source of resentment and dissatisfaction. Subordinates may inwardly or outwardly accuse the supervisor of insincerity. A loss of confidence and respect is the likely product, which usually leads to lowered morale and productivity.

Leadership Characteristics

The traits commonly found in superior leaders would probably be found in most lists of desirable leadership characteristics. Possession of particular traits certainly does not ensure that a person is a good leader. He may be a gentle, kind, and friendly supervisor or a strict, decisive, and knowledgeable one. Neither may be a good leader because he lacks certain indefinable qualities that comprise good leadership.

Ideally, every leader should possess the following traits:[19]

1. *Friendliness, sincerity, affection for others, and personal warmth.*—A long face should be seldom (if ever) be the face of the leader; neither should he have a pessimistic or negative attitude. A sincere expression of pleasure when a greeting is indicated, especially to a subordinate, has inestimable value. A person's birthday, a promotion, his wedding, or the birth of his child is one of the big events in his life. A warm, sincere handclasp or a word of congratulation takes little time and is worth every moment it takes in these and similar cases.

2. *Enthusiasm for the job and all it entails.*—Sincerity and the ability to display it are vital traits of the leader. Zeal to do the right thing and to get the job done is extremely contagious and is quickly felt by others.

3. *Ambition.*—Within reason, ambition is desirable; however, it must be controlled, or it can become a millstone around the supervisor's neck. It should never result in the taking of credit belonging to another. Neither should selfishness and vanity be allowed to corrode the supervisor's career.

4. *Energy and vitality.*—Being a leader requires much physical stamina and a high frustration tolerance. Good leadership and hard work seem to go hand in hand. Diligence and industry are essential to effective leadership.

5. *Moral and physical integrity.*—The real leader has moral as well as physical courage. He has a sense of direction and purpose, with clear goals in mind. He takes personal responsibility. He knows where he wants to go and what he wants to do. He does not make promises he does not intend to keep because his word is his bond. It is

---

[19] William V. WillPratt, "Leadership," in *Selected Readings in Leadership*, 3rd ed., ed. Malcolm E. Wolfe and F.J. Mullholland (Annapolis, Md.: U.S. Naval Institute, 1965), pp. 2–8. See also Bass, *Leadership, Psychology, and Organizational Behavior*, pp. 166–67, 451; Larraine Segil, *Dynamic Leader, Adaptive Organization: Ten Essential Traits for Managers.* (New York: John Wiley & Sons, 2002).

more important that he be trusted and respected than liked. Subordinates expect their leaders to be honorable, to know right from wrong and justice from injustice, and to be fair to all without prejudice. A leader is expected to pursue the truth at all times. He is expected to keep his personal and professional life above reproach and, by his conduct, to be a credit to those in the organization and his profession. "Our values—the core beliefs that drive our behavior—determine our character, our ethics, and our potential as a leader."[20]

6. *Intelligence.*—It has been shown that the successful leader almost invariably has more intelligence than those he leads.[21] He has a sense of imagination and humor. He is capable of making objective observations. He has a questioning attitude that helps him in his search for the truth in all matters. He has vision and insight, for without them he will fail as a leader. He has a highly developed ability to see all sides of a question and draw commonsense conclusions from the evidence at hand.

7. *Technical skill.*—The most successful leader has a technical mastery of his job, including the teaching skill, which often takes the place of order giving, but leadership proficiency is not dependent on technical ability to do the job itself. The supervisor can be highly successful if he has a reasonable understanding of what the job requires and has a mastery of the leadership abilities necessary for getting it done.

8. *Faith.*—The leader has faith and confidence in himself and his subordinates. Employees will seldom have confidence in an individual who has no confidence in himself.

9. *Verbal aptitude.*—A large amount of experimental work supports the conclusion that the most successful leaders are verbally capable.[22] They are persuasive and tactful. Few attributes are more important in dealing with others without generating friction.

10. *Courtesy.*—Common courtesy demands that politeness is a civility that must be practiced at all times. The superior cannot afford to be outdone in it by his subordinates.

11. *Modesty.*—The real leader can afford to be modest and practice humility. His accomplishments will attest to his value without his constantly reminding others of his greatness.

In addition, characteristics of self-control, dependability, empathy for others (short of sentimentalism), good judgment, originality, versatility, and adaptability are usually found in the most successful leaders.[23]

Personality of a Leader

The personality of an individual is a composite of all his personal characteristics. As such, it plays an important part in the development of a leadership style and the ability to apply it successfully in supervising. Every leader has the capacity to be a good supervisor.

---

[20] Paul M. Whisenand and R. Fred Ferguson, *The Managing of Police Organizations*, 6th ed. (Upper Saddle River, N.J.: Pearson Prentice Hall, 2004), p. 22.

[21] Bass, *Leadership, Psychology, and Organizational Behavior*, p. 46.

[22] *Ibid.,* p. 166.

[23] *Ibid.*, p. 451.

Personal traits of successful leaders should be observed and studied by the supervisor in refining his techniques of leadership. Those desirable traits should be adapted to his own natural style whenever possible; those traits he has found undesirable in others should be avoided scrupulously. For example, if he has resented inconsiderate treatment by his superiors in the past, he should avoid treating his subordinates inconsiderately.

He should not assume, however, that any neatly packaged approach that treats employees as a uniformly styled population will always work. It will not. It may only compound his problem and cause him to oversupervise.

Success in supervision cannot be achieved solely by copying the style of other successful supervisors. To know what they do and how they do it does not mean that someone else can make the same approach work. The capability of the supervisor to adapt others' methods to his own particular style is the keynote to supervisory success.

Human Relations and Leadership

The human relations aspect of supervision and leadership has developed to an inordinate degree during the last several decades. It has occupied the attention of leaders and managers to the extent that sometimes their concern for the personal welfare and happiness of the individual employee has been at the expense of the organization as a whole. That consideration for these factors is important cannot be denied, yet some supervisors are so concerned with the principle itself that they have failed to use it with common sense. They often fail to do what must be done for fear of upsetting employees.

With regard to human relations, some researchers have found that there has been too much concern with making people happy. They assert that when the supervisor interprets the human relations doctrine as meaning that he has no right to be critical and dissatisfied with inferior performance, he deprives his subordinates of a standard for determining the level of performance that can be reasonably expected of them. We know that just having happy employees is not enough—they need reasonable goals and a sense of achievement and personal development if they are to be satisfied and productive.

According to Robbins, evidence suggests that productive workers are more likely to be happy workers rather than the reverse. That is, productivity leads to satisfaction. If you do a good job, you intrinsically feel positive about it.[24] Supervisors who put into practice the principles of good human relations without becoming permissive to the degree that the total organization suffers will accomplish more and will have fewer problems and conflicts than supervisors who allow themselves to become strict disciplinarians, with little empathy, compassion, or understanding for others. How the supervisor handles his interpersonal relations and those indefinable, intangible social problems that arise in every organization is an indicator of the degree of his human relations ability. His problems of managing people will be lessened if he reasonably consults with them about things that affect them. This does not imply that he should take a vote before every decision is made, however.

The objective of good human relations should be the greatest production in the shortest possible time with the minimum energy and the maximum satisfaction for the

---

[24] Stephen Robbins, *The Truth about Managing People and Nothing but the Truth* (Upper Saddle River, N.J.: Prentice Hall, 2002), p. 40.

producers.[25] This is the ideal of human efficiency. It is possible to achieve, but it seldom is achieved. It is a worthwhile goal toward which the supervisor should strive.

Industrial psychologist Dr. David Jones reports that many newly appointed leaders fail because of an inability to establish and maintain effective relationships with others, particularly those in subordinate roles.[26] Successful leaders build personal, positive, and professional relationships with those they work with.

Manner of the Leader

The physical, moral, and mental attributes of the supervisor have a powerful effect on his relations with subordinates. These traits are often reflected by his mannerisms, which afford an accurate clue to his state of mind. Body language, such as a look, gesture, voice inflection, physical bearing, or indication of tension, gives away the thoughts of an individual. As has been indicated, how an act is done is often more important than the act itself. For example, the supervisor who makes an accusation to a subordinate before learning all the facts pertinent to an issue will soon lose the confidence of his subordinates. A worker castigated by his supervisor for tardiness when the supervisor has not taken the trouble to learn the reason for the apparent dereliction will be resentful. An employee criticized by one supervisor for doing what another superior had directed him to do has just cause for grievance when the criticism was made without the supervisor learning the reason for the act.

The supervisor will find that a calm, controlled manner will be helpful to him in maintaining the confidence and respect of his subordinates. Frequent irritation, grouchiness, and emotional displays—especially of temper or anger—are indicators that he lacks the self-control desirable in a leader. An outward appearance of impassiveness or calmness may be overdone, however. Sometimes a sincere showing of emotion such as pleasure or a sincere showing of appreciation for a tribute rendered by subordinates is perfectly in order. Indifference is often as out of place as emotionalism.

Language of the Leader

Another outward mark by which a leader can be judged is the language he uses. What he says and the manner in which he conveys his thoughts give a clue to his mental state and the attitude behind it. They also indicate the possession or lack of good taste and breeding. His speech should be unaffected, positive, and direct, not uncertain, indecisive, negative, or apologetic.

Immoderate language habitually used in the presence of others invariably produces unfavorable results. Not only order giving but all communications should be devoid of vulgar, profane, or indecent speech or the sharp-edged tool of sarcastic language. Blunt contradictions serve no useful purpose, nor do inflammatory remarks, name-calling, or labeling. Language implying or expressing finality (as in ultimatums) should be reserved until no other recourse seems available to gain compliance, and then should be used only if the supervisor has the tools to carry out his ultimatum. Special care should be exercised

---

[25] C. David Mortensen, *Optimal Human Relations* (New Brunswick, N.J.: Transaction Publisher, 2008), p. 84.

[26] David P. Jones, *Million Dollar Hire* (San Francisco, Calif.: Jossey-Bass, 2011), p. 210.

to avoid talking down to others or talking over their heads, for to do so will give the impression of affectation or paternalism; either may be resented or cause subordinates to accuse him overtly or covertly of insincerity.

Commendations and Praise by the Leader

The desire of individuals for recognition is a force the supervisor should utilize to substantially increase his effectiveness. A few words of commendation and praise, sincerely given when merited, will do much to induce continued good performance. There are much more effective tools of leadership than condemnation, criticism, or punitive action. The supervisor should follow the adage, "Commend in public but criticize in private." Criticism, like commendation, should not be neglected when it is indicated. It can be constructive or destructive, depending on the manner employed in dispensing it. Supervisors are often so busy seeing that the job is done that they fail to see who does it and give credit when it is deserved.

One of the most frequent complaints of workers is that criticism comes readily but praise seldom.[27] Complimenting or giving praise when it is not merited, however, soon dilutes its value and is seldom effective. Likewise, insincere commendation soon loses its motivating effect. Dale Carnegie used the approach with great success that honest, sincere praise wins friends and influences people but that insincere flattery will backfire and make enemies. The most skillful supervisor will strike a reasonable balance between constructive criticism when it is needed and praise when it is earned.

The One Minute Manager by management experts Ken Blanchard and Spencer Johnson recommends using the one-minute praising technique as follows:[28]

- Tell people upfront that you are going to let them know how they are doing.
- Praise people immediately.
- Tell people what they did right—be specific.
- Tell people how good you feel about what they did right and how it helps the organization and the other people who work there.
- Stop for a moment of silence and let them "feel" how good you feel.
- Encourage them to do more of the same.
- Shake hands or touch people in a [professional and appropriate] way that makes it clear that you support their success in the organization.

Blanchard and Johnson suggest one-minute reprimanding and one-minute goal-setting techniques similar to those listed above. According to these authors, "Feedback is the breakfast of champions."[29]

Criticism and Reprimands by the Leader

The average supervisor all too often does not face up to his responsibilities of giving forthright criticism when it is due. He is often afraid of the repercussions from the social

---

[27] Bob Lee Wall, *Coaching for Emotional Intelligence* (New York: American Management Association, 2007), p. 126.

[28] Kenneth Blanchard and Spencer Johnson, *The One Minute Manager*, 10th ed. (New York: Berkley Trade, 2003), p. 44.

[29] *Ibid.*, p. 67.

Key Biscayne Police Chief Charles Press commends Broward Sheriff's Deputy Osvaldo Petitfrere for saving the life of a Key Biscayne police officer.
(© AP Photo/ El Nuevo Herald, C.M. GUERRERO)

group if he does so. He is afraid to tell employees what they must and must not do. His subordinates must come to understand that when he says something regarding his work expectations, he really means it.[30] If they are not made to understand this, he loses his position of leadership by default.

The supervisor should never lose his temper and become angry or hostile when reprimanding subordinates, nor should he exaggerate and overstate the reason for the criticism. Indeed, effective communication skills, combined with effective interpersonal skills, will allow him to "punish without drawing blood."[31] He should face the issue squarely and inform the employee in private of his unacceptable behavior without equivocation, apology, or sarcasm. The employee should be given an opportunity to make a positive response concerning the issue and to save face. The response should be so structured by the supervisor that it contains some plan for improvement.[32] A "soft," intelligent approach rather than a "hard" one tends to reduce antagonism and resistance to criticism, the object of which is to bring about improvement, not to produce resentment and hostility.

---

[30] W. David Rees and Christine Porter, *Skills of Management,* 6th ed. (London: Cengage Learning, 2008), p. 105.

[31] George Thomson and Jerry B. Jenkins, *Verbal Judo: The Gentle Art of Persuasion* (New York: Harper, 2004), p. 195.

[32] John R. Schermerhorn, *Management,* 11th ed. (Hoboken, N.J.: John Wiley & Sons, 2011), p. 451.

Knowledge of Subordinates

Every supervisor should learn as much as he can about his subordinates, individually and collectively. He should become familiar with each individual's background, experience, education, family relationships, sickness patterns, performance, and any other data that may give him insight into the subordinate's qualifications, aptitudes, potential, and motives. The process of learning about his subordinates is a continuing one. He may find that his first impressions have been fashioned on incomplete or inaccurate information and have been erroneous. As he gains more information through inspection of personnel records, observations, and personal contacts, he will develop a more accurate picture of the individual. He will learn that the personal and performance problems of subordinates may be identified with the brand of supervision they have received in the past. He will learn that he can assist them in resolving most of these preconceived notions.

Once the supervisor has gained the confidence of his subordinates, he will find that they will often come to him for help. He must carefully avoid meddling in their personal lives as long as their work and the organization are not involved. He will become involved only if he is asked to be. By becoming familiar with their drives and motives, he will gain some clues to their reactions as individuals and as a group.

Private information learned about a subordinate that adversely affects his personal or job welfare should remain private unless organizational interests demand its revelation. It should never be allowed to become a basis for unfounded rumor or unjust innuendo.

Supervision of the Marginal Employee

The marginal employee who does just that amount and quality of work that will not give the organization a cause of action against him often is the cause of considerable concern to the supervisor. Such employees are invariably the source of much dissatisfaction within their peer group, which they often contaminate with their anti-organization attitude. Production and morale eventually suffer. Such persons may be (or may think they are) overqualified for the job they are performing and believe themselves suited for a better position, which may or may not be available. They may, however, be underqualified and consequently become frustrated when they cannot achieve the goals they have set for themselves. Additionally, they may be disgruntled, frustrated, or emotionally troubled.

Supervisors often tend to ignore such a problem or try to rid themselves of the employee who is, to them, a source of irritation. They can transfer him, retain him and tolerate his attitude, retain him and attempt to correct his deficiencies, or collect evidence that will support his termination.

Transfer only shifts the problem to someone else, although at times a person performing poorly in one assignment will make remarkable improvement elsewhere because he is better matched with his new job. Retention in his present position may require that he be given special attention, depending on what is causing the marginal performance. If he is unqualified, additional training, education, and guidance, supplemented at times with counseling, may help. The disgruntled employee with a grievance should be given an opportunity to express the cause for his complaint. Imagined grievances are usually corrected easily by encouraging the employee to examine the real facts or by providing the facts he does not have. The disgruntled employee who has been a disciplinary problem in the past is often an extremely difficult and distressing problem to the supervisor. Special counseling and recognition for his strong characteristics will sometimes motivate him to better efforts. There are times, however, despite the best efforts of the superior, when nothing short of transfer or termination will rectify the problem.

The frustrated employee and the troubled one may require special attention. Counseling or referral may help correct their problems, as described in Chapters 7 and 8.

Order Giving

Ideally, order giving involves the complex process of communicating ideas in such a manner that the recipient interprets what he hears in the way the communicator intends. Each order is susceptible to three interpretations: what the person actually says, what he thinks he has said, and what the recipient thinks he said.

Using indistinct speech or poor word selection, giving orders in a disordered or haphazard manner, giving too many orders at one time or too much detail in one order (assuming that the receiver understands clearly what is expected of him), and neglecting to follow up are some of the most prevalent reasons for failures in order giving.[33]

Employees are more likely to resent the way an unpopular order is given than the order itself. Persuasion is much more effective than coercion in obtaining acceptance by those workers affected. The supervisor should consider the time and place in addition to the manner in which orders are given to obtain best results. The orders may be direct commands, they may be framed as requests, they may be implied or suggested, or they may consist of requests for volunteers.

The supervisor should designate one person to direct a task requiring group effort. This will provide for unity of command within the group and accountability for results. Obviously, sufficient authority must be given to the person held accountable to enable him to accomplish the assignment as directed. In deciding the type of approach that should be used in giving orders, making assignments, and delegating appropriate authority in a given situation, the supervisor should consider such basics as the personality of the subordinate, the amount of close direction he needs to do the job, his competency, and his initiative.

Direct Commands

Orders may best be given by command when emergent conditions require direct, prompt action. This method of giving orders may be indicated in dealing with an employee who is lazy, careless, indifferent, or irresponsible or the one who refuses or neglects to obey standard operating rules or fails to respond to suggestions or implied orders. Direct commands are also appropriate in situations where officers know what the right thing to do is but

---

[33] See Chapter 5 for a detailed discussion of interpersonal communications. Barriers to effective communications and means of overcoming such barriers are discussed at length.

may be tempted for a variety of reasons to neglect their duty. For example, when a suspect has been arrested for assaulting an officer and is handcuffed on the ground, the sergeant might say very directly, "Get that man off the ground and into the car NOW." Direct commands can, when used appropriately, get the job done right and actually prevent officers from getting themselves into trouble. When orders are given in the form of commands, they should be simple and direct. If they are hesitatingly given, they will usually be obeyed in a like manner.

How many times do we see it on the 6 o'clock news? The media helicopter catches the end of a pursuit, the take-down, and the arrest. The video on occasion shows the bad guy who is not resisting getting punched or kicked at the end. It then goes on YouTube. This kind of occurrence can be prevented by a supervisor who takes effective control of the situation.

Requests

Most orders should be framed as requests. Employees will often resent an authoritarian, dictatorial method. The capable, conscientious, responsible subordinate usually requires nothing more than a request. He will construe it as an order. Older employees usually respond similarly. Orders to sensitive, nervous, or easily offended persons are usually best framed as requests. Experience clearly indicates that cooperation is most readily obtained through requests rather than commands. Cooperation cannot be demanded; it must be won. The process of achieving it by demand will likely become a frustrating experience for the supervisor because his demands will be construed as ultimatums. If he does not follow up to ensure that they are being complied with, his authority is weakened. Obviously, the supervisor should make requests to others of equal rank or status instead of making demands if he expects to gain their cooperation.

Implied or Suggested Orders

Implied or suggested directives can be employed to good effect with the reliable employee who readily assumes responsibility for a task. They are also useful in developing the initiative of subordinates, since they allow considerable latitude in the method of accomplishing an assignment when immediate action is not essential.

The supervisor will express the degree of confidence he has in his subordinates by the amount of control he wishes to retain over their efforts. The amount of latitude he gives them will depend on their reliability and capabilities and on the nature of the assignment. The amount of confidence he has in them may be indicated by his instructions to them: "Do what you think needs to be done, and then let me know what you did"; "Keep me informed about what you do"; "Let's talk about what you decide"; "Clear with me before you do anything"; "Don't do anything without discussing it with me beforehand"; "I'll make the decision."

Orders to inexperienced or unreliable employees should be given in a more direct manner than by implication or suggestion. The inexperienced employee will often fail to draw the intended inference or make the proper deduction from an implied order. The unreliable employee will often draw the conclusion that is most convenient or desirable for him. Implied orders are often abstract and deprive the supervisor of a follow-up tool because if orders are subject to more than one reasonable interpretation, they are usually unenforceable.

Requests for Volunteers

Occasionally, a supervisor will call for volunteers to perform a dangerous or disagreeable assignment he cannot or should not perform himself. The call for volunteers should be used with care so that it will not become a simple expedient for escaping the responsibility of making assignments or issuing orders that are in the best interests of the organization. Neither should the supervisor call for volunteers to perform a task that he himself should perform merely because he wishes to shed his responsibility because he considers the job beneath him or because it involves a distasteful act.

Method of Communication

If orders are indirectly given, they will tend to strengthen ideas already present. If they are positive, they are likely to be more effective than if made in a negative vein.[34] For example, "Let's increase our selective enforcement efforts" might result in a better response than "You're not being very selective in your enforcement."

Verbal orders are usually satisfactory for simple tasks (especially if they have been performed before) and in emergency situations. As with many communications, a verbal order can be easily misunderstood, as can the intent of the person giving it. Details can be easily forgotten. Because of these factors, it is sometimes difficult to hold anyone accountable for failure in giving or carrying out an oral directive.

When other than a simple order is given, the person giving it should have it "played back" so that any misunderstandings that have resulted in the communication process can be clarified. It cannot be safely assumed that the absence of questions means that understanding has taken place.

Written orders should be used in situations where complex operations or numerous persons are affected to ensure that all receive the same message. Such orders facilitate systematic follow-up and provide a basis for attaching accountability for failures.

The employee with strong qualities of independence usually knows what his job requires and how to do it. He is likely to be more responsive if he is assigned a task in broad terms and is allowed to use his ingenuity and initiative in carrying out the details. The more dependent workers are likely to prefer and to depend on more concrete and detailed assignments rather than broad assignments that leave them to decide for themselves what needs to be done and how to do it.

Follow-Up

The supervisor surrenders his authority little by little when he fails to follow up his orders to ensure that they have been carried out. When a subordinate is directed to complete a task by a certain time, he should be required to comply as instructed. Notations regarding deadlines should be made by the supervisor on his desk calendar, pad, or notebook to remind him of the time he has designated for completion of an assigned task.

---

[34] H.L. Hollingsworth and A.T. Poffenberger, eds., *Applied Psychology*, (Darby, Pa.:Darby Books, 1983), pp. 93–95.

Decision Making

One of the most frequent functions the supervisor is called on to perform is that of decision making. It is imperative that he develop his ability to draw conclusions from facts at hand and stick to a decision unless, of course, it is manifestly improper. Even if he occasionally makes the wrong decision, the fact that he has taken positive action when action is indicated is usually better than if he had taken none at all. Decisiveness has a stabilizing influence on subordinates. Indecisiveness is easily perceived and tends to destroy confidence and lower respect. Ultimately, performance is adversely affected.

The decision-making process involves several steps. First, there must be an awareness that a real problem exists. An appreciation of its ramifications and recognition of a need for a decision must be present. The proper answer to the wrong question is no solution to the real problem. To deal with an apparent problem without knowing that it is merely a symptom of the real one may result in an incorrect solution to the right problem or an inappropriate solution to the wrong one. Second, facts must be obtained. Opinions of others may be needed as supportive data when subjective decisions are involved. Third, when sufficient data have been collected, they must be evaluated and analyzed. Reliability of the source of the data must be tested, just as the facts themselves are. Once the real problem has been identified, concentration can be focused on the solution. Personal bias should be eliminated in the analysis. Fourth, alternative approaches leading to a logical conclusion should be decided on, and probable consequences of each should be weighed. Possible conflicts among those who are to implement the decision must be considered. This involves insight. The effect of each alternative on the objective should be considered in determining the best course of action indicated by the facts at hand. Fifth, a decision must be selected from the alternative solutions. This involves value judgments in selecting the solution that allows action to follow in carrying out the decision. Consideration should be given to the time and the setting in which the action is to be carried out and to the long-term results from choosing one alternative over another. The pros and cons should be carefully considered and weighed. Sometimes, a secondary option for carrying out the mission might be necessary as a contingency measure in the event the primary decision is found to be unworkable or cannot be followed because of unforeseen circumstances. Sixth, the decision must then be communicated to those who must carry it out.

Appropriate follow-up should take place so that results of the decision may be checked and evaluated. This procedure may indicate the effect of the decision in changing attitudes, altering performance, improving morale, or revealing training needs.

Drawing of Conclusions

The making of decisions and the drawing of conclusions should not be based on snap judgments. The supervisor who jumps to a conclusion before knowing pertinent facts will find his conclusions more often wrong than right. Judgment of even the most ordinary of supervisors should be right more often than wrong if he is to survive as a leader. For example, the supervisor observing an employee sitting at a desk, leaning back, and gazing out the window may draw any one of a number of conclusions from this observation alone. The odds are against the drawing of the correct one without additional facts. The person might be just resting, he might be thinking or planning, he could be out of work, he might be lazy, he might be daydreaming or bored, he might be observing someone or something, or he might simply be attempting to resolve a personal or job problem.

The wise supervisor will recognize that one cause may affect behavior in many ways.[35] The employee troubled and worried over a serious personal problem may have varied reactions: He may engage in daydreaming or fanciful imagination in attempting to escape from his problem; he may neglect his work or fail to follow safety rules and quality of his work might decline; he may become overly sensitive to supervision; he may develop disagreeable habits, or his relationships with others might deteriorate; his work might suffer by excessive tardiness or absences; he may drink to allay his worry. Any one or all of these reactions may be set in motion by one causative factor. Such problems should be approached objectively. The real reason behind the behavior may not be apparent from the reason given. The supervisor should attempt to ascertain the true explanation rather than accept the proffered one for a particular type of behavior affecting a subordinate's performance.

Moderation in Supervision

Oversupervision is perhaps the most common failing of an inexperienced supervisor. It arises from his failure to delegate tasks, because of either a lack of confidence in his subordinates or a disinclination to relinquish what he thinks are his supervisory prerogatives. When he takes it upon himself to do his subordinates' work, initiative is corroded, and morale invariably suffers. Subordinates do not expect him to do their work and do not respect him for it when he does.[36]

As the supervisor's responsibilities do not permit him to be constantly on hand to help, he must train his subordinates to do what has to be done and then rely on them to do it. If the employee is capable of performing his assigned task, he should be allowed to do so without the supervisor standing over him checking on every detail. If he cannot be trained to do the task properly, he should be assigned to another. Oversupervision, often called "snoopervision," causes loss of respect for the supervisor, creates suspicions in the minds of employees, fosters rumors, and arouses resentment. Judicious contact between the supervisor and his subordinates is welcomed by them. His presence when he is needed and the lending of a willing ear to their problems will tend to give them a feeling of security and confidence and a sense of direction.

The effective supervisor will soon learn how much attention each employee needs and direct attention to each accordingly. Even the most efficient employees want some attention to give them some assurance that their good services are not going unnoticed. If a field sergeant rides with each of his patrol units on occasion, his subordinates will soon learn to expect it and will look forward to an opportunity to show their capabilities. They will not resent his presence if his supervision has been judicious, but they will feel neglected if others receive more attention than they do.

---

[35] See Chapter 7 for a discussion of frustration and aggressive reactions.

[36] Peter J. Frost, *Reframing Organizational Culture* (Newbury Park, Calif.: Sage Publications, 1991), pp. 191–92.

Fraternization

There is always room for forthright friendships between supervisors and their subordinates. The fact that one has been promoted to a higher position, especially when the organization promotes from within, should not mean that old friendships must be severed. Although the new supervisor must always remember where he came from, he also must recognize that he is no longer a member of his former group. The nature of his official relationships with those who are his friends and peers has forever changed! Certainly, the friendship with subordinates will continue after the individual's promotion to supervisor, but the relationships will be changed. The extent of this friendship will vary among individuals.

Friendship alone should not be allowed to become the basis for preferential treatment, however. Formal relationships should be dignified, warm, friendly, and democratic but never boorish. Overfamiliarity and the taking of unjustified liberties by subordinates, purely because of friendship, should be discouraged because they tend to corrupt respect for authority, especially when unrestrained familiarity takes place in the presence of other subordinates. When such conduct occurs between a supervisor of one sex and a subordinate of the other sex, the results are often particularly devastating to the supervisor's position of leadership and to the morale of the organization.

On the other hand, status distinctions between the first-line supervisor and his subordinates should not be allowed to become so great that he gives them the impression that he is an entirely different species. They will resent a patronizing attitude, and it will soon cause effective communications to break down between them.[37]

Example Setting

Even professional officers and supervisors can be influenced by personal interest. Departmental codes of conduct are intended to guide moral dilemmas, but in making ethical decisions, supervisors must remember the principles, not just the rules. "If you have integrity, nothing else matters. If you don't have integrity, nothing else matters."[38]

The respected leader will be imitated—consciously or unconsciously—by those he leads. He will have a valuable tool at his disposal if he sets the right example by the attitude he displays, by his conduct, by the relationships he maintains with others, and by his appearance. Rigid adherence to the requirements of good taste and convention, good breeding and behavior, and lack of pomposity are marks of a good leader.

The supervisor will hardly be in the best position to take remedial action against others if his own conduct is not above reproach. They will look to him to set the standard of conduct by his own demeanor. Upon it will be based much of their respect and support for him.

---

[37] *Ibid.*

[38] Debbie Kudis, "The Start of a New Lifestyle: A Police Officer's Mission," *FBI Law Enforcement Bulletin* (March 2005), 20.

Women Supervisors

The tenets of leadership discussed in this text are as applicable to women supervisors as to their male counterparts. Women supervisors will undoubtedly find that from time to time there are additional challenges in supervising some of their male subordinates. Some males still find it difficult to accept women in authority or to submit to their direction and control. Common sense in dealing with such attitudes will usually dictate an answer.

Most men have grown up in a culture of male dominance, so many expect better performance from female than from male supervisors performing similar duties. A woman supervisor is often required to prove herself over and over. She may find that she is expected to be more circumspect in her personal conduct and performance than the male supervisor because an inordinate amount of attention is focused on her. This condition may be totally unjustified but does exist, and since it occasionally does, she must dispel it as soon as possible to reduce resistance to her supervisory efforts. The solution seems to be for her to develop leadership abilities, prepare herself technically for her position, and scrupulously avoid the commonly recognized leadership weaknesses that often lead to supervisory failure. Some of these include indulgence in wrongdoing or misconduct, vacillation in the decision-making process, and unfairness. If any of these characteristics are observed in a woman, they may only serve to fortify the stereotyped opinions of those who contend that women are not good leaders.

Gender stereotyping has been cited by Haar and Morash as one of the primary sources of stress for female officers.[39] Their minority status is an additional source of stress for female officers. Of all sworn officers in 2000, 13 percent were women, with commanders representing just 7.3 percent.[40] Excellent resources exist, however, to offset these stressors. Professional associations, such as the International Association of Women Police (www.iawp.org), are sources of peer support, training, and mentoring. Supervisors, administrators, and organizational policy must recognize that women are legally and morally entitled to the same opportunities and considerations in the position for which they were employed as are men.

Supervising a Diverse Workforce

We are indeed a multicultural workforce. Our officers hail from all parts of the world. Successful supervisors not only understand and accept diversity, but they embrace it as well. They understand that the makeup of the police workforce has changed. It is now becoming more and more reflective of the community it serves. Again the successful supervisor understands this and respects the individual and cultural differences of his workers.

In law enforcement, working with officers who are of different generations, races, ethnic groups, religions, genders, and sexual orientations is now the norm. The diverse workforce presents additional challenges to the supervisor. Supervisors need to ensure

---

[39] Robin N. Haar and Merry Morash, "Gender, Race, and Strategies of Coping with Occupational Stress among Police Officers," *Justice Quarterly*, 16, No. 2 (1999), 303–306.

[40] Venessa Garcia, "'Difference' in the Police Department: Women, Policing, and 'Doing Gender,'" *Journal of Contemporary Criminal Justice*, 19, No. 3 (August 2003), 336.

subordinates behave in an ethical and professional manner with their coworkers. They must be told that inappropriate jokes, slurs, and offensive comments about different groups will not be tolerated. It's up to the supervisor to set the proper example. If something is being said or done that's inappropriate, the supervisor must intervene immediately.

Perhaps the biggest challenge facing police executives of the twenty-first century will be to develop police organizations that can effectively recognize, relate, and assimilate the global shifts in culture, technology, and information. Changing community expectations, workforce values, technological power, governmental arrangements, policing philosophies, and ethical standards are but a sample of the forces that must be understood and constructively managed by the current and incoming generation of chief executives.[41] Good leaders are not only creative change agents but also practical futurists, exercising foresight and the capacity to see the "big picture" and the "long view."

Today, as we transition into a new information age and multicultural work environment, leaders need to be both transformational and culturally sensitive. That is, effective leaders innovate by:

- Transforming workplaces from the status quo to appropriate environments.
- Renewing organizations and becoming role models by transmitting intellectual excitement and vision about their work.
- Helping personnel to manage change by restructuring their mind-sets and values.[42]

Such leaders deal with all persons fairly, regardless of gender, race, color, religion, sexual orientation, or cultural differences. A leader seeks to empower a more diverse workforce in law enforcement to be reflective of the communities served.

Furthermore, culturally sensitive leaders cut across cultural barriers while combating prejudice, bigotry, and racism wherever found in the organization and the community. Police supervisors, for example, exercise this leadership through anticipatory thinking, strategic planning, creative decision making, and effective communication.[43] Good leaders not only acknowledge their own ethnocentrism, but also understand the cultural values and biases of the people with whom they work. Consequently, such leaders can empower, value, and communicate more effectively with all employees. Developing others involves acquiring or developing mentoring and coaching skills, which are important tools for modern managers.[44]

The more diverse the working population becomes, the more leadership is needed. Shusta and colleagues report that this approach to leadership was echoed in the introduction to *Transcultural Leadership: Empowering the Diverse Workforce.*

[41] *Police Leadership in the 21st Century: Achieving and Sustaining Executive Success* (1999). Bobby D. Moody, President IACP.

[42] Robert M. Shusta, Deena R. Levine, Herbert Z. Wong, Aaron T. Olson, and Philip R. Harrus, *Multi-Cultural Law Enforcement, Strategies for Peace Keeping in a Diverse Society,* 5th ed. (Upper Saddle River, N.J.: Pearson Education, Inc., 2011), pp. 75, 76.

[43] Philip R. Harris, *High Performance Leadership* (Amherst, Mass.: HRD Press, 2005).

[44] Shusta, et al., *Multi-Cultural Law Enforcement, Strategies for Peace Keeping in a Diverse Society,* pp. 75, 76.

Transcultural leadership addresses a new global reality: Today productivity must come from the collaboration of culturally diverse women and men. It insists that leaders change organizational culture to empower and develop people. It demands that employees be selected, evaluated, and promoted on the basis of *performance and competency,* regardless of sex, race, sexual orientation, religion, or place of origin. Beyond that, leaders must learn the skills to enable men and women of all backgrounds to work together effectively.[45]

Law enforcement leaders must be committed to setting an organizational tone that does not permit racism or discriminatory acts and must act swiftly against those who violate these policies. They must monitor and quickly deal with complaints both from within their workforce and from the public they serve.[46]

Women and minority officers should explore, and supervisors should encourage, membership in voluntary professional organizations such as the International Association of Women Police (www.iawp.org), the National Latino Officers Association of America (www.nloaus.org), and the National Organization of Black Law Enforcement Executives (www.nationalnoble.org). Membership in such groups can provide officers with a vital support network as well as opportunities for training and professional advancement. These benefits can be especially helpful for female or minority officers, who are frequently subject to unique stressors on the job.

Two New Orleans Police Officers patrolling at Mardi Gras. (© Paul Wood/Alamy)

---

[45] George F. Simons, Carmen Vazquez, and Philip R. Harris, *Transcultural Leadership: Empowering the Diverse Workforce* (Houston, Tex.: Gulf Publishing, 1993).

[46] Shusta, et al., *Multi-Cultural Law Enforcement, Strategies for Peace Keeping in a Diverse Society,* pp. 75, 76.

Supervising the Multigenerational Workforce

The world and the workplace have changed in countless ways over the past few decades, and these changes are reflected in the distinct characteristics of each generation. Research and experience have shown us that each generation views their personal and professional lives through very different prisms. While this diversity in points of view can bring richness to an organization, it can also bring conflict, frustration, and problems with communication. To understand the motivations and behaviors of others, employees at all levels must begin by understanding the influence of generational experiences on an individual's priorities, preferences, and reactions.[47]

Each generation carries its own array of strengths and values to the workplace. Overseeing the wide range of generational groups can present challenges for a manager due to the diversity between the newest members, for example, Generation Y, and the oldest members, the Baby Boomers and Traditionalists. How do you manage the multigenerational workforce effectively? Listed below is general information about each age group:[48]

Generation Y: Born after 1980, this generation is extremely technologically savvy, have a casual attitude toward employers, expect instant gratification, and seek a fun and flexible working style. They are also referred to as Millennials and the Net generation.

Generation X: Born between 1965 and 1980, this generation wants a balanced work-life schedule including family time. They appreciate mutual respect and open communication.

Baby Boomers: Born between 1946 and 1964, this generation is defined by a strong work ethic, being loyal employees, and climbing their way up the corporate ladder. They also value face-to-face interaction and may feel threatened by the computer and technological skills of younger generations. They have expressed concerns about Generation Y's decision-making and social skills.

Traditionalists: Born before 1946, this generation is characterized by the hard times in which they lived, many during World War II and some growing up during the Great Depression. They are rule followers and computer-phobic. We often see them as volunteers in the police department.

The traits listed above are general, and exceptions may and will be found in your workforce population. A younger employee may have an older mind-set and an older employee may still be "young at heart." That being said, it is imperative that a supervisor be sensitive to generational differences that may exist among his employees.

Magnuson and Alexander cite the following as how to successfully manage a multigenerational workforce:[49]

- **Nurture mentoring relationships.** Gen Y's were raised on email, text messages, Facebook, and Twitter, while Boomers know CRM and other enterprise management tools inside and out. Take advantage of each group's strengths and pair up older and younger workers to mentor each other.

---

[47] *Leading a Multigenerational Workforce* (Alexandria, Va.: International Association of Chiefs of Police, 2012).

[48] Hess and Orthmann, *Management and Supervision in Law Enforcement*, 6th ed., p. 216.

[49] Debra S. Magnuson and Lora S. Alexander, *Work With Me: A New Lens on Leading the Multigenerational Workforce* (Minneapolis, Minn.: Personnel Decisions International, 2008).

- **Create a productive environment.** Each group may have preferences regarding the work environment. Boomers and other generations are often comfortable with traditional office hours but may also appreciate flex scheduling that allows them to vary their work hours.
- **Communicate with a range of tools.** While a Boomer/Traditionalist might prefer face-to-face communication, a Gen Y worker is completely comfortable with an email, text, or other electronic message. Consider disseminating messages in multiple ways to ensure that each group in the multigenerational workforce is likely to read them.
- **Foster a respectful environment.** Each set of the multigenerational workforce brings its own strengths and experiences, meaning that each worker deserves respect and trust. As a supervisor, work to create an environment free of prejudices like those reflected in comments such as "Those darn kids on their smartphones…" or "Those old people just won't change…."
- **Reward good behavior.** Reward the multigenerational workforce frequently and as soon as possible after a positive action happens.

A successful supervisor must be considerate to each group's values and preferences in order to build a productive and efficient team that will get the job done.

Avoidance of Gender Bias and Harassment

All supervisors must exercise exceptional common sense and introspection in their relationships with subordinates, especially with those of the opposite sex. Harassment can take many forms and must be meticulously avoided. It is destructive of morale and needlessly embarrassing to the organization. It is perceived by those subjected to it as an act or series of acts that causes persistent mental distress or worry. Some of it is illegal and might subject the accused to both criminal and civil liability and the organization to civil litigation.

There are a multitude of acts, real or imagined, that might give rise to charges of harassment; and in the interest of good supervisory practices, improprieties should be carefully guarded against by supervisors in their relationships with subordinates. The most common acts that are alleged as a basis for charges of harassment include:

Unjust favoritism
Improper advances with sexual overtones, involving unwanted physical contact, improper verbal or body language
Rude or discourteous language
Deprivation of entitlements, such as in assignments, promotions, work conditions, or employee welfare
Unfair evaluations
Demotions
Deprivation of merit salary increases
Discharges
Salary reductions
Any acts that might be perceived as having created a hostile environment

Sexual harassment in the workplace is prohibited by federal law (29 CFR 1604), and it may be litigated as a civil rights violation under Title 42, Section 1983. The potential for departmental, and individual, liability is enormous. Yet, incredibly, one survey found that 34 percent of police agencies have no written policy against sexual harassment.[50] A responsible supervisor must promote a professional work environment at all times, he must act immediately to stop any sexual harassment, and he must document and investigate (or forward for investigation) all such complaints.[51] Supervisors must take prompt and professional action.

Symptoms of Leadership Failure

There are many symptoms of leadership failure. The appearance of selfishness, suspicion, envy, failure to give credit, hypercriticism, and arbitrariness will usually denote weaknesses, if not downright failure, of an individual as a leader. When these characteristics are present to a marked degree in a supervisor, he is not fit to direct and control others.

Leadership fails more often because it is not provided when it is most needed than because the techniques are flawed.[52] If the level of discipline in an organization is low, if its standards of conduct and performance leave much to be desired, or if the organization is riddled with disloyalty, mistrust, and self-interest, its leaders have failed; failure will inevitably result in reduced productivity, low morale, and poor organizational spirit.

Such failure is often as much a direct result of a supervisor's incapacity to lead as it is a failure of management to train him once he is selected for the position. If it is the former, selection procedures have been faulty; if the latter, the organization has failed.

The mere fact that a person selected for a supervisory position has been a competent, skilled individual producer is no guarantee that he will become a successful leader. He may fail because, as a supervisor, he cannot manage people, he has trouble maintaining effective relationships with subordinates, or he has not developed an ability to delegate tasks well, coordinate the activities of those working for him, or follow up on their performance and take appropriate remedial action when they fail.

Leadership Issues in Community Policing

Contemporary trends in the modern-day policing environment present new and innovative challenges to supervisors. With many police departments turning to community-oriented policing and utilizing problem-solving approaches, Peak, Gaines, and Glensor state the following: "The challenge for the supervisor is to help police officers redefine their role and accept responsibility for following in a constantly changing, transformational environment. The key ingredients in developing an effective

---

[50] Barbara Lindemann and David D. Kadue, *Sexual Harassment in Employment Law* (Washington, D.C.: Bureau of National Affairs, 1997).

[51] Jeff Bernstein and Herbert Williams, *New Jersey Police Situational Management Training Manual* (Davie, Fla.: Bernstein & Associates, 2013), p. 19.

[52] Phil Dourado, *The 60 Second Leader* (London: Capstone Publishing, 2007), p. 134.

leadership–followership strategy are genuine participation, communication, shared decision making, equity, self-control, and interdependence."[53]

Community policing (CP) calls for a partnership between the police and the local community to solve problems on a neighborhood-by-neighborhood basis. CP is generally understood to include components of crime prevention by police officers acting as coordinators, working with community groups to identify priorities and strategies, and mobilizing all community resources.[54]

CP invests a great deal of authority in street-level officers; it requires leadership, management, and communicative skills, coupled with a considerable amount of creativity. It also requires organizational changes in the police department. Traditional bureaucratic structure needs to accommodate by providing more decision-making authority to officers at the level where the work is being done.

The first challenge for the supervisor of a CP program is to adapt to the high level of necessary commitment and community involvement. The neighborhood residents, business owners, community groups, and local workforce all become equal partners with the police department. Most police officers and supervisors will find this a new and very different experience. Leadership, program management, and negotiation skills are critical. Supervisors must be prepared to train and coach their officers in these skill areas. They must also learn to evaluate officers based on these skills rather than on more traditional

Detroit Michigan Deputy Police Chief Joyce A Motley talks about crime and police issues to residents of Detroit's Morningside neighborhood during the community group's monthly meeting. (© Jim West/Alamy)

---

[53] Kenneth Peak, Larry Gaines, and Ronald Glensor, *Police Supervision and Management in an Era of Community Policing*, 3rd ed. (Upper Saddle River, N.J.: Pearson Prentice Hall, 2010), p. 70.

[54] George Kelling, "The Evolution of Contemporary Policing," in *Local Government Police Management*, 4th ed. (Washington, D.C.: International City Managers Association, 2003), p. 17.

measures such as summonses issued, report quality, and arrest statistics. This requires policy guidance and training for CP supervisors.

For community-oriented policing and problem solving to be effective, supervisors must understand its concepts, support its principles, and be a part of it. They must have the characteristics of a good problem-oriented supervisor. The Police Executive Research Forum (PERF) has identified the following characteristics of a good problem-oriented supervisor:[55]

1. Allowing subordinates freedom to experiment with new approaches
2. Insisting on good, accurate analyses of problems
3. Granting flexibility in work schedules when requests are appropriate
4. Allowing subordinates to make most contacts directly, and paving the way when they are having trouble getting cooperation
5. Protecting subordinates from pressures within the department to revert to traditional methods
6. Running interference for subordinates to secure resources, protect them from criticism, and so forth
7. Knowing what problems subordinates are working on and whether the problems are real
8. Knowing subordinates' beat and important citizens in it, and expecting subordinates to know it even better
9. Coaching subordinates through the process, giving advice, and helping them manage their time
10. Monitoring subordinates' progress, and (as necessary) prodding them along or slowing them down
11. Supporting subordinates even if their strategies fail, so long as something useful is learned in the process and the process was well thought through
12. Managing problem-solving efforts over a long period of time, and not allowing efforts to die simply because they get sidetracked by competing demands for time and attention
13. Giving credit to subordinates, and letting others know about their good work
14. Allowing subordinates to talk with visitors or at conferences about their work
15. Identifying new resources and contacts for subordinates, and making them check them out
16. Stressing cooperation, coordination, and communication within the unit and outside it
17. Coordinating efforts across shifts and beats and outside units and agencies
18. Realizing that this style of policing cannot simply be ordered and that officers and detectives must come to believe in it

Supervisors who put into practice these characteristics emulate the ideal police supervisor. Additionally, officers who work for a good problem-oriented supervisor are more likely to follow them.

---

[55] Dennis Jay Kenney and Robert P. McNamara, *Police and Policing: Contemporary Issues* (Westport, Conn.: Greenwood Publishing Group, 1999), p. 48.

Community policing and problem-solving strategies have become more accepted in law enforcement. That, in turn, has caused the growth and evolution of these concepts. Currently, this trend faces a number of challenges.

When the war on terror began, traditional and community policing as we knew it changed. New agencies were created, task forces were formed, and the United States developed a color-coded threat level system to communicate with public safety officials and the public at large. Some say community policing died on September 11, 2001. With monies diverted from community policing to homeland security, a number of police departments altered their style of policing. Nonetheless, community policing and problem solving still exist. Kappeler and Gaines argue the following:[56]

> Community policing provides the best philosophy for police departments to address both the threat of terrorist events and the fear that these events can generate.
>
> What does community policing offer in terms of "community security"?
>
> - Decentralization of police organizations allows for a faster and more efficient response to crisis. A flat organizational structure allows a faster flow of information and communication within the organization, as well as with the public.
> - Community policing's use of a decentralized organization can produce a faster response to incidents because officers are better dispersed across the community.
> - Empowering line officers with decision-making authority and responsibility can make them better "first responders," who have the ability and authority to really "respond" to a situation.
> - Use of fixed geographic beats allows officers to identify security risks and investigate threats. In-depth knowledge of a beat can allow for better collection and development of intelligence data.
> - Community policing officers are more trusted by citizens and are more likely to be given information about suspicious activities or unusual events in the community long before federal officials become involved.
> - Community policing officers are freed from the incessant demands of responding to calls and are free to pursue leads or investigate suspicious activity.

Ensuring that community policing and problem solving are connected to homeland security is a leadership issue. First-line supervisors are in the best position to make sure this gets done.

SUMMARY

Organizational effectiveness is largely dependent on the degree to which supervisors skillfully apply sound principles of leadership to everyday operations. Some supervisors fail in their primary task of directing, leading, and controlling others because they have not been able to apply these principles to their particular position. Some have been discouraged in doing so by superiors who themselves have failed to realize that the scientific techniques of leadership and supervision are, in the long run, more effective than many of the stereotyped, ineffective practices to which they have been exposed.

---

[56] Victor Kappeler and Larry Gaines, *Community Policing: A Contemporary Perspective*, 6th ed. (New York: New York, Elsevier, 2012), p. 510.

True leadership status can be earned by any reasonably intelligent individual if he devotes himself to the development of the traits a leader must have. He does not gain this status from the award of stripes or bars on his uniform; the only real authority he has is that granted him by his subordinates. The best leaders have been the best subordinates, since individuals cannot order and direct others until they have learned to receive and follow orders themselves.

There is no single leader type, although most have certain common traits, among which are friendliness, moral and physical courage, personal integrity and honor, insight, a strong desire for truth, a desire to teach, and the ability to listen. No one trait can be isolated from the others, since they all relate to the total character of the leader and are interrelated.

Perhaps the single function that best marks the good leader is his ability to maintain a high level of discipline, morale, and esprit de corps. These conditions are brought about by common sense approach and by understanding the fundamentals of good supervisory practices. This can be most effectively related to the leader's management activities if he has some practical knowledge of the psychological factors affecting human behavior.

Nowhere are these psychological factors more important than in the giving of orders. The supervisor should recognize that the manner of giving an unpopular order is often more resented than the order itself. If it is framed as a request, it will most often be accepted and carried out without resentment. In some instances when urgent conditions exist, orders must be given as direct commands because prompt action is needed. Implied or suggested orders may be used effectively with reliable, experienced employees; they should not ordinarily be used with inexperienced or undependable workers. On occasion, the supervisor will call for volunteers to perform dangerous or disagreeable tasks that he cannot or should not perform himself. When he uses this form of order giving, he must exercise care that it does not become a means of escaping a disagreeable job that is properly his.

Order giving involves many complex communication processes. The leader's manner, his gestures and inflections, and the time and place in which the order is given will affect the reactions of his subordinates. He should avoid uncertain or vacillating language because uncertainty will often be interpreted as indecision.

Immoderate, vulgar, or indecent language should be scrupulously avoided, as should sarcastic remarks, in dealings with subordinates. These will only alienate them and others, who are quick to interpret such conduct as rudeness and ill breeding.

A good leader will criticize when necessary—but only after he has obtained all facts on which he has based his criticism. He will do so only in private, with rare exceptions. Whenever possible, he will praise an employee publicly where credit or recognition is earned. He will do so sincerely because insincere praise or that given grudgingly is seldom appreciated.

Good human relations practices should be followed at all times, but in so doing, the supervisor must take pains to avoid becoming so concerned with the "sweetness and light" or the "kid glove" principles that he is afraid to criticize when he is dissatisfied with inferior performance or to punish when punitive action is necessary. He will strike a happy balance by being human and compassionate where he can and being firm when he has to be.

The most effective supervisor will motivate his subordinates through a system of positive incentives that tend to satisfy their individual needs. He will provide appropriate recognition when deserved and praise when merited and opportunities for personal development, challenging work, and fair treatment, but he will avoid as far as possible those negative factors that induce performance through fear and intimidation.

The enlightened supervisor will avoid applying different standards in supervising men, women, and minorities. He must recognize that all are legally and morally entitled to the same opportunities and considerations in the positions for which they were employed and are accountable alike for their performance and behavior. He will also use a high degree of common sense in his relationships with women employees because they are quick to sense when the male supervisor is showing too much personal interest in one of them. They will be quick to suspect him of ulterior motives or accuse him of partiality. Ordinarily, he will apply the same general principles of supervision to women employees as to males, but he will recognize that women are sometimes more sensitive to criticism, somewhat more inclined to become emotionally involved in their jobs, and generally more appreciative than are men of his efforts to improve the physical aspects of the job environment.

REVIEW

Questions

1. Why do supervisors often resist leadership training?
2. List three types of leaders, and discuss the characteristics of each.
3. Define command presence, and discuss how it affects leadership.
4. Discuss the principal characteristics of good leaders.
5. What are the objectives of good human relations?
6. What are the basic principles of commending and criticizing others?
7. What are the most prevalent reasons for failures in order giving?
8. List and discuss four methods of giving orders.
9. Discuss the steps involved in decision making.
10. Discuss how oversupervision occurs and the hazards that result from it.
11. Explain how the supervision of women and minority employees sometimes differs from that of white male workers.
12. List and discuss some of the basic techniques of supervising women employees.
13. What are some positive motivators? Describe how they can be used.
14. What are the major symptoms of leadership failure? Give at least one example of each.

Exercises

Checklist for Leaders

The good leader will constantly review his techniques of supervision to assess his effectiveness. He will ask himself the following questions in doing so. Check your leadership ability by honestly and reasonably answering the questions *yes* or *no*, or *moderately well* if in doubt. Ask yourself what you can do to remove the questionable items. Rate yourself on the following scale: 1 point for each item marked *yes*, 1/2 point for each item marked *moderately well*, zero for each item marked *no*.

Totals

Score = 42 or above (You are probably an excellent supervisor.)
Score = 37–41 (You are probably a moderately good supervisor.)
Score = less than 37 (You probably need to improve.)

1. Have I made myself technically and professionally competent?
2. Do I know and appreciate the traditions of my organization?
3. Do I know thoroughly its practices and standard procedures?
4. Have I generally kept myself more fully informed about my profession than have my subordinates?
5. Have I defined my objectives clearly to my subordinates?

6. Have I tried to resolve those objectives that are in conflict?
7. Have I established clear standards of performance for my subordinates?
8. Have I let them know what these standards are?
9. Do I insist that they be met?
10. Do I actively try to reduce substandard performance?
11. Have I set performance and behavior standards for myself and followed them?
12. Do my subordinates know what they may expect from me?
13. Do I avoid self-centeredness?
14. Am I employee-centered?
15. Do I place my organization's interests before my own as I should?
16. Do I communicate well with others below, above, and horizontally?
17. Do I keep my subordinates and superiors well informed on matters affecting them?
18. Have I kept channels of communication open with those with whom I work?
19. Do I actively lead, direct, and control subordinates?
20. Do I face my responsibilities for these functions forthrightly?
21. Do I avoid unjust criticism of my colleagues?
22. Do I avoid public criticism of others in my organization?
23. Do I give credit when it is earned?
24. Do I commend publicly?
25. Do I avoid "credit snatching"?
26. Do I respect my subordinates for what they are?
27. Do I demand respect from them by my conduct, appearance, and decorum?
28. Am I fair and impartial in meting out punishment when it is indicated?
29. Do I keep my emotions from becoming involved when I punish subordinates?
30. Do I back my subordinates to the fullest as a matter of principle when their cause is just and reasonable?
31. Do I refuse to back them when they are wrong even though such refusal may lessen my popularity with them?
32. Do I delegate as far down the line as possible?
33. Do I force my subordinates to develop their sense of personal responsibility and initiative?
34. Do I use my authority sparingly and display it rarely?
35. Do I avoid oversupervision?
36. Does my unit have pride in its accomplishments?
37. Have I actively tried to build its esprit de corps?
38. Do I practice humility?
39. Do I recognize my shortcomings?
40. Do I constructively compensate to lessen the ill effects of my shortcomings?
41. Have I retained my sense of humor in my dealings with subordinates?
42. Can I still admit that I am capable of error?
43. Do I apply the same standards of conduct and performance to men, women, and minority subordinates?
44. Do I provide positive incentives to motivate my subordinates?
45. Do I avoid the use of negative motivators when positive incentives would possibly serve better?
46. Do I make decisions promptly, without vacillating?
47. Are my decisions the right ones in most every case?
48. Do I always obtain the essential facts before making decisions that affect my subordinates?
49. Am I a good listener?
50. Do I practice the Golden Rule?

4

The Training Function

Problems and Approaches to the Instructional Process

Chapter Objectives

This chapter will enable you:

- To become acquainted with the need for and the importance of training
- To become familiar with the principles of learning and their application to training
- To gain an understanding of the learning process
- To display an understanding of how to prepare a lesson plan
- To become acquainted with the five steps of teaching and how each can be accomplished

One of the principal duties of the supervisor and perhaps one of his most important responsibilities is the training of his subordinates. Of necessity, this activity occurs in all types of settings, ranging from the informal meeting with those who are performing their duties in the field to the formal lecture in the classroom. Supervisors are often called upon to provide training at roll call, police academies, and community policing public meetings. In each instance, the supervisor must adapt his approach to the environment in which the need for training reveals itself. The supervisor must recognize that although various training techniques are available to him, all the methods of teaching have as common objectives not only to impart knowledge or change attitudes but also to motivate the student to further his own learning by changing his behavior to more productive avenues than he might have followed in the past.

The supervisor-teacher must constantly strive to establish an appropriate climate for learning. If he is to do this effectively, he must be familiar with the learning process, the obstacles to efficient learning, and the factors that influence it. Most important, he must bring to his training function enthusiasm that will quickly permeate the group. Haphazard, indifferent teaching will produce unacceptable learning results.

Theoretically, job-connected problems result from a failure of management to provide adequate training. It has been stated that the incidence of personal misconduct and of performance failures is related to the quality and extent of the employee's training. This contention cannot be easily refuted, since if training were perfect—if it were to accomplish its objectives totally—every person subjected to it would react flawlessly to every stimulus. There would be no police scandals arising from misconduct, and police effectiveness would be nearly absolute. Unfortunately, methods of accomplishing this state of perfection have not yet been developed. The supervisor can, however, make the greatest use of the time he has available for training by the skillful application of basic but proven techniques of teaching.

Regardless of the quality of material made available to the supervisor-instructor to pass on to his subordinates, the amount of learning that takes place will depend in large part on his ability to teach the information effectively. No two teachers will utilize the same methods with equal success; each must adapt his approach to his audience, to their capabilities and his own.

Importance of Training

If people are not carefully selected based on appropriate potential for performing the tasks of their positions and then adequately trained and properly supervised, costly high turnover will result. Since most law enforcement agencies do not have total authority to select new personnel, the function of training them to perform their basic duties with skill and dispatch is of utmost importance. It is a function vitally related to the introduction of operational rules and regulations, policies, specifications, and procedures of the organization. Its importance in indoctrinating personnel in changing laws, techniques, and police practices as a means of upgrading the service cannot be denied. Stillman[1] observed that "Individuals who have specialized training and who by constant practice enhance their skills, competences and insights...can minimize delays, lack of precision and wasteful losses."

Causes and Effects of Training Failure

Training failures are usually the result of administrators failing to give supervisors an understanding of their responsibilities for this function and some instruction on how to proceed. It has been demonstrated that these failures can be prevented by systematic efforts to qualify supervisors to instruct.

When the training function is performed poorly or not at all, low morale, waste, frustration, and preventable errors inevitably follow. All these are tremendously costly to the organization because they squander human endeavor. Also consider the grave liability that comes with inadequate training. In the landmark case of *City of Canton, Ohio v. Harris* (1989), the city was found liable for failure to train its officers in a critical skill commonly needed in that agency, identification of prisoners requiring medical attention. Use-of-force incidents, clearly a highly critical skill area for police, now lead the list of civil actions against police officers and police departments.[2] Training failures cost the police department in losses both large and small. These might be prevented if police effectiveness is developed to a greater degree by training.

Remedy for Failure

Every organization must program its approach to the training problem or risk loss of organizational effectiveness and the economic loss that follows. Administrators and supervisors should endeavor to make maximum use of the time and wherewithal

---

[1] Richard J. Stillman, *Public Administration: Concepts and Cases* (Boston: Wadsworth, 2010).
[2] David Griffith, "On the Hook," *Police,* September 2005, p. 46.

they have available for training. Personnel merely exposed to it may learn inefficiently and sometimes hazardously through the slow and wasteful process of trial and error or the "sink or swim" method. In the alternative, they can be taught systematically by efficient supervisors who have been trained in the proven techniques of teaching and have been made aware of the great need to take advantage of whatever opportunities present themselves to train their subordinates, whether it is at shift briefing, in the field, or in the classroom. In each situation, the supervisor may be concerned with technical content or with some of the less tangible problems involving working relationships.

Instructor's Approach to Teaching

Customs, practices, or traditions might affect the form the supervisor's instruction will take. If, for example, the techniques of teaching personnel how to shoot have traditionally been adapted for single-action target shooting, considerable resistance might be encountered if he attempts to shift emphasis to combat shooting. He will often be forced to improvise so that his methods will meet the needs of the moment.

The basic techniques of teaching apply to all forms of training, whether it is the teaching of an officer to photograph a crime scene, investigate a traffic accident, or prepare a crime report. If a police stakeout is involved, the instructor may be required to demonstrate how a shotgun may best be carried to the scene. He may be concerned with such simple procedures as loading or unloading the gun, engaging or disengaging the safety, or checking ammunition. He can never be certain that his subordinates are familiar with these critical procedures, and he can ill afford to assume that they will all remember such routine procedures or even that they have been exposed to them. At the scene of a crime, the supervisor may be called on to refresh the new officer in the basic techniques of dusting a surface for latent fingerprints as well as photographing, lifting, and preserving them. He may be required to impart detailed tactical, technical, or procedural information in a more formal classroom setting relative to the control of public disorder or to instruct his subordinates in field deployment plans to be used in their response to robbery or burglary calls. He may be assigned the task of passing on specific information regarding a new procedure and its background, or he may be called on to discuss the specific elements of crimes or selective enforcement procedures.

In each of these situations, his effectiveness as an instructor will be directly related to the degree to which he has acquired knowledge of his subject, has gained an understanding of the learning process, and has displayed a willingness to work at the job of instructing. He will find that learning the rudiments of teaching is a relatively simple task. More difficulty will be encountered in applying them to practical situations. With reference to teaching, Roueche, Milliron, and Roueche state that "Effectiveness is a result of a combination of factors: knowledge of subject, course preparation and organization, clarity and understandability, enthusiasm for subject/teachings, concern for students, availability and helpfulness, quality of examinations, impartiality in evaluating students and overall fairness to students."[3]

---

[3] John F. Roueche, Mark D. Milliron, and Suanne D. Roueche, *On the Front Lines of Teaching Excellence* (Washington, D.C.: American Association of Community Colleges, 2003), p. 44.

Shotgun Familiariza-
tion Training Winslow
Township Police
Department Captain
Michael Bartuccio
with Officer Michael
O'Rourke.
(© Stock Connection
Blue/Alamy)

Instruction as a Supervisory Responsibility

The supervisory officer has a responsibility to train his subordinates by the most efficient and effective methods available to him. This vital function is an integral part of his job, one he cannot afford to omit or perform carelessly. "The supervisor must realize the necessity of training employees because they are an organization's most precious resource."[4] It is his responsibility to study the techniques of instruction so that he may do the best possible job of acquainting his subordinates with the means of accomplishing their many tasks effectively and with the fewest possible errors. Farr, Kamras, and Kopp point out that effective teaching should be defined in terms of student learning. They further state that this success does not rely solely on the student but more so on the instructor's ability to effectively execute his teaching strategies.[5]

Need for Training

There is no end to the need for training. Concepts, theories, philosophies, practices, procedures, and techniques are constantly changing to meet current social needs. These changes are especially prominent in law enforcement. It has become a truism that the need for training police officers in our complex society is as great as the need for their services. "Without training, the best of officers is inadequate at best, incompetent at

[4] Mary Albright, *101 Biggest Mistakes Managers Make and How to Avoid Them* (Upper Saddle River, N.J.: Prentice Hall, 1997).

[5] Steven Farr, Jason Kamras, and Wendy Kopp, *Teaching as Leadership: The Highly Effective Teacher's Guide to Closing the Achievement Gap* (San Francisco, Calif.: Jossey-Bass, 2010).

worst. The foundation of effective law enforcement is established with a good training program."[6] The day when a new officer could be given a gun and a badge and sent into the field to perform police work has passed. Today's public demands more.

Many police administrators believe that they must deploy their personnel for training just as they do for vacations, days off, or sickness. To them, training is a function that requires the expenditure of vast sums of money and time; it must be recognized as a necessary component of public service, which must be paid for by the public that profits from a well-trained police force. The costs of effective training are well repaid by the results it produces.

Many departments, recognizing the importance of this function, allocate short portions of roll-call periods for this purpose. Supervisors can then profitably take advantage of this time to accomplish a tremendous amount of regular training, to refresh personnel about old procedures, or to acquaint them with new ones.

The benefits to be derived from an effective training program are not immediate, nor are they easily measured; long-term results do occur, but these are usually subtle. A reasonably accurate assessment of the benefits of training can be made from the observations of those who are in a position to compare pretraining and posttraining performance. Precise measurements of results in activities such as law enforcement are difficult because of the many abstract reactions brought about by training. Results may be reflected in a multitude of factors such as higher morale, less job stress with its high economic cost, greater esprit de corps, a lessened need for punitive discipline, greater effectiveness in crime suppression, increased public support and confidence, fewer errors, better decisions

Sergeant holding roll call at Bowie, Maryland police station. (© Tom Carter/Alamy)

[6] Richard Holden, *Modern Police Management,* 2nd ed. (Upper Saddle River, N.J.: Prentice Hall, 2000), p. 282.

by the police, and a feeling of security by members of the community. The benefits that accrue to the police agency will, in the long run, be directly proportionate to the efforts expended by supervisory and administrative personnel in establishing and carrying out a progressive training policy.

Principles of Learning

All supervisors should have a basic understanding of the principles of learning. Psychologists and educators have conducted extensive research in this area.[7] Their findings have indicated that people learn according to some simple, well-established basic rules, of which the following have special significance to police trainers.

Principle of Readiness

When conditions in the learner's environment are such that they establish in him an attitude favorable to learning, he is said to be in a state of readiness to learn. The teacher's efforts in establishing such favorable conditions are of vital importance to the learning process. If the job is pleasant, the learner's mind is receptive to learning. If the job or environment is unpleasant, an emotional block is likely to occur and learning will be retarded. The instructor must therefore direct much of his effort toward stimulating the learner so that he will want to learn and will make an effort to do so. Students can become ready to learn through positive motivators or negative motivators: "Learning to speak Spanish will help you manage situations that we encounter frequently in this police department" (positive motivator); "Using sound tactics will keep you from getting shot" (negative motivator).[8] An application of some of the basic techniques of teaching will contribute to this.

Effective learning will rarely take place (and if it does, the process will be slow and inefficient) if the learner is not ready to absorb what is presented to him. Therefore, the instructor must appeal to the learner's self-interests by showing him *why* he needs the things to be learned and *how* he can use them to improve either his proficiency or his personal welfare. The learner must be given the opportunity for early success in some phase of the learning process so that he will achieve some sense of satisfaction from his accomplishment. The instructor will help this to come about if he displays a sincere attitude of interest in the learner as an individual and avoids annoying distractions and pressures that act as obstacles to learning. The student subjected to ill-prepared, disorganized, overly difficult material will soon lose his desire to learn because of utter confusion and frustration. The absence of the satisfaction of accomplishing something or of making progress will often cause him to "shut his mind" to learning. Motivating him to be in a receptive state where he is ready to learn once again may be extremely difficult.

Principle of Effect

When the learner is in a state of mental readiness in a favorable environment, efficient learning is possible. The effect of his success in learning is a pleasurable sense of satisfaction. The student strives to continue that which provides a pleasant effect, so he continues

---

[7] See Edward L. Thorndike, *The Fundamentals of Learning* (Memphis, Tenn.: General Books, 2010 rpt.), pp. 53–194.

[8] *Methods of Instruction* (Trenton, N.J.: N.J. Division of Criminal Justice Academy, 1988).

to learn. Failure to achieve success in applying the information he has received or failure to learn will usually result when the learner is not motivated to learn or when the material is presented to him ineffectively. These failures cause unpleasant feelings of frustration, which may make the student want to quit that environment or avoid that condition and to do something else that may give him a pleasant and satisfying experience instead of an unpleasant, frustrating, or annoying one. In unusual cases, it may be necessary to set up annoyances to overcome bad habits and encourage the learner to perform correctly. The boxer attempting to deliver a blow to his opponent by leading with a right cross soon finds to his annoyance that he is sitting on the mat looking up and will discontinue the procedure that led to that predicament.

Usually, the instructor should give the learner an opportunity to learn each small unit in a complex operation in its proper sequence before moving on to the next so that by completing something, the learner may derive a pleasant feeling of achievement. In addition, the completion of these small units in such operations will enable the learner to perform in a logical, orderly manner and to learn sequentially. Also, when complicated material is involved, it will be most meaningful if a foundation is given that will enable the learner to understand it better. This understanding will give him a sense of success. If commendation for this achievement is given sincerely by the instructor, it will tend to provide a pleasant and satisfying effect, which will prompt a desire for more success and further effort.

Principle of Repetition

When experiences are pleasing or satisfying, there is usually an accompanying desire to repeat the experience. Repetition builds habits that, if correct, lead to success, satisfaction, and a desire to repeat what produces pleasure. Thus, the repeated use of what is learned strengthens the learner's performance; failure to use what is learned weakens performance. Hilgard and Bower refer to this concept as the law of use and disuse.[9]

The instructor can improve the learner's ability to perform an operation by having him repeat it correctly until he is adept at it so that in a stressful situation, he will react automatically in applying the correct procedure. At times, repetition is necessary to refresh his memory if the operation is not performed frequently. Merely having the learner repeat what he learns for the sake of keeping him busy is wasteful—busy work does not necessarily result in productive learning. Repetition, if required, should be purposeful. The amount will depend on the ability of the learner and the adequacy of the instruction he receives.

The better a person learns by using a procedure, the longer he retains that which is learned. The teacher should remember, however, that every learner forgets in varying degrees with the passing of time. Therefore, he must be again exposed to training from time to time to keep him proficient. Reinforcing new information six times from lecture to application has been shown to improve recall from 10 to 90 percent after thirty days.[10] Special weapons procedures, self-defense techniques, and the like are not ordinarily used

---

[9] B. R. Hergenhahn, *An Introduction to the History of Psychology* (Belmont, Calif.: Wadsworth, 2010), p. 374.

[10] Robert W. Pike, *Creative Training Techniques Handbook* (Amherst, Mass.: HRD Press, 2003), p. 35.

with such frequency in the everyday work routine that the individual can maintain satisfactory skills. The supervisor-teacher should thus provide needed refresher training periodically to maintain such skills at acceptable, safe levels.

Principle of Primacy

Things learned first create a strong impression in the mind that is difficult to erase. For this reason, a negative approach to teaching should usually be avoided, since it may suggest what ought not to be done and cause an impression difficult to supplant later with how things should be done.

Principle of Recency

Information acquired last is generally remembered best; therefore, frequent reviews and summarization coupled with repetition tend to fix in the mind the matters taught.

Principle of Intensity

The more intense the matter taught, the greater is the likelihood that it will be retained. Vivid examples of real situations associated with principles taught provide a most effective learning experience and stimulate the memory to longer retention. This principle is of value in teaching subjects involving basic principles and their association to real events, as in a course on criminal law. Reality-based training relies on the principle of intensity. Skills used under stress, such as arresting a combative suspect, are vividly presented and repeated to create an automatic response in actual confrontations.[11]

Learning Process Variables

Some of the factors that psychologists, trainers, and educators have found to vitally affect the learning process are of concern to the supervisor in his training function. The effectiveness of his teaching and the learning efficiency of the student are dependent on how these factors are applied.

Learning Rate

It is commonly recognized that students learn at varying rates, depending on the presence or absence of several conditions. The student's past training and experience, known as his apperceptive base, and his ability to integrate these with his new learning and experiences will materially affect his learning rate. Therefore, the teacher should adapt his approach to the types of students in the group, their past experiences, and their previous exposure to learning in subjects similar to those being presented. He should attempt to link the new knowledge to the old so that the student may interpret it by associating it with his past experiences. Good examples associating newly learned material to past practical experiences are valuable in making teaching more effective.

The personality of the instructor and his teaching abilities may vitally affect the rate at which learning takes place. The overly demanding instructor may or may not motivate

---

[11] Pamela Mills-Senn, "Real Training, Real Results," *Law Enforcement Technology*, 32, No. 1 (January 2005), 45.

his students to speedier learning. He must therefore look to his own techniques whenever students do not learn and must continually test his approach to determine its effectiveness. If it does not work, he should modify his approach and adopt one that may produce better results.

Individual differences in personalities and in physical or mental characteristics of students will cause them to learn at varying rates of speed and efficiency. The shy, diffident, insecure student may learn slowly until he is sparked by the instructor who inspires self-assurance. The student's rate of learning may then climb precipitously.

There are many individual differences among people. Some of these are inherited, so little can be done by the teacher to change them. Size, physical abilities, and mental capacity may have a profound effect on learning. Even in law enforcement agencies that usually screen personnel carefully before hiring them, some hereditary characteristics that detract from a person's learning capacity will be found. The instructor must be aware that these exist, try to recognize them when they are present, and alter his training approach as circumstances may dictate. Patience and understanding are essential if he is to accomplish the objectives he sets for himself.

Many factors, such as class size, time available for training, and physical facilities, will have a bearing on the individual attention that can be given the student by the instructor. Those students with the most pronounced problems will require the greatest personal attention if they are to be brought to the level of the rest.

Numerous individual differences result from the influences of the student's surroundings. The classroom environment itself may contribute adversely to learning. If the student is easily distracted or annoyed by conditions such as noise, poor ventilation or light, excessive heat or cold, or other discomforting conditions, he may concentrate more on the effects these have on him than on the instruction. Factors such as his home conditions, past experiences, economic insecurity, lack of friends or acquaintances, poor grades, and frustrations, either alone or in combination, may affect his learning capabilities. Personal characteristics such as inability to concentrate, lack of interest because of preoccupation, poor general health, faulty vision, or inferior hearing likewise might drastically affect his learning rate. The teacher must appreciate the potential effect of these deleterious conditions and endeavor to compensate for them in his teaching and in his personal relationships with the students.

Adult Learner Differences

Everyone is familiar with learning from their elementary school experiences, but the training role of the supervisor requires a different approach because adults learn differently than children do. Because adults bring greater life experiences to the classroom, they are more self-directed learners. According to the N.J. Division of the Criminal Justice Academy, this produces four key ramifications that trainers should consider in their training approach:[12]

1. More attention should be given to the quality of the learning environment.
2. Adults can be helped to diagnose their own needs for learning.
3. Adults can be involved in planning and conducting their own learning.
4. Adult learners can evaluate their own progress toward their learning goals.

---

[12] *Methods of Instruction.*

Motivation

The degree of motivation by the teacher has a direct bearing on the student's learning rate and performance. Special effort by the instructor to individualize his teaching and encourage students with special abilities will contribute to accelerated learning and improved performance. Brown and Thornton concluded years ago what is still true today:

> Learning proceeds best when the student is motivated to learn—when he *wants* to learn and when he puts forth *effort* to learn. Achievement of these conditions is aided when the learner considers course goals and learning tasks as having intrinsic worth and value for immediate or eventual use, or both.[13]

One of the greatest spurs to motivation is the recognition by the student that his personal or professional growth will be directly dependent on the effort he expends to improve himself, to gain greater insight into the problems affecting his position, and to increase his proficiency. The recognition of these factors, combined with a sense of accomplishment and a feeling of satisfaction gained from his learning efforts, will contribute greatly to his motivation. Here, the teacher can play a prime part.

Interest and Learning Effectiveness

The interest an instructor generates in his students plays an essential role in the rate at which they learn. He must hold the student's attention, since attention precedes effective learning. The degree of a learner's interest, in turn, depends on the internal motivation he gains from a sense of achievement and the external motivation inspired by the teacher through the use of incentives, such as the spirit of competition or grades. The positive use of stimulation is superior to the use of fear to increase motivation and interest. Yet undoubtedly, fear of competition, poor grades, or fear of dismissal because of unacceptable scores would be a powerful (although negative) influence on performance.

Learning Patterns

There seems to be a definite pattern in the learning process. At first the learner gains accuracy, speed, and self-confidence slowly. As motivation occurs and self-assurance increases, speed and accuracy increase more rapidly. The learner's state of mind is directly involved in this process. If he is receptive to training, if he recognizes the value and need for it, and if he gains satisfaction and acquires a feeling of success from the process, the speed with which he learns will accelerate greatly. Self-confidence and a feeling of security will increase in direct proportion to how well the worker learns to perform his tasks.

Ordinarily, from a learning standpoint, it has been found most desirable to teach an operation as a whole in the same sequence that will be followed in practice. If this sequence is logical, it will be most meaningful to the student because he will be able to apply logic and common sense to aid him in remembering what he needs to know. Of course, there are many exceptions to this procedure. In the case of complicated, lengthy operations, sequential learning may not be practicable because the student will not be able to remember all the critical steps on which later ones are based.

---

[13] Brown and Thornton, *College Teaching*, p. 115.

One solution may be problem-based learning, which seeks to immerse learners in practical situations that force them to apply what they have learned through study and lecture. This approach was developed to help medical students apply the vast learning they had acquired when it was found that they had knowledge but lacked treatment skills.[14] Many police supervisors have found that new academy graduates possess more theoretical knowledge than practical problem-solving skills.

Instructional Goals and Specific Objectives

Once a teacher selects or is assigned a subject for presentation in a training session, such as a briefing or roll-call teaching assignment (both of which are more formal than an on-the-job instructional situation), the general and specific objectives to be accomplished should be determined. Information must be gathered, analyzed, and arranged so that it may be adapted to the five-step method of teaching involving the introduction, presentation, review, application, and test, as discussed in this chapter.

The instructional goals and specific objectives that are to be accomplished by a single presentation or a series of lessons must be carefully developed. Instructional goals are defined as broad, general statements about what is to be learned. Learning objectives (often called performance objectives or competencies) are brief, clear, specific statements of what students should know or be able to do at the end of the course that they couldn't do before.[15]

An example here may clarify the difference. If you're asked to conduct in-service refresher training on "Responding to a weapons of mass destruction incident," the goal might be written as follows:[16]

> Upon conclusion of the training, law enforcement officers will be able to perform safely and effectively during incidents involving weapons of mass destruction (WMD).

It is recommended that learning objectives be expressed as outcomes for participants. For example, the objectives might be that at the end of the session, participants will be able to:

- Define WMD incident priorities relative to protection of persons and property
- Describe measures that provide the greatest protection to life during a WMD incident
- Describe decontamination techniques and identify situations appropriate for each technique

Goals and objectives require care in developing. They must be related to the specific desired changes in behaviors, attitudes, or performance that the instructor intends

---

[14] J. Hoover, R. W. Glensor, and K. J. Peak, "The Next Generation Field Training Officer (FTO) Program: A Problem-Based Learning Model." Paper presented at the annual conference of the Academy of Criminal Justice Sciences, Anaheim, Calif., March 9, 2002.

[15] http://web.mit.edu/tll/teaching-materials/learning-objectives/index-learning-objectives. html#what, accessed on November 16, 2012.

[16] Cy Charney and Kathy Conway, *The Trainers Tool Kit* (New York: Anacom Books, 2005), p. 67.

to bring about through his teaching. As Mager[17] stated, the instructor "must then select procedures, content, and methods which are relevant to the objectives [and] cause the student to interact with appropriate subject matter in accordance with principles of learning."

Analysis of Job Tasks and Material Selection

In preparing to teach a subject about a particular job, the instructor must evaluate the task involved and the operations necessary to complete it. These should then be listed in some logical sequence. Key points to be emphasized should be noted so that the training needs of the students can best be met. This job analysis is the basis for the presentation step of the lesson plan.

Relevant instructional material is then collected from the most authoritative sources available. It must be analyzed carefully so that it may be organized into a lesson plan that will aid in a thorough, logical, and systematic presentation. The amount of material taught can be adjusted to the time available, the needs of the particular subject area, and the type of presentation likely to work best with the group. Nonessential detail and material not relevant to the particular subject should be excluded. Ordinarily, in police training, the amount of time available is minimal. Consequently, the instructor cannot afford the luxury of developing in minute detail each point he must present. Unfortunately, training sometimes suffers because of this time limitation. Therefore, he should ask himself what portion of the material the trainee must know to perform his job adequately and what part would only be nice to know. He will then be able to eliminate whatever is least necessary and emphasize what is most necessary, making maximum use of the time available to him.

The bulk of the material retained for the lesson will be used in the presentation step; however, the instructor should be alert for items that can be adapted to meet the needs of the introduction, application, or test. Each of these steps, but especially the introduction, can be strengthened by an artful, imaginative approach.

Lesson Plan

When the instructor has completed the preliminary procedures of developing instructional goals and specific objectives, obtaining lesson materials, and analyzing them, he is ready to prepare his written teaching plans. If these are carefully prepared, they will guide him toward his objectives and help him avoid some of the common teaching failures. Most will agree that blueprints are necessary for the fabrication of material objects, but sometimes it becomes difficult to convince teachers of the need for a planned approach to teaching. Even those with considerable experience can seldom teach effectively without some plan to guide them in presenting their material in an organized, systematic manner.

The instructional plan involves a simple listing in proper sequence of the several steps to be followed in completing a particular job, or it may involve a logical

---

[17] Robert F. Mager, *Preparing Objectives for Programmed Instruction* (San Francisco: Fearon, 1962), p. 1.

arrangement of material if the lesson is to consist of a discussion of a procedure, law, technique, or philosophical concept. The first consideration is that the points to be covered should be arranged in a logical teaching sequence. The instructor should add the knacks, techniques, tricks of the trade, and basic facts that go with each point. These are the "interest-getters" that give meaning to the various points covered. A liberal scattering of pertinent, practical examples that have been well thought out in advance will do much to clarify abstract principles and assist students in applying them to their work. Illustrations, questions, and special procedures should be carefully prepared and included in the teaching plan if the instructor plans to use them during his presentation.

Form

Although the lesson plan is a personal matter for each instructor, it should be more than a scribbled note or two. It should be geared to the five-step plan of teaching that will be explained later in this chapter and should follow a definite format to meet particular needs, as shown in Figure 4-1. This will require the instructor to make definite decisions regarding what he intends to accomplish and how he expects to reach his objectives in each of the five steps.

The plan should cover all stages of the instructional process from the beginning to the accomplishment of the objectives. The plan serves mainly as a guide to systematic teaching. It should consist of a series of notes that will enable the instructor to recall in an organized manner the information he plans to use, and to use the teaching aids he has developed to his best advantage at the most appropriate time. The plan also should be used to review the main points of the lesson, and to test the students to determine the extent of their learning. It may follow a topic outline form, a detailed sentence outline, a narrative with appropriate markings of key teaching points and subordinate items, or marginal references keyed to the main teaching points. Some teachers make effective use of a single word (or phrase) outline to refresh their memories and help them organize their presentations.

Teaching Sequence

The instructor should consider the point of view of the learner when analyzing the lesson material and preparing the teaching plan so that his presentation will be arranged in the most logical order and will best meet current needs. Any one or a combination of several basic criteria may be used in determining the most appropriate sequence to be followed in each presentation. For example, the instructor may wish to progress from the simple to the complex if he is giving instruction in the field use of primary fingerprint classifications. He may wish to proceed from the safe to hazardous if he is discussing such subjects as defensive driving or the use of firearms. The easy to difficult approach may be utilized with good effect in teaching subjects such as disassembling weapons or using physical defense tactics. By giving his presentation so that it proceeds from the known to the unknown, the instructor might best acquaint the students with such subjects as laboratory procedures or accident investigation techniques; he can also utilize this sequence to establish a basis for clear understanding of even the most difficult material relating to law enforcement. But if his presentation involves merely a rehashing of what is already known, little will be accomplished in terms of bringing a greater understanding to the student despite his knowledge, background, status, or personality. These factors have a

Figure 4-1
Lesson Plan Form.

LESSON PLAN

Name _____

Date presented _____

NAME OF COURSE IN WHICH TO BE USED

COURSE: (Title of course or the subject of which this Lesson Plan is a part.)

LESSON: (Title of lesson. It should be short, complete, and descriptive of the content and should be stated in terms of "HOW TO . . . ," e.g., HOW TO SEARCH [suspects, etc.].)

OBJECTIVES: (List of specific knowledge, skills, and abilities students will gain from lesson.)

MATERIALS NEEDED: (List of handout materials, supplies, equipment, and teaching aids needed.)

ASSIGNMENT: (Specific assignment for next session. If outside project is expected, assignment sheet should be handed out.)

REFERENCES: (List of materials used in developing lesson.)

I. INTRODUCTION: (List what has been planned to prepare the student for the information he is to be given. List what will be done to gain Attention, arouse Curiosity, stimulate Interest, and create Desire to learn [ACID Test of Introduction]. Specify what student will be told to stress importance of lesson material.)

II. PRESENTATION: (List teaching points in sequence, in outline form. Key points, examples, and illustrations should be included to make points clear. In this step, the instructor tells how, demonstrates how, presents new information.)

III. REVIEW: (Review briefly main points covered in Presentation.)

IV. APPLICATION: (Cite hypothetical problem that will require students to apply the principles given them in the Presentation to the solution of the problem, or require students to perform under instructor's supervision the task taught.)

V. TEST: (Have student perform the job taught without aid from instructor, or ask how or what questions to test depth of his understanding of the information presented. Specify exactly what the student is to do in the Test step. Include copy of written test questions in Lesson Plan. Oral how or what questions are best for short presentation. These will test understanding and recall and will reduce guessing. Use periodic paper-pencil tests constructed from written test questions.)

bearing on the instructional approach but will not substitute for good planning. This is not to suggest, however, that refreshing the student in practices, procedures, or techniques that he may have forgotten should be avoided.

A good basis for the systematic organization of instructional material might be based on the time element involved in performing a job such as writing a traffic citation, the need for accuracy in such operations as indexing and filing, chronological sequence as in report writing, cause-and-effect relationships, the pleasant to the unpleasant, comparison and contrast, least to greatest, general to particular, an enumeration of items, or some other logical approach that might be involved in a lecture on report writing or interrogation. When logical, systematic plans are employed, "each of the components of the overall lesson plan will assure that material is both comprehensive and objective, having a clear beginning, middle and conclusive end whereby the student comprehension increases throughout."[18]

Regardless of what criteria for logical presentation are used, the objective is to give the student the knowledge or ability that will enable him to perform his duties properly or better. When the arrangement of the teaching plan is completed, the instructor should review it to make sure it is workable, it can be properly fitted into the time allowed, and critical points have not been omitted.

Learning by Association

Things to be learned should be presented so they can be associated with other familiar things. The process of remembering by association is described by William James in his classical statement, "In mental terms, the more other facts a fact is associated with in the mind, the better possession of it our memory retains."[19]

The instructor who has planned well will have constructed his lesson material so that the learner can relate it to his own background and experiences. This process of learning by association is of special importance when the material deals with jobs, operations, techniques, or principles foreign to the learner. The philosophy behind the law, for example, or the psychological principles involved in the interrogation of suspects may be difficult to convey to the student if he cannot associate the material in some way to his past experiences.

When facts and ideas are presented only in isolated bits and fragments, considerable difficulty will be encountered in communicating them to others. They can be transferred profitably when they have been given meaningful associations.[20] The development of pertinent examples will tax the imagination of the teacher, but the returns for his efforts will amply repay him.

Five Steps of Teaching

Even in the most casual, informal contacts where instruction is involved, there must be an orderly procedure for imparting information to the learner if best results are to be realized from the training effort. First, the learner's attention must be focused on the subject and his interest titillated—this is how teaching begins. Then the information must be conveyed to him; this is the substance of which teaching is made. Major points presented must be reviewed to fix them more strongly in the learner's mind. The learner must then be given an opportunity to apply what he has learned under the supervision of the instructor. Finally, the teacher must appraise his own effectiveness in terms of the learner's understanding.

---

[18] Mary-ellen Weimer, *Learner-Centered Teaching: Five Key Changes to Practice* (San Francisco: Jossey-Bass, 2002), p. 187.

[19] William James, *Principles of Psychology* (New York: Holt, 1908), p. 294.

[20] *Ibid.*, p. 14.

Introduction

The introductory step in the instructional process will perhaps tax the imagination of the teacher more than the other four steps of instruction. Introductory remarks should focus the attention of the student on the subject, gain his interest, and place him in a state of readiness to learn. If these conditions are not present, the value of the remaining steps of the process will largely be lost. This is the step in which the ACID test must be applied. The instructor should ask himself:

Have I gained *A*ttention?
Have I aroused *C*uriosity?
Have I stimulated *I*nterest?
Have I created a *D*esire to learn?

The introduction should result in an arrangement of ideas and experiences already present in the learner's mind in such an order that he will be receptive to the new ideas and experiences to be taught. This step does not involve the imparting of new knowledge, but it provides the instructor an opportunity to develop a basis on which instruction can rest. When properly used, this step gives the learner motive and enthusiasm for learning and establishes a relationship between the subject and his past experience.

There are a multitude of ways of securing the attention of the learner, stimulating his interest, and creating in him a desire to learn:

Asking leading questions
Directing rhetorical questions to students
Making use of suggestions, illustrations, or demonstrations
Relating personal or other practical examples
Placing emphasis on present or future needs that learners may satisfy by the information
Citing group or individual experiences
Discussing why it is imperative to learn how to perform the job correctly
Indicating how increased proficiency may benefit learners personally or economically

In the introductory step of the instruction, the instructor often finds the individual approach has several advantages over the group approach. It is a more personal and informal approach to training and can be given at any time or place. No special physical facilities are required, since contacts are usually short and impromptu and occur on the job. Psychologically, the learner is receptive to the training, since he can apply it immediately to the task and ordinarily needs no other motivation. The instructor can alter his approach to allow for individual differences among trainees.

When training is given in a group setting, considerable planning is needed for the introduction, since the entire group must be motivated to learn. The introductory remarks must be adequate for this purpose; however, the introduction seldom achieves this objective if it is devised primarily to appeal to the average learner in this group. The result is that it often fails to provide motivation to learners outside the middle group. Difficulty is sometimes encountered in altering the teaching approach to compensate for individual differences unless the group is quite small.

Presentation

The objective of the presentation step is either to impart new knowledge or skills to the student or to refresh his memory about what he has once learned but might have forgotten. To be most meaningful, the material must be related to ideas and experiences already known to him. This is the process of association discussed previously.

The material should be presented in an orderly, systematic manner by showing, telling, explaining, or demonstrating so that the learner understands the proper procedures and methods of performing a task. Preplanned demonstrations might well supplement the lecture, imaginative teaching aids will assist the instructor in vividly describing concepts to the students, and discussions and relevant examples will give the learners an opportunity to clarify misconceptions. The variety of approaches available to the instructor in making his presentation most meaningful is limited only by his imagination and his effort.

The advantage to be gained by the teacher in presenting information on an individual basis is that he can make allowances for individual differences by speeding up or slowing down his presentation. When it is given in a group setting, he must gauge his speed to meet the needs of the average learner and sometimes loses the interest of the speedier or the slower ones. The amount of emphasis on key points and the pace of instruction must be continuously adjusted to accommodate varying group abilities; however, the information can be presented to more persons in groups than individually. This advantage of the group method cannot be overlooked.

Review

Although a review following each major segment of the presentation step ordinarily is desirable to help fix the material in the learner's mind, the review or summary step should be added after the total presentation as well. This will enable the instructor to include in his lesson plan the several major points in his presentation that should be reviewed briefly. Such a summary is of special value in long presentations, where confusion or lack of retention might occur. It is an excellent means of tying together the material in the presentation step.

Application

In the application step, the learner is provided an opportunity to try out or use the information he has learned under the teacher's supervision. This step should disclose how much of the new material he has grasped and how ready he is to progress to a new area of learning. The instructor should carefully supervise and assist the learner when necessary during the application step to ensure that what has been taught is applied correctly and that bad habits are not formed. The instructor should check key points as they are being performed and require the learner to repeat the operation if repetition is necessary to increase his proficiency to an acceptable level. There is wisdom to the adage that "practice makes perfect."

Problem solving and role playing are excellent teaching devices to determine if the students are able to solve practical problems by applying the principles given them in the presentation. Realistic, simulated field problems are very useful in giving students experience in handling incidents frequently encountered in their work. This form of training is merely an extension of the application step, since students are required to apply what they have previously learned, unless, of course, role playing is intended only to test judgment or common sense. Role playing and the use of field problems are discussed later in this chapter.

The instructor can more closely supervise the individual in this step than he can a group. He can also answer questions more readily as the need arises and can detect and correct errors more quickly. In the group setting, equipment needed by students to apply what they have learned is often unavailable and participation thereby suffers. In addition, errors may occur without prompt detection, bad habits can develop more readily, and retraining is needed more frequently.

Test

The fifth step, the test or follow-up, is the last step in the instructional process and consists of an evaluation of the learner's progress. Like the application step, the test enables the instructor to determine the present ability of the learner and his readiness to proceed to a new phase of instruction. The learner must know the extent of his successes and failures and why they occurred to encourage him to further effort and to enable him to correct his weaknesses. Regardless of the type of tests given (oral, written, or manipulative), they must be constructed so that they will measure the effectiveness of the teacher through an evaluation of the learner's progress or lack of it. This step is closely related to the application step in which the learner demonstrates the extent of his learning and his ability to apply what he has learned. On occasion, the test step can be appropriately combined with the application step. "How" or "what" questions are best when asked orally in testing the student's understanding of the principles presented.

As diagnostic instruments to show gaps in learning and as a medium for applying principles to practice, tests have unquestioned value. Testing to determine what the student has or has not learned is perhaps the most fruitful part of the teaching process, so the test should never be relegated to a place of unimportance in teaching. Test questions should be based not on trivia but on objectives. Although tests are not easy to construct, they deserve a great deal of attention because they will, if properly formulated, give the teacher some clues to whether he is achieving his general goals and specific objectives.

General Problems Affecting Teaching Method

The real problems encountered by the instructor in applying the five-step method of teaching are not failures of the method but failures of the instructor to make proper use of the steps and to alter his approach to teaching as necessary when confronted with specific training problems. The method has been widely used with great success, as the training of massive numbers of military troops by similar methods will attest. The theory and method are sound and can be adapted to any teaching situation. The emphasis placed on each step of the method depends on the particular training need that must be met.

On occasion, the instructor can eliminate the introduction because the learner is self-motivated. He may reveal this by asking a question or requesting instruction. The instructor may then proceed immediately to the second step. A review is always a valuable aid to learning and should follow, in summary form, the presentation. The application step may not be required because the test may serve two purposes. All steps in the process are important at times, but the appropriate emphasis for each changes. The instructor must make his own value judgments regarding his method of approaching a particular training situation in the classroom or in the field.

In addition, no method suitable for one instructor is necessarily suitable for others. Uniform training material can be provided to an instructor, but the effectiveness of the specific methods he employs to impart knowledge to his subordinates depends on his individual teaching repertoire and his ability to avoid the pitfalls that contribute to teaching failures. He can be told what methods have been found effective and he can be acquainted with the many and varied techniques of teaching, but unless he diligently, enthusiastically, and imaginatively applies himself to his teaching responsibilities, he will achieve little more than mediocrity in this activity.

Common Causes of Teacher Ineffectiveness

Perhaps one of the most common faults in presenting instructional material arises from oversimplification, leaving to the student the task of drawing a conclusion without adequate facts. The inexperienced teacher is often prone to include too much detail in his lesson because he fails to allow for the basic intelligence of the learner. When he includes too much material for the time available, he will have a tendency to "cover the ground at any cost." Either too much is attempted—in which case learners retain few of the key points because time limitations make it necessary to gloss over them, the teacher uses the allotted time without completing his objectives, and he fails to complete the steps of instruction—or he improvises at the last moment and proceeds without an organized plan. In any event, the student suffers by having been exposed to too much and having learned little, which is called "overloading."

Another common weakness contributing to teaching ineffectiveness is aimlessness. Rao observed, "Aimlessness and indifference in teaching are the greatest obstacles in the development of educational skills."[21] Aimlessness usually results from a failure to plan and organize teaching material properly. Deficiencies in teaching often result from the inclusion of unnecessary or irrelevant material in the teaching plan. The cause usually can be traced to the failure of the teacher to discriminate between necessary material and trivia that is only nice to know. Once a cluster of information has been accumulated, the teacher often finds it extremely difficult to discard any of it, but he must strip his material to the essentials or risk failure.

Too frequently, the teacher assumes that the learner knows more about the job than he actually does. This ill-founded assumption often causes the instructor to leave out points that are essential, to gloss over them without sufficient emphasis, or to fail to define unusual terms. The learner thereby fails to grasp the necessary facts; he misunderstands or fails to understand. The result is performance failures and costly errors.

Often, a lack of competency or a failure on the part of the supervisor to prepare himself for his training role is the cause of teaching ineffectiveness. It is highly desirable that he be occupationally competent to perform the task he expects his subordinates to learn about, but having technical proficiency does not ensure that he can impart the knowledge to others. It would be erroneous to assume that just because an individual is an excellent burglary investigator, he could effectively teach others how to catch burglars.

---

[21] R. Ranga Rao, *Methods of Teacher Training* (New Delhi: Discovery Publishing, 2006), p. 38.

Rather, the technically competent supervisor who is also a good teacher will achieve a high degree of success in the training function because his ability in one area will complement that in the other.

Teaching Methods

There are numerous approaches to teaching, each with its own characteristic advantages and disadvantages. The instructor must recognize that there is no ideal approach for all situations and that no single method can be used to the exclusion of others. Some of the most common techniques of implementing the five-step method of instruction are included here as reminders to the supervisor-teacher of the need for an imaginative approach to teaching.

Lectures

The pure lecture method of instruction is greatly overworked because many instructors find it the easiest way to present instructional material. Good demonstrations, use of teaching aids, questions and discussions, and development of the more sophisticated supplements to teaching require time and energy that many instructors do not feel are worth the results. The contribution of these various approaches to learning will, however, more than offset the time required to prepare them.

The lecture method of teaching is quite often the least effective method, since it assumes that all members of the class progress at the same rate; it can be used advantageously if the lesson is presented in extremely short sessions, however. Even under this condition, the presentation should be supplemented by some teaching aids, even if nothing more than the chalkboard, which is readily available and easy to use. Some humor, showmanship, and even a little histrionics at times will help to improve the learning environment.

When explanations are made of procedures, techniques, or manipulative tasks, they must be simple, clear, and concise to be most effective. They should be given in language suitable to the backgrounds of those being taught. Recruit officers will be less familiar than seasoned officers with police jargon, so an unfamiliar term used without definition or explanation may hinder a learner's understanding of the entire lesson. Unusual jargon, vernacular expressions, or technical terms should be defined or avoided in favor of language with which the learner is more familiar.

Often, the teacher makes an erroneous assumption that his material is understood because questions are not raised, but in reality, questions may not be asked. Perhaps a learner desires to remain inconspicuous in the group. Another student might feel self-conscious about not understanding what he assumes is common terminology. Sometimes, lack of questions is brought about simply by disinterest. The teacher should ask himself what he failed to do to stimulate a desire to learn; then he should do something about it to avoid further waste of time.

Questions from students should be handled carefully, since they may indicate that understanding has not taken place or that review is needed. They should be treated patiently by the instructor. He should be guided by the nature of the question in determining the extent of the answer required, but he must answer it to clarify any misunderstanding. Bugelski indicated many years ago, and it is still true today, that

"Misunderstanding and understanding can occur with exactly the same feeling of assurance."[22] The student may believe he has understood the instructor perfectly when he has not done so at all. The only clue to the instructor that misunderstanding has occurred might be a simple question. The absence of questions cannot, however, be considered a reliable indicator that understanding has taken place.

Guest Speakers

Frequently, experienced detectives, vice officers, investigators of juvenile crime, and the like can be utilized to give training sessions relating to their areas of expertise, especially when matters arise that should be brought to the attention of patrol officers.

Role Playing and Field Problems

Role playing in a wide variety of field problems developed to simulate (as nearly as possible) common incidents likely to be faced frequently by officers in the field is an extremely useful training device. This gives trainees experience in a practical setting by dealing with typical situations they are likely to face on the job. Such problems must be carefully developed and orchestrated, however, so that the maximum practical, real-life effects can be realized.

The scope of simulations and field problems is limited only by the imagination and ingenuity of those responsible for the training. For best results, they should be carefully planned, preferably in a conference setting in which experienced personnel provide subject-matter information and the criteria for appraising results. Scripts should be prepared to guide each actor in the problem; experienced personnel should be used in the various roles to make the simulations most lifelike.

Each trainee should be evaluated by experienced personnel as the problem proceeds. At the conclusion, the trainee's performance should be critiqued so that he might gain maximum benefits from his mistakes.

Stress Management Simulations

Role-playing problems can also be easily adapted to stress management training. Although they are not foolproof in training personnel perfectly in every stressful situation, such simulations will provide them with an opportunity to gain a mastery over their emotional and physical responses in real, lifelike situations.

Job-related stress[23] has been recognized by progressive administrators in recent times as a costly concomitant to most occupations, especially police work. Although some of this stress can be prevented by the elimination of those organizational factors that unnecessarily cause it and by improving managerial and supervisory techniques that contribute to it, little can be done to reduce the work pressures an officer must face in performing his daily tasks. These also cause stress, but his responses to such pressures can be made more positive by improving his ability to cope with them through training.

---

[22] B. R. Bugelski, *The Psychology of Learning Applied to Teaching* (Indianapolis, Ind.: Bobbs-Merrill, 1964), p. 202.

[23] See Chapter 8 for a discussion of occupational stress.

His physiological responses to everyday stressful situations are called arousal.[24] They cause subtle physical and emotional reactions that may range from slight to severe, usually depending on the adequacy of his training and his experiences in handling similar incidents. If the person is properly conditioned by training, his reactions are likely to be positive and stress will be minimal. If his reactions are negative and cause distress, they are usually reflections of skill deficiencies.

Adequate training directed toward remediation of these deficiencies can prevent many of the negative reactions from stress. The objective of such training should be to give the trainee a higher tolerance of stress and an increased repertoire of techniques useful in managing it. Even though the field problems are simulations, the exposure of the trainee to them tends to condition him psychologically so that he is better able to cope with stressful problems he encounters in the field. "Under stress, an officer will do what [he is] trained to do under stress."[25] Training that does not improve stress management will fall short in critical situations.

Workshops

Workshops and small discussion groups in which trainees can talk, listen, and compare experiences with others under the guidance of experienced personnel can give participants added insight into the perspective and experiences of others. In addition, such discussions may be suggestive of new approaches to difficult situations.

Demonstrations

Instructors and students find relief from the boredom of the pure lecture method when planned demonstrations with actual equipment or implements are used to supplement other teaching techniques. Although demonstrations are a useful device in almost any training situation, they are of particular value when manipulative skills are the subject of instruction. The student can be shown one step of the procedure at a time, allowed to apply what he has learned under the watchful eye of the teacher. He can then advance to the remaining steps, one at a time, until he has received instruction in and has been able to perform satisfactorily the entire job.

The object of the demonstration should be made clear to students. They should be told the important portions to look for and their overall relationship to the completed task. The student is thus prepared for the instruction by being familiarized with the ways he can utilize the information to help him do his job.

Ideally, the teacher should place himself in a position where students can observe him performing the demonstration from the same relative position as they would assume when actually performing the operation. An explanation of why the operation is performed in a certain way will give the student a greater understanding of the procedure and will tend to fix the steps in his mind. The task should be repeated as many times as necessary

---

[24] Robert J. Rotella, "The Psychology of Performance under Stress," *FBI Law Enforcement Bulletin,* 53, No. 6 (June 1984), 2, 3. See also Ayola M. Pines, Elliott Aronson with Ditsa Kafry, *Burnout: From Tedium to Personal Growth* (New York: Free Press, 1981), pp. 115–16.

[25] Phil Messina, "Confrontational Simulations," *The Law Enforcement Trainer* (July–September 2005), 29.

to ensure student proficiency at about the level where he could effectively and safely execute the task on the job. The need for too much repetition should cause the instructor to reassess the effectiveness of his teaching techniques; changes in his approach might be indicated. As the demonstration is conducted, the instructor should test students by asking them how to perform the next step and why it is done to ascertain the degree of learning that has taken place and the effectiveness of his methods of presentation.

There are as many types of demonstrations as there are tasks a peace officer performs daily. Many of these demonstrations can be used to make training sessions more lively and interesting and to permit participation by members of the audience. Some examples might be to call on a member to demonstrate such common field procedures as searching a person arrested for a narcotics violation or stopping a vehicle for a variety of reasons. Objective critiques by other members of the group will enhance the benefits of such training. Care must be exercised, however, to establish an appropriate basis and value for the demonstration to prevent a potential deadening effect brought about when calling on a student participant to assume the position of a teacher.

Group Discussions

A change of pace may be of great value in reviving lagging interest, fostering participation, and refocusing attention on the subject. The instructor may often accomplish this by stimulating discussion among the students. Problem solving by students with the accompanying benefits derived from their participation provides them with opportunity to contribute pertinent information, evaluate it, and draw conclusions. This procedure is extremely useful for synthesizing a vast amount of information from a variety of sources. It is also a useful device for determining the extent of learning that has taken place, since it involves the application of stated principles to practical problems. In fact, the use of several techniques in some sessions is often desirable to spice up the training, provide balance to the presentation, give it vitality, and add color and interest.

An instructional technique involving a presentation by specialists with audience participation permitted is called a forum. When the discussion is between a group of specialists without audience participation, the technique is referred to as a panel discussion, and a modification of this procedure is to permit the audience to ask questions of the panel. It is an excellent problem-solving medium and is very useful in clarifying complicated issues that cause insecurity and misunderstanding among personnel. Such a training technique has the disadvantage of limiting the content to the information imparted by the panel.

Panel Discussions

Panel discussions can be used productively, especially at or near the end of training sessions for experienced officers. Members chosen for their expertise can clarify issues involving the application of policies and procedures to the regular operational duties of the trainees. Often, questions can be obtained from trainees to aid in selecting appropriate panel members.

Conferences

Conferences are splendid training mediums that have been utilized frequently and have produced notable results in many cases, especially at the operational level in police work. These meetings need not follow formal procedures and can be easily adapted to current needs. For example, they are well suited for simple briefings, for progress briefings, or for development of workable plans. Conferences can be used to disseminate information, to share problems in need of resolution, to examine possible solutions, and to coordinate the efforts of participants with common concerns in large-scale or complex investigations or operations.

Staff Meetings

Well-conducted meetings with subordinate personnel provide the supervisor an excellent opportunity for training. These meetings, usually called staff meetings, may be scheduled periodically at specified intervals or only as needed. In a newly established unit or in one with newly assigned superior officers, staff meetings probably should be held frequently at first, but once the operational personnel become acquainted with any changes in policy or procedure, such meetings will be necessary less frequently.

Staff meetings are useful in passing on new information and in solving problems within the organization. As a means of developing coordination and integrating efforts, they are without equal if properly handled. They are sometimes held as coffee or breakfast meetings, which give them a desirable degree of informality.

Usually, staff meetings are called by superior officers, although every supervisor should take advantage of this medium for training. Those with common interests, even though assigned to another unit, should be invited to participate. The patrol supervisor would miss a splendid opportunity to achieve greater coordination between uniformed personnel in his unit and investigators in another unit if he failed to invite to such meetings the detective supervisor and possibly from time to time various members of his staff.

Planning

The most "mileage" can be gained from staff meetings if the supervisor responsible for their conduct prepares a plan of action. Problems that require discussion should be noted as they occur so that they can be included in the agenda. Facts necessary for complete resolution of the problems should be collected and organized, and an agenda should be prepared and transmitted to concerned personnel before the meeting so they will have time to think about the items to be discussed. If the meeting is to produce maximum results, a portion of it should be devoted to training. A specialist, one of the members of the unit, or a representative of another allied unit might be asked to prepare a short training presentation for the group on some pertinent topic of current importance.

Follow-Up

Minutes of the proceedings should be prepared so that policy determinations, solutions to operational or other problems, and group decisions will become a matter of record. Follow-up observations or action necessary as the result of the decisions arrived at by the group should be made by the supervisor or his delegate.

Use and Misuse of Procedures

Staff meetings are usually conducted in one or a combination of three ways: as a democratically led conference, as an autocratically controlled assembly, or as a training session. When they are conducted democratically, by use of the conference method, employees are encouraged to participate in the decision-making process by expressing their opinions and making recommendations. By being encouraged to become involved in the solution of problems that affect them, they will likely accept the decisions made as their own.

If the supervisor looks on staff meetings as a place in which he can give orders and monopolize the time by doing all of the talking and none of the listening, the meetings will eventually turn into silent sessions with little or no response from those assembled, who will soon consider such meetings as ordeals, with themselves as a captive audience. Many supervisors recognize that the problems arising within a unit are their responsibility. They are, therefore, inclined to tell their subordinates what to do about the problems rather than solicit their ideas for solving them.

Supervisors tend to become one of several types, as Sutherland classifies them.[26] The absolute dictator falls into the habit of telling his subordinates what they have been doing wrong, seldom telling them what they have done right; he rarely listens effectively. The benevolent dictator discusses; his subordinates listen, often only to his philosophy. The responsibility dodger does not dictate, but he does not lead either. The democratic leader shares problems with his subordinates; he also shares his decision-making power by encouraging suggestions and initiative.

Use of Questions

Questions to students requiring thinking and reasoning can be used to reveal the extent to which they have absorbed the material needed to perform a task or have gained an understanding of the more abstract types of instruction. Additionally, such questions can be used to spot-check the student's progress or to reveal the need for review.

The questions used may be of several types. Overhead questions are those directed to the entire group, with the instructor then choosing one student to answer. This type of question is the one most commonly used. Sufficient time should be allowed for the named student to formulate an answer, and every effort should be made by the instructor to aid him, without actually answering the question, to give the learner a feeling of success and achievement. Relay questions, those asked by one student and relayed by the instructor to another member of the group for an answer, can also be a useful tool of instruction. The instructor should avoid using the relay question as a means of evading a response to a question that he is unable to answer. The reverse question is one that the instructor "throws back" to the person who asked it. It can be used to advantage to help the student solve his own problem, perhaps with some prompting by the teacher or others if necessary.

Questions should never be used as a club to embarrass, chastise, or reveal the ignorance of a student. Using questions in this way tends to close students' minds and set up barriers to effective learning. However, a simple question, tactfully asked, is sometimes a useful device to gain the attention of an inattentive student.

---

[26] Sidney S. Sutherland, *When You Preside,* 5th ed. (Danville, Ill.: Interstate Printers and Publishers, 1980), p. 135.

Use of Teaching Aids

The aids available to the teacher to help him carry out his teaching function are practically unlimited. Too often he relies only on the spoken word to put his material across, yet investigation has revealed that the largest portion of a person's knowledge has been gained not through the auditory sense alone but through the use of this sense combined with the others, principally sight. The teacher who performs his instructional function most effectively is the one who utilizes every possible means to assist him in carrying his message to the student in a manner calculated to enhance learning efficiency.

Instructional aids help the teacher to avoid too much telling and too much reliance on words to carry ideas. They will help him and the student to develop meanings in common and, when used properly, will help prevent misunderstandings arising out of merely verbal presentations. They do not supplant good verbal instruction but supplement and improve it because they stimulate other senses used in learning. Student interest and participation are enhanced by the addition of color and variety to the instruction and the presentation of live problems and situations. Monotony can be avoided by the use of these teaching supplements when they are imaginatively employed to vary presentations. Many avenues of learning are opened when senses other than hearing are brought into play and combined with it.

Knowledge is acquired through the senses and stored in a system of symbols. Teaching is concerned with the art of stimulating a desire to learn and developing the ability to perceive symbols accurately and clearly. When this is done, increased learning is possible. It will be enhanced by any communication media that aid perception and understanding.[27] Ideally, as many senses as possible should be appealed to when the teacher presents ideas, principles, facts, and problems. Although he should use as many aids as are available to him, no one type should be used to the exclusion of all others; each type has its own value and should be used to serve a particular purpose. This is particularly important in the introduction and presentation steps.

Types of Teaching Aids

Elaborate aids are not essential. Simple, inexpensive ones can be used to fill a real need. Sometimes the aid made with a felt pencil or a wax crayon on butcher paper is more effective than a sophisticated, expensive mock-up.

Display Aids

The simple chalkboard, whiteboard, or specially prepared chart can be effectively used for display purposes to supplement oral instruction. Such aids are especially useful when material is being taught in a small area where the entire class can see them. Pictures, diagrams, charts, or other matters depicted must be large enough to show details clearly if the teacher expects them to be effective. Color adds variety and value to posters and should be used whenever possible to stimulate student interest. Discretion and good taste are always in order. If charts, tables, or diagrams are prepared beforehand and are complex, parts

---

[27] Edward Conrad Wragg and George Brown, *Explaining* (London: Routledge, 2001), p. 39.

should be used separately to focus the span of the student's attention. When the chalkboard is employed, the material placed on it should be well arranged, simple, and clear. If the teacher desires to draw diagrams while lecturing, he should plan carefully what he wishes to depict so that the drawing will not detract from his presentation; a series of tiny dots previously arranged on the board will guide his drawing if it is other than a simple one. In all cases, display aids should follow the maxim, "White space and bold face, because nobody reads fine print."[28] Visual aids should be clear and easy to read from the back row of the classroom.

Duplicated Aids

Duplicated aids can be prepared by a multitude of mechanical processes now available to the teacher. These aids may consist of instruction sheets, information sheets, diagrams, charts, illustrations, PowerPoint outlines of the fill-in type, conventional outlines, or other types of data useful to the student. The material should be punched so that it may be included in the student's notebook. These handout materials should not be made available to the student as substitutes for study. The information should represent matter that is difficult to obtain, but valuable to the student's progress.

Projected Aids

The teaching aids available for projection on a screen are almost unlimited. Some are easily and cheaply prepared and make a splendid contribution to teaching. The equipment necessary to project these materials, however, is often expensive and not easily available. PowerPoint, DVDs, webcasts, overhead projection equipment, and a multitude of other devices will add greatly to the teacher's instructional efforts if they are properly used. The instructor, however, must not rely on them as a crutch; they should be only a complement to his own efforts. Neither should this type of aid be looked on as a form of recreation for the student.

When video presentations are used, it is essential that they be ordered sufficiently in advance so that they may be delivered and the necessary equipment set up for their use prior to the time of the class meeting. They are part of a planned lesson and must be used carefully and with discrimination to be most effective. A few selected slides, for example, studied carefully by the student might provide more learning than the use of many, which may only cause confusion. Students should be prepared in advance to observe important points—careful introduction paves the way for learning. Note taking during this type of presentation generally should not be required, since it tends to distract attention from the film and is difficult in darkened rooms. Ideally, students should note and discuss key points after the video has been observed, discuss major concepts depicted, and answer pertinent questions to demonstrate the amount of learning that has taken place.

Three-Dimensional Aids

Equipment parts, cutaways, mock-ups, simulated scenes common to police work, table models, and other such devices overcome the difficulty of depicting items on a flat surface. Flannel and magnetic boards are very useful in giving the student an overall perspective of

---

[28] Herbert Williams, *Exploring Crime Analysis* (Overland Park, Kan.: IACA Press, Crime Analysis Publications, 2004).

a problem, although these ordinarily have flat surfaces. They do, however, have the advantage of simplicity of preparation, economy, and portability. Mock-ups do not have these advantages. In addition, flannel or magnetic boards give the student the opportunity to deal with movable objects. This type of aid is unmatchable in some presentations having to do with police tactics and field operations, since it places the learner in a position that simulates those encountered in practice. He is also afforded an opportunity to exercise his judgment or apply principles in a hypothetical setting. Problems involving such police incidents as civil disorder, major disasters, barricaded subjects, fires, demonstrations, or other unusual occurrences can be simulated to give the student experience in the classroom. Any number of smart devices may be used to enhance the learning process as well.

Electronic Media Devices

Although expensive and sometimes not available for training on a daily basis, all sorts of electronic media devices can be used as training aids to liven up training sessions. Video presentations offer a vast variety of training opportunities. They often encourage audience participation and add alternatives to ordinary training. Many police academies are now using sophisticated devices, such as driving simulators and FATS (firearms training systems), to give trainees a "virtual-reality situation."[29] This training allows officers to learn from their mistakes and improve their professional judgment, without injuries or lawsuits.

Field Trips

Trips carefully planned to accomplish a specific objective are a useful type of teaching aid that allows students to learn firsthand through observation about an actual operation. They should be oriented in advance to the objectives of the trip and pertinent points to look for so that the trip might be most meaningful. Trips should be carefully controlled to prevent them from becoming purely recreational.

Additional Training Resources

Training updates, information on student and instructor development, teaching aids, curricula, and many other resources are available on the Internet:

- www.communitypolicing.org is the site for the Community Policing Consortium, the leader in promoting and assisting in the development of community-oriented policing.
- www.policeforum.org is the site for the Police Executive Research Forum, a source for cutting-edge information on best practices in policing.
- www.theiacp.org is where you can find the International Association of Chiefs of Police, which provides a wide variety of professional information, including volumes on training.
- www.ncjrs.org is the premier site for criminal justice reference material.
- http://police.sas.ab.ca/ links to CopNet, which has information and links to unlimited law enforcement–related websites.

---

[29] Donna Rogers, "WILL Interactive Helps Trainees 'Play It Out Before They Live It Out,' " *Law Enforcement Technology,* 31, No. 3 (March 2004), 116.

SUMMARY

A principal duty of the supervisor is the training of his subordinates, since the level of their proficiency is directly related to the amount and quality of the training they receive. Personnel constitute the most important and costly of all items in the police budget. The supervisor-teacher must therefore make the greatest possible use of the time he has available for training. He must take advantage of every opportunity that presents itself to improve the performance of his subordinates through the most efficient training methods available to him. Inefficient, careless teaching methods must give way to effective, artful instruction. Without it, low morale, waste, and costly errors inevitably infiltrate the police operation.

Training failures that allow personnel to sink or swim by the slow process of trial-and-error learning will eventually take a toll on the resources of a force in the form of lowered public confidence brought on by ineffectual law enforcement, costly lawsuits arising from performance derelictions by police personnel, and a general withering of the morale and esprit de corps of the organization.

The effectiveness of the supervisor in his training function is dependent on his knowledge of the various components of the job, his understanding of the learning process, and his common sense, imagination, and willingness to work at his training task. The techniques he uses will depend on the setting in which training takes place. Much of this will occur on the job, and some will be of a more formal type in the classroom, but wherever it takes place, the basic principles of teaching will be applicable, with perhaps only a change of emphasis in the specific methods used.

Once a teacher selects or is assigned a subject for presentation in a training session, such as a briefing or roll-call teaching assignment (both of which are more formal than an on-the-job instructional situation), the general goals and specific objectives to be accomplished should be determined. Information must be gathered, analyzed, and arranged so that it may be adapted to the five-step method of teaching involving the introduction, presentation, review, application, and test, as discussed in this chapter.

When the subject matter has been selected for training, the instructor must first decide on the general instructional goals and specific objectives he wishes to accomplish by the instructional process. The teacher should look on them in terms of the desired changes in attitudes or behaviors that he wishes to bring about by training.

After the instructor has established his objectives, material should be collected from the most reliable and authoritative sources available. It must then be analyzed to determine what operations are most necessary to complete the job and how much of the material can be presented in the time available. That which is of secondary importance should be discarded; only that which is pertinent and can be presented in the allotted time should be retained.

The instructor should then prepare a written plan to teach. It should be devised to guide him in presenting the subject matter to his students in a logical, systematic manner. It should be adapted to the five-step method of teaching and should include notations regarding when and how the teaching materials and aids are to be used in each step. Proper, careful planning is essential to proper application of this five-step method.

The introductory step is useful to motivate the student to learn, to secure his interest, and to focus his attention on the subject. The objective of the presentation step is to develop understanding, impart knowledge, and prepare the learner better to accomplish a task. The review step should be used to summarize main points in the presentation. In the application step, the learner is given an opportunity to apply what he has learned. The test step enables the teacher to evaluate his effectiveness in teaching and the learner's comprehension of the subject matter.

The teacher must be cognizant of the advantages and disadvantages of the various approaches to teaching to minimize failures. He should recognize that the five-step method is basically sound.

Failures are the result of the instructor's shortcomings in applying the proven principles of teaching. He fails to accomplish his objective when he tries to teach too much in the time available, when he fails to discriminate between necessary and trivial material, or when he oversimplifies or overcomplicates his presentation. His teaching effectiveness is also reduced when he fails to appeal to the learner's several senses and to supplement verbal presentations through the proper use of teaching aids of all kinds.

If the teacher does not relate the material he presents to his students to things they already know or if he fails to convince them of the importance of the information in terms of either what it can do to make the job easier, safer, or more effective or how it can personally benefit them, they likely will not retain it. If the information is not presented so that the student can see clearly what he is supposed to learn, confusion will result. The student who is unable or unwilling to make use of what he has learned will not remember it long and will probably have wasted his time and that of the instructor.

REVIEW

Questions

1. What are some of the effects of training deficiencies?
2. How might traditions, customs, and habits affect the teacher's approach to training? Give examples.
3. How can an administrator or supervisor determine the effects of training?
4. Define the principles of readiness, effect, and repetition, and give an example of how each may be applied to the learning process.
5. How are these three principles interdependent?
6. What are some of the factors that affect the learning rate of students?
7. What is meant by motivation? How can a teacher bring this condition about?
8. What are teaching objectives?
9. How should an objective be written?
10. What factors should an instructor take into consideration in analyzing his teaching material before presenting it?
11. What is a lesson plan? How may it be used?
12. What should a lesson plan contain?
13. What form should a plan follow?
14. Why is learning by association important to the student?
15. List the five steps of teaching discussed in this chapter, and explain what each step should accomplish.
16. What are some ways of stimulating attention and securing the interest of the learner?
17. What are the advantages of the individual approach to teaching over the group approach in each of the five steps of instruction?
18. What are the advantages of the group approach over the individual approach in each of the steps?
19. What step controls the learning process most? Explain why this is so.

20. List the most common causes of teaching ineffectiveness. Discuss briefly what can be done to avoid them.

21. Discuss the advantages and disadvantages of at least three of the most common methods of teaching.

22. Name three types of questions, and explain how they can be used in a teaching situation.

23. Name four general categories of teaching aids, give a specific example of each, and explain how each might be used in a training session.

Exercises

1. List as many individual differences as you can, and indicate how each might affect learning.

2. List at least ten environmental factors that might affect learning, and indicate which of them might be controlled by the teacher. Explain how this might be accomplished.

3. List at least ten bases on which a teacher can establish a logical sequence in his teaching, and give a concrete example of how each might be used in a practical teaching situation.

4. Prepare a lesson plan from information you have collected for a fifteen-minute roll-call training session on one of the subjects listed below. Be prepared to give your lesson from this plan to the class. Limit the subject chosen where necessary.

How to handle a fire call in an apartment building
How to make a juvenile arrest report
How to mark evidence (choose a specific kind)
How to handcuff two arrestees
How to prepare for a promotional exam
How to operate an automated license plate reader
How to use verbal judo
How to search for a prowler
How to recognize a stolen vehicle
How to work a stakeout
How to handle an "unknown trouble" call
How to respond to a robbery-in-progress call
How to handle a "burglar there now" call
How to search a crime scene for evidence (of a particular crime)
How to mark shell casings
How to handle a major disorder
How to issue a traffic citation
How to handle a sexual assault call
How to drive under emergency conditions
How to handle a mentally ill person
How to conduct a field interrogation
How to work a special event
How to direct traffic
How to recognize a narcotics violation
How to make notifications and issue warnings about an approaching brush fire
How to drive in pursuit
How to stop a vehicle
How to fingerprint an arrestee
How to lift fingerprints
How to make and use a primary fingerprint classification
How to search a vehicle for narcotics

How to make a vehicle inspection

How to handle a barricaded sniper

How to conduct a search for a lost child

How to handle a bomb threat call

How to handle a plane crash in a business district

How to respond to a terrorist incident involving chemicals or biological agents

5. Prepare and use at least two teaching aids other than the chalkboard in your teaching exercise.

6. Constructively critique a staff meeting you have attended, describing what was done that could have been done better, and how; discuss what was done that should have been avoided, and why. Discuss the favorable aspects of the meeting. Do not identify the meeting unless you feel that its identity adds to your description.

5

Interpersonal Communications

Chapter Objectives

This chapter will enable you:

- To gain an understanding of the need for clear, concise communication in management activities
- To become acquainted with the barriers to effective communication and the techniques of overcoming such barriers
- To become familiar with some techniques of preparing effective written communication

The ability to communicate clearly and concisely is the most important single skill of the supervisor because it is basic to understanding the subordinate's point of view and passing on to him the objectives of the enterprise. Yet, among supervisors, communication is commonly the greatest area of weakness and the one most neglected.[1] Too often people are prone to take for granted that understanding takes place when they converse with each other. The old adage, "I know you believe you understand what you think I said, but I'm not sure you realize what you heard is not what I meant," is an important caveat the supervisor must always consider in his communications.[2]

Burrow, Everard, and Kleindl report that the number one problem of management, and the number one complaint of workers, is communication difficulties.[3] Without understandable communications, there can be no coordination of effort; without coordination, there can be no constructive organization.

It is important for the supervisor to realize that ideas and decisions can more readily be translated into the desired action when they are communicated to others with some consideration given to the emotional needs of the recipient and to his environment. Good communications are accomplished not only with words but with tones and deeds. Often these are more important than verbal expressions. There is much truth in the ancient adage that "actions speak louder than words." A gesture, the display of an attitude, or an inflection in the voice will often convey more meaning than will the spoken word. It is

---

[1] Mary E. Guffey and Dana Loewy, *Business Communication: Process & Product,* 7th ed. (Mason, Ohio: South-Western, 2011), p. 4.

[2] Kenneth D. Moore, *Effective Instructional Strategies: From Theory to Practice* (Thousand Oaks, Calif.: Sage Publications, 2012), p. 70.

[3] James L. Burrow, Kenneth Everard, and Brad Kleindl, *Business Principles and Management*, 12th ed. (Mason, Ohio: Thomson South-Western, 2008), p. 239.

therefore good for the supervisor to review from time to time the basics of good communications practices, since they all too often tend to become submerged in the day-to-day routine.

Few opportunities in the organizational setting offer the supervisor a greater chance to make his mark than the occasion to prepare a competent report and then convey its content to superiors and subordinates alike.

Cultural, Environmental, and Psychological Factors

Communications between persons and groups are very delicate, complex processes involving many factors—cultural, environmental, and psychological. The connotations of certain words can be highly offensive and provocative. The environment in which a communication takes place will often determine its effect. Even seemingly harmless and common words can be considered insulting, depending on the time, place, and circumstances in which they are used. Accordingly, supervisors should refrain from criticizing subordinates in the presence of others, whether outsiders or peers. Likewise, a patrol officer should address his superior by title in public, regardless of the closeness of their acquaintance. Psychologically, the reserved or shy individual could be dealt with more effectively perhaps with a tactful "soft" approach rather than the direct "hard" approach that is sometimes necessary in dealing with the aggressive extrovert. Indeed, in today's increasingly mixed-gender workplace, supervisors are wise to consider that the differences in how men and women communicate have been compared to "cross-cultural communication."[4]

Processes of Communications

Symbols and signs are the means a speaker uses to translate ideas to his listener. Word symbols are used to express thoughts. Words in themselves mean nothing; they are merely arbitrary symbolic representations of something.[5] Unless they are associated with some past experience, they are meaningless. For example, the word *cow* does not look like a cow and means nothing to a person who has not seen one or had one described to him. It is merely a symbol. Conversely, signs are the meanings that emanate from what is perceived. One expresses himself by words, gestures, facial expressions, inflections, and actions—but mostly by imprecise words—to the recipient, who hopefully absorbs what he perceives, interprets it, and reacts by words or actions. The communicator then responds to the recipient's reactions. If this sequence of interaction is distorted or unbalanced, unilateral communications take place. This may result in a failure on the recipient's part to respond as expected, or, worse, it may result in no action at all.

---

[4] Deborah Tannen, *You Just Don't Understand* (New York: HarperCollins, 2001).

[5] Jonathan L. Friedman, *Introductory Psychology*, 2nd ed. (Reading, Mass.: Addison-Wesley, 1982), pp. 154–55.

Barriers to Effective Communications

The effectiveness of organizations is highly dependent of necessity on good upward, downward, and lateral communications. The latter is most important to the activity of coordinating the efforts of organizational units.

Before real communications can take place, those who desire to engage effectively in this interaction should be aware that certain barriers must be recognized, understood, and removed. When they attain this awareness and do something about it, then and only then will their communications with others become truly effective.

Failure to Listen

A principal obstacle to good communications is the failure to listen to what others are saying.[6] This may result from many causes. Some of these are lack of interest in what is being said, personal problems causing mental preoccupation, egocentricity, or some other psychological condition that causes inattention or inability to concentrate. Mostly, however, failure to listen results purely from a lack of effort to engage actively in this process. One cannot truly communicate with others by merely hearing in a passive manner what is being said. Such passiveness will more often than not stifle understanding between individuals, since it will usually be interpreted as a reflection of disinterest. This is often shown by one party frequently changing the subject of the conversation or habitually losing eye contact (a nonverbal communication), which destroys the continuity of the conversation. The result is communication failure.

Status Differences

The greater the difference in status or rank is, the greater the difficulty in achieving effective communications. Communications are easier if they travel downward from the superior than if they go upward from the subordinate. Likewise, the greater the prestige of the communicator, the greater is the likelihood that his communications will be effective. Some researchers have found that "speakers having prestige significantly influence listeners more than those who do not."[7] Eisenson, Auer, and Irwin also found that "listeners tend to accept ideas from those who have prestige. . . . Listeners also tend to reject equally good ideas from those who lack prestige. . . . Speakers have prestige when listeners like them, accept them as authorities, defer to their judgment or attach importance to what they say."[8]

Status difference can be helpful, or it can be a hindrance. It will be helpful if the supervisor has earned the respect of his subordinates through the proper use of his authority. Earning respect is also enhanced by considering the human elements of communications; when a supervisor addresses a subordinate by his or her first name, it "often has an exhilarating effect on an officer."[9] It can be a hindrance, however, if the supervisor has grown apart from subordinates to the extent that he has become unapproachable.

---

[6] See Chapter 6 for further discussion of the listening process.

[7] Jon Eisenson, J. Jeffrey Auer, and John V. Irwin, *The Psychology of Communication* (New York: Appleton-Century-Crofts, 1963), p. 284.

[8] *Ibid.*

[9] Robert R. Johnson, "Personal Relationships with Subordinates," *Law and Order*, 53, No. 3 (March 2005), 105.

Psychological Size

Denominating all appearances of superiority, inferiority, or personal inadequacy as complexes has become a hackneyed practice, yet such psychological conditions exist and set up obstacles to interpersonal relations. Sometimes referred to as psychological size, these feelings often cause a bad "climate" between supervisor and subordinate and adversely affect their capacity to communicate effectively. Especially damaging to these relationships are those manifestations of superiority or impatience exhibited by supervisors in dealing with their subordinates. Often subordinates will resent having the boss talk down to them and will resent even more a paternalistic attitude.

Should the subordinate tend toward feelings of inadequacy or inferiority, he may become especially sensitive to a "hard" approach and is likely to resent it. As a result, he will tend to withdraw even further, making two-way communications with him more difficult.

The failure of the supervisor to recognize the importance of the psychological aspects of the communication process creates barriers that will be difficult to overcome. An atmosphere of openness in communications is conducive to improved interchanges between people; however, one can harm his relationship and his ability to communicate well with another by being overly frank unnecessarily. "When a message is delivered, it should be in such a way that it is not perceived as negative."[10] Likewise, an atmosphere of secrecy, evasiveness, and pressure will clog channels and impair communications.

Noise

Noise in communications is referred to by theorists as the static that interferes with the transmission of messages. This static tends to bring on redundancy—the repetition of the message, perhaps in a different way, to ensure that it gets across. Redundancy is inefficient in that it wastes time in repetition, but it is efficient if it helps to clarify and get the message across better.[11] The extent to which noise is reduced as a distractor will largely determine how effective communications are. Psychological stress from the outside or inside, failure to listen actively, environmental distractors, and even abstractions can be considered noises that hinder communication.

Language Barriers

Because of selection standards, the police supervisor will seldom encounter problems resulting from inability of his subordinates to express themselves in the language of the profession. He will, however, encounter many degrees of lucidity among his subordinates; their capabilities of understanding will likewise vary.

When the receiver passes the state of clear understanding because he does not have the capacity for it, he starts to make mistakes, and a total breakdown in communications may follow. Ambiguities contribute to this condition and do nothing but cause confusion. Perhaps the most common form of everyday misunderstanding results from the assumption that what is perfectly obvious (apparently) to the sender is clear to the

---

[10] Ken W. White and Elwood Chapman, *Organizational Communications: An Introduction to Communications and Human Relations Strategies* (New York: Simon & Schuster, 1996).

[11] Roger H. Davies and Adam Davies, *Value Management: Translating Aspiration into Performance* (Burlington, Vt.: Gower Publishing, 2011), p. 217.

receiver. The ability of the supervisor to express himself not only clearly, concisely, and simply but also understandably will largely determine his effectiveness.

In the interests of effective communications, words must be put together so that they mean the same thing to the listener as they do to the speaker. Distortion of meaning or the garbling of communications is usually brought about by a failure to use language that has a precise meaning to others. This failure may be overcome by projecting oneself into another's viewpoint, which is called empathy.

Semantic blocks do occur at times regardless of how perfect one thinks his communications are. Complete understanding is seldom achieved, but the chief aim of communications can be realized if meanings are conveyed to others in a way so that what is said will be understood.

Samovar, Porter, and McDaniel state that the 500 most used words in our language have about 14,000 meanings, an average of 28 meanings per word.[12] It is thus obvious that a great need exists for clarity and precision of expression if communications between individuals in an organization are to be effective.

Fear of Criticism

Many individuals avoid making positive declarations because they fear being criticized for what they say or think. They often feel so insecure that they dislike giving others occasion to attack their observations. As a result, they too often couch their expressions in vagueness and abstraction, always leaving "an open back door" through which they can retreat if their statements are challenged. Communicating in such cases becomes difficult, if not impossible. The supervisor will contribute to this condition if he editorializes on each bit of information he receives, embellishes on it, or overevaluates its importance. The tendency to make merit evaluations on each opinion or each comment made will have a deadening effect on communications, and soon those who must communicate with him will avoid doing so.

Jumping to Conclusions

Jumping to a conclusion on incomplete information before hearing a subordinate out is a tendency supervisory personnel must suppress. Such acts will be interpreted as impatience, disinterest, and discourtesy and will contribute greatly to communication failures. The speaker trying to converse with another who refuses to listen soon will become discouraged and will discontinue his attempts because, to him, "The boss has already made up his mind, so why confuse him with facts?" Perhaps no action of the supervisor will cause more resentment than his failure to allow a subordinate to have his "day in court" before his case is judged.

Filtering

As information is passed from individual to individual, usually a distortion or dilution of content occurs, which is called filtering. It is a natural occurrence resulting from the tendency of individuals to repeat or remember that part of what they have heard or otherwise learned that has had the most impact on them.

---

[12] Larry A. Samovar, Richard E. Porter, and Edwin R. McDaniel, *Communication Between Cultures*, 6th ed. (Belmont, Calif.: Thomson Learning, 2007), p. 172.

In medieval times, it was not uncommon for the bearer of ill tidings to be subjected to harsh treatment—even death—by a king who did not wish to hear bad news. This desire to escape unpleasant situations is not an unusual phenomenon. Some supervisors at times seem to prefer to avoid hearing the truth when it is disagreeable, thinking perhaps that they can thereby immunize themselves from responsibility or liability for what has happened by such remarks as "Don't tell me about that" or "I don't want to hear about it," but ignorance is rarely an excuse for inaction when action is indicated, nor does it reduce a supervisor's liability or accountability. This is especially true when the supervisor could keep himself reasonably informed about incidents in his unit—both good and bad—by insisting that his personnel let him know what is happening so that he can evaluate the information himself and act accordingly.

If a supervisor's attitude indicates that he is unreceptive, however, he will soon be operating in a vacuum. He will shut off his sources or will hear only the pleasant information or that which his subordinates think he wants to hear. Thus, the supervisor is shielded from the unpleasant truth by those who believe that they are doing him a favor by keeping him in ignorance or in good humor. Actually, they are doing him a great disservice and are exposing him to even greater liability by forcing him to make value judgments based on partial, inaccurate, or distorted information or information taken out of context through the filtering process. If such information puts him on notice that something is wrong, he is bound to make further inquiry to determine the full facts that would enable him to take whatever action is deemed proper. Employees sometimes give the supervisor filtered information as a means of letting him know that all is not what it appears to be because they feel a responsibility to inform him in a subtle manner of an existing problem he should know about without giving him all the details they might have. This is especially true in the police service where breaching the "code of silence" is generally looked on, by some, with disfavor.

The process of filtering also affects the supervisor in his downward communications. Giving employees filtered information is sometimes worse than giving them none. Besides the adverse effects filtering eventually will have on the confidence of personnel in their leader, such distorted information will often cause rumors that are harmful to morale.

Individual Sentiments and Attitudes

Like it or not, management must accept the fact that people in all phases and at all levels of an establishment communicate either within their own system or in the organization's system. Each employee interprets those communications received according to his own particular past experiences. He is likely to see what he wants to see based on his perceptions of what has been said and done.

The acceptance of a communication depends a good deal on the receiver's needs and his experiences, as well as the environment in which the message was received. If the communication is a threat to his own goals, he may refuse to acknowledge it or may accept it even though he disagrees with it, depending on how well he has been conditioned to accept discipline in the organization. If he has a feeling of true identification with the group, he will probably accept without question most communications that are of a directive nature. In the end, the important thing is how he accepts them and how they cause him to react.[13]

---

[13] Elaina Zuker, *Mastering Assertiveness Skills: Power and Positive Influence at Work* (New York: American Management Association, 1983), p. 96.

Feelings between individuals vary widely. Their likes and dislikes of other persons may aid or harm their communications. Attitudes, moods, and emotions likewise have a direct bearing on the type of interaction between individuals. These interactions will vary from time to time depending on the intensity of emotions, the receptive mood of either of the two persons attempting to communicate, or the attitude of one toward the other. These factors should be considered by the supervisor in selecting the time and place for communicating with his subordinates.

Intentional Suppression or Manipulation of Communications

Intentional suppression of information that should pass from the superior to his subordinates will eventually cause a breach in upward channels. When he blocks information they should have, eventually they will suppress information he should have. Information that should flow from the employees to management will thus be reduced; the net result will be misunderstandings. These more often than not will result in friction and the consequent lowering of production because they tend to be perceived as personal matters rather than those in the best interests of the organization.

At times, a supervisor is approached by a subordinate who suggests directly or indirectly that a particular problem be dealt with in an irregular, improper, or illegal manner. The supervisor may rationalize to himself that the objective justifies the means used but, fearing liability, may give an "official" answer for "the record" while implying by word or expression that he condones, or at least will not stand in the way of, the proposal. His less-than-forthright manipulation of such information usually is easily exposed. This kind of situation could be exceedingly embarrassing (if not actually illegal) and subject him and his organization to considerable liability or unnecessary criticism.

Complexity of Communications Channels

The channels through which communications pass are called the communications net. The complexity of these channels will directly affect the speed and accuracy of messages flowing through them. The larger the number of persons involved in the interpretation of messages, the greater is the possibility that the end product will be distorted.[14] In this regard, the official chain of command can actually work against good communications. "Rigid compliance with formal channels can be harmful, mainly in terms of time, creativity, and experience."[15] When channels are overly complex, messages will tend to be delayed at bottlenecks, which in themselves are obstacles difficult to overcome. The total effect is that senders and receivers are not brought into contact. Communications are thus stifled almost at their source.[16]

Overloading of Communications Channels

Overloading of channels causes jamming much as in the case of bottlenecks. Overloading results from lack of discrimination in separating relevant and irrelevant information. This suggests that each communicator should constantly control the quality of his

---

[14] Harold J. Leavitt and Homa Bahrami, *Managerial Psychology:Managing Behavior in Organizations,* 5th ed. (Chicago, Ill: The University of Chicago, 1988), pp. 193–95.

[15] Paul M. Whisenand and R. Fred Ferguson, *The Managing of Police Organizations*, 7th ed. (Upper Saddle River, N.J.: Pearson Prentice Hall, 2008), p. 93.

[16] Zuker, *Mastering Assertiveness Skills*, pp. 98–99.

messages—more messages do not mean more information. If the supervisor does not establish some priorities, he will soon become bogged down in paperwork or will spend too much of his time listening to trivia rather than doing what really has to be done.

It is good for the supervisor to insist that subordinates keep him informed, but too much insistence may cause resentment. The employee may feel that he is not trusted. The demands of the supervisor should be reasonable in this respect; however, his right to know what is going on to protect himself and his organization cannot be challenged. The astute supervisor will require his subordinates to keep him apprised of matters of concern to him, especially in critical operations such as vice and narcotics law enforcement. He should demand that they inform him of any occurrences when they are in doubt as to their importance. His subordinates should understand clearly that if they fail to do so, he will assume that they acted in bad faith and will treat them accordingly. It is true that the imposition of such requirements on employees will tend to place a heavy burden on communications channels, but too much information is better than too little under these conditions. Where supervisor–subordinate relationships have developed in a culture of mutual trust and respect, channels will not be unduly burdened.

Overstructuring of Communications Channels

Too much insistence that employees follow formal communications channels will tend to sterilize the passing of information upward, downward, and across organizational lines. Research has shown that adherence to formal channels within the hierarchy facilitated communications but that morale was better in systems involving informal channels.[17]

The direction of communications has been found to play an important part in their effectiveness. Two-way communications are apt to be more accurate than one-way communications, and although unilateral communications are faster, they do not provide for feedback as a means of measuring understanding. Therefore, they are likely to end up in talk only.[18]

Overcoming Communication Barriers

Rarely will a supervisor overcome all the barriers to effective communications. He can, however, overcome most of them most of the time by preparing to communicate before doing so and by employing the basic techniques of expression that have been proven successful. He must remember that communication has not really taken place until an accurate message has reached the mind of the receiver. "That message may be received through formal or informal channels. With respect to informal channels, the grapevine typically operates with great strength in most organizations."[19] Some studies have shown that employees rely on the grapevine when they feel threatened, are under stress, when there is a pending change, and when employees feel that communication from management is

---

[17] Suzanne M. Crampton, John W. Hodge, and Jitendra M. Mishra, "The Informal Communication Network: Factors Influencing Grapevine Activity," *Public Personnel Management*, 27, No. 4 (1998), 569–84.

[18] Leavitt, *Managerial Psychology*, pp. 115–17.

[19] Crampton, Hodge, and Mishra, "The Informal Communication Network."

limited. Additionally, researchers have found that the grapevine tends to be quite accurate. Supervisors must be aware that the grapevine can never be completely eliminated and will still carry some valuable insights into "what's really on the minds of the workforce."[20]

If the supervisor is to achieve better understanding between himself and his subordinates, he will be well advised to concentrate on removing the impediments to effective communications wherever possible. He will be materially aided in accomplishing this by adhering to the following admonishments.

Determine Objectives

Before communicating, the supervisor should be sure his ideas are clear in his own mind because if they are not, he will have scant success in conveying them to others. He should carefully analyze the matter to be communicated to determine what objectives he expects to accomplish. He should avoid trying to accomplish too much with each message. The more complex the communication, the more analysis it requires. He should consider the views and attitudes of those to whom the communication will be directed and those of other affected persons.

Before an order or directive is given, the supervisor should be certain of what he really wants others to do. If he does not understand himself, it is certain they will not. Is the communication intended to obtain information, change attitudes or thinking, or alter performance? What is the most important objective? Once these questions have been answered, the supervisor can adapt his language to the accomplishment of his objective. He will realize that the more he structures his communication toward his primary goal, the more likely are his chances for success.

There is a direct correlation between the effectiveness of communications and the total setting in which they occur. Communications will accomplish most of what is intended if they are timely. They must take into consideration customs and practices and the human element, including the moods, attitudes, and emotions of the recipients. Communications should take place in the proper physical setting at the most propitious time in order for it to be effective. The purpose of communications is also achieved if they are clear and simple; if they are made to appeal to those affected; and if the recipient is prepared to receive them. If they do not meet these requirements, they are likely to fail, and usually do.

For example, if an order is given to officers for the first time the evening before Christmas that they must work on that holiday, unless some emergency is obvious to them, the directive is not likely to be relished. On the other hand, if they had been previously prepared for the possibility of being required to work, the directive would have considerably more acceptance and would affect officers' morale less. As obvious as this principle may seem, such breaches of good communication practices occur with appalling frequency.

A change in equipment, such as a particular sidearm mechanical holster (which might be especially liked by many officers), has been observed to cause a considerable amount of resentment because those affected were not prepared for the change. They construed the change as arbitrary because the basis for the decision was not understood.

---

[20] Carole Moore, "If There Must Be Gossip, Use It for Good," *Law Enforcement Technology* (May 2004), 110.

When the purpose of the communication or the evidence on which it was based is conveyed to the recipients, it is far more likely to be well accepted than if no efforts have been made to prepare them for the change.

Practice Empathy

"Seek first to understand, then to be understood. This principle is the key to effective interpersonal communication."[21] The supervisor should consider the views of those to whom the communication will be directed. Before issuing directives that will have any substantial and widespread effect on employees, he should confer with others to gain insight into the problem. He may thus gain a better understanding of the thoughts and feelings of those affected. A variety of points of view will give greater objectivity to those issuing directives. These will receive greater acceptance if others are permitted to participate in their development; they will also be carried out faster and with greater precision.

Obtain Feedback

Feedback is perhaps the most important of the supervisor's tools in learning if he is communicating well. "Feedback is the breakfast of champions! In other words, winning leaders demand feedback. Without feedback, police managers are saddled with unnecessary uncertainty and excessive risks."[22] It involves simply the process of learning what the listener's verbal and nonverbal responses are by observing, inspecting, and questioning whether understanding is taking place. The manner in which a message is given and the tone of voice, inflections, and facial expressions have a great impact on the acceptability of communications (as previously discussed). The overtones accompanying these messages provide clues to the communicator as to the extent of the listener's comprehension. Such overtones are often as important in getting a message across as the basic content itself. Subtle shades of meaning brought about by choice of words will often greatly influence the listener's reception of the message. If it is possible for employees to read hidden meanings into words and overtones, the supervisor should expect them to do so and attempt to prevent this from happening.

The considerable effort that goes into the development of good communications may be wasted if the supervisor fails to follow up to determine how effective they have been. Such follow-up is essential if useful feedback is to be obtained.

Keep Subordinates Informed

A supervisor should keep his subordinates informed as much as possible about matters affecting them such as work plans, schedules, policies, decisions, and programs. Employees will react best to changes in plans, operations, or working conditions when they have been given some background to aid them in understanding the need for change. Before making changes managers should anticipate how employees will react.[23] Workers are not always

---

[21] Stephen R. Covey, *The Seven Habits of Highly Effective People* (New York: Simon & Schuster, 2005), p. 235.

[22] Whisenand and Ferguson, *The Managing of Police Organizations*, p. 87.

[23] Laird W. Meabiea, "Employee Resistance to Change: A Learned Response Management Can Prevent," *Supervisory Management*, 23 (January 1978), 16–22; Robert N. Lussier, *Management Fundamentals: Concepts, Applications, Skill Development* (Mason, Ohio: South-Western, 2012), p. 213.

Police promotional orientation class- Officers preparing for a sergeant, lieutenant, and captains exam are given an overview of the new exam format.

entitled to explanations from management as a matter of inherent right, but management will do well to explain the why of orders or directives whenever practicable or risk failure to gain acceptance. Management is under no obligation to justify every decision made— to do so would clutter the decision-making process so badly that operations would be seriously impeded. On the other hand, operations can be enhanced if management "sells" its decisions to employees as often as reasonably possible.

If the supervisor looks at management from the point of view of the subordinate and takes the subordinate's interests into account when formulating communications vital to his interests, greater managerial success will be achieved in the all-important function of communicating. If he makes little or no effort, the grapevine, with all its potential hazards, will take over.

The skilled supervisor often is able to use the grapevine to good advantage. When he does so, however, he is always faced with the problem of starting the spread of more misinformation than information. Most supervisors will be well advised to use more formal and conventional methods.

Rumors can seriously impair good communications and harm morale if allowed to spread. The further they spread, the more they are likely to be embellished and the more employees tend to believe them. Therefore, the supervisor should be alert for harmful rumors so that he can promptly counter them with the truth. Once discredited, they quickly die.

Be Consistent in Communicating

Communications that are devised to bring about lasting results should be consistent with the long-term goals of the organization. Policies, rules, or procedures should not be changed willy-nilly. To make frequent unnecessary changes would cause confusion and result in a general lowering of confidence of employees in management. For example, if an organization declares its intent to refrain from filing personnel complaints that are shown to be without merit in the concerned employee's personnel file, perhaps all such files should be reviewed and purged of such information in the interests of consistency. This would be of special importance if the personnel files were to be used for promotional purposes by oral examining boards or for merit increases in salary. This example, of course, is a policy matter to be determined by the highest authority under existing law or employee agreements.

Similarly, it would be eminently unfair for the supervisor to postpone communicating with his subordinate merely because both might find the interchange disagreeable. Adverse personnel evaluations or incident reports concerning unacceptable behavior or performance should be discussed with the concerned employee as promptly as are the favorable ones commending him, yet many supervisors avoid making negative incident reports when they are required to discuss the matter with the concerned employee and allow him to see the report before it is filed in the personnel jacket. Neither should the application of punishment for misconduct be delayed merely because it is an unpleasant task for the supervisor. The way these activities are performed by him will have long-term effects on morale and all its concomitants.

Make Actions Speak Louder Than Words

The admonishment to "practice what you preach" has become a management principle. It is perhaps nowhere more important than in the supervisor's relationships with his subordinates. The most persuasive communications involve what is done, not what is said. This adage implies a consistent application of rules and policies to all employees. It means that the supervisor must not prescribe one course of action for his subordinates and follow another more favorable course himself.

Listen, Understand, and Be Understood

The ability or the willingness to listen to what is being said, to understand the expressed and the true meaning of interpersonal communications, and to convey clear and understandable messages to others is dependent on the background, experience, and motivation of the communicants. Hayakawa said, "The meanings of words are *not* in the words; they are in us."[24] Communicating is a two-way process. It involves good listening as well as good expression. One learns little by talking but a great deal by listening. The ability to listen well is truly an art. Talking is an excellent secondary means of learning, but only as a supplement to listening. It is the oil that lubricates the process of listening and provides a foundation for it.[25] The supervisor must develop his listening ability if he is to achieve success in his communications consistently. He does so by developing the "big ears, little mouth" philosophy, which is one of the most important and most often neglected skills in communicating.

Attentiveness to responses and concentration on what is being said are necessary to understanding. The most effective communicator will listen not only to what the speaker says but also to what he means. If this listening is halfhearted, effective communication will not occur. Rogers and Roethlisberger have observed most appropriately, "The biggest

---

[24] Samuel I. Hayakawa, *Language in Thought and Action* (New York: Harcourt Brace Jovanovich, 1992), p. 258.

[25] Techniques of active listening are discussed in detail in Chapter 6.

block to personal communications is man's inability to listen intelligently, understand-ingly, and skillfully to another person."[26]

Characteristics of Communications

Communications, like the leaders who initiate them, may be categorized into three broad groups: autocratic, democratic, and free rein. Each has its characteristic advantages and disadvantages.

Autocratic Communications

Autocratic communications can be issued with relative ease, since concurrence by those affected is not sought. They have the advantage of speed and are well adapted to emer-gency conditions. They have the characteristic disadvantage of arbitrariness. Difficulty is often encountered in achieving general acceptance by workers because they are not afforded an opportunity to participate in decisions affecting them.

Democratic Communications

The two-way passing of information makes democratic communications easy to under-stand. It permits the development of ideas and enables those affected by decisions to par-ticipate in making them. Information readily passes in both directions, making it simple for the supervisor to keep informed of activities below him. Democratic communications

A perimeter is established by members of the Miami-Dade, Coral Gables and City of Miami Police departments at a building located in Coral Gables, Florida after a double homicide. (© Roberto Koltun/MCT/ Newscom)

---

[26] Bob Levoy, *222 Secrets of Hiring, Managing and Retaining Great Employees* (Sudbury, Mass.: Jones and Barlett, 2007), p. 198.

lack the speed and directness of those that are autocratic, and while they hold the greatest promise for success in most normal operations, the supervisor will find that he must forgo consultation with his subordinates when speed of operations is essential.

Free Rein Communications

Free rein communications provide for a minimum of contacts, thereby leaving subordinates to operate in isolation. Leadership and guidance are often absent, and subordinates do not realize the benefits of two-way communications. As a consequence, misunderstandings, misapprehensions, and mistakes flourish.

The supervisor is well advised to adjust his communications to the setting in which they occur. Each type has its place and none should be employed to the exclusion of others. The type most appropriate for one set of circumstances might be totally inappropriate under other conditions.

Types of Communicators

Attempts by the supervisor to improve his ability to express himself cannot be successful until he has analyzed his shortcomings and has made a positive effort to overcome them. Eisenson, Auer, and Irwin list several types of communicators.[27] A supervisor should consider what type of communicator he is. Is he a noncommunicator, who says no more than he thinks the situation requires? Has he failed to say something that should be said? Is he a logical speaker, troubled by anxieties or compulsiveness? Is he unconcerned with the impact his statements have on others? Is he the undertalker, who often fails to communicate when communicating is indicated? Is he the tiresome overtalker, who often communicates well but does not know when to stop? Is he a tangential speaker? Does he fail to give direct response as expected, responding instead to irrelevant side issues? Is he the so-called helpless speaker, full of self-pity and self-apology? Does he apologize for asking a subordinate to do something he is expected to do? If he does the latter, any respect his subordinates have for him will soon be eroded.

Written Communications

The supervisor is judged to a great extent throughout his career by how well he expresses himself not only orally but also in writing. His ability to study a problem, find a solution, develop proper and workable plans, and record his thoughts, ideas, conclusions, recommendations, or findings in writing will be a measure of his competency in the eyes of his superiors and subordinates. Poorly written, unintelligible communications will usually result in confusion and misunderstanding and will invariably reflect unfavorably on the ability of the writer.

Any effective writing involves an organization of thoughts and ideas in a manner that will enable the reader to know exactly what the writer wants him to know. In a literal sense, anything written by a person in his official capacity involves a staff function and can be called a staff writing. Fundamentally, there is little difference between reporting and staff writing. Staff papers may consist of correspondence of all kinds, orders, directives, or

---

[27] Eisenson, Auer, and Irwin, *The Psychology of Communication*, pp. 347–56.

briefs of formal documents. Whatever the type, the writer should follow the requisites of good staff writing and should adhere to the principles of completed staff work.

Clarity of Expression

In written communications as in oral communications, words and ideas must be clearly expressed. In fact, clarity is more essential in writing, since the readers are not permitted the opportunity to clarify misunderstandings, as is the case in face-to-face, two-way oral communications. They can only ponder what was meant.

Excessive use of abbreviations should be avoided. If they are necessary, authorized abbreviations or those with clearly apparent meaning may be used. In police writing, the same principles apply to section numbers of criminal and procedure codes. These should be avoided without descriptive terms unless their meaning is so commonplace that it is unmistakable.

Clarity of expression is all-important. If this requirement is not met, the reader will waste time trying to decide what was meant. Confusion will result. Ideally, writings should be so explicit that their meanings cannot be misunderstood.

Simplicity

Writers should think about the reading ability of their readers and scale their writing accordingly. Short sentences composed of simple words and careful punctuation to make the meanings clear are preferred to complex sentences and difficult words; the former are much easier to read and comprehend. Costly mistakes occasioned by misinterpretations can be reduced if this practice is followed. This fact should constantly be kept in mind by the writer as he prepares his communications. Writers should always consider the intended reader and tailor the document accordingly. "If you have a reputation for giving officers the information that they want, the way they want it, they will be more likely to read what you write."[28]

The elimination of trivia, redundant items, and nonessential details will save time not only of the writer but of the reader. The type and speed of action taken as the result of a report may well depend on its clarity and the rapidity with which it is understood.

Accuracy

When a written communication is in the form of a report concerning a research project, it should be based on the most reliable and authoritative data available. Findings must be accurate, even in the most minute detail, to prevent misleading those who are to rely on the report. The writer should test the accuracy of a report he prepares by asking himself if his superior could safely stake his reputation on it; if not, it should be rewritten until it meets this test.

Arrangement

Ideas should be arranged logically so that they may be easily followed and understood by the reader. Systematic arrangement of a paper may be accomplished with the aid of a checklist of subjects or items to be covered, an outline, and a rough draft or two.

---

[28] Herbert Williams, "Crime Analysis Publications," in *Exploring Crime Analysis,* ed. Christopher W. Bruce, Julie P. Cooper, and Steven R. Hick (Overland Park, Kan.: IACA Press, 2004), p. 354.

Important key points that the writer wishes to emphasize can be made more emphatic by the use of underlining, italics, boldface, script letters, or other distinctive markings to call such points to the reader's attention.

Style

The so-called newspaper style of writing ordinarily simplifies expression and facilitates understanding. The first paragraph expresses the essential elements of the paper and is called the topic paragraph. The first, or topic, sentence should likewise express the essence of the paragraph it introduces. Succeeding paragraphs explain and amplify the opening paragraph in such a way that each is almost self-sustaining. Thus the report proceeds from the most important ideas to the least important details, which make the main ideas more meaningful.

Summary, Conclusions, Recommendations, and Plan of Action

Final paragraphs should present conclusions, recommendations, solutions, or a plan of action. Summary statements are often placed at the beginning to enable the reader to capture the important aspects of the report without reading the details. Indexing these summary statements to pages in lengthy reports helps the reader to easily find those details he might wish to refer to in the body.

Format

The heading of the report should obviously indicate the title or subject, the body presents the main ideas or findings, and the closing incorporates the conclusions, recommendations, and plan of action. The name of the writer should be included for purposes of accountability.

The U.S. Navy uses the technique of placing well-chosen cues in the left margin as guides to the material in the text. This enables those who have to do a massive volume of reading to scan the guides for material they wish to read and to concentrate quickly on only the points in which they have an interest at the time.

Email

Most police agencies communicate through email at workstations, via in-car computers, and with personal digital assistants. The primary advantage of this form of communication is speed. A common problem is that users tend to become too casual and mistake it for informal conversation. Microsoft recommends the following guidelines:

- Use clear, brief subject lines. They help your reader get straight to the point. This is especially important when sending a message to handheld devices, which have small display screens.
- Keep it short and businesslike.
- Proofread your message.
- Check the "TO" and "CC" lines to make sure the message goes only to the intended readers.
- Don't use email when face-to-face conversation is feasible.

- Use security features for confidential matters.
- Consider your emails as departmental records.

Used as one communication channel, but not the only one, email is an effective tool.

Effectively Managing Your Email

Having a good system for managing your email inbox is important. If you do, you will be more efficient and effective at work and at home. Most of us need to clean out our inboxes and develop better habits for managing our email. For many, the thought of hitting the delete button is scary. There is often concern about deleting emails. Additionally, some folks suffer from the "What if I need it" syndrome.

Sally McGhee offers four key factors for processing and organizing your email more efficiently:[29]

1. *Set up a simple and effective email reference system*—The first step toward an organized inbox is understanding the difference between reference information and action information.
   - *Reference Information* is information that is not required to complete an action; it is information that you keep in case you need it later. Reference information is stored in your reference system—an email reference folder, your My Documents folder, or a company intranet site, for example.
   - *Action Information* is information you *must have* to complete an action. Action information is stored with the action, either on your to-do list or on your calendar.

      Most people receive a considerable amount of reference information through email. Sometimes as much as one-third of your email is reference information, so it is essential to have a system that makes it easier to transfer messages from your inbox into your email reference system. For example, storing reference information in a series of email folders will ensure that you have easy access to it later.

2. *Schedule uninterrupted time to process and organize email*—How many times are you interrupted every day? It's nearly impossible to complete anything when there are constant interruptions from the phone, people stopping by your office, and instant messaging. So it's critical that you set aside uninterrupted time to process and organize your email.

      Many email messages require you to make a decision. The best decision requires focus, and focus requires uninterrupted attention. Establish a regular time each day to process your email so that you can empty your inbox. Of course, you can scan your email during the day for urgent messages or requests from your boss.

3. *Process one item at a time, starting at the top*—When you sit down to process your email, the first step is to sort it by the order in which you will process it. For example, you can filter by date, by subject, or even by the sender of the email message. Resist the temptation to jump around in your inbox in no particular

---

[29] http://www.microsoft.com/atwork/productivity/email.aspx, accessed May 30, 2012.

order. Begin processing the message at the top of your inbox, and move to the second one only after you've handled the first.

4. **Use the "Four Ds for Decision-Making" model**—The "Four Ds for Decision-Making" model (4 Ds) is a valuable tool for processing email, helping you to quickly decide what action to take with each item and how to remove it from your inbox.

The Four Ds for Decision-Making Model

Decide what to do with each and every message

How many times have you opened, reviewed, and closed the same email message or conversation? Those messages are getting lots of attention but very little action. It is better to handle each email message only once before taking action—which means you have to decide what to do with it and where to put it. With the 4 Ds model, you have four choices:

1. Delete it
2. Do it
3. Delegate it
4. Defer it

Generally, you can delete about half of all the emails you get. Some of you may shudder when you hear the phrase "delete email" because you're hesitant to delete messages for fear you might need them later. That is understandable, but ask yourself honestly, What percentage of information that you keep do you actually use? If you use a large percentage of what you keep, your method is working. But many of us keep a lot more than we use. Here are some questions to help you decide what to delete:

- Does the message relate to a meaningful objective you're currently working on? If not, you can probably **delete it**. Why keep information that doesn't relate to your main focus?
- Does the message contain information you can find elsewhere? If so, **delete it**.
- Does the message contain information you will refer to within the next six months? If not, **delete it**.
- Does the message contain information that you're required to keep? If not, **delete it**.

Do it (in less than two minutes)

If you can't delete the email message, ask yourself, "What specific action do I need to take?" and "Can I do it in less than two minutes?" If you can, just do it.

There is no point in filing an email or closing an email if you can complete the associated task in less than two minutes. Try it out—see how much mail you can process in less than two minutes. I think you will be extremely surprised and happy with the results. You can file the message, respond to the message, or make a phone call. You can probably handle about one-third of your messages in less than two minutes.

Delegate it

If you can't delete it or do it in two minutes or less, can you forward the email to an appropriate team member who can take care of the task? If you can delegate it (forward it to another team member to handle), do so right away. You should be able to compose and send the delegating message in about two minutes. After you have forwarded the message, delete the original message or move it into your email reference system.

Defer it

If you cannot delete it, do it in less than two minutes, or delegate it, the action required is something that only you can accomplish and that will take more than two minutes. Because this is your dedicated email processing time, you need to defer it and deal with it after you are done processing your email. You'll probably find that about 20 percent of your email messages have to be deferred. There are two things you can do to defer a message: turn it into an actionable task, or turn it into an appointment.

Use the 4 Ds model every day

Using the 4 Ds model on a daily basis makes it easier to handle a large quantity of email. Experience shows that, on average, people can process about 100 email messages an hour. If you receive 40 to 100 messages per day, all you need is one hour of uninterrupted email processing time to get through your inbox. Our statistics show that of the email you receive:

- Fifty percent can be deleted or filed
- Thirty percent can be delegated or completed in less than two minutes
- Twenty percent can be deferred to your task list or calendar to complete later

Manuals—Orders

As the amount of administrative requirements, statutory and case law, and developing professional practices continues to grow, the job of the police supervisor becomes only more complex. A policy management system is absolutely necessary to keep rules organized in a way that facilitates operations. The Commission on Accreditation for Law Enforcement Agencies (CALEA) says that "a comprehensive, well thought out, uniform set of written directives . . . is one of the most successful methods for reaching administrative and operational goals, while also providing direction to personnel."[30]

Policies, procedures, orders, and rules and regulations can be easily codified into a numbered decimal system and fashioned into a manual by even the smallest agency. The manual can be used as a simple but effective means of communicating to employees uniform, detailed rules, regulations, procedures, and directives relating to the operations of the organization.

Some agencies develop separate manuals for policies, procedures, and rules and regulations. Others combine all such written guidelines into one manual, which is appropriately numbered and arranged homogeneously into segments.

As in the case of any order, manuals must be constantly reviewed to ensure that their provisions are kept current. These reviews and recommendations for needed changes are of major importance to supervisors if they are to carry out the objectives of their organization effectively.

---

[30] http://www.CALEA.org/content/law-enforcement-accreditation, accessed April 23, 2012.

Modification of manuals can be accomplished as the need arises by a system of general, special, or operation orders. General orders establish policy, the broad rules describing general objectives of the organization. These are somewhat permanent declarations of organizational policy and, as such, should not be changed frequently. Special orders are issued to establish procedures or rules and regulations necessary in carrying out policy; these are changed occasionally to keep organizational practices consistent with current needs. Operation orders are used to describe the procedures to be followed and the goals to be achieved in a particular event. These should remain in effect only for the duration of the operation to which they relate. Although part of the manual and orders system, they are usually not consolidated within the manual itself. Some operation orders are used repeatedly for athletic events, parades, fairs, and the like and require minimal changes to keep them current, while others are of use for one event only, after which they become inoperative. Notices are forms of orders relating to matters of general interest, such as routine notifications and scheduled events.

Most agencies make provisions to give personnel in supervisory and command positions authority to issue formal orders relating to the operation of a particular unit. As in the preparation of any written directive, great care must be exercised so that such communications will clearly state their purpose, the policy or rule established, or the procedure to be followed. Ideally, they must be written so that they are incapable of being misunderstood by even the least astute person affected.

Briefing

An employee will sometimes be asked to reduce a lengthy report or dissertation to give his superior a concise account of the contents. The total report should be carefully analyzed to select the important ideas or points to be covered in the brief and these should be listed. Sufficient collateral detail should then be selected from the report to provide a basis for understanding. Care must be exercised in this process to preserve the meaning of the base report and to prevent any distortion or garbling of the author's meaning; likewise, the person preparing the brief must avoid taking the excerpts out of context. His superiors should be able to use the brief with confidence that it faithfully and accurately represents the whole writing.

Proofreading and Editing

Brown suggests:[31] "In any writing that you do, it is very important that you proofread your work. Read your writing twice: once for content and once for spelling and punctuation errors. Use whatever references you need to help you. If you ask yourself if a word is spelled or used correctly, you probably need to look it up. If you are unsure of a grammatical or punctuation rule, either change the sentence or look up the rule in a reference. Make any required revisions."

---

[31] Jerrold G. Brown, *Report Writing for Criminal Justice Professionals,* 2nd ed. (Cincinnati, Ohio: Anderson Publishing, 1998), p. 42.

Typical Deficiencies in Writing

Written communications fail to achieve what is intended for three main reasons. First, the writer, because of a lack of care or an inability to discriminate between fact and nonfact, confuses his communications by misinterpreting the data on which they are based. Second, the writer fails to use the most specific and concrete words to make his meaning clear. Third, the writer fails to support his conclusions by factual data.

SUMMARY

The ability to communicate clearly is one of the most important and often the most neglected of supervisory skills. It is a very delicate process involving cultural, environmental, and psychological factors and can easily become thwarted by barriers between persons. The supervisor must constantly review his communicating habits to determine how effectively he is transmitting messages to others.

Communications are affected adversely by many factors. Failure to listen actively to what is being said; feelings of superiority, inferiority, or inadequacy reflected by impatience or lack of confidence; language difficulties that cause misunderstandings; and fear of being criticized or challenged, which sometimes causes the speaker to express himself vaguely or abstractly, are among the prime obstacles to effective communications. If the supervisor is prone to jumping to conclusions before learning all the facts, he will frequently shut himself off from his subordinates because they will consider it useless to go to him with their problems or information. Filtering, which often causes distortion and dilution of information as it is passed from person to person, will also hamper effective communications. Rarely can all the hindrances to good communications be removed, but they can be minimized by the supervisor if he will clarify his ideas in his own mind before they are transmitted to others—if he decides what objective the communication is to achieve and directs his efforts toward accomplishing that objective by clarity and simplicity of expression.

The wise supervisor will recognize that the manner of disseminating communications will affect their acceptance. He will realize that subtle shades of meaning often cause messages to be misunderstood and that misinterpretations of orders or directives often result in costly errors. A supervisor will be able to profit from his communication mistakes only if he follows up to determine how they occurred and how he can avoid them in the future.

The most persuasive communications are brought about by deeds, not words. The supervisor should not establish one course of conduct for himself and preach another for his subordinates; neither should he expect one standard of conduct from some of his subordinates and a different one from others. Impartiality and consistency of actions must be his guides. His subordinates are justified in expecting that he will consistently apply the rules to all. He must not postpone communicating with them when they are entitled to information that affects them, even when it is an unpleasant task.

Written communications require even more attention than do oral ones because readers have no opportunity to clarify meanings intended by the writer by questioning him. They can only ponder what was meant. Therefore, the supervisor must give particular attention to written orders, directives, or procedures. To be most effective, these should be clearly and simply written and logically organized so that the reader will have no difficulty understanding what was intended.

REVIEW

Questions

1. Give a practical example of how cultural, environmental, and psychological factors affect communications.

2. Describe what takes place in the process of active listening.

3. How do status differences affect communications? Give examples.

4. What is meant by psychological size? Explain how this condition affects communications.

5. What is noise in communications?

6. Why does the fear of criticism often have a harmful effect on communications?

7. What is meant by filtering, and how does it affect the process of communications?

8. Give an example of how attitudes affect communications.

9. Explain how the barriers to effective communications can be largely overcome.

10. List the three broad categories of communications, and discuss the advantages and disadvantages of each.

11. List five types of communicators, and explain how their peculiarities affect their communications.

12. What is the newspaper style of writing?

13. What are the main parts of a written report? What should be included in each of these parts?

14. What is a brief? What are the requisites of briefing?

15. What are the main deficiencies in most written communications?

Exercises

1. Write a policy statement that your superior might wish to issue to members of your organization concerning pursuit driving. As a basis for this policy statement, assume that there have been an inordinate number of accidents resulting from pursuits and that your superior wishes to reduce these by establishing guidelines for personnel exposed to the hazards of driving under such conditions. Write a procedural order to implement this policy.

2. Write a policy statement on the use of force on offenders. Consider legal aspects, civil liability, and any moral issues involved.

3. Write a procedural order by which the policy statement in Exercise 2 can be implemented.

6

Principles of Interviewing

Chapter Objectives

This chapter will enable you:

- To become acquainted with the principles of good interviewing practices
- To become familiar with the techniques of interviewing
- To be able to demonstrate ability in applying the principles of interviewing

An interview is an interchange of views and ideas between two or more persons. Its primary purpose is to obtain or impart information or influence attitudes or behavior. In each interview, some functions common to others are involved, but each also has its own characteristics involving psychological interactions between two people with different knowledge, attitudes, feelings, and objectives. Sometimes it is difficult to reconcile these individual differences with the goals of the organization simply because an appreciation of such goals has not been adequately instilled in the minds of the members. For example, on occasion, an employee will feel he has a valid grievance because his employer has not permitted him to engage in certain outside employment that involves a conflict of interest with his primary police position. The employee might find it easy to justify his rationale in such situations but difficult to accept the viewpoint of his supervisor, who demands that his subordinates consider their police employment to be of first importance.

Consulting with people is not solely the personnel officer's responsibility. It is one of the prime activities of every supervisory officer at all levels and requires a great portion of his time. If it is done effectively, the time spent will reap huge rewards. The skillful supervisor learns about his subordinates by hearing about them, by analyzing their work through the inspection process, by observing their performance, but mostly by talking with and listening to them—the last being one of his most important activities. The degree of his success in this activity is directly related to the effort expended. His technique will vary depending on the objective to be accomplished. If he is to fulfill his objective in the most effective manner, he must develop his ability to motivate others, to change attitudes, and to obtain willing cooperation through purposeful face-to-face communications. He must also develop his working knowledge of the general principles of interviewing and counseling so that his methods can be adapted to meet the overall objective of a particular type of situation.

Interrogation versus Interview

Interrogation, unlike interviewing, involves a process of questioning with the investigator usually assuming a dominant role in the relationship. According to Reid, "Interrogation is an art whereby, through the use of questioning and observation, the truth is elicited from a suspect by sound reasoning and understanding without the use of threats or promises."[1] True, both interrogations and interviews are often calculated to produce information; but the interviewer, unlike the interrogator, must often exchange his views with those of the person being interviewed. The interrogator seldom will place himself in a position of "giving" information; his job is to obtain much information while imparting little. If the latter practice is followed in the interview situation, it will often result in failure to accomplish the objectives of the meeting.

Major Functions of the Interview

The major functions of the interview are to obtain information (about work or another situation, about the employee, or about a grievance); to communicate or give information (about policies or practices, or about services, behaviors, or employee relationships); to motivate employees for the purpose of improving cooperation, production, or performance; to help solve personal and group problems through the consultation process; and to appraise the past, present, or future situation of the employee (with respect to his career, transfers, education, extra-departmental activities such as secondary employment, or personal problems).

The significant characteristic about these functions is that they are involved (at least in part) in almost every interview. The differences in objectives to be accomplished will determine the amount of emphasis to be placed on one or more of these functions. For example, the consultative approach is involved in differing degrees in many employee interviews, such as those relating to personal problems, discipline, and work progress as reflected by service ratings or job performance.

Preparation for an Interview

Good preparation for a personnel interview is just as essential to its success as it is in the case of interrogation of a suspect. Each interview requires forethought and planning. The objectives to be achieved should be carefully analyzed so that the interviewer may best direct his efforts toward those ends.

Preliminary Planning

The degree of planning necessary will vary somewhat from interview to interview, since each will require special consideration, depending on the reason for conducting it. A written outline is often useful as a guide to assist the interviewer in covering salient points that he may wish to develop. This preliminary planning will be most useful if

---

[1] Robert A. Shearer, *Interviewing: Theories, Techniques and Practices* (Upper Saddle River, N.J.: Pearson/Prentice Hall, 2004), p. 63.

the facts available about the person to be interviewed are studied beforehand. Applications, personal history statements, files, correspondence, and other data that may give the interviewing supervisor some insight into the background of the person to be interviewed will give clues that may require further development during the interview. For example, misspelled words or poor grammar in a badly prepared application would provide many clues regarding personality that should be pursued in the interview. Preliminary planning should also involve an analysis of the point of view of the person to be interviewed—if evidence is at hand to permit this—so that potential misunderstandings may be avoided. The interviewer should analyze his own predilections and biases as well as those of the interviewee to avoid unnecessary conflicts. On occasions such as employment interviews, discussion of some subjects, such as religion, political beliefs, and sexual preferences, is forbidden by law and should be carefully avoided.

Gathering information beforehand will help to verify the issues that are the subject of the interview. For example, a sergeant planning to discuss an officer's request to transfer to a detective assignment should review the officer's personnel file and evaluations, as well as reports written by the officer. A sergeant interviewing an officer about a performance problem would review complaints about the officer, reports on the particular incident, and relevant regulations or procedures.[2]

The interview should be planned so that it need not be hurried. Sufficient time should be allowed to permit a relatively full development of facts and observations relevant to the situation. On occasion, there will be a need for a second or third session, depending on the nature of the information required. In any event, the objectives should be reached without undue haste or any waste of the supervisor's or interviewee's time.

Privacy

The hazards of conducting an interview in the presence of others should be recognized. Usually, the interviewing supervisor should make every effort to conduct it in privacy to help avoid possible inhibitions, which often limit frankness when persons other than those concerned are present. Exceptions are those group interviews where it is desirable to compare several individuals, such as in assessment center interviews.

Types of Questions

Questions should be prepared that may be used at first to establish the habit of answering if the question-and-answer technique is adopted. These should be framed so that they can be easily and willingly answered. Obviously, ambiguous, dual, or multiple-meaning questions should be avoided to prevent misunderstanding and confusion. Unnecessary use of such questions might hamper free communications. Furthermore, questions should be prepared with the objective of obtaining a true, unequivocal response. If the reply requires the interviewer to draw an inference from what is said, often such responses will be misinterpreted and further questioning will be required to obtain accurate information needed to qualify or explain the initial response.

---

[2] Jeffry Bernstein, *N.J. Police Situational Management Manual* (Davie, Fla.: Bernstein & Associates, 2013), p. 19.

Well-planned questions are sometimes necessary. They can be used to obtain maximum accuracy and completeness from responses about certain facets of the interview that are necessary but sometimes overlooked or forgotten. Inaccurate responses resulting from ill-prepared questions can be minimized if the interviewer has in mind the general and specific information he desires when he prepares certain alternative questions. These should be calculated to guide the interview into channels from which such information may be derived.

Conducting an Interview

The supervisor conducting an interview should employ a friendly, empathic attitude toward the employee interviewed. Questions, conduct, or signs conveying an appearance that may be interpreted as a threat to the employee's security should be meticulously avoided. These would probably produce results just the opposite of those desired, and deceitful or misleading responses would be a likely outcome.

Interview Opening

The interview should start on a note of obvious sincerity and reasonableness, with the interviewer stating the reason and objective simply and clearly. It should be developed in an atmosphere of friendliness, beginning on a pleasant topic, if possible, to help the interviewee to gain poise and a feeling of ease. "The beginning is a warm-up period, the time when the interviewer must establish rapport."[3] In almost every interview, the initial

Sergeant and Captain reviewing paperwork during an interview. Sheriff's Office, Nebraska, USA.
(© Mikael Karlsson/ Alamy)

[3] Charles R. Swanson, Neil C. Chamelin, and Leonard Territo, *Criminal Investigation,* 11th ed. (New Jersey: McGraw-Hill, 2011), p. 132.

conversation can relate to a matter of interest to the interviewee. Such an approach usually stimulates responses from him.

Use of Questions

In using questions, an interviewer must recognize that they may guide the interview away from its true purpose. They may, however, be used to good advantage in starting the conversation or delving deeper into a specific area. Since utmost accuracy in response to the interview question is desirable, such a question should be framed in positive terms. British psychologist B. Muscio found in early studies that questions framed in negative terms had a tendency to elicit inaccurate responses more frequently than did positive questions because negatives are somewhat more suggestive and cause a lessening of caution in response and decreased reliability.[4] Open-ended questions should be framed so that the trend of thought cannot be stopped by a "yes" or "no" answer; rather, they should be framed so that continuity of thought will result and an issue can be developed as fully as need be. Likewise, questions should not lead the interviewee into a directed answer because he may try to please and, in doing so, avoid giving a true response. Questions such as "You don't think the supervisors are stupid, do you?" or "Don't you like this graveyard shift?" may lead the interviewee into a structured answer. The question "How do you feel about working the graveyard shift?" may elicit the true feelings of the individual.

It is true that the question-and-answer technique often plays an important part in police work, especially in the interrogation of suspects. However, using this procedure in the interview is not entirely successful, since questions seldom elicit the whole story. More frequently than not, the exclusive use of this procedure produces barriers and interferes with full communications.

Interviewer Attitude

Any semblance of a domineering, overly authoritative, or paternalistic attitude should be avoided, since this might close avenues of communication. Ideally, mutual trust and confidence should be fostered between interviewer and interviewee. To this end, a sincere, frank, and helpful attitude will do much to encourage the person interviewed to cooperate so that exaggeration and deceit may be minimized.[5]

In those interviews where the supervisor has been approached by his subordinate for advice or "just talk," the supervisor should get to the problem at hand as soon as rapport is established. He should determine as clearly as possible the nature of the problem. Once the initial problem is isolated, it may require revision as the interview proceeds, since the *real* problem often does not appear until it is detected from subtle indicators noted during the course of the interview. These are the clues that often lead to the true nature of what is meant. A grievance comment such as "You know what he's like" says little, but the direct question "Just what is he like?" might force the employee to provide a more specific response.

---

[4] John Heritage, "The Limits of Questioning: Negative Interrogatives and Hostile Question Content," *Journal of Pragmatics,* 34, No. 10 (2002), 1427–46.

[5] John C. Campbell, "Communications Skills Are Required for Interview/Interrogation," *Law and Order,* 32, No. 9 (September 1984), 71–73.

The wise supervisor will realize that sudden and pronounced behavioral changes in his relationships with subordinates might be viewed with distrust by them and might hinder his rapport with them. He should, therefore, approach an interview with his usual manner, preferably friendly and calm. Especially when they have solicited his help, any abruptness that might be inferred from the "Now, what's on your mind" approach may defeat the purpose of the interview from the beginning, so an attempt must be made to develop rapport from a theme of mutual interest in their performance or continued service. These mutual interests can usually be illustrated by the problem at hand. For instance, in an interview involving a grievance, the supervisor might well at the start express his desire to remove causes for existing grievances in the interests of morale.

Rapport can be strengthened by a meticulous avoidance of argument, fault-finding, or recrimination, since these acts will often force the employee to fight back to save face and, in doing so, might well destroy any accord that may have developed. The employee will seldom welcome a lecture on morality or cross-examination from the interviewer because these may be interpreted as an attack on his self-esteem and result in loss of cooperation. Criticism for the sake of criticism seldom accomplishes anything, but when it is directed toward performance rather than the person, it can be effective without being considered a personal attack if it is accompanied by a sincere, objective, and constructive manner. The employee can often be led into a constructive solution to his own problem if he is encouraged to look at it objectively; the supervisor can then avoid direct criticism, which is often construed as offensive.

By displaying sincere interest in and consideration for the employee, the supervisor will start the process of building the employee's confidence. Respect, tolerance, and understanding of the employee's viewpoints will contribute to success in the interview, and if the employee is permitted an opportunity to engage in catharsis, he may vent his true feelings and state his real opinions. The hostile employee often will not.

The arbitrary supervisor who cannot (or will not) see both sides of a problem and allows this one-sidedness to color his judgment will seldom make an interview an outstanding success. Even an officer who is lazy will resent the "Why don't you get off the dime?" attitude of the supervisor who has made no attempt to use positive means to motivate him.

Employee-Centered Approach

In each interview, the person being interviewed should be the central figure at all times. This employee-centered characteristic requires that the supervisor suppress any tendency to be the dictator and that he actively engage in the "understanding listener" role. It is often said that as many superior officers climb the ladder of authority, their ears shrink and their mouths grow. Little is learned by talking; much can be learned by listening. Therefore, the wise interviewer will adopt a "big ears, little mouth" approach to the interview. He should always bear in mind that certain interviews will succeed only if the employee leaves feeling that at least he had his say. If he does not gain this impression but merely acquiesces, feeling that he "didn't have a chance," the interview must be considered a failure, and as such, it tends to increase the barriers to good supervisor–employee relationships.

Active Listening

In the interview, the successful interviewer will utilize the technique of listening, and when true communication takes place, the interviewer should adopt an attitude of active listening, which will encourage the interviewee to express himself freely and stimulate continuing responses. No face-to-face communication can be effective without some listening on the part of the communicators. Skill in listening is a primary qualification for the position of first-line supervisor.[6] There is ample evidence that the best listeners are the best interviewers. This conclusion applies to the criminal investigator and the supervisor-interviewer mainly because good listening, like good interviewing, requires patience, restraint, and a degree of insight.[7]

The greatest learning occurs not through speaking but through listening, an art difficult for some supervisors. Understanding is a by-product of listening, through which one gains some insight into the speaker's desires, ideas, concepts, and attitudes. It is not a passive but an active function, which requires that the listener be actively attentive to what is said. It requires effort to listen actively and involves much more than hearing only that which one wants to hear. Listening must be a positive function so that the person speaking will be encouraged to reveal his real rather than his superficial feelings.

In order that listening may be truly rewarding to the interviewer, it must be accompanied by an effort to understand what the speaker is really saying, to understand what he really means. This requires not only that the interviewer listen carefully to the declared problem but also that he be observant to the hidden clues that might indicate the real problem. Up to two-thirds of any message is nonverbal; these communications, called "body language," often speak more clearly than words.

Employment of the active listening technique is often difficult for supervisors simply because they are not aware that the final objective of interviewing cannot be accomplished until the first objective of listening *and* understanding has taken place. This process involves considerable skill. All too often, supervisors are not good listeners because, as managers of people, they become habituated to speaking rather than listening, giving orders and directions more frequently than receiving them, and making decisions that affect others. They often have an insistent desire to tell others or to get them to reveal something rather than to encourage free discussion and communications interplay between themselves and others. Often the supervisor's objective is to convince his subordinates of something or to acquire from them certain information on which to base judgments and conclusions. Because of this, there often exists the tendency on the part of the supervisor to impose his viewpoint on the interviewee from the beginning rather than to attempt to understand that person's views.

In order to gain real understanding, two things must exist: a sincere desire on the part of the interviewer to gain a better understanding of others—their problem situation and the degree of their involvement in that situation—and a forthright approach to the interview designed to make such understanding possible. Basically, this involves a sensitivity on the part of the interviewer not only to the interviewee's words but also to his underlying feelings, attitudes, and motives. Therefore, the interview should not be so

---

[6] Robert R. Johnson, "Listening—When Management Values Input, Morale Improves," *Law and Order,* 44, No. 2 (1996).

[7] Edgar M. Miner, "The Importance of Listening in the Interview and Interrogation Process," *FBI Law Enforcement Bulletin,* 53, No. 6 (June 1984), 16.

closely structured as to discourage the person interviewed from airing his problem; rather, he should be encouraged to engage in the process of mental catharsis so that his repressed feelings at the very base of the problem may be brought out.

The interviewer should respond in a limited way to encourage such reactions. The interviewee should be helped to talk, not be subjected to it. This might best be accomplished by brief natural responses to his comments—by an attentive manner, a nod of the head, a smile, an encouraging remark—or by a question framed from the interviewee's last statement. For example, if the interviewee remarks, "Supervisors don't seem to take the interest in their subordinates they once did," the interviewer might repeat, "As they once did?" or "How is that?" Or if the interviewee says, "No matter how hard I work around here, I never seem to get any credit for it," the interviewer might then repeat, "You never seem to get any credit?" A particular expression reflecting the attitude of the interviewee might be rephrased in the form of a question, but such a response should be framed with care to prevent adding new ideas and thoughts or directing the interview away from the real issue. For example, the person interviewed might exclaim, "I don't seem to be one of the fair-haired boys. I was passed over on the last promotional exam, so I'm thinking about quitting." The response might be, "Do you feel the department has discriminated against you for some reason?" The mutual exchange that occurs produces an opportunity for the interviewer to develop rapport and for both parties to gain better acceptance of each other's viewpoints.

The process of active listening gives the person being interviewed an opportunity to understand himself better and, in so doing, to gain a different interpretation of the problem at hand. The interviewer also gains the opportunity to better understand the situation and the degree of the employee's personal involvement. In addition, the process provides a good opportunity for the interviewer to broaden the base on which he must make judgments and take action.

The supervisor-interviewer must develop the skill of discriminating between symptoms and causes of problems in his relationships with his subordinates. In an attempt to put out the fire (the real cause of the problem), he must not get lost in the smoke screen of symptoms. This skill is one that can be gained by practice and experience.

It is not suggested that the supervisor-interviewer merely listen during the interview. This would rarely enable him to achieve his true objectives. Each situation will involve some giving and receiving of information. The procedure does suggest, however, that the process of listening be emphasized, at least until the point is reached where understanding of the employee, his attitudes, and his views has developed sufficiently to enable the supervisor to make sound judgments and to take action as indicated. Having taken the action, he must listen to evaluate its effectiveness. On occasion, such as in the employment interview, the results will be most productive if the prospective employee is given the opportunity of free, unstructured expression; however, ordinarily the interview must be controlled to some degree to prevent excessive wandering from the subject at hand. Such necessary structuring can often be accomplished best by the skillful use of questions.

Elimination of Bias

In his dealings with subordinates, every supervisor should avoid allowing his personal prejudices and biases to color his judgment. This is especially important in the interview situation, where he must interpret overtones and draw conclusions from the oral interchange.

The effective supervisor will recognize the tendency of employees to say the things they think might impress him and thereby set up another barrier to clear understanding. He must make every effort to remove such barriers if he is to succeed in the interview. Unsound conclusions and faulty interpretations are apt to occur if he allows himself to subjectively react to the interview and permit his likes and dislikes to color his judgment. For example, merely because the supervisor has an intense dislike for drinkers, he should not shut his mind to the underlying cause of a drinking problem of a member of his unit that might be corrected and result in "saving" the employee for many productive years of service.

Confidential Agreements

On occasion, information will be offered to the interviewer only under a "confidential agreement" arrangement. Should the interviewee proffer information under such conditions, the supervisor must carefully weigh the circumstances surrounding the offer before committing himself to accept it as a confidential communication. Once he has committed himself, he must not breach the confidence, for to do so would grossly reflect on his moral integrity. If such information turns out to be vital to the organization, he should endeavor to induce the employee to reveal it voluntarily. Keeping all information given to him under such conditions in strictest confidence is a basic requirement. If this cannot be done, the interviewer should avoid such agreements.

The supervisor-interviewer, however, must be prepared for unusual disclosures on occasion. When he is confronted with them, he should not display surprise or shock, nor should he attempt to support the employee's rationalization or give the impression of implied approval. He should avoid making any commitment or giving the impression that the information will be suppressed or withheld in confidence if misconduct is involved. Once he becomes a party to such information, he is responsible for taking whatever action is appropriate based on common sense and good judgment. He is accountable for failing to do so.

Advice Giving

Often, an employee with personal problems seeks out his supervisor for advice. Care should be exercised in this type of consultation to avoid providing a crutch to the employee who makes a feeble attempt (or even none) to solve what to him seems a dilemma that perplexes him. In this situation, the interviewer should avoid solving the employee's problem but should assist him in considering its ramifications and possible solutions by focusing his attention on things that might have been overlooked. No supervisor can afford to deprive a subordinate of the opportunity to engage in self-analysis and direction, nor can he afford to assume the responsibility for decision making, which should rightly rest on the shoulders of the employee.

Ordinarily, by encouraging an employee to air his problems, by giving him the reassurance he may be seeking, by suggesting alternative points for him to consider, and by enlisting his active participation in the matter at hand, the supervisor can guide the employee to his own solution by a process of reflection. When the employee's problem has resulted from a lack of information, the interviewer should concentrate on furnishing it rather than on giving advice.

Whisenand and Ferguson describe detailed guidelines for helping employees with personal problems. If after two thorough counseling sessions, however, the employee is not making progress, the supervisor should consider referring him to a professional therapist.[8]

Psychological Reactions in the Interview

The interviewer should recognize the basic psychological aspects involved in the communication process and should avoid conditions that produce barriers or lead to faulty conclusions. He should be aware that his judgments cannot be sound if they are based on appearances alone. This factor, often called the halo effect, simply implies that because persons look alike, one cannot accurately assume they will react alike. Thus, each individual will require an independent approach in the interview.

Likewise, the tendency to generalize or carry over a judgment from one particular trait or appearance to another must be avoided to prevent misconceptions and errors resulting from the belief that a person's habitual responses are transferred from one situation to another. The mere fact that a person has a reputation of being a practical joker does not mean that he can be excused from all his acts because they were only practical jokes.

Often the interviewer will allow an unconscious imitation to influence his judgment. This condition might result from the subtle moods that often permeate the interview and are transferred from it to the interviewer. Anger and hostility are emotions that are most often transferred from one person to another. Such a transfer may cause an overly stern or overly cordial mood not in keeping with the situation.

When the face value of information is questionable, it should be verified if possible; however, any hasty accusation might be best avoided until the accuracy of the information is determined. At that time, an explanation from the interviewee might be indicated.

Types of Personnel Interviews

The most common interviews are those of an informal nature involving day-to-day personal contacts between the supervisor and his subordinates, those conducted for the purpose of evaluating a candidate's fitness for employment or job placement, those utilized to inform the employee of his progress on the job, those initiated by the employee who has a grievance or a problem to be solved, those related to disciplinary actions, and those involving separation from the service. These will be treated in some detail in the following pages.

There are numerous other types of situations, however, in which particular research projects require the interviewing of employees for specific purposes, such as in job analysis and classification studies, personnel audits to fill specific personnel needs, labor relations studies, attitude surveys, polls, or salary studies. These types of interviews are not treated here, since they involve special research procedures not relating necessarily to the functions of the supervisor.

---

[8] Paul M. Whisenand and R. Fred Ferguson, *The Managing of Police Organizations,* 7th ed. (Upper Saddle River, N.J.: Pearson Prentice Hall, 2008), p. 187.

Informal Interview

Perhaps one of the most productive sources of information that might be used by the police supervisor is the day-to-day informal contact he has with his subordinates in office visits, during inspections, at briefing sessions, in the locker room, or in the field. In each of these contacts, the adroit supervisor will employ the techniques of listening and patient understanding as much as possible. He will listen to what is meant rather than what is said because people often convey messages by subtle implication, preferring that approach to one involving direct statements.

The wise supervisor will allot some of his available field time to riding with patrol officers engaged in performing their field duties, talking informally with them, and observing their work. "Don't make the mistake of thinking you can lead with your feet up on the desk. You lead by your feet being constantly on the ground and constantly visible to your staff—in other words, managing (leading) by walking around (MBWA)."[9] On occasion, the supervisor might make good use of an opportunity to join a subordinate while eating lunch or while making a follow-up investigation. Likewise, effective supervisors will make themselves available for after-hours interchanges with subordinates. The opportunity for coffee room conferences should not be overlooked; these are exceedingly productive means of learning about personnel.

The supervisor should, however, exercise great care to avoid making subtle comments or innuendoes concerning either subordinate or superior personnel that might be misquoted, misinterpreted, or misunderstood, since distortions or "filtering" may start rumors, create reactions harmful to morale, or erect barriers detrimental to good communications. In informal contacts with his personnel, he should proceed on the assumption that they are likely to read hidden meaning into his comments.

A friendly approach coupled with an expression of genuine interest in the employee and his family, problems, and interests will do much to foster true communications. Any appearance of prying should be avoided, however. The supervisor gains a splendid opportunity in such informal contacts to establish a climate for his subordinates—to let them know, through many easily read, subtle clues, his expectations of them and to make himself approachable to them.

Employment Interview

The employment interview has as its prime objective the appraisal of an applicant's qualifications for employment. The mental picture the interviewer obtains of the candidate's fitness or unfitness for the position is an excellent supplement to the more objective data obtained from the application and medical, psychological, intelligence, and other such examinations.

This interview is a useful device for obtaining clues to other sources of information about the prospective employee such as former employment success or failure and other personal information. It provides an excellent opportunity for observing personal characteristics, behavior, and judgment under varying contrived situations and may be used as a tool for obtaining subjective information such as beliefs, opinions, and attitudes not easily available from other sources. Of secondary importance is the giving of information about the position and the employing agency.

---

[9] Whisenand and Ferguson, *The Managing of Police Organizations,* p. 229.

For purposes of full evaluation, the interviewer must inquire into those traits that are the best predictors of success—moral integrity, ability to make decisions, insight into problems of society, approaches to dealing with people, personal interests, poise, confidence, and temperament, which cannot be measured well by other tests. The supervisor must be aware, however, that the interview cannot measure with great precision slight personality differences between individuals.

The keynote of such an interview, whether it be in a group or individual setting, is that of patient listening coupled with the skillful use of suggestive questions to encourage the applicant to talk so that maximum perception can be gained into his inner nature, his mental processes, his real character, and his ability to express himself.

One of the most common pitfalls the interviewer falls into is to assume that if the applicant fits a given pattern in one trait, he will follow the same pattern in other similar traits. Obviously the rating of observable characteristics such as articulation or poise can be judged more precisely than abstract psychological traits such as temperament or courage, but by focusing attention on specific characteristics, the interviewer is forced to make an overall judgment by relying on many such traits rather than on only one general impression, which if based on only one favorable attribute may create a misleading halo effect.

Ordinarily, such interviews are too short, so additional time should be made available whenever possible. It is suggested that a fifteen-minute interview be at least doubled. The expenditure of this added time will be well repaid if it results in the rejection of just one applicant whose unfitness for law enforcement work might not have been detected in the shorter interview. Much information regarding the candidate's personal background can be obtained from a well-planned personal history form completed by the applicant; however, such data often fail to reveal personality or temperament defects, which might be detected by the interviewer in a face-to-face conversation.

The interview should be conducted in a cordial, informal atmosphere and in an honest, straightforward manner, with the interviewer or interviewers attempting to place the applicant at ease. Any appearance of bias, discrimination, favoritism, or political patronage must be scrupulously avoided. It should be recognized that a certain amount of tension, inherent in the interview situation, will affect the applicant's responses to varying degrees. Normal discomfort about being interviewed will help expose the verbal and nonverbal characteristics that are symptomatic of the truthfulness of the person being interviewed. Similarly, deceptive subjects engage in a variety of physical activities to reduce the tension associated with lying, such as leaning away from the interviewer when uncomfortable subjects come up, rubbing and wringing the hands, and bouncing legs.[10]

The interviewer should be alert for casual remarks made by the applicant on taking his leave after the formality of the interview situation has ended. Much insight can often be gained into the inner thoughts and character of the interviewee at this time, since he will often say revealing things he might not have considered important during the interview. Likewise, comments made in an unguarded moment over a cup of coffee or lunch often provide much insight into an applicant's character.

---

[10] F. E. Inbau, J. E. Reid, J. P. Buckley, and B. C. Jayne, *Criminal Interrogation & Confessions,* 4th ed. (Sudbury, Mass.: Jones & Bartlett, 2004).

The interviewer should bear in mind that as a representative of management, he has an obligation to establish a favorable impression in the applicant's mind concerning the organization. The applicant should be left with a warm, friendly feeling toward the prospective employing agency, not with a feeling of bitterness which might result from an ill-prepared interview by the employer's representative who has neither the desire nor the ability to display compassion, courtesy, and understanding even toward the most unacceptable police candidate.

Information about the employing agency should be made available in an employment announcement; however, occasionally during the interview, the prospective employee will express a desire for information that is not available from the literature provided. He should be given such data honestly and factually, and it should include not only favorable information but also unfavorable aspects of the position sought. Such information should be made available promptly, since it might furnish the basis for an affirmative decision by the desirable applicant who has not yet decided to accept employment.

Progress Interview

The progress interview can be used effectively to inform the employee of his progress, to review his past performance, and to give constructive guidance concerning improvement required. The objective of the interview is to aid him to engage in self-appraisal. All too often, in those agencies that use periodic service rating procedures, the service rating interview is delayed until long after such reports have been prepared, if it is conducted at all. Such an interview is frequently avoided by the rating supervisor because of his reluctance to discuss any low ratings with the concerned subordinate. Progressive systems require such discussion with the employee, however, since rating reports furnish a basis for corrective training and provide opportunity for the employee both to view himself as others view him and to learn from his supervisor how his past and present performance are rated and what improvement might be indicated in the future.

The wise supervisor will avail himself of all such opportunities to discuss the employee's performance as a means of aiding the substandard employee to improve it and commending the high producer for a job well done. Properly conducted, such interviews will have a very positive and beneficial effect on the morale of employees. The effect the discussion may have on the morale of the particular subordinate should be carefully considered, and the approach should be varied for each employee accordingly.

Facts pertinent to the discussion should be clearly in mind. The interviewer may find it necessary to prove a disputed point to avoid demoralizing the employee. The strengths and weaknesses about which the conversation will revolve should be reviewed before the interview takes place, and available information should be reviewed concerning the employee's background, rating reports by other supervisors, medical history records, and other personnel data in preparing for the interview.

Sufficient time should be allotted for the discussion. If it is a hurried affair, the employee is likely to gain the impression that the interview is merely a formality and that the supervisor would like to get it over with as soon as possible because he is busy with more important things. Yet few of the supervisor's duties, in reality, are more important than this training function.

The interview should not be utilized merely as an excuse to "lower the boom." "The goal of the Sergeant should be to handle the interview in such a way that officers (with the exception of incompetents and malcontents) will return to their job with an enthusiastic attitude and a genuine desire to improve their own on-the-job performance."[11] The interview should be conducted in a relaxed, friendly, helpful, understanding, and constructive atmosphere. The supervisor must remember that he is always in charge of the meeting and should avoid becoming apologetic or defensive about it; neither should he make excuses for his ratings. Points should not be argued—a specific and constructive approach should be taken.

The interview should be conducted in a manner that will include specifics about the employee's performance, not his personality, unless certain characteristics are being appraised on the evaluation report. Employees seldom like vague, general comments about their performance, so the interview should be as specific as possible about what is to be accomplished by it. Good performance should be stressed at the outset, with sincere praise for the employee's strong points. This should then be followed by telling him in specific constructive terms what is wrong and how he can improve. This sandwich technique allows the employee to receive objective criticism in small bits rather than in large, often harmful, bites. Weaknesses should be discussed in a factual, objective manner. Personal criticism should be avoided to avert stifling the discussion. The employee should be encouraged to solve his own problems whenever possible, but the supervisor should be prepared to aid him if necessary.

The objective of the meeting should be constantly kept in mind so that collateral issues not relevant to the discussion can be avoided. It is imperative for the supervisor to convince the employee of their mutual goals, objectively and constructively, in a manner calculated to avoid bitterness and recrimination. Once this difficult problem has been overcome, a prime objective of the evaluation procedure—to improve performance—will have been accomplished. The City of Miami Police Department counsels its supervisors with reference to the personal development interview: "The guiding principle is that the supervisor should provide the member with a firm sense of direction for self-improvement, based on those factors needed by the member to bring about his maximum development."[12]

Excessive leniency by the supervisor seldom provides good results, nor does it often produce desired reactions of changing attitudes because level of performance is largely dependent on attitudinal factors. Supervisors should not fall into the trap of being too understanding and mild (police employees rarely respect a timid or meek type of supervisor), yet common courtesy and discreet forthrightness are always appreciated. The overly mild conversation may weaken the supervisor's position if he is later required to take disciplinary action against the employee for unacceptable performance. Tribunals reviewing the action may attach considerable significance to any failure on the part of the supervisor to inform his subordinates of substandard or unsatisfactory performance. Usually, they will expect that such employees will have been placed on notice that improvement is required; in the absence of such notice, disciplinary action cases are frequently dismissed or reversed.

---

[11] Harry W. More and Larry S. Miller, *Effective Police Supervision,* 6th ed. (Cincinnati, Ohio: Anderson, 2011), p. 269.

[12] Jeff Bernstein, *Supervisors Situational Management Training Handbook* (Miami, Fla.: City of Miami Police Department, 2003), p. 100.

Every attempt must be made to avoid comparing the interviewee to other individuals because this will only result in bitterness and personal animosity. Undue emphasis on the police employee's production based on raw statistics from accomplishment records should be avoided because the validity of such records as a sole criterion for personnel evaluations is subject to attack and will seldom convince the employee that he has been rated fairly. The adroit supervisor will base his discussion of the substandard employee on careful analysis of those specific factors that will reflect qualitative and quantitative performance as well as those that reflect personal relationships with other employees and the public. Fundamental to this interview is an objective and constructive manner.

The employee should be encouraged to express how he feels about his performance, and disapproval should not be shown when he does so. The art of listening should be developed and applied to each interview (as was described in detail previously). The fair supervisor will be prepared to acknowledge any problem he may have caused the employee because of the supervisory methods followed without apologizing for them. This acknowledgment should be used judiciously, however, so that it will not provide a crutch for the employee to use for rationalizing his deficiencies. The supervisor should be aware that his relationships with his subordinates may have been interpreted by them differently from the way he had anticipated. He should look at his supervisory methods through his subordinates' eyes whenever possible to gain better insight into the effect these methods have on them.

The interview that results in neither satisfaction nor constructive guidance for the employee is wasted. It achieves nothing and should not have occurred in the first place. The interviewee should leave the interview feeling, at least, that something has been accomplished; that his efforts have been recognized; that he has gained a fresh, revitalized viewpoint; or that he has had some reassurance from the supervisor.

Each interview should be followed up to determine—by casual questions, observations, or inspection—if any changes have occurred in the employee's outlook, attitude, or performance. If further interviews seem indicated, they should be held as circumstances dictate. They should also be made easily available to the employee should he so desire.

Grievance Interview

Every supervisor should be sensitive to the needs of employees who have a real or imagined grievance. He should recognize that even imaginary grievances are always "real" in the mind of the person who feels he has been wronged. As a result, resentment and hostility arise and quickly spread if other personnel are convinced that a fellow employee has been wronged or that a wrong has not been corrected. It is therefore incumbent on the supervisor to provide the employee an opportunity to air his grievance at the earliest moment. The cause of real grievances should, if possible, be corrected without delay. Conditions causing grievances that are not easily correctable should be analyzed carefully. Wherever possible, an opportunity should be provided for the employee to participate actively in the solution of the problem.

The employee with imagined grievances, though requiring an approach similar to that used in discussing real grievances, should be given the opportunity to see the problem in its true perspective. He will often recognize the imaginary nature of his belief that he has been wronged and usually respond to patient reassurance, which often reestablishes his feeling of security.

The employee with an ill-founded grievance, perhaps resulting from punitive action imposed on him because of his own misconduct, often fails or refuses to recognize the need for maintenance of the particular brand of discipline to which he feels he has been subjected. He should be allowed to talk out his problem in the process of mental catharsis, and the supervisor must provide ample time for the employee to give his reasons for believing he has been wronged. Recriminations should be avoided by the supervisor, since this will tend to aggravate the feeling of hostility that usually exists in this situation. The supervisor should explain forthrightly and patiently that the important consideration of the effect such punishment might have on the officer's future career is not the severity of the punishment but the attitude with which it is received.

Unless such interviews are conducted privately, with ample time, in one or more separate interviews to allow for complete ventilation by the employee and unless they are held in an objective, constructive atmosphere, the employee may forever be lost to the agency as a productive, happy officer. Instead, he may become a disgruntled, marginal producer and may try to contaminate every other employee who will listen. Candor is a virtue but should be tempered on occasion by discretion and restraint on the part of the interviewer to avoid irreparable damage to the employee's pride and to prevent further recrimination and bitterness.

Problem-Solving Interview

The supervisor frequently finds it necessary to help his subordinates solve personal problems or otherwise adjust to a particular situation.[13] Often called a consultation or chaplain interview, its function might be likened to that performed by a military chaplain or a police counselor.

The supervisor must approach such a meeting with a decision to allow the troubled subordinate to air his problem. Frequently, merely by talking about it, the troubled employee finds his own solution through reflection and self-analysis. Viewed in the calm atmosphere the supervisor provides, such problems seldom appear as difficult to resolve as they do in the imagination of the employee. Often the supervisor is credited with a simple solution when in reality he has provided only a patient, understanding ear, leaving the solution to the subordinate.

Disciplinary Action Interview

An employee against whom a disciplinary matter is pending should ordinarily be interviewed in two settings. He should be interviewed during the investigation.[14] Then he must be informed of the findings, conclusions, recommendations, and penalty (if any) stemming from the investigation when the matter has been finally resolved. It is the obligation of the supervisor, unless it is assumed by a higher authority, to notify the subordinate of the findings in a disciplinary investigation and the conclusions drawn from them as promptly as possible after conclusion of the inquiry. There are few situations that affect an officer's performance more adversely than an investigation

---

[13] Counseling to help employees solve many of their personal problems is discussed in Chapter 8.

[14] Interviews in connection with disciplinary investigations are discussed further in Chapter 11.

into his conduct. While prompt interview and notification are usually indicated, the supervisor should make certain that he can perform this task objectively before attempting it. Rarely is it advisable to interview a derelict employee until the cooling-off period has passed to prevent anger from coloring the judgment of the interviewing supervisor.

The informative interview with the subordinate to notify him of the disposition of the investigation should be conducted promptly upon conclusion of the inquiry. This provides an opportunity to clear the air if the investigation proves that the allegations of misconduct were unfounded or if the complaint has not been sustained by the available facts. If investigation has revealed facts resulting in suspension, surrender of days off, cancellation of accumulated overtime, reprimand, admonishment, or other penalty, the supervisor should accept the responsibility for informing the employee of the action to be taken. Regardless of whether the penalty is less or more than the accused person expected, the supervisor should assume some responsibility for it if his recommendation played an important part in the assessment of punishment. He should avoid any implication in his manner or speech that he blames a severe penalty on someone "above" or that a light penalty resulted from some defensive action he might have taken on behalf of the derelict employee. "Some supervisors occasionally need to be reminded that the fundamental responsibility for direction and control rests with the immediate supervisor at the operational level, not with the law enforcement executive."[15] The supervisor's responsibility for maintaining discipline does not include participation in a popularity contest.

Separation Interview

One of the frequent failures of supervisors' human resource management functions that has a long-term adverse effect on the organization's image results from the neglect of someone in authority in the employing agency to discuss circumstances surrounding an employee's separation from service. An interview should be conducted regardless of the cause for separation, whether it is from voluntary or forced resignation, termination for cause, or retirement. Such an interview is especially helpful in determining useful or harmful hiring procedures. The techniques of using it should be included in supervisory training to acquaint those in supervisory positions with the need for improvement in questionable practices that might cause unnecessary and costly employment turnover.

It is most important to learn the true reason for a resignation rather than the expressed reason. Perhaps the employee has indicated that family pressures, a fearful spouse, lack of adequate pay, or adverse working conditions are the reason when the true reason involves work pressures or a capricious supervisor, either of which is correctable. Every effort should be made to isolate as specifically as possible the real reason for leaving; whether or not an attempt should be made to persuade the employee to change his mind will depend on the circumstances of each case.

---

[15] *Internal Affairs Policy and Procedure* (Trenton, N.J.: Department of Law & Public Safety, September 2011), p. 12, http://www.state.nj.us/lps/dcj/agguide/internalaffairs2000v1_2.pdf, accessed November 15, 2012.

Every means must be taken to prevent the employee from terminating his employment with the feeling that the organization is a poor place to work. If the separation results from personal dereliction or incompetency, the interviewer seldom gains friendship for his organization if recriminations and hostility are allowed to creep into the interview. It should be conducted in as friendly a manner as possible so that the employee leaves with as little bitterness as possible because an unfriendly former employee can do inestimable harm to the organization.

Special effort should be made by supervisory personnel to take advantage of any opportunity to express gratitude to the retiring employee. Each has contributed something to the organization and should not be permitted to leave with a feeling that he was treated as if "they couldn't wait to get rid of me." It is especially important that a separation interview be conducted by the personnel officer, whatever his rank, since he speaks with the formal authority of his position. All too often, the supervisor excuses his failure to "extend a friendly hand" to the retiring employee because of the press of other business, but what other activity could return so much goodwill, or ill will, minute for minute?

Recording of Results

When a record of the interview is desirable upon its conclusion, the results, both general and specific, and the observations of the interviewer should be recorded promptly to prevent omissions, inaccuracies, and faulty information from filtering in. Often, it is desirable to prepare notes as the interview progresses (rather than to rely solely on memory) to avoid such shortcomings in the report; however, great care must be exercised in doing so to prevent any stifling of the interviewee's responses.

Evaluation of Results

The skill of interviewing can be developed, just as the skill of interrogation can. Once the interviewer has learned how to listen, has made a diligent effort to learn the patience required in the process of gaining true understanding of others' viewpoints so that he may make allowances for views that may differ from his own, has diligently attempted to avoid past mistakes, has applied the general and specific principles others have found helpful, has learned to control his own biases so that he may objectively treat the problems posed by subordinates, and has made a conscious effort to focus the interview on essentials, he will have mastered the initial steps that must be taken in becoming an expert interviewer. Experience and practice are necessary to learn how to interview well, but these waste time and are slow processes unless the interviewer profits from a systematic review of his strengths and weaknesses, modifies and improves his strengths, and avoids further errors from his deficiencies.

An interviewer's skill can be improved by analyzing what was said to determine the motives, feelings, views, and attitudes expressed and comparing these conclusions with those made during the interview. The interviewer must also analyze the techniques he used to ascertain if they produced free expression or stifled it. If such procedures suppressed the interviewee's responses, what might have been said or done to encourage a better response? Finally, consideration must be given to the total objective: Was the objective accomplished? If not, how might it have been achieved? Would a change in technique have brought about better results?

Causes of Unsuccessful Interviews

There are many limitations imposed on the interview procedure and many combinations of factors that contribute to failures. Some interviews are unsuccessful because of a failure of the parties to communicate what is meant or to understand what is said. Others fail because of ignorance, faulty recollection, tendency to say what one thinks he is expected to say, or distortions that creep into the reporting of results when the facts are interpreted on the basis of subjective impressions rather than objective facts.

Success of the interview is dependent on factors such as the ability of the interviewer in eliciting accurate responses and the personalities of both parties—their idiosyncrasies, attitudes, and biases. The interviewer's failure to analyze the problem confronting him and to decide on the best method of approaching it, or his failure to prepare for the interview by mastering background data and using the data to best serve the purpose, or his failure to plan the wording of questions might further lessen the effectiveness of the interview. When it fails for these reasons or if the interviewer cannot gain the interviewee's cooperation or understand him, techniques should be devised for preventing future failures. Most failures occur because the proven principles and techniques of interviewing are not adapted to the needs of a given situation. By selecting and applying the best procedures—those found to have been most effective in many interviews—the supervisor will enjoy a continuing sense of satisfaction from the results.

SUMMARY

The effective supervisor will spend a large portion of his time talking with his subordinates, in addition to inspecting their work and observing their performance, if he is to gain the greatest understanding of them. Purposeful face-to-face interchanges with them will enable him to motivate them, change their attitudes when necessary to comport with the objectives of the organization, obtain their cooperation, or help them to resolve problems.

An interview differs from an interrogation in that the latter is primarily interviewer-centered, with the dominant role played by the person asking the questions. In the interviewee-centered situation, the person responding to the prompting is most important, with the interviewer only "priming the pump" to elicit complete responses. This is the supervisor's role in his verbal interchanges with subordinates. The amount of emphasis he wishes to place on this or that technique will be dependent on what he wishes to accomplish.

The informal interview may have as its objective the general gathering of intelligence or information to determine the level of morale or group responses to organizational objectives. The employment interview has as its objective the evaluation of those abstract traits in a prospective employee that may qualify him for employment or promotion or that may constitute cause for his rejection. The progress interview is primarily directed toward giving the employee some insight about his performance and progress on the job. If he has a grievance, the nature of the interview will generally dictate a different approach, one primarily of listening to learn the truth rather than the ostensible reason for the grievance. Telling is reserved for clarifying misunderstandings on which the grievance may be mistakenly based.

An interview may involve problem solving, in which case the supervisor may be asked to help the employee reach a solution to his problem; the supervisor will then lend a willing ear and indirectly encourage the employee to air his problem and arrive at his own solution. The disciplinary action interview is concerned with an investigation of the employee's conduct. The supervisor first interviews the subordinate complained against to determine his side of the matter, and the employee is interviewed the second time to inform him of the action to be taken as the result of the investigation. The separation interview is utilized to determine the reason for termination so that corrective action can be taken if a voluntary resignation is based on dissatisfaction related to the work environment.

In every case (with perhaps an exception for informal interviews), the supervisor conducting the interview with a subordinate should plan ahead what he wishes to accomplish and how he will approach it. He will maintain a patient, objective attitude and will plan his questions according to his objectives. He will refrain from giving advice; instead, he will expertly guide the discussion into constructive channels suggested by the interviewee himself.

REVIEW

Questions

1. What is the difference between an interrogation and an interview?
2. What are the major functions of an interview?
3. List the types of interviews, and discuss briefly the characteristics of each.
4. What is meant by the principle that interviews should be employee-centered? Discuss how the employee-centered interview can be achieved.
5. Discuss the active listening technique.
6. Discuss how questions might best be used in the interview process.
7. How should the interviewer generally handle an offer to give information under a confidential agreement?
8. What is meant by the term *unconscious imitation,* and how might it affect an interview?
9. Discuss some of the most prevalent causes of interview failures.
10. Why should an interviewer ordinarily refrain from giving advice to the interviewee?
11. What are some of the broad steps a supervisor should take in preparing for an interview?

Exercises

Case 1: The Transfer Interview

    I. The Facts
        A. Personal
            1. Detective Leo Sparks is age 32.
            2. He was appointed eight years ago; his wife recently died, and they had no children.
            3. He has received no promotions but has been assigned to the investigation division for five years.

    4. He is the senior officer in his division.

    5. He has been heard to say that he would quit the job if he ever had to leave the investigative assignment.

  B. Assumptions

    1. Sparks has had several minor (almost trivial) complaints from victims of crimes that he has been assigned to investigate.

    2. His golf clubs have been found in his police car.

    3. It is rumored that he is not paying attention to duty.

    4. His clearance rate for cases has recently been the lowest in the division, although formerly it was the highest.

    5. You have been instructed to drop one man from the division and have selected Sparks because of the factors noted above, even though he is the senior man and was (until recently) one of your most productive detectives.

    6. Sparks is very upset, having learned of the pending transfer before you were able to inform him.

II. The Problem

  A. You are to interview this officer to tell him of the transfer, since he has brought up the issue in the coffee room.

  B. Your main concern is to "sell" him on the transfer and to prevent his threatened resignation.

  C. Employ the principles of interviewing as discussed in this chapter.

Case 2: The Grievance Interview

I. The Facts

  A. Personal

    1. Robert Heath is age 35.

    2. He was appointed twelve years ago.

    3. He is a very satisfactory producer and does a very acceptable job in any assignment.

    4. He has a very happy home life but is becoming unhappy with working conditions on the job.

  B. Assumptions

    1. This officer has complained to his city councilman that he has been discriminated against by his supervisors (without naming them) in respect to assignments, days off, and vacation. He is threatening to quit his job because of it.

    2. He has allegedly had a position offered to him at a considerably higher salary.

    3. Your department can ill afford to lose its seasoned officers, since you now have several vacancies that you are having difficulty filling.

    4. Your councilman, Mr. Jackson, is a strong supporter of the department and thinks someone should talk to the officer. He learned of the situation informally from the officer at a social event. Your chief agrees that the officer is worth making an effort to save.

    5. Make whatever additional assumptions are required for the interview. There is no factual evidence that the officer has been discriminated against as alleged.

II. The Problem

  A. You are to interview this officer to ascertain the nature of his grievance.

  B. You are to try to change the attitude of this officer. He has become known around the station as a person with grievances but has not approached his supervisors about them.

Case 3: The Problem-Solving Interview

I. The Facts
   A. Personal
      1. Officer Sam Peters is age 40.
      2. He was appointed fourteen years ago.
      3. His performance is very good.
      4. He is married to Margaret, and they have three children, ages 9, 12, and 14.
   B. Assumptions
      1. Margaret Peters has come to you, her husband's immediate supervisor. She states that Officer Peters respects you highly.
      2. She then states that during the last two years, Officer Peters has been "chasing" another woman and that his conduct is rapidly becoming a neighborhood "scandal."
      3. No complaints have been received by the department, and his conduct has apparently not affected his work.
      4. Officer Peters has no record of previous disciplinary action.
      5. According to his wife, Officer Peters's conduct is such that the department will undoubtedly be embarrassed soon if something is not done promptly.
      6. Make other assumptions as required.

II. The Problem
   A. You are to interview Officer Peters in an attempt to protect your department.
   B. This is an initial interview.
   C. Neighbors have not been interviewed, nor have the allegations of Margaret Peters been supported by other evidence at the time you were asked by your superior to do whatever is necessary to prevent possible embarrassment to the department.
   D. Other personnel have heard rumors to the effect that Officer Peters has become involved with a woman, but none of them will admit that they have any firsthand information to support the rumor.

7

Some Psychological Aspects of Supervision

Chapter Objectives

This chapter will enable you:

- To gain an appreciation of the need for a reasonable application of the principles of human relations in dealing with others
- To become acquainted with some of the psychological factors that affect behavior
- To become familiar with the techniques of dealing effectively with some of the psychological problems of subordinates

The contemporary attitude toward human nature and human engineering is an increasingly discussed concept of management. Too often, people in management rise to high positions with little knowledge of the psychological factors that interfere with the productivity of their personnel. Persons who are highly successful in developing certain specialized skills often are placed in supervisory positions with considerable power, where some prove to be bunglers in applying the fundamental skills of dealing with others.

The approach of the human relations school toward supervision is an important science, a science of managing human beings, which grew out of other sciences. It was long in coming, but when it arrived, it showed great promise. The new thinking was applied to a preposterous degree by some; others refused to accept or apply it at all. The most successful managers and supervisors recognized the value of getting things done through the democratic process and saw that people would perform better if they were made to want to perform better. As a result, where this approach was applied, production and morale improved.

Dale Carnegie made a fortune by teaching people how to get someone to do what they want. Whatever this approach is called—the charm school approach or the democratic method—it can bring excellent results when applied sincerely, with common sense, and with good intentions. If applied superficially and insincerely, it eventually will produce bad results.

The Western Electric Company spent a great deal of money in a long study of people at work in their plant in Hawthorne, Illinois. These studies, still accepted as valid by experienced supervisors and managers, revealed that the performance of workers is more affected by factors in the psychological and social environments than by factors in the physical environment. Evidence is clear that output is affected to a greater degree by workers' feelings about their jobs, their colleagues, and their supervisors, as well as the happenings about them, than by their attitudes about the physical working conditions.[1]

The rise of worker dominance and merit systems has made it necessary for management to seek positive methods of gaining an understanding of workers and leading them into a desire to produce. Vast sums have been poured into human relations training of supervisory personnel by management in recent times. Most of this training has stressed cultural background and psychological differences between people and the effects these factors have on human behavior. Undoubtedly, some good results have accrued from these efforts, but without question, some poor results have also come about where superiors have allowed the democratic approach to degenerate into permissiveness. As a consequence, it is readily apparent that discipline has deteriorated and leadership has generally weakened in some organizations. The ideal, of course, is a good blending of strong leadership, good discipline, and palatable human relations.

Drives, Satisfactions, and Needs

All persons have certain basic drives that motivate their behavior. They have certain satisfactions that need fulfillment and psychological needs that, in large part, govern their demeanor. If the efforts of the supervisor to prevent or relieve many of the emotional problems of his subordinates are to be most meaningful, it is imperative that he understand the basic relationships of their drives, satisfactions, and needs to their behavior patterns.

Drives

The commonly recognized basic human drives are the wish for security, based on fear, apprehensiveness, and avoidance; the drive for response, derived from love, friendship, and affection; the wish for recognition, gained from status, prestige, and social approval; and the drive for new experiences, including curiosity, adventure, and the craving for excitement.[2] Some add the service motive as a fundamental drive,[3] but many disagree that this aspect of human behavior should be included as a drive. Certainly, the satisfaction derived from serving others well is important in law enforcement.

Satisfactions

The fundamental satisfactions that the individual strives to fulfill will be found in the lists prepared by most authorities. These are (1) affection, acceptance, and security; (2) a sense of personal adequacy; (3) recognition as a personality; (4) an opportunity for

---

[1] Fritz J. Roethlisberger and William J. Dickson, *Management and the Worker* (London: Routledge, 2003), p. 615.

[2] Joanne Belknap, *The Invisible Woman: Gender, Crime and Justice* (Belmont, Calif.: Wadsworth, 2006), p. 34.

[3] Raymond J. Corsini and Danny Wedding, *Current Psychotherapies,* 9th ed. (Belmont, Calif.: Brooks/Cole, 2011), p. 624.

accomplishment; (5) an opportunity for independence; (6) an opportunity to obtain new experiences; and (7) an opportunity to possess something or someone.

Needs

Adair lists the basic psychological needs of an individual as a feeling of security, a sense of adequacy, a sense of self-esteem, and a sense of social approval.[4] These have a vital bearing on the behavior of individuals. Every well-balanced person needs to feel secure in his judgments, in his work, and in his relationships with others. He needs a strong sense of adequacy and confidence in his ability to perform well in the job he has selected and to meet the needs of his social environment. He needs to have self-esteem, a sense of pride in his accomplishments, and a feeling of worth in himself; he also needs a sense of social approval by his family, associates, peers, and society. Unfortunately, law enforcement personnel too often come to believe that the society they serve does not approve of them or what they stand for, which can force them into a harmful psychological isolation from the public.

When these basic needs become imbalanced in a person to a degree that he loses his ability to cope with the stresses of his work, he will eventually lose some of the control he has over his behavior. He then could become an annoying problem for the supervisor.

Inferiority Complex

Alfred Adler used the phrase "inferiority complex" to describe the psychological feeling of inadequacy and applied this concept as a partial explanation of some of the problems of the emotional human animal. He believed that persons have a drive for superiority and that the frustration coming from a feeling of inferiority thwarts this basic drive. Some accept it, retain their feelings of inferiority, and engage in daydreaming or fantasy to compensate. Others compensate for their inadequacies by increased effort and make themselves productive members of society.

The normal individual always thinks of himself in the best possible light, and it is difficult for him to recognize his weaknesses, accept defeat, or admit failure. He will often resort to all kinds of subterfuges—even self-deception—to escape any ill thought of himself.[5] In attempting to avoid the feelings of inferiority, the individual may set unrealistic goals for himself; in his efforts to achieve these goals, he often develops a desire to gain dominance at all costs, and this desire often leads him to all sorts of antisocial behaviors, from bullying and boasting to acting in a tyrannical manner.

The types of overcompensation developed by such overdriven individuals in the form of intensified and exaggerated strivings to compensate for their strong feelings of inferiority become an imposing challenge to the supervisor because to bring about the emotional balance of such individuals, it is crucial that their self-confidence be restored.[6]

---

[4] John Adair, *Develop Your Leadership Skills* (London: Kogan Page, 2010), pp. 37–38.

[5] Wayne Weiten, Dana S. Dunn, and Elizabeth Yost Hammer, *Psychology Applied to Modern Life: Adjustment in 21st Century*, 10th ed. (Belmont, Calif.: Wadsworth, 2012), p. 43.

[6] Richard A Griggs, *Psychology*, 2nd ed. (New York: Worth Publishers, 2009), p. 267.

Training might help to improve the individual's proficiency and confidence. An assignment to a position where he can achieve added success and the satisfaction that results from it often increases his self-esteem; the sincere and judicious use of praise when it is deserved often brings about similar results.

Catharsis

Sigmund Freud, the father of psychoanalysis, attempted to discover the causes of some psychological diseases that baffled him as a physician. He reasoned that if he could bring these problems into the open, he could learn more about their basic causes and possibly discover a cure more readily. He found that if he allowed his patients to talk about their psychological ailments—to engage in catharsis—by bringing them to consciousness and giving them expression, their fears, problems, and complexes were often alleviated.

The process is particularly helpful in reducing feelings of anxiety, guilt, fear, hostility, and failure. Rogers, in describing catharsis as the process of "talking or acting things out" in a permissive atmosphere, states, "We have learned that catharsis not only frees the individual from those conscious fears and guilt feelings of which he is aware, but that, continued, it can bring to light more deeply buried attitudes which also exert their influence on behavior."[7]

Lack of knowledge or understanding is often the direct cause of debilitating anxieties, fears, and feelings of insecurity among employees. These can often be materially reduced by the supervisor if he provides those affected individuals an opportunity to talk about their feelings in an informal environment, where he provides the necessary information that usually reduces or eliminates such apprehensions. This might be done in privacy in the coffee room, while riding with the officer on patrol, and the like. Patience, sincerity, and an attitude of helpfulness are essential if the best results are to be achieved.

Fixation and Regressive Behavior

If left unresolved, emotional ills often result in various psychological conditions. Adults often seek infantile ways of solving their emotional problems. The adult's psychological character is generally thought to be largely a product of childhood conditions. If by screaming a child can get his way or if discipline is the result of the erratic and inconsistent behavior of his parents (sometimes succumbing to the child's tantrums and giving in to his demands as the course of least resistance, and sometimes refusing to do so), the child gains a sense of insecurity. Psychological fixation may occur at this stage of development, with the probability that the child will become a screaming, tantrum-raising man at forty or regress or develop compensations in his behavior for the shortcomings he experiences in his environment.

Symonds describes regressive behavior as a "step taken by the individual in order to avoid meeting and solving some difficulty or present problem. It is an escape from reality"

---

[7] C. R. Rogers, *Counseling and Psychotherapy* (Cambridge, Mass.: Rogers Press, 2008 rpt.), p. 21.

and describes the condition of fixation as a "defense against anxiety by stopping the process of development."[8] It involves a concentration on some particular infantile situation that tends to block maturation. Childlike or immature reasoning, in connection with some problem situation, usually will not solve the dilemma but will likely lead instead to increased anxiety. These conditions sometimes lead to serious emotional problems, as discussed later in this chapter.

Supervisory Problem: The Frustrated Employee

The supervisor is constantly dealing with people who, in one respect or another, have regressions, fixations, or overdrives caused by frustrations. When individuals are prevented from fulfilling certain conscious desires or impulses, when their basic drives or needs or satisfactions are not realized, when they are thwarted in reaching their goals, frustrations are likely to develop. These are called goal frustrations (as opposed to those due to mental disorders).[9] Accompanying them will be numerous problems for the supervisor to resolve.

The behavior reactions of aggression, regression, or fixation commonly found in frustrated persons will demand attention.[10] The supervisor's course will be determined in large part by the psychological impact of the frustrations on his subordinates. One thing is certain: When psychological problems interfere with performance, the supervisor must do something to resolve them because if he does not, they will invariably become more pronounced and troublesome to him, the organization, and the individual involved.

It would be an oversimplification to state that a single underlying cause of abnormal behavior can be easily isolated or even that such behavior can be attributed to any one causative factor. Ordinarily, many factors contribute, and the supervisor must consider that a particular type of human conduct is usually the result of multiple stimuli. On occasion, however, one predominant factor can be pinpointed as the primary cause of a particular course of conduct. For example, a supervisor observes an issue developing among a group of his subordinates. They have had an increasing problem of getting along with others, their performance has deteriorated, they seem to be preoccupied, they have missed calls, and they have had an inordinate number of conflicts with other coworkers and superiors. The supervisor finds that one officer has become involved in financial difficulties and that the problem lately has become particularly acute. He is worried about his security. The second officer is worried about his health; he has been ill and is troubled because of his failure to improve as rapidly as he thinks he should. The third employee is bored, feels he has outlived his usefulness in his present job, and wants to transfer. He is looking for new experiences.

---

[8] Percival M. Symonds, *Dynamics of Human Adjustment* (Westport, Conn.: Greenwood Press, 1984), p. 204.

[9] *Diagnostic and Statistical Manual of Mental Disorders*, 4th ed., text rev. (Washington D.C.: American Psychiatric Association, 2000), p. 13.

[10] Norman R. F. Maier, *Frustration: The Study of Behavior without a Goal* (Westport, Conn.: Greenwood Press, 1982), p. 16.

The fourth feels that he has not been given sufficient recognition for his work and that others are getting more than their share. All the officers' problems may be but reflections of these various circumstances; the results are generally the same, but the causes may vary widely.

The supervisor must develop a clinical approach in dealing with the emotional problems of his subordinates that he encounters day to day. He must attempt to understand how these problems arise and deal with them in a practical, commonsense way. Sometimes a workable solution cannot be found—perhaps none could be found even by a professional who specializes in the study and treatment of emotional disorders. Ordinarily, the degree of success achieved will be directly related to the supervisor's patience and understanding and the effort he expends in helping his subordinates solve their problems.

To deal most effectively with the lack of emotional adjustment in others, the supervisor himself must be well adjusted. He must exhibit complete control of himself before he can supervise others. He should display a mature philosophical attitude in his dealings with subordinates, realizing that each has a unique personality that can best be developed along certain lines. He should govern his relationships with them accordingly.

Sometimes giving subordinates an opportunity to talk, providing a bit of information, or giving a simple explanation is all that is required to correct an incipient problem. Although symptoms of lack of adjustment may be similar, causes usually are not. If the basic causes of lack of adjustment rather than the symptoms can be treated effectively, a most valuable service will be rendered to the individual as well as to the organization.

Nature of Frustration

When the route to an important goal is obstructed, the usual reaction is to go around the obstacle, remove it, attack it head-on, or accept defeat. If the goal is unimportant, forget it, ignore it, or deny that it ever existed.

As a practical approach to such goal obstruction, people may circumvent it and find other ways to reach their goal. Sometimes they will find a way to remove the obstruction (deviously or forthrightly) or they may become aggressive and attack it properly or improperly. Others may decide that the cost of aggression or circumvention is too great and give up in resignation. The last recourse may be avoidance or denial, avoiding the responsibility for doing something or denying the problem exists.

The course followed in meeting obstruction involves problem-solving behavior, since it requires some adjustment to circumstances. This is the essence of personal development.

The adjusted person is capable of meeting normal problems and solving them without undue psychological strain. Gradually, he develops the ability to meet and solve more difficult personal problems. The individual who finds it difficult to adjust to his problems develops a sense of failure, which causes frustration, irritation, emotional conflicts of all sorts, and reduced flexibility in handling other problems. If he is unable to find a satisfactory solution, his failure becomes a barrier. With it comes frustration, and the vicious cycle starts all over again.

The supervisor who ignores or is unaware of the employee's drive to attain a certain goal is often the very cause of frustration—he becomes the barrier. If he notices the acceptable efforts of his subordinate and indicates approval of those efforts, he assists the employee in his drive toward his goal. He must not, however, accept or condone improper or unethical methods employed in goal achievement.

Barriers Causing Frustration

A drive toward achievement of a goal may be blocked by external or internal barriers, which may be man-made or environmental. Although it is not possible or even desirable to eliminate all barriers that contribute to frustration, many can readily be removed and should be, as they are unnecessary impediments to smooth operations. Any reasonably astute supervisor can easily assess the work environment to determine what changes should be made to improve performance and where changes should not be made. He must be careful, however, to avoid an overprotectiveness of subordinates that will be harmful to the development of their problem-solving abilities or their capacity to cope with ordinary job problems.

External Barriers

Physical things in the environment of the individual, such as a malfunctioning flashlight, a sticking door, or bad brakes on an automobile, may constitute barriers to which the individual must adjust. Human barriers might be a nagging spouse or an incompatible partner or supervisor. Situational barriers may consist of unpopular rules or policies, inadequate salaries, or onerous situations that affect the individual.

The supervisor should set about to correct those things he can remove as barriers. Some of them he cannot, but he can make an effort to lessen their impact by giving the employee a better understanding of why such barriers exist.

Internal Barriers

Conflicts in motives existing within the individual may constitute internal barriers to personality adjustment. Often these obstacles are brought about by failure of the person to make adjustments to the environment in which he finds himself. The individual desiring a new and better assignment is often torn by internal conflicts that arise because he fears the added responsibility of the new position.

Frustration and Performance

As has been pointed out, frustrations may appear when job motives encounter barriers. The individual experiencing frustrations to which he is unable to adapt will usually become emotional, irritable, and inflexible, which will affect his performance. It therefore appears desirable for the supervisor to examine the factors contributing to frustrations and to isolate the common symptoms so that he may recognize them when they are present. He then must set about to eliminate the conditions in the job environment that lead to unnecessary frustrations and work intelligently toward the relief of the consequences when frustrations occur.

If expected earnings are not realized, an employee may feel a lack of economic security, or he may feel personally insecure if he is made to believe that he is inferior to coworkers. If he is frequently criticized by supervisors, if he is not kept informed regarding matters that affect him, if he does not receive adequate training for the job to which he is assigned, if he is not informed where he stands, or if he is not accepted by the group, feelings of emotional insecurity may develop. Appearances of favoritism, inconsistent application of rules and policies, and other reflections of instability in the job environment may also give rise to such feelings.

An individual may become frustrated if he does not receive recognition for his efforts or accomplishments or if he fails to gain expected promotions. He may not understand why this happened because he lacks insight into the reason for his failure, or he may believe that an unfair promotional system was the cause. If he feels a lack of appreciation for his contributions to the entire operation, he may also experience frustration; the same results will be likely if he is not provided with an opportunity for self-expression on the job. Frustration might be brought about by a feeling that his job is too simple for his talents or that his job is boring or monotonous. Failure to give the worker a sense of active participation in the total organizational objectives, a lack of encouragement for him to develop new skills and take on added responsibility, the exercise of excessive dominance over him by his superiors, or their failure to help him gain insight into his shortcomings may contribute to the development of frustration.

Additionally, employees often become frustrated when they are deprived of a feeling of personal dignity as the result of the failure of the supervisor to consider their pride and self-esteem. Excessive, inconsistent, arbitrary, or unduly strict discipline, giving rise to a feeling that they have been stripped of reasonable freedom of action, is often a cause of frustration.

Frustrations connected with the employee's off-the-job life may be reflected in his job performance, and the reverse is also likely to occur. If the employee is subjected to frustrating conditions on the job, he often takes his problems home, with the result that his home life becomes a series of frustrating experiences.

Many organizations have found that family problems are materially reduced by a program in which spouses of new employees are encouraged to meet with representatives of the organization to discuss the social, economic, and psychological restraints the job often places on the worker and his family.[11] Such programs are usually made a part of the initial training program that a new employee attends. However, even the more progressive attempts to help officers and their families cope with job pressures are not totally effective in resolving all the family problems that are bound to exist. In these cases, the supervisor must recognize his limitations; if he concludes that he is not qualified to give the necessary assistance, he should recommend that the employee seek the help of skilled professional counselors.

Unsatisfactory home conditions or social experiences, ill health, unpleasant job conditions, or the inability to maintain a satisfactory standard of living will often have a vital bearing on the way the employee responds to his job. Stability in the home or job environment is likely to help the individual withstand the frustrations in the other.

---

[11] Ellen Kirschman, *I Love a Cop: What Police Families Need to Know* (New York: Guilford Press, 2007), p. 215.

Some Common Reactions to Frustration

Susceptibility to frustration varies with individuals. The threshold level at which frustrations have different effects on behavior is called the "frustration tolerance."[12] The same situations do not cause frustration in all individuals or may cause different degrees of frustration in different people and, consequently, different reactions. The emotionally mature, stable person has fewer frustrations and is more capable of finding a solution to potentially frustrating conditions than is the unstable person with infantile emotional development.

Sometimes the speed with which an individual abandons his attempts to find a solution to a problem or the intensity of his frustration reaction seems to be out of proportion to the apparent cause of the reaction. A sequence of minor events may trigger abnormal behavior, and the individual's frustration tolerance may seem to have disappeared. A simple explanation may or may not be available. The cause may be a sequence of minor frustrations: Perhaps he had little sleep the night before, overslept, missed breakfast, had an argument with his spouse, found no place to park when he arrived at work, and was berated by his supervisor for being late to roll call. Although each incident in itself probably would cause little emotional disturbance, the combination of small incidents may well exceed an individual's threshold of frustration.

Intense frustration might be the result of the blocking of a great desire to attain a goal or the inability of the individual to accept a substitute goal. The nearer the goal when the individual is thwarted in reaching it, the greater the frustration and disappointment, and the greater will be the reaction to it.[13]

Usually, if the cause of the condition is not obvious, it can be uncovered by patient counseling by the alert supervisor. Often the cause can be easily eliminated. The supervisor should realize that things cause less frustration than people because cooperation and understanding are not expected from things. Where frustrations are caused by people, the problem can usually be removed by commonsense action. If two partners are unable to get along, obviously the simple solution might involve determining the nature of the conflict and the reason for it and dissolving the partnership if the conflict cannot be resolved. The supervisor should be constantly aware, however, of the possibility that the apparent cause of conflict may not be the real cause.

Some of the more common reactions to frustrations frequently encountered by the supervisor on the job cannot be prevented because they are spontaneous. Other reactions may be tempered or causes of frustration might be eliminated if the supervisor is alert to the symptoms of conflict.

Aggression

Since human beings cannot remain static for long, they tend to meet frustration with aggression. When the aggressive behavior conflicts with social standards, suppression takes place, but with suppression comes more frustration, and what has been suppressed

---

[12] David H. Jonassen and Barbara L. Grabowski, *Handbook of Individual Differences, Learning and Instruction* (Hillsdale, N.J.: Lawrence Erlbaum Associates, 1993), p. 343.

[13] W. Warner Burke, Dale G. Lake, Jill Waymire Paine, *Organization Change: A Comprehensive Reader* (San Francisco, Calif.: John Wiley & Sons, 2009), p. 345.

will seek expression in some manner.[14] It must be kept in mind, however, that not all aggression is necessarily the product of frustration. Other causes may have contributed. Frustration does not inevitably lead to aggressive action; instead, other reactions may follow.[15] These reactions will be described in the following pages.

Some forms of aggression resulting from frustration are direct and undisguised, and others are indirect and subtle. Hostility may be present with or without physical or verbal attack or noncooperation. Attack or noncooperation may not always be recognized and understood because these responses vary widely in individuals and because often the individual does not attack the barrier directly. Instead, he will often make loaded remarks and accusations, assign blame, or label others.

If anger or hostility is smoldering inside, it may result in sudden or unexpected reactions of a physical, mental, or verbal nature directed at a person or thing.

When a person is afraid to express anger or annoyance outwardly, he often engages in passive hostility symptomized by sullenness, uncommunicativeness, or grumbling. He may carry out the boss's wishes to the letter and to a ridiculous extreme, but the motive is often to make the boss suffer because of his own words. The opening of communication channels might help to reduce these feelings. If the subordinate is made to state his complaint clearly even though what he wants cannot be done, he can at least be made to realize that he has had an opportunity to express himself and that his feelings have been considered. If the supervisor overreacts, he will only reinforce the subordinate's act of complaining.[16]

Talking back, picking arguments, finding fault, name-calling, excessively criticizing, belittling others, and engaging in sarcastic or bossy behavior are examples of direct verbal attacks. Indirect verbal attacks may take place in the form of rumor-spreading activities, uncomplimentary stories and jokes, and disparaging remarks about the object of the attack.[17] Noncooperation may occur in the form of loafing, work slowdowns, sabotage, destruction of property, waste, excessive rest periods, absenteeism, departure from the job before the end of the day, attitude of doing only what is required, failure to help resolve common problems occurring in the work situation, or other acts indicating marginal job interest. Belligerence may be reflected in the "chip on the shoulder" attitude, sullenness, irritability, quarrelsomeness, and so forth. A physical attack on equipment or other physical facilities or even an attack on an individual may be the concomitant result of frustration.

The tendency of the aggressor is to attack the source of the frustration. At times, he is afraid or unable to attack the person he feels is the obstacle, so he vents his anger senselessly on substitute persons or objects because they happen to be convenient. These scapegoats are innocent victims of displaced aggressive acts. For example, a motorist, a minor offender, or an innocent bystander may become the symbol of the frustrating

---

[14] Randy Joe Nelson, *Biology of Aggression* (New York: Oxford University Press, 2006), p. 118.

[15] Robert A. Baron and Deborah R. Richardson, *Human Aggression,* 2nd ed. (New York: Plenum Press, 2004), p. 23.

[16] Pieter J. D. Drenth, Henk Thierry, and C. J. De Wolff, *Handbook of Work and Organizational Psychology: Personnel Psychology* (East Sussex, U.K.: Psychology Press, 2001), p. 191.

[17] Nora Doherty and Marcelas Guyler, *The Essential Guide to Workplace Mediation and Conflict Resolution* (Philadelphia, Penn.: Kogan Page, 2008), p. 158.

barrier and be subjected to verbal or physical attack.[18] Usually, such substitutes are easy objects of aggression because they are often unable to strike back. A citizen, a subordinate, or even a spouse may become the victim of an aggressive act.

At other times, the frustrated individual himself becomes the object of his attack through self-criticism for failure or even self-punishment.[19] He may drink excessively, overwork, worry, engage in self-pity, or develop feelings of guilt. When the attack cannot be directed toward a specific object, the frustrated individual may remain hostile and search for other avenues of escape.

In these attack situations, the individual may become so absorbed in his reaction that he will temporarily forget his original goal. The supervisor may then have considerable difficulty in understanding the motive of the attack and may have even more difficulty in attempting to satisfy the motives of the individual.

Aggression has two main functions. The view generally accepted is that the first of the two functions of aggression involves the extraction of satisfaction from the outside world in the drive toward a goal that is blocked; the second involves a desire to hurt or destroy the source of the pain, those things or persons who are symbols of the barrier.[20] Both motives may require satisfaction before the attack reaction ceases. If the individual receives satisfaction of his attack motives, he may end the attack, but if the initial frustration remains, the attack may recur. In other situations, the attack may continue for some time after the frustration stimuli have been removed. Tests with animals and humans have shown that when a need is thwarted, the frustration that occurs is likely to persist long after the original frustration-producing stimuli have ceased. When gratifying activities are interrupted and not brought to a successful conclusion, the individual is likely to continue the interrupted activity, or to have a desire to do so, long after the interruption, especially when the interruption is threatening to the individual or the desire to achieve the goal is intense.[21] This may explain the intense desire in some individuals to gamble or drink or otherwise indulge in what to them is a pleasant pastime. This may also give rise to a condition wherein the supervisor must engage in follow-up to any corrective action he may be required to take to prevent a recurrence of the unacceptable conduct, but he must do so in a constructive way or his acts may be misinterpreted and only worsen the problem.

If these attack motives are blocked and the person is not able to take aggressive action, he may engage in other substitutes such as noncooperation instead of criticism or a different type of reaction such as rationalization or giving up. In other cases, the individual will repress his aggressive tendencies.

The "pleasure-pain" principle will apply to the amount of control the individual exercises over his behavior. If the pain from punishment he is likely to sustain exceeds his pleasure from the aggressive acts, he will probably discontinue them.

---

[18] Katherine W. Ellison, *Stress and the Police Officer*, 2nd ed. (Springfield, Ill.: Thomas Books, 2004), p. 35.

[19] J. Dollard, N. E. Miller, L. W. Doob, O. H. Mowrer, and R. R. Sears, *Frustration and Aggression* (New Haven, Conn.: Yale University Press, 1939), pp. 44–47.

[20] Robert A. Baron and Deborah R. Richardson, *Human Aggression* (New York: Plenum Press, 2004), p. 23.

[21] Mortimer Ostow, *Spirit, Mind and Brain* (New York: Columbia University Press, 2007), p. 152.

Supervisors should be sensitive to their subordinate's body language, which may be an indicator of the officer's mental state. (© Lisa F. Young/Fotolia)

Attitude of Resignation

When emotional conflicts with their resultant frustrations are frequent or continuous and attack reactions are not available to the individual, he may give up all attempts to satisfy a motive and adopt an attitude of resignation. His hope for a solution will be absent, as will his esprit de corps. Discouragement will often cause bitterness or apathy. The individual will not ordinarily be responsive to praise or criticism, so he must be approached patiently, given renewed hope and self-confidence, and helped with establishing new goals and interests. Sometimes this can be accomplished by giving him added responsibility and an understanding that someone has confidence in him. If his self-esteem is not reestablished, this type of individual often becomes the marginal producer. There are frequently no readily available solutions for such a mental attitude if it involves true resignation; however, the condition may be a temporary one reflecting a depressed state of mind and, as such, can usually be corrected along the lines just discussed. As a last resort, separation of the individual from the service may eventually be in order to preserve the morale of the organization.

Escape

An individual who finds that the efforts needed to fulfill an objective are greater than he desires to make, who faces what appears to him to be an insoluble problem, or who lacks self-confidence in his ability to perform often attempts to escape from his dilemma by physically or mentally withdrawing. If he has a problem the solution to which seems beyond his reach, he will run away from it. He will try to make himself believe that this course of action will relieve his obligation to himself or others for meeting the problem head-on. He may revert to daydreaming or become ill; he may remain absent from his job, ask for a transfer, resign, or just avoid doing the task assigned him. He will often spend more effort avoiding it than he would spend doing it.

Escapism should not be confused with laziness or lack of motivation, wherein the employee will avoid doing what he is supposed to do because he is not inclined to put forth the necessary effort; rather, it is a condition involving a lack of fortitude brought about by any one of a number of factors. If a means can be found to motivate the employee or convince him that it would be to his advantage to face his problem with resolve, it can usually be easily corrected.

Psychosomatic illnesses such as headaches, stomach upsets, or nervous disorders are often caused by anxieties or frustrations. They are not always physically caused illnesses but are nonetheless very real to the individual. Often they are physiological manifestations intimately dependent on the external environment.[22] Often, when the unpleasant external conditions are removed or when the individual is helped to face his problems realistically, the symptoms disappear and his desire to escape ends.

[22] Gordon Edlin and Eric Golanty, *Health and Wellness*, 10th ed. (Sudbury, Mass.: Jones and Bartlett, 2010), pp. 30–32.

Sometimes the individual escapes from frustrating situations by an imaginary accomplishment of his goals. This daydreaming is harmless when it stimulates him to real accomplishment, but it is more often harmful because it is not constructive. It may provide satisfaction without achievement, or it may substitute for action and effort. It usually results only in loss of time.

Excuses and Rationalizations

Sometimes an individual will develop certain defenses in the form of excuses to help save face or preserve his pride and to justify his failure to achieve his goals or fulfill his responsibilities. He will attempt to justify some action he has taken or failed to take. He may attempt to save face by blaming poor tools, improper or no training, deficient education, or some physical factor. He will do almost anything but accept the blame himself. When he assigns such blame to some external object rather than to himself, he is said to have engaged in projection.[23] He may pass the responsibility on to the supervisors, saying that he should have been told of his poor work or how to improve it, or he may try to pass the buck to others, blaming them for his failures. Blaming someone or something else may help him absorb the impact of his failure.

The person may insist that what he wanted and did not get was not important anyway. This "sour grapes" attitude tends to reduce in his mind the importance of the goal and makes the frustration attending the failure easier to endure.

Rationalization is a common reaction to failure. When it causes a person to refuse to assume personal responsibility for anything, it is harmful; when it impairs a person's ability to perceive things as they are and respond to reality, it becomes destructive. It becomes a serious problem when the individual fools himself into believing that his relationships with others are good and that he is carrying out his duties and responsibilities well when, in fact, it is commonly known that neither is true.

This is perhaps one of the most common and one of the most insidious defense mechanisms because it usually cannot be dealt with subtly. Although a direct approach is often indicated, care should be exercised so that it is not so unnecessarily harsh that it will destroy the employee's self-esteem. Occasionally, the individual lacking confidence in himself and not expecting to achieve a goal he has set for himself will manufacture excuses in advance by magnifying all possible difficulties and then really not trying to achieve the goal. Finding excuses may protect him from the effects of frustration to a degree, but it prevents him from facing the situation and making a real effort to solve the problem confronting him. For example, he may attempt to blame a lack of recognition for his efforts on a supervisor's favoritism rather than face the real issue of his own poor work. He is blind to the fact that he is using excuses because he regards them as sound reasoning. The excuses may not be the real reasons for failure, but to him, they are good reasons. The nonperformer is likely to rationalize: "You don't get into trouble for what you don't do, but for what you do." Excuses of this nature are so easily used and their face-saving protection is so satisfying that their use tends to become habitual.

Rationalization practiced by a supervisor is particularly damaging to the organization when he uses it to relieve himself of the necessity of seriously tackling problems that

---

[23] Richard A. Griggs, *Psychology* (New York: Worth Publishers, 2012), p. 294.

are likely to be frustrating. The harm can be incalculable if he blames subordinates for his failures, if he blames the boss for an unpopular order instead of selling such an order to the workers and telling them that he expects it to be carried out, or if he refuses to confront a problem employee because "there's nothing you can do with a person like that." All he feels he can do is hide his head in the sand and hope the problem will go away. Other employees will soon begin to suspect his fortitude. By such failures, the supervisor will place a premium on nonconformance.

Often, these reactions will be combined with others. An individual may give up all attempts to satisfy his motives; in addition, he may mentally withdraw from the situation in an attempt to escape from reality. At other times, he may engage in finding excuses and may at the same time become aggressive (with or without verbal hostility). He may even rationalize his own aggressiveness and blame it on provocation.

Regression

At times, a frustrated individual will abandon problem solving for an immature or even infantile type of regressive action. He may regress to a stage where his problem began or he may revert to earlier, less mature methods of performing his work. Some will weep or revert to infantile temper tantrums; some will develop highly sensitive characteristics. Temperamental outbreaks become frequent with such employees because they develop extremely low frustration tolerance levels. Often, they do not react objectively to criticism and have learned that they may gain their way more often than not by throwing a temper tantrum. Many supervisors will back off rather than undergo the vitriolic attacks and abusive treatment they are often subjected to by this type of individual. Their retreat may be prudent at times but generally will only tend to erode their authority. If their position in the matter is correct and justified, the attack should not deter them from doing what needs to be done. Calmness and common sense are needed at such times.

Regression in a supervisor has particularly damaging effects. It may cause him to depart from his philosophy of firm supervision, which he feels has detracted from his popularity even though it earned him respect in the past. He may retreat to the weaker permissive form of supervision if he can gain ego satisfaction from it, or he may stop delegating work, feeling he has lost confidence in his subordinates.

Immature reaction resulting from regression substitutes for growth and problem-solving ability. The greatest danger, however, is that it lessens a person's adequacy to perform his job.

Adler's psychology assumed that individuals tend to repeat infantile acts when they have found such behavior helpful in achieving their desires.[24] The screaming child seeking gratification of a desire will continue to use this device so long as it achieves results. The weeping employee will weep when results are achieved thereby.

The supervisor can accomplish much practical supervision if he understands Adler's concepts. Regressive reactions may be a means to avoid unacceptable behavior. The individual avoids seeing his emotional conflicts maturely and tries to deal with them

---

[24] Robert Withers, *Controversies in Analytical Psychology* (New York: Brunner-Routledge, 2003), p. 324.

by reverting to infantile behavior. Some display childlike reliance on their supervisor to make decisions that they themselves are perfectly capable of making, and if the supervisor permits them to escape the responsibility that is theirs, he will only contribute further to employees' regressive reactions, which will eventually result in a complete breakdown of normal employment relations.

Fixations

When an individual experiences a fixation, he keeps repeating a response even if it is not effective. His development is arrested and alternative approaches are not tried. For example, if an employee is criticized too severely for the way he performs an operation, he may become "frozen" or fixated in using the wrong method over and over. The individual often becomes inflexible in meeting new situations. His attitudes do not change: They persist despite seemingly conclusive evidence that a contrary attitude would serve him better.

Frustration Prevention

The most obvious means of preventing frustrations arising out of the work environment is the discovery and removal of underlying causes. This is often an extremely difficult task, since the causes may not be readily apparent. Management personnel must recognize that many problems result from the human and physical factors related to the job. Most important, the supervisor should appraise the nature of his relationships with his people: Are his supervisory techniques so flawed that they may be the underlying cause of his subordinates' frustration? Is he arbitrary or capricious with them? Is he impatient and unreasonably demanding of them? Such shortcomings generally can easily be corrected.

The work situation is a fertile source of frustration because it restricts the worker's freedom of action and, at the same time, imposes on him positive demands. He is responsible for meeting performance standards and is also expected to conduct himself in a manner that best serves the needs of the organization, and these dual responsibilities are sometimes incompatible. The law enforcement officer might ask, "How can I do an effective traffic enforcement job and make the motoring public like it and what I stand for?" The demands of selective traffic enforcement, general public welfare, and good public relations are seemingly at odds. The officer feels the pressures from his supervisor if he does not perform his enforcement duties reasonably well; he is more often than not castigated by the errant motorist for a traffic citation and simultaneously often accused of being an "eager beaver" by his fellow officers if his performance records exceed theirs. No wonder he often becomes frustrated.

Stress and tensions arising from the work environment can be reduced significantly by improving supervisory practices. Knowing that frustration reactions tend to be emotional and seemingly pointless at times, the supervisor working toward reduction of frustration-producing situations must recognize the limited value of threats, coercion, arguments, or appeals to logic as means of corrective action when aberrant behavior occurs among his employees. Instead, he will maintain a tolerant, objective, and helpful attitude without retreating to a point of permissiveness. He will keep in touch with employee attitudes and moods so that he may perceive possible causes of frustrations that can and should be remedied and will remove them wherever possible. He will keep channels of communication open with his subordinates and superiors so that pertinent information may flow up, down, and across organizational channels. He should continuously strive to make frustrating situations more acceptable if they cannot be removed.

The supervisor should make every effort to satisfy the motives of his subordinates by helping them develop feelings of security through the process of informing them about matters affecting them and by providing them with means of self-expression. He should keep in mind that the individual who is not well liked or the one who feels inferior or lacks social adjustment may need additional attention to help him in overcoming his sense of insecurity. Extra encouragement and attention to the training of the individual who lacks confidence in his ability may be indicated to help in relieving his feelings of inadequacy. Special effort may be needed to help such individuals achieve a level of performance that conforms at least generally with the group average. When employees are unable to reach this average, they become easily discouraged and frustrated.

Many frustrations can be prevented if the supervisor makes an effort to place his subordinates in the assignments for which they are best suited. Ordinarily, if he does this, the employee will feel more adequate, perform best, and develop fewer frustrations arising out of his job activities. While in these assignments, employees should be empowered to solve problems and make decisions.

Likewise, the supervisor will assist his subordinates greatly in reducing job-connected frustrations if he helps them to establish realistic goals. Fryer stated, "When goals are adopted which are impossible or unreal, frustration is likely, resulting in uncontrolled anger, psychomotor tension, depression, remorse, embarrassment, and sometimes withdrawal from reality and a complete change of personality."[25]

The supervisor is bound to be confronted with many emotional conflicts in his subordinates. He will reduce their effects whenever possible even if he cannot eliminate the conflicts themselves. He will make every effort to provide a work environment in which each employee can satisfy his basic drives in a manner that best comports with organizational objectives.

Relief for Frustration: Some Commonsense Approaches

The supervisor will not always possess the technical ability to provide relief for a frustrating condition—often, he will not even be able to ascertain the cause. However, if he is alert, he may readily recognize symptoms of distressful emotional conflicts. He can then go about taking action to relieve the condition by helping the troubled individual overcome his frustrations or see them in a different light. Studies have indicated that persons are more likely to follow the suggestions of the supervisor if he has demonstrated an ability to help others solve their problems.[26]

---

[25] Douglas H. Fryer, "Motivation and Self-Direction," in *Handbook of Applied Psychology,* ed. Douglas H. Fryer and Edwin Henry (New York: Johnson Reprint Corp., 1969), p. 99.

[26] Gerard Egan, *The Skilled Helper: A Problem Management and Opportunity Development Approach to Helping* (Belmont, Calif.: Brooks/Cole, 2010), p. 69.

If the frustration reaction involves aggression that the individual is unable to suppress because of his deficient control mechanisms, it would seem that relief is most adequately achieved by directing the aggression into harmless channels.[27] The individual may be directed toward constructive activity by means such as a challenge to show others what he can really do, assignment of added responsibilities, or placement in a position that absorbs more of his energy.

The provision of an opportunity for self-expression as an important corrective technique is generally recognized.[28] Patient nondirective counseling wherein the individual is given the opportunity to engage in catharsis by talking out the situation will provide an outlet for reducing his anger, developing some objectivity, and gaining insight into his problems. It will tend to make seemingly intolerable situations tolerable. This often reveals the inconsistencies of his problems and is one of the best means of changing his interpretation of the situation. If he can be encouraged to assume an objective rather than a purely subjective view, frustration can be relieved without permitting expressions that will only worsen the matter.[29] He can usually be made to see the abusive citizen, for example, as a problem that needs to be solved rather than a source that causes frustration. If he can be given some insight into problems such as this, he might be able to change his interpretation of a particular problem by placing himself in the position of the other person. If aggressive behavior is involved, however, the supervisor must avoid indulging it to a point where he is only reinforcing violent behavior.

The supervisor should help relieve his troubled subordinate of frustration by providing an opportunity for the achievement of a feeling of success. If motivation results, the frustration need not be a harmful experience, but if it results in continued failure from trying to make old methods work, the effects can be devastating for the individual. Since frustration is normally associated with goals of some sort, the supervisor should be cautious to avoid action that will be harmful to goal achievements. When an individual gives up his desire to achieve positive constructive goals, he is likely to give up efforts to better himself.

Since sensitivity to frustration is greater during ill health or fatigue, rest or medical attention may be considered at times. Employee Assistance and Stress Reduction programs may also be helpful. If the frustrating conditions produce severe emotional or mental disorders that persist, professional attention might be in order.

Some people tend to pick up a few stray principles of psychology and psychiatry and try to apply them without a basic understanding of human behavior. A little information may be a dangerous thing. It is best, therefore, that the supervisor, in attempting to determine why certain behavior occurs, confine himself to those aspects of the personality that can be readily observed. Even the professional therapist encounters substantial difficulties in analyzing human behavior and determining the cause of many emotional problems. Finding an effective cure seems to be an even more difficult task.

---

[27] Konrad Lorenz, *On Aggression* (London: Routledge, 2002), p. 64.

[28] Maier, *Frustration*, p. 216.

[29] *Ibid.*, p. 107.

Summary

A motive is a conscious or unconscious drive that prompts an individual to take action to achieve a goal. When motives are obstructed, frustration often occurs. The individual usually tries in different ways to solve his problems. If the goal is not important, he may disregard the frustration and forget the matter; if the goal is important, the usual reaction is to go around the obstacle, remove or attack it, or compensate by finding substitute goals to replace the original ones.

Stable, emotionally mature persons are usually capable of meeting normal problems and solving them. The unstable, infantile individual is less able to adjust to problems, has a lower frustration tolerance, and develops a sense of failure, irritation, and emotional inflexibility. His reactions then become a real challenge to his supervisor.

The barriers blocking goals may be external or internal. Physical obstacles, human impediments, and situational factors are some of the external barriers, while internal barriers involve emotional conflicts. Either a single barrier or a combination of obstacles may give rise to frustration.

The individual experiencing frustration who is not capable of adapting to it may develop aggression symptoms. He may attempt to physically attack the person or thing that obstructs the realization of his goal, he may verbally attack the barrier, or he may become noncooperative.

A common reaction to conflict involves hostility on the part of the individual. This reaction may be expressed by aggressive behavior against a person or thing. Either may be the cause of the frustration and become the object of aggression, or some other person or thing may become the scapegoat in the attack. On other occasions, the individual may adopt an attitude of resignation, make a mental or physical withdrawal, or try to rationalize his failures and shortcomings by blaming others. Each of these reactions poses a special problem for the supervisor. He should provide an opportunity for emotional security wherever and by whatever means possible. He should give his subordinates opportunity for self-expression.

Frustrations may best be prevented if the underlying causes are discovered and removed. Threats, arguments, and appeals to reason have limited corrective value in relieving frustration. The supervisor needs to assist his subordinates troubled with frustration by encouraging them to view such conflicts in their true perspective and by helping them to gain objectivity and insight into their problems. He will give each individual an opportunity to vent his feelings through the technique of nondirective counseling. He will assist him in developing attainable goals or subgoals if he has selected unreasonable ones; he may change the subordinate's assignment to give him an opportunity to adjust under more favorable conditions or to regain his emotional stability in a new environment. Rest or medical attention may be indicated in extreme cases. As a last resort, when other efforts have failed to find a workable solution to the individual's conflicts, professional attention may be desirable.

REVIEW

Questions

1. Distinguish among drives, satisfactions, and needs.

2. Define *catharsis,* and explain a simple method by which the supervisor might use it with a subordinate.

3. Discuss some of the reactions that might result from frustration.

4. What are some of the overt manifestations of frustration? How may frustration reactions be covertly expressed?

5. What is the most obvious means of preventing frustration?

6. Discuss some of the means of relieving frustration reactions once they have occurred.

Exercises

1. If you were called on for assistance, explain how you would help an officer's spouse to adjust to his work. What factors would you stress?

2. Assume that one of your subordinates was passed over for promotion when he was at the top of a promotional list and someone below him was appointed. The subordinate becomes extremely frustrated and his work has deteriorated. Explain how you would approach this problem.

8

Special Problems in Counseling and Remediation

Chapter Objectives

This chapter will enable you:

- To become acquainted with the characteristics of common problems that require counseling

- To become familiar with the behavioral effects brought about by these problems

- To gain an understanding of the techniques that can be used to prevent or remedy psychological problems of subordinates

At times, the supervisor must assume the role of counselor to his subordinates when information comes to his attention that they need his help or when they seek it either directly or indirectly. Sometimes his observations reveal that the employee's work is deteriorating. The symptoms may suggest that the employee is troubled with any one or more of a host of personal problems such as those arising from domestic difficulties, a developing physical or psychological illness, excessive drinking, or the use of drugs.

Although the supervisor cannot be expected to administer a program of professional therapy to subordinates with serious emotional problems, he can familiarize himself with the symptoms usually characteristic of these conditions so that he may recognize them and initiate timely and appropriate remedial action. It is in the early stages that most of these disturbances will respond best to treatment. The application of proven techniques of counseling, whether provided by the supervisor, peers, or a professional, is perhaps more essential in such cases than in most other situations involving oral interchanges between persons.

Nature of Problem Drinking

According to the American Council for Drug Education, alcohol dependence is without question the most serious drug problem in the country.[1] It has increased in severity and extent substantially in the last fifty years, with the largest percentage concentrated among males in their most productive years, between

---

[1] Amitava Dasgupta, *The Science of Drinking* (Lanham, Md.: Rowman and Littlefield Publishers, 2011), p. 11.

thirty-one and thirty-four.[2] "The problem has become one of considerable significance to law enforcement agencies in light of the fact that one in four officers may have a problem with alcohol.[3] This is a concern not only from an enforcement standpoint, but also from one involving personnel management." Consequently, many agencies are taking steps to reduce its impact by training supervisors to recognize its common symptoms so that timely corrective action may be taken.

There is insufficient evidence that alcoholism can be attributed to personality predispositions. It must, therefore, be assumed that any predispositions must be associated with other influences, which tend to press one toward alcoholism before addiction occurs.[4]

By its very nature, police work is conducive to problem drinking. It attracts and tends to hold young men and women in the age bracket in which alcoholism is most frequent. According to Swanson, Territo, and Taylor, the stresses inherent in police work, and the commonplace social drinking found in the police culture, create an environment especially conducive to alcoholism.[5] The occupation is very stressful and competitive, with pressures seldom duplicated in other endeavors. If selection procedures are defective or if supervisory controls break down, the characteristics of the job sometimes contribute to the development of excessive drinking.

Stresses associated with a person's job, family, relationships with people, or economic responsibilities may cause confusion, anxiety, insecurity, frustration, unhappiness, or loneliness and often lead the individual to drink to relieve them. Whatever the cause, when drinking develops into a problem, his ability to perform his job becomes impaired. He eventually becomes a major concern to his supervisor because he cannot function effectively as a police employee. In fact, aside from physical and emotional impairment and the poor image an officer portrays to the public when he smells of alcohol or demonstrates some alcohol-induced aberration in connection with his work, he often becomes a downright hazard to himself and his coworkers.

Tests involving speed and precision have revealed that the performance of the problem drinker is considerably reduced in the early stages of alcoholism. As he approaches the middle stage, a progressively greater loss of coordination becomes apparent.[6]

It might be asked, "Does not management share some of the responsibility?" "As the problem develops, not spontaneously but over a considerable period of time, why was remedial action not taken before the problem became aggravated?"

There is usually a threefold answer to these questions. First, the supervisor may not recognize the symptoms of deviant drinking in the early stages because he has not

[2] Donald W. Goodwin, *Alcoholism: The Facts*, 4th ed. (New York: Oxford University Press, 2008).

[3] Robert A. Fox, "The Blue Plague of American Policing," *Law Enforcement News* (May 15–31, 2003), 9.

[4] Goodwin, *Alcoholism*.

[5] Charles R. Swanson, Leonard Territo, and Robert W. Taylor, *Police Administration*, 8th ed. (Upper Saddle River, N.J.: Pearson Prentice Hall, 2011), p. 539.

[6] Keith Weanes and David M. Warburton, "Stress and Drugs," in *Stress and Fatigue in Human Performance*, ed. Robert Hockey (New York: John Wiley & Sons, 1983), pp. 220–22.

been trained to do so. Second, if he does recognize them, he may not care to make an issue of the problem and may thereby tacitly allow it to develop into a major one. He often justifies this failure because he chooses to classify the employee as a "heavy social drinker" rather than a problem drinker bordering on alcoholism. Last, the supervisor may be forced to take disciplinary action because of misconduct by the employee brought about by drinking.

Regardless of how he rationalizes his failures, the supervisor still has an obligation to protect his agency from the needless and expensive loss of what otherwise might have been a highly productive employee. It, therefore, behooves him to familiarize himself with the characteristics of the problem and the options available to him in handling it. He must be able to recognize the difference between the chronic complainer, the hypochondriac, and the person with a psychosomatic disorder as previously described. The supervisor, however, should be aware that certain symptoms that are associated with excessive drinking may also signal the presence of other illnesses besides alcoholism. He will then be in a position to make an appropriate referral to professional medical aid when necessary.

Some practical methods the supervisor might use to cope with the drinking employee are discussed in the following sections.

Development and Symptoms of Problem Drinking

The development of problem drinking will be discussed in the context of psychological, medical, social, or job problems resulting from the condition. Emphasis is placed on those common symptoms any alert supervisor can easily detect. The most prominent are the employee's preoccupation with alcohol, the self-deception "games" he plays in denying a problem or justifying his drinking, his guilt feelings (reflected in many ways), memory lapses, and the anxiety and depression he often suffers.

The medical problems that often accompany problem drinking are legendary. These may extend to any part of the body and usually require medical attention. The social problems are the most troubling for the supervisor; these involve the employee's family, his job, and his relationships with others.

Development of the Problem

As social drinking develops into problem drinking and then into an actual physiological and psychological dependence on alcohol, the individual progresses through several distinct phases. Jellinek and others have categorized these phases into three stages: an early stage, a middle or intermediate stage, and a late or acute stage. Each has its characteristic symptoms.[7] These stages may consume many months or years, with no abrupt transition from one stage to another. The progression often goes unnoticed.

A drinking problem may exist without the affected person being aware of it. The individual's social drinking habits begin to deviate from the usual drinking standards of his associates, or he begins to solve his real or imagined emotional problems or to obtain satisfaction with the aid of alcohol. These reactions place him on the broad road to

---

[7] Peter Myers and Richard Isralowitz, *Alcohol* (Santa Barbara, Calif.: Greenwood, 2011), p. 33.

addiction. He develops a variety of motives for his conduct—excitement, relaxation, increased social ability, an escape from real or imagined problems, a release from pressure, a sense of euphoria, or a simple feeling of well-being.[8] His job, home life, and social life gradually become impaired, and he suffers emotional and physical damage. Finally, he loses his ability to consciously control his drinking once he starts, even though he recognizes its harm.[9] It is then that he is addicted.

Symptoms of the Problem

Problem drinking is exactly what the name implies. In a broad sense, when someone is repeatedly affected adversely by alcohol, he is a problem drinker, regardless how slight or grave the effects are.[10] He may manifest minor symptoms such as a developing tendency toward arguments, tardiness, absenteeism, or frequent hangovers, or he may be involved in more serious breaches such as an arrest for drunken driving or a traffic accident. Typical physical indicators, such as bloodshot eyes, slurred speech, and other symptoms that are readily apparent, especially to peace officers, may demand immediate attention by the supervisor.

Many of the individual's early symptoms of problem drinking go unnoticed by even his closest associates. It is believed by some that the best clue to what is developing is the recurring memory blackout.[11] He may have acted normally and may have been fully conscious, but he cannot remember the following day what happened while he was drinking.

When these symptoms begin to appear in an officer, the supervisor should carefully watch for personality changes. Undue tensions, frequent periods of nervousness or irritability, and temperamental outbursts that did not occur before afford clues that all is not well; attempts to avoid his supervisor while working may also indicate that something is wrong. The development of unusual drinking habits off the job should be a cause for concern.

Growing domestic and financial troubles may also signal a drinking problem. The family usually is vitally affected because personal and financial irresponsibility are often associated with a drinking problem. Disharmony and anxiety within the family are also often concomitant problems.

When the drinker's tolerance for alcohol increases or when he needs several drinks to obtain the effect that one drink gave him before, he is developing the pattern of a drinking problem. It is easily recognizable but is a difficult condition to counter because a considerable tolerance for alcohol has become a prestige factor among certain segments of our society.

The deviant drinker often manages to drink more than others by sneaking drinks now and then, by drinking faster than others, or by supplying others with drinks so that he can conceal the quantity of his own drinking. He may not be an uncontrolled drinker at this point but may begin to rely more and more on alcohol to bolster his tolerance for

---

[8] *Ibid.*

[9] Elizabeth Connell Henderson, *Understanding Addiction* (Jackson, Miss.: University Press of Mississippi, 2000), p. 4.

[10] Raymond Goldberg, *Drugs Across the Spectrum* (Belmont, Calif.: Wadsworth, 2010), p. 128.

[11] *Ibid.,* p. 128.

the pressures he feels. A vicious cycle often occurs: The person with stress and tension takes alcohol to relieve the tension in the early stages; later, when the alcohol produces undesirable effects, more alcohol is taken to counter those effects.[12]

When his drinking patterns are called to his attention, his resentment is symptomatic of his problem. He becomes defensive, usually denying that he has any problem at all.

An extension of problem drinking is alcoholism, in which the individual drinks compulsively—never intending to drink too much but invariably doing so. He can seldom stop on his own accord but must be given assistance because he has lost control of his addiction. At this stage, it is often said that one drink is too many and that one hundred are not enough.

With the approach of the intermediate stage of the disease, the employee's work habits start to deteriorate and absenteeism increases. Usually the supervisor can recognize the clues if he is familiar with them. The employee more and more often leaves his post temporarily, offering lame or unusual excuses for his absence. Lunchtime drinking, mood changes after lunch, and loud talking are behavioral signs reported by alcoholic officers and their supervisors.[13] The quantity and quality of his work are lower, and his hangover symptoms and bleary eyes become more evident. "Sick" patterns begin to develop. These might be uncovered by close examination of a calendar prepared to show his "sick" record over a period of several years. Recurrent inadequately explained absences following pay-days or a series of days off when other officers usually return to duty may reveal to the supervisor that he should be alert for other symptoms that might suggest a developing drinking problem.

Gradually, with the continuation of his drinking, the employee loses control over his drinking behavior. His insistence, if he talks about it at all, that he can stop drinking any time he wants to grows more and more obvious. In many cases, he constantly hopes secretly that some miracle will happen to help him out of his dilemma.

As his loss of control develops, he may begin to lie about his drinking, denying it when it is perfectly obvious to others. He is prone to develop one or more of three defense mechanisms: denial, wherein he denies using alcohol or claims that he can take it or leave it alone; rationalization, wherein he denies the existence of any problem; and projection, wherein he projects the blame for his problem (if he admits he has one) onto other people or things, such as work pressures, a nagging spouse, or financial difficulties.[14] He rationalizes "taking a belt" to settle himself down after a particularly stressful day, he may make excuses for his recurrent hangovers, or he often claims that some other chronic health problem is the cause, often misquoting his doctor.

He becomes a real supervisory headache because an inordinate amount of the supervisor's time must be devoted to him. The instances of his calling in sick without advance

---

[12] Mark Edmund Rose and Cheryl J. Cherpitel, *Alcohol: It's History, Pharmacology and Treatment* (Center City, Minn.: Hazelden Foundation, 2011), p. 63.

[13] Clive Tobutt, *Alcohol at Work: Managing Alcohol Problems and Issues in the Workplace* (Burlington, Vt.: Gower Publishing Company, 2011), p. 62.

[14] Harold E. Doweiko, *Concepts of Chemical Dependency*, 8th ed. (Belmont, Calif.: Brooks/Cole, 2012), p. 349.

notice increase and require more and more last-minute changes in work schedules. He becomes a threat and an annoyance.

If his supervisors reject him because of his problem or do not understand it, he may withdraw and turn increasingly to alcohol. His tendency to brood in isolation usually grows. He may isolate himself from others, even to the point of antisocial behavior.

He starts forcing the supervisor's hand. Some supervisors will give him warning after warning but will do little else in these initial episodes. The employee is apt to become aggressive, and his conduct may become offensive with colleagues and the public, increasing complaints against him. Other officers may refuse to work with him or may protest when assigned to do so. When they are pressed for the reason, they will often become evasive, fearing criticism for "snitching" on him or for allowing him to drink on duty. Accidents and fighting off the job are clues that should not be overlooked, especially when they occur repeatedly. Such acts are common with the problem drinker.[15]

He may try to gain control over his drinking by setting a limit on when, how much, and what types of liquor he can drink. In reality, he is making the management of his drinking a central concern of his waking hours.[16] Much of his productive work seems to be governed by his desire for a drink.

The intermediate or middle stage of a developing drinking problem is a critical period for him. Deceiving others, especially his supervisors and associates, about his drinking becomes common for him. If decisive action is taken when it is evident that a drinking problem is developing and is impairing his performance on the job, some highly desirable results can usually be attained. However, if the supervisor delays because of vacillation and indecisiveness, and if the little help offered is given grudgingly, the employee will probably continue on to the acute third stage.

Physical deterioration often sets in during the third stage. The entire spectrum of the employee's drinking behavior becomes increasingly more aggravated until he is physically and psychologically dependent on alcohol and becomes totally unsuited for the demands of police service. If it is at this time that severe negative corrective action is first deemed necessary, then the employee invariably becomes a total loss to the organization, through either a long-term suspension or a permanent separation from the service. When positive corrective action has been delayed until this stage, even if it is desirable to treat the person rather than punish him, the probabilities of restoring him to full productive capacity are greatly limited.

Some Options in Treating the Problem Drinker

Supervisors should be aware that drug and alcohol addiction is covered under the provisions of the Americans with Disabilities Act (ADA). When dealing with employees whom you suspect of having possible drug or alcohol problems, it's a good idea to consult with

---

[15] Frederick Rotgers, Marc F. Kern, and Rudy Hoeltzel, *Responsible Drinking: A Modern Management Approach for Problem Drinkers* (Oakland, Calif.: New Harbinger Publications, 2002), pp. 15–16.

[16] Albert Bandura, *Self-Efficacy: The Exercise of Control* (New York: W.H. Freeman and Company, 1997), p. 292.

your personnel or human resources department. This doesn't mean you can't act right away. You can if it's necessary. Those addicted to drugs and alcohol are a potential danger to themselves and others. The ADA doesn't stop the supervisor from acting on performance concerns. It does, however, grant confidential status to diagnosis, treatment, and record keeping.[17]

Like any disease, problem drinking is more easily corrected in its early stages than when it becomes acute. The emotional problems associated with it are usually exceedingly difficult to reverse at the last stage, and physiological harm may be irreversible.

When drinking adversely affects the employee's performance on the job or when his resultant misconduct off the job cannot be tolerated, punitive action may be indicated. Negative disciplinary action for substantive violations of rules or regulations is ordinarily taken, following established procedures. However, this is not the sole recourse for the supervisor. Treatment is a much more positive course if the employee can be persuaded that he needs it. Sometimes, punishment brings him to this realization, but if punishment or persuasion fails to do this, his separation from the organization may become necessary. Termination is stage four in alcoholism.[18] When this happens, everyone suffers—the employee, his family, his friends, his colleagues, and the organization.

Off-the-Job Problem Drinking

The problem of the police employee whose deviant drinking behavior has not yet directly involved his job but is a matter of common knowledge may become a distressing experience for the supervisor. He is often torn between hoping the problem will correct itself and becoming involved in what many say is the employee's private matter.

Unfortunately, the supervisor will rarely be sought out for help by an employee who believes he has an incipient or actual drinking problem. Such help may be solicited by a spouse, another member of the family, or a close friend, but usually only after the drinking has been going on for some time. Sometimes, a partner or colleague recognizes what is happening and calls it to the supervisor's attention. Invariably, there are many subtle indicators of what is happening—even in the early stages of problem drinking—but the supervisor must be alert for them and must develop the capacity to recognize them when they are present.

When counseling by the supervisor or intervention by a close friend is not practicable, the employee might be directed to secure a medical examination from the organization's physician. Professional help then becomes involved. If the physician is given full details, he is in a position to recommend further referral to a professional counselor or an agency specializing in such cases; however, the critical objective of convincing the employee that he needs outside help is usually exceedingly difficult to achieve. Shearer theorized that officers are reluctant to access psychological services for fear of being stigmatized and losing promotional opportunities or even their jobs.[19]

---

[17] Gerald W. Garner, *Common Sense Police Supervision* (Springfield, Ill.: Charles C. Thomas Publications, 2008), p.135–36.

[18] Jack Halloran, *Supervision: The Art of Management* (Englewood Cliffs, N.J.: Prentice Hall, 1981), p. 341.

[19] David J. Thomas, *Police Psychology* (Santa Barbara, Calif.: Praeger, 2011).

The problem drinker will usually deny to others and to himself that he has a problem, especially during the early stages of the disease. He will seldom believe that he needs help to solve a problem he does not acknowledge. In fact, the most significant hurdle to overcome in the whole corrective cycle is that of bringing him to a realization that he has a problem and needs someone to help him resolve it. This is usually a more important step than the treatment itself because he will never seek treatment until he is ready to admit that he needs it.[20]

He will often resist any attempt by the organization to interfere in his private affairs. Although such resistance may be passive, he may not accept aid even if it is forced on him. The organization may then find it necessary to withhold action until the employee's drinking behavior causes his performance to deteriorate or results in an incident that requires disciplinary action.

Indirect Solicitation for Help

Sometimes, a trivial, seemingly unrelated question or problem will be used by an employee as an excuse for seeking help when he has a deep-seated anxiety brought about by excessive use of alcohol. It is not necessarily true that he must hit bottom before he realizes that he needs help—many persons reach this conclusion long before they reach the acute stage of alcoholism.[21] Under these conditions, much of the problem is solved because the employee can be helped effectively when he wants to be. Guiding him toward appropriate help is then a relatively simple task.

Job-Related Problem Drinking

When problem drinking causes the employee's job performance to deteriorate or results in misconduct that justifies negative disciplinary action, the supervisor is obligated to take action. Sometimes, several other drinking-connected incidents have occurred, although a written record may or may not have been made of what specific action was taken. The supervisor must recognize that the longer he waits, the less likely will be the chance of constructive behavior changes.

A decision must be made: Will the matter be treated as an illness and the employee retained (with or without punishment) and given an opportunity to correct the problem, or will it be handled solely as a dereliction of duty, calling for punitive action? If discharge is indicated, the supervisor's immediate problem is resolved, although such severe action might have been avoided had something been done earlier to remedy the problem.

If the course of action involves retention and treatment, the impact of what has occurred must be brought forcefully to the employee's attention. It is most important that corrective action be initiated before he becomes so deeply involved in further drinking-induced derelictions that he must be terminated. The authors have experienced numerous cases in which employees terminated for unacceptable behavior brought about by a drinking problem have indicated that they would not have lost their jobs had their supervisor "knocked their ears down" when the problem first became evident.

---

[20] Edward C. Donovan, "The Boston Stress Program," *The Police Chief*, 52, No. 2 (February 1985), 38–39.

[21] Frederick Rotgers and Beth Arburn Davis, *Treating Alcohol Problems* (Hoboken, N.J.: John Wiley & Sons, 2006), pp. 49–50.

Disciplining a subordinate for derelictions resulting from a drinking problem is not necessarily incompatible with efforts to treat the condition. Sometimes, punishment applied to preserve organizational integrity brings about the crisis needed to make the employee realize that his job is at stake. In such cases, the reason for punitive action should be made clear to him at the outset, and he should be told what is expected of him in unmistakable terms. It is then up to him to live up to those expectations.[22] These situations often present an opportunity for the employee to voluntarily seek help for his condition. He needs to be guided toward the recognition of his problem and the realization that he needs help to overcome it. If this cannot be done because he refuses to acknowledge that a problem exists, it is unlikely that much will be accomplished by way of real treatment.

Drinking and Deteriorating Job Performance

Just as in the case of other misconduct brought about by the use of alcohol, when drinking causes an employee's work to deteriorate or drop to an unacceptable level, the supervisor is responsible for corrective action. Deteriorating performance has revealed many cases of early and intermediate stages of alcoholism before other visible or physical symptoms of the disease have appeared. If such a condition is ignored, it is unlikely to become better through the employee's efforts alone; it probably will only become worse. "Economic loss through increased absenteeism, interpersonal problems, errors of judgment and safety, increased discrimination and harassment complaints, and a reduction in employee morale are bound to follow."[23]

Careful documentation of specific instances of unsatisfactory performance should be prepared promptly when they are observed by the supervisor. These are the bases for corrective action needed when an employee's performance becomes unacceptable because of substantive misconduct. Facts indicating the cause of the deteriorating performance should be recorded, with observation for symptoms of excessive drinking in that connection being especially desirable.

Counseling for the Problem Drinker

The A-DIME problem-solving method, appropriate for a wide range of performance problems, may be used when counseling the problem drinker (see Table 8-1).

The supervisor should gain an understanding of the problems of deviant drinking and must accept the objectives of his role in dealing with it if he is to effectively counsel the employee. If he does not accept problem drinking as a treatable condition but looks on it only as misbehavior meriting punitive action because the employee lacks willpower and moral responsibility, such an attitude will hinder any effort to resolve the matter.

---

[22] Stewart Liff, *Managing Government Employees: How to Motivate Your People, Deal with Difficult Issues and Achieve Tangible Results* (New York: American Management Association, 2007), p. 82.

[23] Audrey J. Aronsohn, "Substance Abuse: Is Your Company's Policy Up-to-Date?" *Loss Prevention and Security Journal* (June 2003), 34–35.

Table 8-1
A-DIME Problem-Solving Method

A	Analysis	Review all relevant information and documentation; verify problem areas; review options
D	Develop a Plan	Meet with employee; gain input; generate strategies; discuss consequences; set goals and timelines; end on positive note
I	Implement	Initiate action plan; remind employee of your availability
M	Monitor	Hold follow-up meetings with employee; compare progress to goals; make course corrections as needed; document
E	Evaluate	Assess performance improvement; document progress; commend and praise improvement; institute positive progressive discipline for failure as agreed

Source: Jeffry Bernstein, *Situational Management and Supervision of Chicago Police Training Manual* (Davie, Fla.: Bernstein & Associates, 2006), Section 2, p. 11.

Every supervisor can gain an adequate working knowledge of such problems and how he can best handle them by studying the literature and by becoming familiar with departmental resources and referral agencies in the community. The important factor in a supervisor's ability to counsel well is his capacity to recognize a drinking problem and to know not only when he is not equipped to handle it but also where the person can be referred for the type of help he needs.

Preliminary Action

As with other interviewing situations, the supervisor should familiarize himself with all pertinent facts available concerning the employee. He should review the employee's personnel file, attendance records, performance evaluations, and his disciplinary history. Proper preparation for the counseling session is critical. By guiding the problem drinker toward a realization that he has a drinking problem, that he needs help in solving it, and that he cannot otherwise maintain an acceptable capacity for his work, the first step may be taken in a course of treatment.

Counseling Sessions

At the earliest practicable time after the supervisor has noted a deterioration in a subordinate's performance, he should discuss the matter with him, with the objective of helping the employee improve. The circumstances of each case will dictate what specific action may be needed to bring this about. The existence of symptoms of excessive drinking concurrent with worsening performance may suggest the approach to be taken.

The interview should be held in private, as is any progress interview. Sufficient time should be allotted to preliminarily explore the matter and establish a satisfactory basis for future sessions. It should be anticipated that several sessions may be required to lead the subordinate to an understanding of his problem (several short sessions may be more desirable and effective than fewer longer sessions in giving the employee an opportunity to reflect in more detail on what took place in the short sessions). Although the supervisor may conclude quite accurately what the problem is, telling the person involved might be precisely what ought *not* to be done. The supervisor cannot be expected to make a medical diagnosis of the condition, nor should he try—that is a function of the professional. However, some notably successful results have been achieved by lay counselors.[24]

All the interviewing techniques at the supervisor's command should be used to make the session most constructive. Prior to discussing performance concerns, the supervisor should develop a rapport with the counseled employee. A short ice-breaking period is appropriate. The initial discussion might be on an area of interest for the employee. A positive tone should be set at the beginning. A transition can then be made to the purpose of the meeting. For example, "John, the purpose of the meeting today is to review some concerns that I have in regards to your performance." The initial conversation should ordinarily be directed toward the subordinate's performance rather than toward him as an individual. Although he may be resentful of having his performance challenged, if the supervisor exhibits a sincere desire to be of help and encourages the subordinate to talk about what he thinks is interfering with his work, resentment and hostility will begin to disappear. If the supervisor talks at the right time without irritation, anger, or reproach and without any appearance of judgment, he will help the person see himself as he is.

Being attentive to what is said, looking at the problem from the employee's point of view, and establishing a comfortable relationship during the session are the three basic ingredients in effective counseling.[25] The supervisor should actively listen without shock or surprise while encouraging the employee to express his feelings, no matter how embarrassing they may be.

The technique of nondirective or employee-centered counseling, in which the supervisor stimulates the individual to discover his own problem and decide on a course of action to correct it, has been found to be extremely productive. It may not accomplish everything that can be done, but it can do no harm so long as it doesn't become abrasive. The person is more apt to respond to a solution he works out for himself than to one the supervisor works out for him.

It's important to get the employee actively involved in the discussion. What is his assessment of the problem? How does he think it can best be addressed? By following this procedure, the supervisor can avoid giving advice or opinions, diagnosing the problem, and directing the subordinate in solving it; rather, interest can be focused on how to help him gain insight into his problem.[26] The supervisor should guide the employee discussion while making it clear that he will not tolerate substandard performance. The text might go something like this: "John, you and I have worked together for many years. You have always been an excellent officer. However, over the last three months, I have noticed a

---

[24] Donovan, "The Boston Stress Program," p. 39.

[25] Charles Truax and Robert Carkhaff, *Toward Effective Counseling and Psychotherapy: Training and Practice* (Piscataway, N.J.: Transaction Publishers, 2008), p. 110.

[26] Gene Hawes and Anderson Hawes, *Addiction-Free: How to Help an Alcoholic or Addict Get Started on Recovery* (New York: St. Martin's Press, 2003), p. 128.

decline in your job performance. I'm concerned about you. Help me to understand why that has happened." This type of dialogue should help to get the employee actively engaged in the discussion. Once the employee has explained and the supervisor has addressed the performance issues point by point, an agreement should be reached on a performance improvement plan. The supervisor should not attempt to interpret everything that is said, however; he should listen and ask the right questions without talking about the alcohol problem until after the subordinate "discovers" it himself.

Simply restating in question form what has been said will force the subordinate to reflect and gradually move toward a clarification of his own problems. It will tend to bring him to a point where he realizes that something is wrong.

Questions should not be overused, as they tend to absorb too much of the subject's attention, and they should not be asked in a manner that will incite anger, fear, or suspicion instead of cooperation. Questions of an accusatory nature may defeat their purpose. They may appear to be innocuous enough but may imply an accusation that will be resented. For example, a question such as "Did that [act] give you a guilty feeling?" rather than "How did you feel afterward?" may undo much that has been done to establish rapport because it might imply some wrongdoing. Properly phrased questions are useful for encouraging the subject to talk. They should also be used to obtain information or to lead the conversation toward matters that are more pertinent.[27]

Criticizing, censuring, belittling, moralizing, or degrading the employee or telling him how low he has sunk will do no good. These actions will only cause him to lose face and contribute to his resentment; he will then resist help even more. Such conduct on the part of the supervisor will often have a fatal effect on the chances of persuading him to do something on his own accord to correct his problem.

It is important that the employee's ego be preserved because he cannot be helped until he wants to be. He must be allowed to make his own evaluation of himself and gain insight into his problem through the process of gentle prompting. It is true that he can be forced to obtain treatment or go through the motions of it, but he cannot be forced into accepting it through fear.

Fear, unfortunately, is used too often in counseling as a prime technique, but rarely does it serve any real constructive purpose in situations involving the problem drinker. There is apprehension enough when he faces his supervisor and knows that his failures are at issue. The supervisor should reduce this fear, not by making assurances (which might be construed as a commitment to overlook the problem) but by asking the employee what the trouble is without challenging everything he says. The greatest need is to bring out the real problem so that a solution can be reached. Fear and accusations will usually result in defensiveness, rationalization, projection, and evasiveness.

Note Taking

Although a record of contact with the employee should be kept, the taking of notes during the counseling sessions should be avoided as this procedure will only contribute to the subject's apprehensions and may aggravate his suspicions and increase his defensiveness.

---

[27] Don C. Locke, Jane E. Myers, and Edwin L. Herr, *The Handbook of Counseling* (Thousand Oaks, Calif.: Sage Publications, 2001), pp. 243–44.

Note taking will also tend to divert the attention of the supervisor and the employee from the real issues.[28] However, as soon as possible after the counseling session, notes should be prepared for the file and for other necessary reports.

Referral

It does not take an alcoholic to treat one any more than it takes a thief to catch one, nor is professional training a prerequisite to success in dealing with the problem drinker; however, a good deal of patience and common sense are needed if the matter is to be handled constructively—patience to weigh the issue objectively and enough common sense to recognize when immediate resources have been exhausted. The supervisor may achieve good results in many cases despite his lack of professional training if he realizes that he does not have all the answers and recognizes when he has exhausted his own resources and those of his organization.

When the employee begins to realize that he has a drinking problem and makes a purposeful effort to help himself find the scientific reasons for it, the supervisor might suggest some appropriate literature or websites on the subject. Then, when the employee begins to understand that he needs to find some way of facing his problems other than with alcohol, it might be suggested to him that he learn about available treatment options. He should then be guided into some positive effort to find appropriate assistance. At a latter point in the employee discussion, the supervisor could always say, "John, I believe you have a personal problem that is contributing to your job performance problem. You said you feel the employee assistance program could benefit you. I believe that if you get the assistance you need you will return to being the fine officer you once were. Let's make the call and the appointment right now." Many employers have excellent employee assistance programs (EAPs)—services provided typically include diagnosis, treatment, and referral. Those in need should be encouraged to contact the EAP. Other resources include medical doctors, peer counseling, clinical psychologists, faith-based counseling, private treatment centers, and Alcoholics Anonymous.

The various chapters of Alcoholics Anonymous usually are the core to any successful referral program. The organization has built an enviable record of success with its program, which extends anonymity, confidentiality, sincerity, and help to those in need.

Objective of Professional Counseling

The important objective of professional counseling is not only to get the problem drinker to give up drinking but also to lead him to the realization that he can never be a moderate drinker and that he can never again use alcohol. Once he has come to this realization and makes a positive effort to do something about it, to find ways of meeting his problems other than with alcohol, the counseling mission has been successfully accomplished.

Emotional and Personal Problems

Every supervisor sometimes will observe a marked behavioral change in a subordinate whose personality has been stable and controlled in the past. This should alert

---

[28] Allen E. Ivey, Mary Bradford Ivey, and Carlos P. Zalaquett, *Intentional Interviewing and Counseling* (Belmont, Calif.: Brooks/Cole, 2010), p. 225.

him that something might be wrong, especially when a number of symptoms occur together. They might be an early sign of the development of a serious emotional disturbance.

Many of the symptoms that may be interpreted as clues to the onset of emotional distress are not necessarily positive indicators of such a condition—they are often transitory in nature and occur in most people from time to time. They may be relatively simple matters to deal with and will often disappear of their own accord, as they may only be reflections of low morale or poor supervisory practices. When such basic causes are corrected, it is remarkable how often the symptoms disappear. Common sense, objectivity, and a large amount of patience, compassion, and understanding are called for in dealing with such conditions. But if the symptoms persist over an extended period, they should be cause for concern, as they may signal the onset of chronic distress.

Psychological Symptoms

Among the most prominent of the psychological indicators that may occur singly or in conjunction with others are uncontrolled emotional outbursts, excessive irritability, excessive altercations with colleagues or the public, loss of self-confidence, loss of job interest, insecurity, hopelessness, frequent short absences from the job, feelings of remorse or guilt or self-pity, loss of ability to concentrate, pessimism, sadness, indecisiveness, sleeplessness, recurrent talk of giving up or quitting the job or committing suicide, withdrawal from others or an inability to get along with them, and feelings of persecution.

Physiological Symptoms

Physiological symptoms such as chronic fatigue or other marked changes in bodily functions range from relatively minor muscle spasms, headaches, upset stomach, and other real or psychosomatic disorders to severe conditions that are life-threatening. The appearance of some of these symptoms may dictate that medical attention should be secured, especially if they are a substantial deviation from the normal physical or mental state of the individual.

Supervisory Role

The supervisor is often the first and most readily available source of help. If he is familiar with these signs and what they may signify, he is in an ideal position to initiate some timely action that will help the employee.

As previously described, there are two occasions when the supervisor is obligated to become involved in a subordinate's personal affairs: when the employee asks for help (in which case his problem becomes the supervisor's also), and when the problem has affected the subordinate's performance. Sometimes, however, there is a reluctance on the supervisor's part to add to the burden of an individual who is already suffering from personal problems. The easiest alternative may be to do nothing. In such cases, the supervisor may find it easy to rationalize his inaction and continue to do nothing, or he may react by becoming exasperated and irritated because he must divert attention from his own affairs to the subordinate. As a consequence, he may take arbitrary punitive action of one form or another against the employee for the slightest infraction and end up causing a problem worse than the original one.

There are those who contend that job-related stress in an employee is only a reflection of the worker's indolence or is downright malingering. With the alarming increase in pensions granted because of job-related stress, it is understandable that such a conclusion is often drawn. As a matter of fact, the stressed employee frequently exhibits characteristics that are likely to be interpreted as indolence, laziness, disloyalty, hostility, and the like, but there is substantial evidence that stress is sometimes disabling. The supervisor, therefore, should not be too hasty about concluding that the existence of these symptoms is merely an indication of an employee's inherent dislike of work but should look at his own brand of supervision and those factors within the organization that might be the real culprits in causing undue stress. If it reasonably appears that this is the case, he should objectively think through how he might have contributed to the condition and take or recommend what remedial action seems appropriate.

At times, the supervisor may not even recognize that something is wrong because he has not been trained to do so or has not bothered to familiarize himself with the signs, or if he observes that an employee has developed symptoms of frustration, insecurity, hostility toward management, or other emotional problems, he may know that something is wrong but can do little to help because he has not prepared himself to cope with even the simplest of these problems. Perhaps the supervisor is prone to classifying persons with such problems as disturbed or difficult and shrugging off his responsibility to do more, not realizing that if their attitudes can be changed so that their tensions are reduced through counseling, the entire organization will profit.

Sometimes, the emotional problems the supervisor is faced with are extremely complex and beyond his capacity to resolve. He must, therefore, learn to recognize his limitations and know when referral to professional help should be made.

Counseling for the Emotionally Troubled Subordinate

Although certain techniques are common to all types of counseling, each has its own characteristics, depending on the objectives to be accomplished. If these techniques are applied with forbearance and understanding, the supervisor might find them useful on occasion in helping to prevent a troubled employee from becoming emotionally disabled.

When a subordinate with an emotional problem approaches the supervisor for help, the supervisor's first objective should be to examine the basic difficulties to determine if the employee has come to the right person. When the symptoms indicate a deep-seated psychosis or other serious emotional problem, professional help would be indicated. Additionally, if the supervisor believes the employee may be a danger to himself or others, a psychological fitness for duty evaluation would be appropriate. Most departments have an order, policy, or procedure that indicates the steps to be taken.

Often, however, the matter is a simple one and can be solved with ease. Any competent supervisor with a little patience and empathy can give help to an employee who has a concern that has caused some emotional stress and anxiety. By simply making himself available and actively listening to the employee, the employee and the agency both benefit. This type of case involves the simple matter of encouraging the employee to examine the true facts so that he can recognize they are not necessarily what he has interpreted them to be.

As with other counseling situations, some persons unravel their problems quickly, while others will take considerable time before they come to that point. A considerable amount of patience is needed if the supervisor is to come to grips with the true problem.

In those cases where the supervisor has brought up the matter because the subordinate's performance has been apparently affected by some emotional problem, the employee might feel offended that the matter has even been brought up. He may become evasive, devious, and noncommittal. He may ask a hypothetical question (usually about a friend, seldom about himself) that calls for an answer to his own dilemma. The wise supervisor will see through this ruse and will quickly be able to arrive at the core of the matter by sifting fact from fiction. He should not allow his attention to be distracted by this common tactic and should keep his focus on what his work expectations are.

It can reasonably be expected that a subordinate will do something about conditions that adversely affect his performance. If he is given an opportunity to talk, he can be helped to realize that there is something wrong that can be corrected. The processes of nondirective counseling and reflective thinking, coupled with patient listening, are useful in bringing this about.

At the close of the session, the subordinate should be given an opportunity to summarize the conclusions he has reached about the problem and the course of action he has decided to take. A definite commitment to execute the solution decided on should be obtained so that the employee will not continue aimlessly as before. A further session or two might be needed in helping him to resolve the problem. If some degree of improvement is not achieved by this time, however, referral to an EAP, professional counselor, a physician, an organizational peer group (if available), or a religious organization might be indicated.

The process of referral need not be a traumatic experience for the employee, but the need should be sold to him. The explanation that to receive help from a professional counselor is the same as accepting help from any other professional might help make the thought easier for him to accept. The supervisor should then assist him to obtain the most appropriate help available. There are a number of excellent resources available. Referral to an EAP is a great start. The police psychologist, clergy, peer support groups, hotlines, Alcoholics Anonymous, Narcotics Anonymous, and Gamblers Anonymous are also good resources.

Management and Remediation of Emotional Distress

The following discussion relates to some specific problems the supervisor frequently encounters and some commonsense solutions that he will find helpful as a lay counselor.

Occupational Stress

Excessive job stress, or that resulting from personal frustration and inadequate coping skills, is referred to as "burnout."[29] This psychological condition is also referred to as

---

[29] Phillip J. Dewe, Michael P. O'Droscoll, and Cary L. Cooper, *Coping with Work Stress* (Hoboken, N.J.: John Wiley & Sons, 2010), p. 76.

BOSS (burnout stress syndrome). It has been found to be involved in the whole gamut of physical, emotional, spiritual, intellectual, and interpersonal exhaustion and is commonly associated with alcoholism, all sorts of mental illnesses, drug problems, suicide, and marital conflict.[30] It results from both work-related and organizational factors.

Police work is one of the most stressful occupations. It may be tedious and boring or filled with excitement and danger. This characteristic, coupled with the irregular working hours and the unusual types of persons officers must deal with, contributes to job stress. The requirements of the profession force officers to develop a lifestyle different from what they have been accustomed to. Sometimes they are faced with problems of adapting to a work environment containing a subculture or ethnic group different from their own; also they must resolve troubling conflicts between their personal lives and official responsibilities. Too much criticism and too little praise may bring on a feeling of stress and depression in some, causing them to isolate themselves increasingly from a society that seemingly does not recognize or appreciate the true worth of police service.

It has been found that organizational factors involving what are perceived as poor or inadequate supervisory practices have been a major cause of employee burnout.[31] Lack of administrative support, inadequate equipment, and an unjust disciplinary system contribute greatly to frustration and job stress. Crank and Caldero found that organizational stressors top the list of sources of stress, regardless of an officer's rank, assignment, or area of service.[32]

Some persons manage these stressors well because they learn to develop a philosophy that they cannot cure all the evils of society or their profession and that emotional involvement will not help but will only make matters worse. Others react emotionally, and often negatively, to factors that cause stress. If these factors are present over a prolonged period, they will often result in chronic distress, which frequently causes those afflicted to regress because their psychological growth regresses. They often become more immature and react in a childlike manner in their relationships with others (as described in Chapter 7). Sometimes the distress is converted into a defense mechanism, causing the officer to become insensitive to the human misery with which he must deal; as a result, he is likely to become callous to the pain he causes others. The controls he might have developed are no longer effective.[33] He then becomes a risk to his organization and a problem for his supervisor.

---

[30] D. Bracy, "Police Stress—The American Response," *England Police Journal*, 50, No. 4 (July–September 1979), 263; F. Barry Schreiber and Jack Seitzinger, "The Stress Pressure Cooker: A Comprehensive Model of Stress Management," *The Police Chief*, 52, No. 2 (February 1985), 40–49; J. T. Reese, "Life in the High-Speed Lane: Managing Police Burnout," *The Police Chief*, 41, No. 6 (June 1982), 49–53; Whiton Stewart Paine, *Job Stress and Burnout* (Beverly Hills, Calif.: Sage, 1982), pp. 11–13.

[31] Richard L. Daft and Dorothy Marcic, *Understanding Management* (Mason, Ohio: South-Western, 2011), p. 358.

[32] John P. Crank and Michael A. Caldero, *Police Ethics: The Corruption of the Noble Cause*, 3rd ed. (Burlington, Mass.: Elsevier, 2010).

[33] Laurence Miller, *Practical Police Psychology: Stress Management and Crisis Intervention for Law Enforcement* (Springfield, Ill.: Thomas Books, 2006), p. 89.

Every supervisor should be alert for indications of such emotional and physical changes that cause a deterioration in the performance and interrelationships of his subordinates. Often, his help is solicited by the affected employee who is experiencing psychological problems but who avoids seeking professional help because he thinks to do so would be a reflection on his capacity for police work. The employee's immediate supervisor may be instrumental in giving the help he needs. Obviously, the condition cannot be ignored, and it will not be solved merely by transferring him because usually this will only shift the matter to another supervisor. Termination might eventually occur if nothing is done to correct the existing problem and to salvage a valuable human resource.

Disability retirement, however, is a brain drain on the system and accomplishes little for the organization and employee. Efforts to rehabilitate the employee are, therefore, the most reasonable alternative. The affected employee should be given an opportunity to talk about his problem in the process of catharsis (as discussed in Chapter 7). During the process of explaining his feelings, he should be provided an opportunity to do so in a nonjudgmental atmosphere. He should feel that he has his counselor's full support and understanding. If he does not feel that he has such genuine support, little is likely to be accomplished. In conveying this appearance, the counselor must utilize all the positive listening skills at his disposal.

Once the problem has been fully explored, the supervisor should assess whether it is so severe that it is beyond his capacity to resolve. If so, measures should be taken to refer the involved employee to professional help.[34] Sometimes, however, as previously stated, a sincere and patient manner, a friendly ear, and a few helpful suggestions by the supervisor are all that is needed.

The second phase of the counseling procedure involves an assessment by the counselor of the problems presented. These should be summarized so that the employee clearly understands what they are. The various courses of remedial action available should then be explored. There are a number of proven stress reducers that might be recommended. Diet changes may be required to provide balanced nutrition (officers often comment that every meal is breakfast). Shift changes are likely to alter eating habits so drastically that nutritional deficiencies usually result, and these are acute stressors. Physical exercise that causes cardiovascular benefit, such as bicycling, running, and swimming, is readily obtainable, under supervision if needed, in almost any community. Many departments have also initiated wellness programs. These programs are usually beneficial, and involve instruction on proper nutrition, exercise, smoking cessation, and stress management. Periodic retraining, devised to increase the officer's stress tolerance and coping abilities, should be made available by the organization as part of any stress-reducing effort.[35]

Should evidence reveal that other organizational factors discussed in preceding paragraphs are causing unnecessary stress, recommendations should be made by the supervisor to his superiors for corrective action. Under the patient guidance of the supervisor, the employee should be encouraged to select the options he considers will best suit his needs and should then be assisted in every way reasonably possible to accomplish the course of action he has chosen.

---

[34] Marianne Schneider Corey and Gerald Corey, *Becoming a Helper*, 6th ed. (Belmont, Calif.: Brooks/Cole, 2011), p. 24.

[35] See Chapter 4 for a discussion of stress remediation by training.

Depression

Depression may result from even a short exposure to stress and may cause reactions that seriously impair performance. The symptoms may develop from a sense of loss or a threatening situation commonly associated with job pressures, a fear of failure (especially in a competitive occupation), or an overmagnification of the importance of a goal. When these conditions cause a person to become depressed, he usually loses his objectivity and sense of perspective. He tends to give up, to shun diversion that he once enjoyed. He considers himself a failure and may contemplate suicide. Physical symptoms such as heartburn, back pains, stomach trouble, and headaches are common. He may recognize these as stress symptoms or he may not, although almost everyone with whom he associates does.[36] The National Institute on Mental Health reports that serious depression is often masked in men by alcohol or drugs or by the socially acceptable habit of working excessively long hours.[37]

Everyone suffers depression of a transitory nature from time to time. According to one authoritative website, 16 percent of Americans will have (clinical) depression during their lifetime.[38] They do not become depressed because they want to, and in most cases, the passage of time, together with understanding, encouragement, and assurance that all will be well, will eliminate the problem. If the depression lingers, medical attention might be indicated. The physician can usually relieve the problem, but in severe cases where the condition does not respond to medical treatment, psychotherapy may be required.[39]

When a serious, conscientious, sensitive employee with an intense job interest makes what he considers a serious blunder and blows it out of proportion, developing a depressive reaction from his guilt feelings and self-chastisement, his self-esteem can be restored if he is made to realize that the matter was not as serious as it appeared to him. Although mistakes are not to be condoned by the supervisor, the experience gained from an honest unintentional error often more than compensates for the harm caused. The matter may be a constructive learning experience for the employee.

Grief and loneliness brought about by the normal experiences of life may result in depression that may drastically affect performance, but the depression can be lessened if the supervisor reacts with compassion and patience. The mere passage of time usually will bring about a cure. Each day that the person copes with his problem helps him to face the next day with more composure and greater equilibrium.

The employee mourning over the loss of a loved one can be helped if his attention can be diverted from his grief toward some physical activity, especially when his energy and interest can be focused on helping someone else. The person should not be encouraged to take a vacation "to get away from it all" because this will only tend to increase his depressive reactions by focusing his attention more on his own problem than diverting it to something or someone else. Medical attention—sometimes coupled with psychotherapy when severe psychological aberrations are present—usually does much to relieve

---

[36] Brian Luke Seaward, *Managing Stress: Principles and Strategies for Health and Well Being* (Burlington, Mass.: Jones and Bartlett Learning, 2012), p. 24.

[37] www.nimh.nih.gov/publicat/depression.cfm.

[38] http://www.depression.com, accessed July 15, 2012.

[39] Wes Burgess, *The Depression Answer Book* (Naperville, Ill.: Sourcebook, 2009), p. 121.

these conditions, but a good deal of patience, tact, and understanding are required in dealing with such problems.

Suicide Awareness and Prevention

Tragically, too many times suicide becomes the way officers deal with the horrors they have witnessed in the daily performance of their duties, along with internal stressors from their department and external problems in their personal lives. Relationship problems, coupled with alcohol abuse and the accessibility of a firearm, create a recipe for disaster among troubled officers who may view suicide as the only way out. They are in so much pain that they cannot see any other option.[40]

Supervisors are in a unique position to prevent some suicides. All supervisors should be able to recognize risk factors and warning signs and be able to identify the myths and facts about suicide. Additionally, supervisors should be aware of resources and referral options, and understand prevention strategies.[41]

Some of the suicide warning signs of which all supervisors should be aware include:

- Depression
- Previous suicide attempt
- Increase in use of alcoholic beverages
- Overly aggressive or violent behavior
- Any changes in mood or behavior that are out of the ordinary
- Changes in work habits
- Behavioral clues of suicidal thoughts
- Anger or irritability
- Concern expressed by family/friends/colleagues

Supervisors also should be aware of direct and indirect verbal clues, including comments such as:

Direct

I'm going to kill myself.
I wish I were dead.
I'm going to commit suicide.

Indirect

I can't go on any longer.
We all have to say goodbye sometime.
I can't take it anymore.

---

[40] Orlando Ramos, "Police Suicide: Are You at Risk?" *FBI Law Enforcement Bulletin* (May 2010), http://www.fbi.gov/stats-services/publications/law-enforcement-bulletin/May-2010/perspective, accessed May 29, 2012.
[41] N.J. Police Training Commission (NJPTC), "Suicide Awareness and Prevention Training for Law Enforcement Professionals." Curriculum approved by NJPTC, Trenton, N.J., June 2010.

There are a number of myths about suicide. Here are some of the myths, along with the real facts:

- *Myth:* People who talk about suicide won't complete the act. Suicidal officers keep their plans to themselves.
- *Fact:* Most suicidal officers communicate their intent sometime during the week preceding their attempt.
- *Myth:* No one can stop a suicide; it is inevitable.
- *Fact:* If a law enforcement officer in crisis gets the help needed, that officer may never be suicidal again.
- *Myth:* Only experts can prevent suicide.
- *Fact:* Suicide prevention is everyone's business, and anyone can help prevent the tragedy of suicide.
- *Myth:* Confronting an officer about suicide will only make the officer angry, and increase the risk of suicide.
- *Fact:* Asking someone directly about suicidal intent lowers anxiety, opens up communication, and lowers the risk of an impulsive act.

Supervisors need to intervene if they believe an officer is at risk for suicide. Violanti advises that the supervisor should not be afraid to ask the question, "Are you thinking of killing yourself?" Although it's a hard question to ask, it should be done if the warning signs are there. He reports that once the supervisor asks the question, he will actually have brought relief to the person. The employee will feel like, "man, there's somebody out there that finally understands how I feel."[42]

Supervisors need to intervene immediately. The chain of command should be informed, help should be located, and someone should stay with the person. If a supervisor believes that an employee is at significant risk of suicide, immediate professional assessment and treatment are necessary.

In addition to treatment resources already discussed in this chapter, other assessment and treatment resources include:

- Suicide Prevention hotline: 1-800-273-TALK (8255)
- Cop to Cop hotline—telephone counseling: 1-866-COP-2COP (267-2267)
- Medical or mental health evaluation counseling
- Hospital emergency rooms
- Peer counseling

The employee may or may not seek treatment voluntarily. If he is not open to referral, the supervisor will have to initiate the proper departmental psychiatric emergency protocols. This is to ensure the officer's safety, as well as the safety of others.

Family Discord

When burnout occurs and the employee cannot resolve stress on the job, he often transfers it to his home, where it plagues his marital relationship. The resulting discord, in turn, increases the stress, so a vicious cycle results. Job stress may be only a contributing factor to marital problems, or may be the direct cause. However, whatever part it plays, the supervisor must recognize that family discord almost invariably will result in stress that will bring on reactions

---

[42] John M. Violanti, "Suicide Prevention for Cops Starts Here...," *New Jersey Cops Magazine* (May 2012), p. 42.

that frequently affect an individual's performance. Sometimes the reactions can be extremely severe. The affected subordinate may, for a time, give up. He may suffer severe depression, which in time may turn into resentment and anger; in this critical period, the employee might react aggressively toward others, especially the source of his trouble. It is then that the need for help is greatest. The supervisor can help temper the problem by displaying an understanding, warm, friendly, and helpful attitude that will give the subordinate an opportunity to ventilate should he so desire.

A vast array of complex causal factors is usually involved in such conflicts, and the behavior patterns that result are equally varied. In fact, a number of mental health issues are frequently associated with marital difficulties. Such conflicts often involve delicate physical or psychological relational issues between two people. If the supervisor becomes too deeply involved, his position in the matter will become untenable. He may eventually be accused by each (either overtly or covertly) of siding with the other.

When a marital conflict involving a subordinate has become critical and the supervisor's help is sought, he should confine his participation to listening to enough details to indicate whether outside professional help is needed. If it is, he should encourage the employee to seek it and should help him in any way possible.

Cop to cop phone counseling is available 24 hours, 7 days a week.

The supervisor cannot be expected to be a marriage counselor. He can, however, at times start the subordinate on a road toward gaining some insight into his problem and making some progress toward saving his marriage. When a subordinate (especially a youthful one) comes to the supervisor with a job problem related to an incipient marital conflict, he should be encouraged to discuss the matter with his spouse rather than withdraw from the marital relationship. The supervisor should stress the value of such discussions. If they are objective, friendly, and considerate, the discussions can be a wonderful remedy for a failing marriage. The parties themselves can do much to resolve their problems. If the discussions take place in an emotion-charged setting full of anger and hostility, little will be accomplished. Many marriages that have failed might have been saved had the parties made an effort to open and keep open the channels of communications between themselves and to talk about their problems—especially with each other. Often this has the effect of causing each to appreciate more the perspective of the other.

Should the subordinate's problem appear to have developed because he has, without realizing it, allowed his job to become more important than his family life, he should be guided toward a realization that he must not attempt to derive all his satisfactions from his work at the expense of his family relationships. The phenomenon of high job satisfaction is common in police work because of its nature. It is therefore reasonable to expect that marital disharmony might result from this fact on occasion, especially before the police spouse learns to adjust to the conditions surrounding the other's position. The supervisor should be alert to such an eventuality so that he may take preventive action should the need arise. His role is to prevent job-connected problems that might impair the performance of his subordinates without becoming involved in their marital relationships. He can hardly dissuade an employee from enjoying his work, but he can help him reach a balance between it and his marriage.

In some instances, transfer to a less demanding assignment might help. For example, it is commonly known among peace officers that many police spouses have strong objections—although they do not always express them—to assignments such as vice enforcement given to their partners. If the work begins to jeopardize the marital relationship, eventually the marital conflict jeopardizes the employee's performance. If the requirements of the employee's assignment are demanding an unreasonable amount of time, an adjustment might be made in order to correct the condition.

Because of the tremendous emotional impact some marital breaches have on the parties involved, the supervisor should practice a considerable amount of forbearance and understanding of the turmoil experienced by a subordinate; the condition should never be an excuse for misconduct, however. Normally, the depressive reactions brought about by such domestic difficulties are temporary and will correct themselves if given time.

The casket of Ogden police officer Jared Francom is escorted by officers through the Ogden City Cemetery after his funeral in Ogden, Utah.
(© Reuters/George Frey)

Trauma-Producing Incidents

Officers involved in traumatic incidents, such as shootings, severe car accidents, death or injury to a fellow officer, or catastrophic events, sometimes develop rather severe psychological reactions shortly after such occurrences. These reactions can acutely affect their performance and job relationships and usually require some attention so that further aggravation can be minimized. Posttraumatic stress disorder is often reflected by feelings of isolation, flashbacks, sleeplessness, anxiety, and a loss of work interest, causing a deterioration in performance.[43] When these symptoms begin to appear (usually soon after the incident), the supervisor is obliged to take remedial action. Many police departments have organized employee assistance programs that have been used effectively in such matters. Coworkers who have experienced similar traumas as well as supervisors can be of great help in providing the involved officer with an opportunity to vent his feelings.

---

[43] *Diagnostic and Statistical Manual of Mental Disorders*, 4th ed. (American Psychiatric Association, 2000), p. 467.

Peer counseling programs, such as the Critical Incident Stress Management Program, have also been very successful in helping officers involved in shootings and other highly traumatic incidents.[44] Supervisors should be aware of such resources so they can refer their officers to effective confidential counseling.

Most progressive departments have a mandatory critical incident stress debriefing process. This is the right thing to do and is typically policy. Additionally, patient listening is the key to catharsis, and several sessions may be necessary to accomplish positive results.[45] Steps should also be taken, as appropriate, to allow the officer to resume his job gradually at a reasonable speed. Such simple procedures can achieve remarkable results in relieving stress in affected officers.

In this phase of the remediation procedure, it is essential that supervisors convey to the troubled subordinate a feeling that he can discuss the matter freely. The techniques of active listening (as described in Chapter 6) should be followed. This will tend to develop rapport with the affected employee and is essential in convincing him that the supervisor is ready and willing to help. In the event that professional assistance (the counsel of a psychologist or psychiatrist) appears necessary, the supervisor should be prepared to report this observation upward in a timely fashion so that an appropriate referral can be made.

SUMMARY

Alcoholism, as the most serious drug problem in the nation, involves nearly 17.6 million persons. Most of these persons are in the age group that encompasses the most productive years. The problem has become one of considerable significance to law enforcement because the occupation attracts and holds the type of person often affected and contains the stresses that tend to move a person toward alcohol addiction.

As the social drinker develops into a problem drinker, he commonly progresses through three distinct phases—early, middle, and acute stages—each with its characteristic symptoms. It is believed that recurrent memory blackout is the most significant symptom of the start of problem drinking, although other symptoms, such as the presence of frequent hangovers, absenteeism, and unusual drinking habits off the job, tend to support the conclusion that the person is in the early stages of addiction. Work performance begins to deteriorate in the second stage. He begins to lie about his drinking and denies it when it is perfectly obvious to others. As his denials become stronger, he begins to rationalize his drinking; then he starts to blame his habit on others. He begins to become a real supervisory problem as he turns more and more to alcohol. In the third stage, a physical deterioration begins to set in, and the employee so afflicted becomes physically and psychologically dependent on alcohol.

The employee often disqualifies himself from his job by acts of misconduct due to his addiction; his performance may begin to deteriorate. The prospect of losing his position may be the very crisis that brings him to the realization that he has a problem and needs help in solving it. The

---

[44] Leonard Territo and James D. Sewell, *Stress Management in Law Enforcement*, 2nd ed. (Durham, N.C.: Carolina Academic Press, 2007), p. 378.

[45] See Chapter 7 for further discussion of catharsis.

supervisor can do much to help him: He can help the officer to gain insight into his needs through listening and attentiveness, as well as nondirective counseling.

When the employee begins to realize what course of action he must take to correct his problem, the supervisor might help him find the scientific reasons for it. He might suggest appropriate literature and websites on the subject and then suggest that he become familiar with available treatment options. The employee should be guided into some positive effort to find appropriate treatment. Many employers have excellent employee assistance programs (EAPs). Services provided typically include diagnosis, treatment, and referral. Those in need should be encouraged to contact the EAP. Other resources include medical doctors, peer counseling, clinical psychologists, faith-based counseling, private treatment centers, and Alcoholics Anonymous.

The important objective of professional counseling is to help the problem drinker realize that he must give up drinking and that he can never again use alcohol. Once this has been done, the objective of counseling has been achieved.

Counseling, however, has other valuable uses. It can be used as a means of helping the frustrated, insecure, tense, or hostile employee who has developed anxiety or depressive reactions that are interfering with his duty performance. The techniques applicable to the counseling of the problem drinker are generally effective in dealing with the employee who has an emotional problem. The supervisor must apply patience, understanding, and tact in his relationship with the emotionally troubled subordinate. When the anxiety or depression is deep-seated, referral should be made to professional help.

REVIEW

Questions

1. Why is problem drinking so important to law enforcement?

2. What is primarily the cause of problem drinking?

3. What are the three stages of problem drinking?

4. What are three defense mechanisms the alcoholic will often use?

5. Why is listening so important in counseling?

6. What is nondirective counseling?

7. When might a supervisor request a mandatory psychological fitness for duty evaluation?

8. Why is it necessary that the counselor avoid giving the problem drinker advice as part of the counseling procedure?

9. What are the three main uses of questions in counseling?

10. Why is it important that the problem drinker's ego be preserved as a technique of counseling?

11. Why should note taking not be practiced during a counseling session?

12. When should the problem drinker be referred to professional help?

13. What is the objective in counseling the problem drinker?

14. What are some common causes of depression?

15. What are some of the warning signs a supervisor should be aware of in a suicidal employee?

Exercises

1. Describe the early symptoms of problem drinking.

2. Describe what usually happens during the second stage in the development of alcoholism.

3. Explain what the supervisor might do if a subordinate's work has begun to deteriorate as the result of his drinking. Assume that the drinking is becoming a problem of habituation.

4. Conduct a simulated counseling session with a person who (it is assumed) has developed a drinking habit that has caused his work to deteriorate drastically. Assume further that his work has deteriorated to a point that he could be terminated; however, that course of action is to be reserved as a last resort. The person has no record of misconduct that has been induced by drinking.

5. List potential professional resources available to supervisors.

6. Describe how the supervisor might best handle an employee who develops depression after he loses a child.

7. Explain why time is a great healer in some cases of depression.

8. What should the extremely sensitive person with a high job interest and very conscientious nature be told if he has developed a depressive reaction because of a serious but honest mistake he made?

9. What should the young officer be told by his supervisor when it appears that the officer has allowed his job to become more important than his family relationships? Assume that the subordinate has solicited the help of the supervisor.

10. List three facts in regards to suicide.

9

Employee Dissatisfaction and Grievances

Chapter Objectives

This chapter will enable you:

- To become acquainted with the most common causes of employee dissatisfaction

- To gain an understanding of options in dealing with employee grievances

- To be able to recognize several symptoms of employee dissatisfaction

Every supervisor should be sensitive to the needs of employees who feel a real or imagined dissatisfaction or grievance arising from their relationships within the organization. These often result from supervisory or management practices perceived by workers as a threat to their personal rights or their right to fair treatment or as an infringement on their right to privacy.

Dissatisfaction may not be expressed, but the mere fact that it is present may have the same effect in eroding ambition and initiative and causing a deterioration in morale and performance as if it were verbalized. Grievances, should be recognized by the supervisor as being "real" in the mind of the employee who feels he has been wronged. If the supervisor is indifferent to them, resentment and hostility will occur. This will quickly spread if other personnel are convinced that a fellow employee has been treated unjustly or that a wrong has not been corrected.

Studies have revealed that worker reactions to management controls and the work environment in many occupations have changed little in the last half century. Such studies have consistently shown that employee dissatisfaction and grievances arise from factors that can be broadly categorized into four areas: the work environment; harsh, abusive, tyrannical, or inept supervision; misunderstandings about policies and procedures of the organization; and management failures of various types.[1]

By developing a sensitivity to the feelings of others and being alert to their reactions to these factors, the supervisor can gain many clues concerning how police officers and other employees frequently perceive

---

[1] John A. Wagner and John R. Holenbeck, *Organizational Behavior: Securing Competitive Advantage* (New York: Routledge, 2010), p. 131. See also International Association of Chiefs of Police, *Managing for Effective Police Discipline* (Washington, D.C.: International Association of Chiefs of Police, 1976), pp. 200–12; James Auten, "The Supervisor's Role in Handling Complaints and Grievances," *Law and Order*, 32, No. 6 (June 1984), 47–50.

organizational controls and supervisory practices that affect their personal and professional lives. He may then draw certain unmistakable conclusions about his own brand of supervision and how it may have contributed to employee discontent.

Crank and Caldero have identified organizational practices as the primary source of stress for police officers.[2] Once a supervisor recognizes his shortcomings, he can set about to correct them. If he is honest about this self-evaluation, he will recognize where his performance as a supervisor might need modification.

It is not known what percentage of these reactions to organizational controls is valid or to what degree they exist at any particular time in any particular group; however, the fact that they are present is indicative of a problem that requires some attention. Those that are invalid should not be ignored if giving an explanation will change an employee's attitude or correct a misconception; at least he will feel that his complaint has been considered. There are no standard methods for handling these matters. Each must be approached with common sense and fairness.

Dissatisfaction with Work Environment

Physical factors in the work environment give rise to a large portion of employee dissatisfaction. Bad lighting, improper temperature, uncleanliness or inadequate restroom facilities, unsatisfactory operational equipment, and other workplace deficiencies are factors that usually require capital outlay to correct. In such cases, the supervisor is often powerless to make the necessary corrections directly but should call such deficiencies to the attention of higher management. If maintenance or service employees are subject to his direction and control, he will frequently find that more attention to their supervision will bring about a noteworthy improvement. He must recognize that adequate physical facilities and equipment contribute to the maintenance of a high level of production and vitally affect employee morale.

Inept Supervisory Practices

Poor supervisory practices account for a large share of dissatisfaction and negative feelings of employees. Failure to give recognition to employees when they believe they have earned it, use of intemperate language by the supervisor, harsh arbitrary methods in dealing with subordinates, display of favoritism, existence of dual standards of conduct, unfairness of supervisors in the application of rules to subordinates, excessive supervision, existence of cliques—and all of the bad connotations usually associated with these issues, whether or not the supervisor is part of the problem—are commonly cited as causes of employee dissatisfaction with their leaders.

These dissatisfactions are a prime cause of grievances and complaints of various types and contribute markedly to a lowering of morale. Such employee reactions cannot be regarded merely as trivial, nor can the supervisor afford to downgrade or minimize

---

[2] John P. Crank and Michael A. Caldero, *Police Ethics: The Corruption of Noble Cause*, 3rd ed. (Burlington, Mass.: Elsevier, 2010).

their importance. He must learn and apply the tenets of effective leadership in dealing with the problems associated with such reactions. (These principles are discussed in detail in Chapter 3.)

Misunderstandings of Policies, Rules, and Procedures

Observations indicate that managers in law enforcement agencies tend to communicate organizational policies and procedures rather well. However, since effective communications are essential to effective leadership, the supervisor must constantly work at improving his skill as a communicator so that he can minimize all problems resulting from poor communications. (Suggestions for accomplishing this objective are discussed in Chapter 5.)

Management Failures

Failures of management give rise to many negative reactions of workers. Toleration by supervisors of wasted time, effort, and physical resources; unjustified abuses of equipment; supervisory negligence in protecting the interests of the organization; violations of employee due process rights; infringement on what workers believe are their rights to privacy; and arbitrary enforcement of rules and regulations are quickly recognized by employees and tend to erode organizational pride, morale, and efficiency. Employees are quick to sense the attitudes of management personnel, especially operation-level supervisors. When supervisory personnel are indifferent to the best interests of the organization, employees are prone to adopt the attitude, "If the administration wants it that way, that's the way they'll get it."

Indifference of supervisors to the squandering of organizational resources and other wasteful practices contributes to inefficient operations. Most law enforcement personnel remain in public service because they like the work. They conscientiously strive to perform their duties effectively and efficiently and resent supervisory practices that make their jobs more difficult.

Rules of Conduct

Studies among peace officers have revealed some distinct dissatisfaction about organizational rules and regulations and how they are applied by supervisors.[3] Individuals who had the strongest opinions about the regulation of their personal conduct by their organization were rather explicit in their reactions: They indicated that their greatest concern was that such rules and regulations placed undue restrictions on their personal rights; they were opposed to controls governing their off-duty employment, their hairstyles or mustaches or beards, their criticism of the organization, and their places of residence. Personnel who had strongest feelings about department rules and regulations relating to the operation of vehicles, courtesy to the public, use of physical force, use of firearms, and other general departmental restrictions on conduct and performance perceived these as

---

[3] International Association of Chiefs of Police, *Managing for Effective Police Discipline* (1977), pp. 200–12.

interferences with their ability to do good police work. Officers who had the strongest opinions about organizational controls of their moral conduct, personal debts, off-duty use of alcohol, and the like believed these matters to be an invasion of their right to privacy and none of the department's business.

Rule Enforcement

Employees often oppose the manner in which organizational rules are enforced more than the rules themselves. The most frequently cited reason for opposition is the inconsistency of supervisors in enforcing the organization's rules.

Failures of supervisors to follow the same rules that officers are expected to follow invariably cause strong negative reactions. Overly severe punishments for violations of rules are also likely to be resisted and criticized by employees. Undoubtedly, many of these can be prevented by the supervisor if he learns how to motivate and direct his subordinates (as discussed in Chapter 3).

Due Process Violations

Employees react strongly and often challenge management in court when they feel they have been arbitrarily deprived of some due process right. "Procedural due process is near and dear to the heart of every unionist. . . . Procedural due process is considered sacrosanct and non-negotiable by virtually all rank-and-file police officers."[4]

It is obvious that officers' demands for greater freedom from management controls are growing. In the last decade, they have insisted on greater and greater procedural safeguards to protect them against management infringements on their personal rights, and these demands have been reflected by due process statutes enacted in many states providing for a police officer's "Bill of Rights." These statutes usually confer on an employee a property interest in his position. In addition, contractual agreement, common practice under existing rules, or understandings, like statutes, may give employees, even those who are not tenured, a property or liberty interest in their employment. In cases where either of these interests is affected by the employer's action, courts will require that procedural due process be provided.[5]

A property interest in his position is present when the tenured employee has a legitimate claim to his job as conferred by statute, contract, or existing rules or understandings. An employee's liberty interest is involved if the employer's action in dismissing him significantly damages his reputation or standing in the community or stigmatizes him to such a degree that he is unable to take advantage of future employment opportunities. Dismissal of a nontenured employee itself probably will not give rise to procedural due process requirements unless it is based on unfounded charges that injure his reputation. Under these circumstances, fair play and justice, which are at the heart of procedural due process, require that he be given an opportunity to clear his name and restore his honor and reputation. A liberty interest is involved only when the employee is able to show that he suffered a damaged reputation as a result of public disclosure of the reasons

---

[4] Edward A. Thibault, Lawrence M. Lynch, and R. Bruce McBride, *Proactive Police Management*, 8th ed. (Upper Saddle River, N.J.: Prentice Hall, 2010), p. 373.

[5] *Perry v. Sinderman*, 408 U.S. 493 (1972). See also *Board of Regents v. Roth*, 408 U.S. 564 (1972).

for the discharge and that he was stigmatized to such a degree by the disclosure that he was unable to obtain employment.[6]

It is therefore imperative that supervisors become thoroughly familiar with statutes, contract provisions, and existing rules or understandings between employer and employee so that procedural due process requirements can be meticulously adhered to in disciplinary cases that might affect the employee's property or liberty interest in his position. Courts will reverse on appeal any action by an employer that arbitrarily deprives an employee of such due process rights. Such reversals can generally be avoided if the employee is notified of the charges against him in a timely fashion so that he can prepare his defense and is given an opportunity to present such defense.[7]

The U.S. Supreme Court held in *Cleveland Board of Education v. Loudermill* that a tenured public employee is entitled, under due process, to oral or written notice of the charges against him and an opportunity to tell his side of the story before he is terminated.[8] The majority opinion did not specify what form the procedure should take except to declare that it "need not be elaborate." The Court declared that "the formality and procedural requisites for the hearing can vary, depending upon the importance of the interests involved and the nature of the subsequent proceedings." However, a minority opinion indicated a mood to require more detailed due process procedures, much as previously delineated by the Court in *Morrissey v Brewer*.[9] The *Morrissey* procedures (described in Chapter 11) would be the safest course to follow in important disciplinary cases.

These extensions by the courts and legislators of constitutional guarantees to protect public officers' rights have further restricted organizations in exercising management controls once considered commonplace, yet a surprising number of supervisors believe that they can still supervise as they once did. They soon learn that some of their practices run counter to the law as court rulings become increasingly protective of employee rights. Since these decisions have varied widely from place to place, it is incumbent on every supervisor to acquaint himself thoroughly with those applicable to his jurisdiction.

The supervisor should exercise considerable care in attempting to punish his subordinates for conduct of a purely personal nature not involving their job performance or the public image of the organization and its real interests. Such occurrences sometimes place him in a situation requiring a choice between two undesirable alternatives: Either he takes action contrary to legal rules protecting the employee and risks a court challenge that might overrule him, or he is forced to overlook conduct that he considers improper and takes no action at all.

Generally, courts have ruled that an employee cannot be penalized for his acts unless it can be proved that his conduct was related to his performance of duty *and* that it

---

[6] See Chapter 10 for a discussion of the training value of publicizing disciplinary actions within the organization and avoiding the liberty interest brought about by public disclosure. *Johnson v. Martin,* 943 F.2d 15 (7th Cir. 1991).

[7] *Arnet v. Kennedy*, 416 U.S. 134 (1974); *Paul v. Davis*, 424 U.S. 693 (1976); *Bishop v. Wood*, 426 U.S. 341 (1976).

[8] *Cleveland Board of Education v. Loudermill, et al.*, 105 S. Ct. 1487 (1985).

[9] *Morrissey v. Brewer*, 408 U.S. 471 (1972). See also *Goldberg v. Kelly*, 397 U.S. 254 (1970) and *Arnet v. Kennedy*, 416 U.S. 134 (1974).

impaired his efficiency, seriously interfered with the operational efficiency of the organization, or interfered with the maintenance of good order within the organization, or it was common knowledge that the particular conduct was prohibited.[10] This imposes a rather heavy burden on the supervisor, especially when the subordinate's behavior involves the question of whether or not the department can legally dictate non–job-related standards of conduct. Some of the issues raising the most doubt about whether or how the supervisor should become involved are those arising from conduct such as off-duty employment, off-duty use of alcohol, bankruptcy, failure to pay debts, and immoral conduct not involving an unlawful act.

Supervisory Influence on Non–Job-Related Employee Behavior

In dealing with behavior that is non–job-related, the supervisor must be aware that his options are limited in the eyes of the law, yet he may feel impelled to do something to correct a subordinate's demeanor when he believes it to be contrary to the best interests of the organization and the individuals in it. He must consider the legal justification for his action as well as the morality of what he does if he is to set a professional tone within his sphere of influence.

It is in cases such as these that the supervisor's persuasive abilities are truly tested. If he is respected by his subordinates, he will be able to exert a great influence in controlling or preventing what he considers objectionable conduct that might not be legally actionable. Since people generally need a model to follow, the supervisor should find occasion to communicate his convictions to his subordinates without sermonizing. "We preach a better sermon with our life than with our lips."[11] He must strive to develop and maintain in them the high standards and ideals that are characteristic of a true professional and should direct his greatest efforts toward those who have difficulty abiding by the conduct norms recognized and accepted within the organization.

The so-called freeway therapy, transfer treatment, or the wheel, which may involve frequent transfer from one place, one shift, or one assignment to another, is sometimes used to remove an employee from an unwholesome environment to one of lesser exposure. Frequently, such treatment is more injurious (if not more immoral) than the conduct it is designed to cure.

Transfer may correct a problem but more often does not. All it usually does is shift it from one place or from one supervisor to another. It may well be that transfer from one environment to another is the only solution to a problem, but it should not be done without consideration of other useful alternatives, such as additional training, counseling, or change of assignment or partner within the unit.

---

[10] *Bence v. Breier*, 501 F.2d 1185 (1974); *Perea v. Fales*, 114 Cal. Rptr. 808 (1974).

[11] Paul M. Whisenand and R. Fred Ferguson, *The Managing of Police Organizations*, 7th ed. (Upper Saddle River, N.J.: Pearson Prentice Hall, 2008), p. 59.

Recognition of Employee Dissatisfaction

When employee discontent is not verbalized, it may become more grievous to the supervisor—and the organization—than expressed grievances, and its effects may be just as devastating. The typical symptoms that should alert a supervisor to the existence of dissatisfaction among his subordinates are similar to those symptoms of frustration described in Chapter 7. Other manifestations of dissatisfaction might be increased "blue Monday" absenteeism, growing inattention to duty, excessive tardiness, indifference to job requirements, hostility and irritability of employees, general deterioration in performance and morale, and similar reactions.

Once the supervisor recognizes the symptoms that strong feelings of discontent are growing among his subordinates, he should try to determine what the cause might be. In doing so, he will look to a cross section of his subordinates for clues. Interviews with affected personnel (as discussed in Chapter 6) may provide additional evidence.

Supervisory Approaches to Employee Dissatisfaction

Although much employee dissatisfaction is valid, some is not. Many of the causes for employee complaints can be prevented by the supervisor if he consistently adheres to the basic tenets of leadership. When the work environment causes discontent that cannot be or was not prevented, the supervisor should do whatever is possible, reasonable, and just to remove the causes of dissatisfaction.

Some of these problems cannot be resolved directly by him because they involve established organizational policies or practices. Often, he can only inform his superiors of the effects of such factors and recommend what changes need to be made.

In some cases, discontent may be caused by unfulfilled employee expectations concerning salary increases, the work environment, fringe benefits, rules and regulations and their enforcement, and like matters. When employee demands are rejected as unreasonable, reactions often become hostile, but the adroit supervisor can do much to temper such strong feelings by wise counsel. He must avoid commiserating with employees in such cases; rather, he should counsel them to seek any redress they believe they are entitled to by submitting objective justification for their demands to arbitration between their representatives and management.

Employee Grievances

When some factor in an employee's work environment causes him to complain orally or more formally, in writing, it is usually referred to as a grievance. Those grievances involving some factor not related to a contractual agreement are resolved primarily by the first-line supervisor unless he is the subject of the grievance; then the matter is usually resolved by his superior. According to Holden, "Where possible, grievances should be handled at the lowest possible level. This saves time, resources and egos."[12] Those that allege management

---

[12] Richard R. Holden, *Modern Police Management*, 2nd ed. rpt. (Upper Saddle River, N.J.: Prentice Hall 2000), p. 257.

has breached some contractual agreement with the employees are usually handled according to procedures specified in the contract. In either case, the technique is similar.

It is critical that supervisors be attuned not only to verbalized grievances but also to those not verbalized. Grievances "provide a measure of contentment among officers…, [indicate] hostility toward management…[and] serve as an indicator for the need for a greater action on the part of the administration."[13] Grievances provide critical feedback to the astute supervisor.

Noncontractual Matters

Most grievances that do not involve a contractual matter can be resolved by the first-line supervisor without referral to higher authority. He must first determine the true cause of the grievance by making it easy for the subordinate to discuss the cause of his complaint. When the supervisor is unable to resolve the difference, he should fully document the problem and submit it to higher authority. Some recommended techniques for conducting such interviews and for arriving at solutions to problems are described in Chapter 6.

Contractual Violations and Grievances

When employees complain because they believe the management in an organization has breached an agreement of their contract, a more formalized procedure is usually required. Typically, four steps are involved when dissatisfaction degenerates into formal grievances. In the first step, the supervisor or the employee representative receives the complaint; often the issue can be resolved at this level. If the supervisor's inquiry reveals a true basis for the complaint, he can take appropriate corrective action and resolve the issue then and there. Reasonableness and fairness on the part of the supervisor, the employee, and the employee representative are essential to prompt resolution. Should attempts fail to resolve the matter at this level, the matter becomes an official grievance. This is the second step, in which the complaint is referred to an intermediate level of management for resolution. Third, should disagreement continue, the grievance is transmitted to the top level of management within the organization. When attempts to reach a resolution fail at this step, the matter then proceeds to the fourth step—voluntary arbitration. It should be noted that 90 percent of grievances brought to an arbitration hearing involve discipline brought against an officer.[14] The typical work contract usually provides that both parties accept as binding the decision of an impartial arbitrator.[15]

In such matters, the first step in the procedure is most critical to the employee, the supervisor, and the organization. Because of the economic cost associated with the processing of grievances through the various stages and their adverse effects on employee morale, the supervisor must make every effort to resolve such matters at the earliest stage. Usually, an objective approach, coupled with sound supervisory practices, fair play, and common sense, will provide the answers to these problems.

---

[13] *Ibid.*, p. 256.

[14] Charles R. Swanson, Leonard Territo, and Robert W. Taylor, *Police Administration*, 8th ed. (Upper Saddle River, N.J.: Pearson Prentice Hall, 2012), p. 545.

[15] Constance E. Bagley and Diane Savage, *Managers and the Legal Environment: Strategies for the 21st Century* (Mason, Ohio: South-Western, 2010), p. 92.

Working with Unions

Carpenter and Fulton offer several important guidelines for the supervisor in dealing with unions:[16]

1. *Know the Union Representative*—This is an important relationship that should be developed. Many issues can be resolved informally. Let the representative know you are available to resolve disputes.
2. *Have a Good Working Knowledge of the Contract, Rules, Regulations, and Policy*—Ensure that you have an updated copy of everything so that when issues arise, you will know what is and is not appropriate. The provisions of the contract should be followed.
3. *Follow the Grievance Procedure*—If you tried but could not resolve a grievance at your level, it must proceed to the next step. You should document your actions and pass it to the next level. Make sure you adhere to the contractual time limits.

SUMMARY

Supervisors must be alert to detect factors within the work environment that cause employee dissatisfaction. They must recognize that prompt corrective action is essential if morale and productivity are to be maintained at high levels.

Employee dissatisfaction arises from many factors, which can be categorized into four broad areas: the work environment, inept supervision, misunderstandings about policies and procedures in the organization, and management failures of various types.

Physical factors in the work environment may or may not be correctable by the supervisor (unless he has some direct supervisory responsibility over maintenance personnel), because they ordinarily involve capital outlays over which he has little control. Most of the dissatisfaction resulting from inept supervisory practices can be avoided if the supervisor applies the basic tenets of leadership in his day-to-day dealings with his subordinates. In police agencies, few complaints are made by personnel about their misunderstandings of policies, rules, and procedures; however, many adverse reactions arise from the failure of management personnel to protect the resources of the organization.

Much of employee discontent can be associated with their opposition to rules and regulations they construe as being an infringement of their personal rights. Of greater significance, however, are employees' adverse reactions to the manner in which such rules and regulations are enforced by management personnel, especially those at the working level. These employee reactions afford many pertinent clues to the wise supervisor who continuously engages in self-appraisal of his brand of supervision so that he may eliminate his bad practices and strengthen his good ones.

The supervisor who discovers among his subordinates non-job-related behavior that is not legally actionable but that is contrary to the best interest of the organization may feel compelled to do something. In such cases, he has several options. He can take action without legal support and risk being overruled in a court if challenged, or he can overlook the conduct and do nothing. The third option will test his persuasive ability to eliminate the unacceptable demeanor by convincing his subordinates of the value of high professional standards and ideals.

---

[16] Michael J. Carpenter and Roger Fulton, *Law Enforcement Management: What Works and What Doesn't* (Flushing, N.Y.: Looseleaf Law Publications, 2010), pp. 115–17.

REVIEW

Questions

1. What are the four categories into which employee dissatisfaction can be grouped?

2. What are some of the most prominent failures of management personnel that contribute to adverse employee reactions?

3. What supervisory practices do employees oppose most in the enforcement of rules and regulations?

4. Describe and give an example of a due process violation.

5. What is a formal grievance?

Exercises

1. You learn from a resident in your area that one of your units has been parked in a secluded location near his home two or three times a week at 4:30 A.M. when he leaves for work. The vehicle is assigned to a male training officer who has been working with a woman officer on probation for the past several months. Explain what you would do.

2. Describe what you would do if an employee's representative submitted a grievance to you involving a clique in your unit. What would you do if the complaint accused you of being a party to the clique?

3. Discuss the merits and demerits of transfer treatment or freeway therapy.

4. Describe some of the typical symptoms of employee discontent when dissatisfaction has not been expressed.

10

Discipline

Principles, Policies, and Practices

Chapter Objectives

This chapter will enable you:

- ■ To become acquainted with the principles and requisites of discipline
- ■ To become familiar with the effects of positive and negative discipline
- ■ To be able to recognize the relationship between discipline, morale, and esprit de corps

Discipline is often thought of in a limited sense as meaning punishment or penalty, a negative connotation. However, the term means, more nearly, instructing, teaching, and training. Its main purposes are to facilitate coordination of effort, develop self-control and character, and foster orderliness and efficiency.

One of the primary measures of the level of discipline within the police force is the orderliness with which it operates. The degree of this orderliness is directly related to the conduct of the employees, which, in turn, is largely dependent on how well the supervisor performs his duties. The preeminent organizational theorist Henri Fayol wrote in the nineteenth century: "Poor discipline is the result of poor leadership. Good discipline exists when workers and managers respect the rules governing activities in the organization."[1]

The principal responsibility for maintaining an appropriate level of discipline in his unit should rest on the immediate line supervisor, and he is responsible for enforcing obedience to organizational rules even though he may not personally favor them. Subordinates are bound to obey lawful orders regardless of their feelings.[2] Failure to do so will disrupt smooth operations.

If the supervisor refuses or neglects to consider complaints against his subordinates, if he fails to investigate their delinquencies that are called to his attention, or if he fails to take proper action when they are derelict in their duties or unprofessional in their conduct, he not only is doing himself a disservice but is doing an injustice to his organization and other employees as well. The ability to maintain a high level of discipline is probably the single most important characteristic of the strong leader.

---

[1] Henri Fayol, *General and Industrial Management,* revised by Irwin Gray and David S. Lake (1987).

[2] Robert Adams and Peter Villers, *Police Leadership in the Twenty-First Century: Philosophy, Doctrine and Development* (Winchester, U.K.: Waterside Press, 2003), p. 121.

Forms of Discipline

The word *discipline* comes from the root word "disciple," which denotes one who receives instructions from another or who follows devotedly the expressions and actions of a respected leader. It is more accurately a term used in modern administration and management to denote a form of moral or mental training, education, subjection to control and regulation, correction, and, finally, chastisement when other, more positive means of corrective action fail.

Positive Discipline

That form of training and attitudinal conditioning used to correct deficiencies without invoking punishment is known as positive discipline. It is constructive in nature. Sherman and Lucia define positive discipline as a systematic approach designed to instruct or guide employees in such a way that they become loyal, dedicated, responsible, and productive members of the organization.[3] Its influence engenders a habitual or conditioned reaction from within the individual to the established values of the organization and its customs and traditions. It is present when employees willingly follow the directions of their supervisors and adhere to standards of conduct prevalent in the organization.[4]

A well-disciplined organization is one that is highly trained. It follows that an effective, efficient organization is a well-disciplined one in which the principles of positive discipline have been recognized and practiced. The members have the same individual objectives as those of the group. Such a state can only be achieved, however, when the group objectives are made known to the members and they adopt these objectives as their own.

If supervisors are thoroughly indoctrinated in their responsibilities; if they are expert planners, trainers, and leaders; if they assist their subordinates by demonstrating, guiding, and counseling; and if they set a good example by their conduct, positive discipline will prevail and the need for punitive discipline will be lessened. Indeed, the skill with which supervisors use this positive tool to a large extent determines the quality of their leadership and the effectiveness of the organization. Iannone stated, "An organization may be considered to have been brought into the ideal state when there exists a maximum of efficiency and satisfaction [of its members] generated by techniques of positive discipline, with a minimum use of the punitive or negative discipline."[5] Punishment for well-intentioned mistakes will quickly remove officers' enthusiasm to employ creativity and extra effort; police departments must have reasonable tolerance for "mistakes of the head," though not for "mistakes of the heart."[6]

Negative Discipline

Discipline that takes the form of punishment or chastisement is known as negative discipline. When positive methods fail to achieve conformity with accepted standards of conduct or performance, a negative type of action, punitive in nature, must follow to

---

[3] Mark Sherman and Al Lucia, "Positive Discipline and Labor Arbitration," *Arbitration Journal*, 47, No. 2 (1992).

[4] R. Wayne Pace, *Organizational Dynamism: Unleashing Power in the Workplace* (Westport, Conn.: Quorum Books, 2002), p. 64.

[5] Marvin D. Iannone, *A Descriptive Study of the Internal Disciplinary Program of the Los Angeles Police Department* (unpublished master's thesis, California State University at Los Angeles, 1967), p. 13.

[6] Tanya Erzen, *Zero Tolerance* (New York: New York University Press, 2001).

preserve the integrity of the organization. This action will generally follow a progressive approach. Delpo and Guerin describe progressive discipline as a system of escalated penalties made known to employees in advance and imposed with increasing severity for repeated infractions; normally such a system includes the following:[7]

1. Oral warning
2. Written warning
3. Disciplinary layoff or suspension
4. Discharge

Often, loss of regular days off, annual leave, or accumulated compensatory time when permitted by the rules is preferable to outright suspension with full loss of pay because the employee's family is not made to suffer financially for the officer's derelictions. Indeed, in today's affluent society, the loss of time that might otherwise be used for recreation may be a better deterrent than the loss of salary.

Use of these punitive forms of discipline should be reserved for the unadjusted, discontented nonconformist who has not been amenable to other, more positive methods. Punishment, then, is the first step in the process of either changing his behavior or removing him from the organization for the good of the service.

Adverse Effects of Punishment

Although punishment may produce some undesirable effects, it must be administered at times because no alternative method of coping with a problem of misbehavior is appropriate. Some of the adverse reactions to punishment may be tempered, however, if it is administered promptly, intelligently, fairly, and consistently and if the employee can be made to understand that it was necessary because of his own misbehavior, not because of someone else's.

The person punished may react with hostility and childlike behavior, especially if he considers the action arbitrary or unfair. He may become frustrated, and if he is a nonconformist with an emotional problem, he is likely to be the very one who will be most often punished. Punishment may cause him to become paranoid rather than responsible.

To many employees who have been punished, such action poses a challenge to devise ways and means of avoiding discovery of their derelictions. For example, the misbehavior of the sleeper on the job will be harder to discover after he is once caught and punished.

Actual punishment (or the prospect of it) may cause a hostile, negative attitude toward the job, and marginal performance is the likely result. The employee will do just enough to avoid being punished for unsatisfactory performance and may sabotage the work efforts of others at every opportunity.

The threat of punishment and the fear it creates may be less effective in changing behavior than are the more positive methods of motivating people. This does not suggest, however, that sanctions against improper behavior are not needed.[8] If the primary

---

[7] Amy Delpo and Lisa Guerin, *Dealing with Problem Employees* 6th ed. (Berkeley, Calif.: Nolo, 2011).
[8] Kavita Singh, *Organizational behavior* (New Delhi: Pearson, 2010), p. 95.

focus of negative sanctions for derelictions is on behavior control rather than on training, some personnel may concentrate on avoiding bad behavior rather than doing good. Punishment might actually become a challenge to them to devise ways and means of avoiding discovery of their derelictions. In these processes, fear of punishment may effectively suppress their desire to perform well. They may try to avoid a distasteful situation that may lead to unpleasant consequences rather than attempt to resolve it forthrightly.

Detection of Problem Employee Behavior

All police departments should have some type of system in place to monitor the behavior and performance of its officers. In every agency, there are a small number of officers who receive a disproportionate number of complaints. Recent court decisions have made it clear that law enforcement agencies have a duty to identify these officers and prevent them from engaging in inappropriate behavior. It should be noted that most officers cooperate with their supervisors and respond positively to feedback on performance issues.

However, supervisors should be able to identify officers with performance and conduct issues. The goal here is to detect these problem officers early. Some police agencies have adopted programs such as the early warning and intervention system. Such systems are designed to identify patterns of behavior by police officers that may be inappropriate and that warrant intervention.

The New Jersey Attorney General's Office recommends that police agencies use certain data to help identify the problem performer:[9]

- Citizen complaints
- Use-of-force incidents
- Motor vehicle stop data
- Search-and-seizure data
- Claims of duty-related injury
- Arrests for resisting arrest
- Incidents of arrested persons injured
- Vehicular pursuits and accidents
- Cases dismissed by the court

An analysis of these kinds of data by the internal affairs unit is suggested. As potential problem officers are identified, the information is passed along to the individuals' immediate supervisors. The supervisors would then review the data and conduct additional fact finding. After a thorough review, if the supervisors believe some form of intervention is necessary, counseling, training, or close supervision may be the result.

For the early warning and intervention systems to be effective, supervisors need to be trained and have a variety of intervention options available to them. The goal is to detect the problem behavior before it becomes more serious and then to intervene with appropriate remedies. Intervention may also include either positive or negative discipline.

---

[9] *New Jersey Attorney General Guidelines on Internal Affairs* (Trenton, N.J., September 2011), page 52.

Police Officer Writing a Traffic Citation.
(© Lisa F. Young/Fotolia)

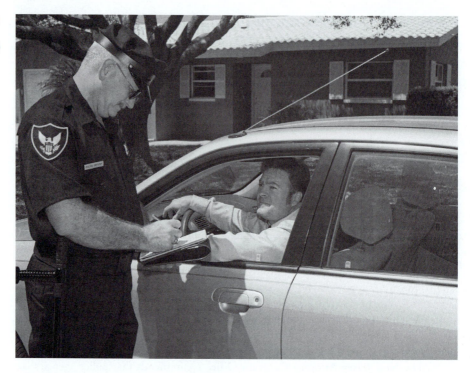

Requisites of Punishment

While punishing an employee does not guarantee that his future conduct or performance will improve, it will not demoralize others in the organization if it is sensibly applied in a fair, consistent manner. Most employees will understand the need for it when a colleague's conduct tends to reflect adversely on them. In fact, most employees are highly critical when a supervisor fails to take prompt disciplinary action they know is long overdue.

Certainty

To be most effective, punishment for even the mildest of infractions must be certain. This characteristic is perhaps the greatest deterrent to further misbehavior. Keynes has attributed to George Bernard Shaw the remark that "deterrence is a function of certainty, not severity."[10]

The fear that misconduct will certainly be discovered and inevitably punished in one way or another is a powerful deterrent force for individuals. The fear of losing face with peers or being ostracized by one's fellow employees, especially when the act has been reproachable and is one from which all will suffer, is sometimes greater than the fear of punishment itself. Unfortunately, fear must be used as a management tool to gain conformity from some employees, but its indiscriminate use is seldom justified; when its use is indicated, it should be employed with common sense.

---

[10] John Maynard Keynes, *The Economic Consequence of the Peace* (Los Angeles, Calif.: IndoEuropean Publishing, 2010), p. 476.

Swiftness

Punishment not only must be certain but also must be meted out as swiftly as possible after detection and proof of the wrongdoing if it is to be most effective. According to McGregor's hot stove concept, "The sooner the disciplinary action is taken, the more automatic it will be and the more closely it will be associated with the errant, disruptive, or deviant behavior."[11] Interminable delays in making necessary investigations and administering penalties while the superiors of the derelict employee mull over the matter only serve to embitter the employee involved because anticipation of what might or could happen is often more traumatic than the penalty itself—procrastination is a strong stressor in the job environment. If a necessary delay is involved in the application of a penalty, the employee should be kept informed. Punishment will seldom have the desired constructive effects when finally applied if it is too far removed in time from the conduct that brought it about.

When the supervisor is confronted with a need for disciplinary action against a subordinate, he should not hesitate to administer it. An unnecessary delay might be interpreted as weakness because both the offender and other members of the group expect some action to be taken. Failure to act when action is indicated may result in the supervisor abdicating his position of leadership.[12]

In cases where criminal charges are to be made against an employee, ordinarily disciplinary action contemplated should be held in abeyance pending resolution of those charges to avoid prejudicing him unduly in court. Too long a delay, however, may prove to be more harmful to the interests of the organization than proceeding with the administrative action.

Fairness and Impartiality

When punitive action is taken against a derelict employee, it will seldom have the desired effect if it is not fairly and impartially administered. Arbitrary or capricious punishment will be resented not only by the involved employee but often also by his peers. Likewise, if punishment is not applied in a constructive setting, it will have little corrective value. Nor should it be imposed as revenge for an "affront to the establishment." As Newman stated many years ago, "it should not be given in a spirit of retribution, or for the prime purpose of humiliating the offender. The purpose of discipline is to bring about improved conduct in the future."[13] This is certainly still true today.

Often, punishment is meted out by a supervisor who has allowed his anger to color his judgment. Such emotion should never be allowed to cloud fairness or to trigger capricious or arbitrary punishment. Therefore, the supervisor discovering misconduct on the part of a subordinate should allow his emotions to cool (if they have become heated) before taking punitive action against him. Misbehavior all too frequently causes

---

[11] Richard W. Plunkett, *Supervision: Diversity and Team in the Workplace*, 10th ed. (Upper Saddle River, N.J.: Prentice Hall, 2002)

[12] John C. Maxwell, *Developing the Leader Within You* (Nashville, Tenn.: Thomas Nelson, 1993), p. 139.

[13] William H. Newman, *Administrative Action*, 2nd ed. (Englewood Cliffs, N.J.: Prentice Hall, 1963), p. 400.

supervisors to react angrily and to show the extreme irritation that sometimes colors their judgment. Such reactions tend to stifle constructive and more positive methods of changing behavior. Punishing a subordinate is a simple approach, but not a positive one, since often the supervisor can more easily punish a person for doing a poor job than show him how to do it properly.

Punishment that is intemperately or unfairly applied will be resented by employees more than when it is overly severe. It should never destroy the employee's desire to make amends for his mistakes, nor should it become a demoralizing influence on other employees, who are quick to sympathize with and support another whom they believe has been treated unfairly even though they do not condone his conduct.

The wise supervisor knows that he himself may bear some responsibility for many of the derelictions of his subordinates because of his failure to communicate clearly with them or to train them properly. Bodie asks, "Could the officer have done it right if his life depended on it?" If the answer is "No," then negative discipline would be unfair and training is probably the solution.[14] The wise supervisor will recognize that reprimanding or punishing a subordinate for a minor deviation often will serve no useful purpose. This is because the well-disciplined employee will usually be the first to recognize his own mistakes and prevent a repetition of them in the future.[15]

The supervisor who finds it necessary to take corrective action against a subordinate should do so only after he has made every effort to determine if the dereliction was a "mistake of the head" or "mistake of the heart." An inadvertent deviation from standards or an act of carelessness is one thing; intentional misconduct is quite another. The supervisor should differentiate between the two and take action accordingly, keeping in mind that the training value gained from an error may far exceed the harm done by it.

Consistency

Punitive action for similar breaches of conduct should be somewhat uniform, providing such derelictions occur under like conditions. A useful guiding rule is to apply just that amount of punishment that will prevent further derelictions of the same nature. The penalty should fit the offense, but it should also fit the individual. This is the ideal state but is seldom achieved.

Some supervisors contend that all employees who have committed the same infraction under similar circumstances cannot be treated alike, since some will respond more quickly to a lesser penalty than will others. If rehabilitation is accomplished without destroying the employee's morale, then what does it matter that penalties are not always equal? Other supervisors ask, "But how about the morale of other employees?" Certainly, the employee's past performance should be considered in meting out punishment, but this does not suggest that one employee's breaches of conduct should be "winked at" while punishment is administered to another for the same dereliction. To do so would violate the basic principle that requires that punishment be applied somewhat consistently.

---

[14] David Bodie, "Basic Supervision in a Community Policing Environment" (Bodie Consulting Services, 2000), p. 114.

[15] Felix A. Nigro and Lloyd G. Nigro, *Modern Public Administration*, 4th ed. (New York: Harper & Row, 1977), pp. 286–90.

Overly severe or excessively lenient penalties may cause a reaction from employees just the opposite to that intended by the supervisor. Such penalties may make the recipient a martyr or indicate that management considers the dereliction inconsequential.[16] In neither case will the punishment accomplish what it should; rather, it may set a dangerous precedent that may tend to bind management to an undesirable course of action in the future.

Deterrence for Others

Punitive action should not only serve as a deterrent to the employee against whom it is applied but also be a form of training for other employees to orient them to the types of acts the organization cannot and will not tolerate. Fuller has pointed out that taking punitive disciplinary action against an employee may cause others to shape up when they realize the supervisor will make difficult decisions when necessary.[17]

Telling employees what is expected of them is a primary requisite in the establishment of an effective disciplinary program. To accomplish this training, some organizations publish in their house organ or by special notices the disciplinary actions taken against personnel. Some contend that this publication places the chastised employee in double jeopardy, while others believe the benefits to the total organization more than offset the hazards of such procedures. If the results of disciplinary actions are published within the organization for training purposes, organizational policy will dictate whether the names of those disciplined are omitted and only the penalties and the derelictions on which they were based are briefly reported. Although it is argued that this approach accomplishes the objective of letting others know the types of actions that result in punishment, the procedure has some inherent dangers. Rumors, inaccurate guesses, and downright false conclusions are easily nurtured, especially in larger organizations when only brief incomplete accounts of disciplinary actions are publicized.

Obviously, then, if such accounts are to be circulated throughout the organization for training purposes, they should be carefully prepared with sufficient detail to prevent speculations, guesses, and rumors. Statements of charges such as "Neglect of Duty," "Conduct Unbecoming an Officer," and the like reveal little information of deterrent value to others. This suggests that more explanatory information should be included about the nature of the act that constituted the breach of discipline. In small organizations, the facts of any particular case are usually matters of common knowledge and require little elaboration.

Supervisors should acquaint themselves with sufficient details of more complex disciplinary cases so that they may explain to their subordinates when necessary the basis for punitive actions taken against employees and thus reduce morale-destroying rumors. Discussions of such matters with other employees (if deemed essential) should be conducted in an objective, matter-of-fact manner, with a minimum of editorializing, so that maximum training may be achieved.

---

[16] Newman, *Administrative Action*, p. 400.

[17] George Fuller, *The First-Time Supervisor's Survival Guide* (Upper Saddle River, N.J.: Prentice Hall, 1995), p. 188.

Publishing the names of derelict employees and concise information on which charges against them were based can be considered one aspect of the penalty that obviously enhances its deterrent value. Except in the largest agencies, those punished for infractions are usually well identified, in any event, long before penalty sheets are published. Information of this nature travels swiftly through organizational grapevines.

Plaintiffs in civil action suits against police officers can ordinarily obtain information regarding an officer's course of conduct through discovery proceedings.[18] The organization should not jeopardize the confidentiality of its records by placing bulletins concerning disciplinary actions in locations readily accessible to the public; however, these should be easily available to members of the organization. This is especially important if the details of a disciplinary proceeding might lose their confidentiality through publication and thereby become ammunition that can be used against the officer in a civil suit arising from his actions while on duty.

Furthermore, as discussed in Chapter 9, a tenured employee is entitled to due process if granted such right by statute or otherwise. Even a nontenured employee is entitled to due process (at least notice and hearing) if his liberty interest in his position is involved, such as when there is a public disclosure of the reasons for dismissal that damages the employee's reputation to such an extent that he is unable to secure employment. While most agencies follow a policy of disclosing to the media the results of serious disciplinary actions (as described in Chapter 11), the supervisor should recognize and comply with the due process implications in applying the policy because the employee's interests are superior to those of the news media in such matters. If doubt exists in connection with disclosure in such cases, it should be resolved in the officer's favor. Where public disclosure is not involved or such public disclosure does not stigmatize the employee to the extent that he is deprived of future employment, it can be assumed that due process based on the employee's liberty interest alone is probably not required. In such cases, there is no liability for a constitutional violation of a liberty interest for placing records of an employee's dereliction in his personnel file.[19]

Discipline by Example

A supervisor must be able to control himself before he can control others. If he follows his own set of rules but expects his subordinates to follow a more rigid pattern of conduct, he can hardly expect them to respect him. If he cannot engage in self-discipline, he will not be able to discipline his subordinates effectively, and if he cannot follow the orders of his superiors, he can scarcely expect his orders to be followed. According to Whisenand and Ferguson, "The most meaningful act of responsibility that leaders can do is to control their own state of mind."[20]

---

[18] *Brady v. Maryland*, 373 U.S. 83 (1963); *Ogilvie v. City of New York*, 353 N.Y.S.2d 238 (1974); *Boyd v. Guilett*, 64 F.R.D. 169 (1974); *Gaison v. Scott*, 59 F.R.D. 347 (1973); and *United States v. Reynolds*, 345 U.S. 1 (1953).

[19] *Johnson v. Martin*, 943 F.2d 15 (7th Cir. 1991).

[20] Paul M. Whisenand and R. Fred Ferguson, *The Managing of Police Organizations*, 7th ed. (Upper Saddle River, N.J.: Pearson Prentice Hall, 2009).

Upward Discipline

Subordinates can exercise a form of discipline against their supervisor just as he can against them. They can do so by thwarting his attempts to exercise leadership, by forcing him to maintain constant pressure on them to gain compliance with his directions, by withholding information from him, and by doing a myriad of other things calculated to indicate their displeasure.[21]

Interdependency of Discipline, Morale, and Esprit de Corps

Morale is a state of mind reflecting the degree to which an individual has confidence in the members of his group and in the organization, believes in its objectives, and desires to accomplish them. The exact state of morale at a particular time within an establishment is difficult to measure since it is dependent on a multitude of factors: the quality of leadership to which the group members are exposed, the level of discipline in the organization, extraneous pressures, the existence or absence of attainable goals, the remuneration received by employees, fringe benefits, and other working conditions.

Morale is a fluctuating condition existing within individuals and in groups. It may be high or low, moving up or down as it is influenced by a variety of stimuli. An ill-conceived act of a supervisor, an intemperate outburst, the application of an unjustified penalty, a display of partiality, an act of unfairness, or the like may adversely affect the morale of the group or the individual.

In a broad framework, morale may be measured by factors such as the quality or quantity of work, the rate of turnover, the number of disciplinary cases, the number of grievances (imagined or real), the amount of absenteeism, acts of disloyalty to the organization, a sharp increase in bickering and arguments among its members, incidents involving the careless use of equipment, and the misuse of sick time, but the most obvious indicator that morale is slumping is a general deterioration in the appearance of personnel, which is usually a gauge of organizational pride. Alert supervisors will constantly attempt to assess the level of morale in the group by the extent to which these and other symptoms of employee dissatisfaction exist. Supervisors who assume that morale is always high will be mistaken all too frequently.

Esprit de corps, like morale, involves the existence of a sense of common endeavor and responsibility within the group. It embodies devotion to the group enterprise, cooperation among its members, and pride in its accomplishments.

Discipline, morale, and esprit de corps are of equal importance, since they are interdependent. Each may flow from the others, or each may adversely affect the others.[22] High morale is usually accompanied by a high level of discipline and esprit de corps; neither a high level of morale nor esprit de corps commonly accompanies a poorly

---

[21] *The U.S. Army Leadership Field Manual* (Washington, D.C.: Center for Army Leadership, 2004), p. 13.

[22] U.S. Department of the Army, *Military Leadership,* FM 22-100 (Washington, D.C.: U.S. Government Printing Office, 1990), p. 38.

administered disciplinary program. When these three occur together at a favorable level, however, efficiency will be in direct proportion. Thus, the supervisor must constantly appraise the methods he employs in carrying out the disciplinary function so that he can avoid those pitfalls that lower the levels of morale and esprit de corps of his group.

Reversals of Administrative Actions

A common belief exists among a large segment of the public that a civil service employee cannot be fired. Such a belief is untrue as long as supervisors responsible for maintaining standards of performance and conduct properly fulfill their duties when called on to make disciplinary investigations. Experience indicates that management is generally upheld by reviewing tribunals upon appeal by employees who have been punished for breaches of discipline in the public service.

It is true that many supervisors who initiate disciplinary action against subordinates often feel that they, not the derelict employee, are on trial when they are called on to testify in administrative proceedings and are required to support the action taken against the defending employee. They are often subjected to a vigorous cross-examination; however, if they have properly prepared a case based on hard facts rather than on convincing inferences, speculation, emotion, or unsupported conclusions and if they have meticulously complied with procedural requirements established by law or contractual provisions, their case, not the appellant's, will be upheld in almost every instance.

Results of Unsustained Disciplinary Actions

Invariably, the poorly prepared case, carelessly investigated and lacking in documentation, reflects adversely not only on the supervisor who investigated it but also on the organization if it based punitive action on it. As a result, the offending employee, who probably should have been removed for the good of the service, is returned to the job on appeal. More often than not, from that day forward, he becomes an embittered marginal performer, producing just enough to avoid further punishment and contaminating others at every opportunity. Not only does his morale suffer greatly, but the morale of all who must work with him is affected as well. All too often, his fellow employees who have heard only his version of the story will commiserate with him. It should be clear that a poorly done investigation and the failure to prepare adequately have long-term consequences.

To be sure, the prestige of management and the confidence of its employees will be lowered by each reversal of a disciplinary judgment it has made. The supervisor whose case has not been sustained frequently becomes reluctant to take further action against the same or another delinquent employee because of the failure; as a result, his effectiveness and that of the entire unit he directs are lowered. In those agencies where excessively liberal rules have been enacted by overzealous civil service commissions or legislators to protect employee interests, supervisors will often tolerate a substandard employee rather than remove him and contend with defending their case against him on appeal.[23]

---

[23] Cynthia Estlund, *Regoverning the Workplace* (New Haven, Conn.: Yale University Press, 2010), p. 175.

Complaint Investigation Policy

Procedure

Organizational policy will dictate the procedure to be followed in receiving and disposing of complaints against personnel. Progressive organizations will adhere to a firm policy of inquiring into each and every complaint made concerning the misconduct of personnel, with perhaps only two exceptions. Complaints against official procedures followed by the organization are not usually handled as personnel complaints, nor are those allegations too trivial to dignify as true complaints of misconduct that justify a full investigation (such as the complaint of a citizen that he saw an officer wearing his uniform hat at an improper angle). The allegation should be treated as a complaint, however, if the supervisor receiving it is in doubt as to its classification. Ordinarily such incidents will cause little problem, but the organization should protect itself by a policy that requires that doubtful cases be treated as complaints. Thus, the supervisor is held responsible for his judgment errors so that the likelihood of his being overly lax in his application of the policy will be lessened. Furthermore, the public confidence in the organization will be enhanced by a forthright policy of accepting and determining the merits of all personnel complaints through the process of investigation, and supervisors within the organization will not be unnecessarily exposed to the inherent danger attending a loose rule permitting acceptance of those complaints appearing valid and rejecting (sometimes purely on an emotional basis) those that do not appear to be bona fide. Application of such a policy would be contrary to all the precepts of investigation, which hold that a conclusion should not be drawn before the facts are known. Experience has proved that some of the complaints that at first seem to be the least plausible are found to be most authentic; the reverse is also often true.

Objectives

The primary objectives in the administration of an effective personnel complaint investigation policy are to protect the integrity and reputation of the force, to protect the public interest, and to protect the accused employee from unjust accusation.

Public confidence in an organization will be fostered if it demonstrates its willingness to accept complaints against its personnel forthrightly and to give them prompt attention. Supreme Court Justice Oliver Wendell Holmes's famous quote, "Sunshine is the best disinfectant," has been updated by More and Miller: "Openness serves as an antidote to suspicion and distrust."[24] Protection of the public interest is an equally important objective of a progressive complaint investigation policy. Insistent demands for police review boards and like procedures rarely originate and gain momentum in a community served by a force that has gained public confidence because it has given evidence of its desire to police itself and has recognized that it is in the best interests of the public and the agency to rid itself of unfit or derelict personnel.

It is also of great importance that the personnel complaint investigation policy act as an effective protection for the employee against unjust accusations of misconduct. These accusations often have as their objective the establishment of a basis for a civil action against him, his superiors, and his employer.

---

[24] Harry W. More and Larry S. Miller, *Effective Police Supervision*, 6th ed. (Cincinnati, Ohio: Anderson, 2011), p. 371.

Vicarious Liability

In many jurisdictions, public entities (agencies of state, county, and local government) have been traditionally immune from civil liability resulting from wrongful acts by their employees. This immunity was based on the ancient philosophy of sovereign immunity, commonly known as the divine right of kings. Public employees have always been liable for their own negligent or wrongful acts and have been liable for compensatory as well as exemplary (or punitive) damages. The former were damages resulting from actual loss of wages, medical expenses, or pain and suffering; the latter were damages awarded by the courts to punish the defendant, especially when malice, fraud, corruption, or connivance was involved in the acts that were the basis of the litigation.

Under the doctrine of *respondeat superior*, however, a public entity is liable for the wrongful acts or omissions of its employees who are acting within the scope of their employment. This is the essence of *vicarious liability*, which is defined by *Black's Law Dictionary* as: "Liability that a supervisory party (employer) bears for the actionable conduct of a subordinate or associate (employee) because of the relationship between the two parties."[25] The employee was formerly liable by himself for both compensatory and exemplary damages, and he is still liable for exemplary damages. In some jurisdictions, the public agency that employs him is liable along with him for compensatory damages and may elect to assume liability for punitive damages in certain instances when the acts or omissions were committed or omitted while he was acting within the scope of his employment. The "empty pockets" doctrine of the past wherein, as a practical matter, it was useless to sue a person with empty pockets no longer applies, since the treasury of a public agency may now be exposed to civil suit for the wrongful deeds of its employees. If the employee abuses the position given to him by the state and deprives another of a constitutional right, the conduct may be actionable in state courts, as well as under the Civil Rights Act in federal courts.[26]

As the result of such changes in the philosophy of courts and of the legislative bodies that have enacted similar laws regarding civil liability throughout the nation, litigation in which the officer's conduct is at issue has increased dramatically and can be expected to continue. Thus, the supervisor's responsibility in making personnel complaint investigations is increased materially. He must consider an entirely new dimension in conducting his investigations, since the financial security of his organization may be involved. Evidence that may be required for the purpose of a civil defense must be considered in addition to that involved in determination of the merits of the complaint. He must be especially alert for clues that would indicate that a civil action might be filed against the officer and the department in connection with the issue under investigation.

The supervisor should also be mindful that a criminal act depriving a person of a constitutional right or a death proximately resulting from police action ultimately might involve action under Section 1983 of the federal Civil Rights Act.[27] Allegations are being

---

[25] Bryan A Garner, *Black's Law Dictionary*, 4th ed. (St. Paul, Minn.: West Group, 2011).

[26] *West v. Atkins*, 487 U.S. 42 (1988); *Mary M. v. City of Los Angeles*, 285 Cal. Rptr. 99 (1991).

[27] Title 42 U.S.C. § 1983 provides: "Every person who, under color of any statute, ordinance, regulation, custom, or usage, of any State or Territory, subjects, or causes to be subjected, any citizen of the United States or other person within the jurisdiction thereof to the deprivation of any rights, privileges, or immunities secured by the Constitution and laws, shall be liable to the party injured in an action at law, suit in equity, or other proper proceedings for redress."

raised with increasing frequency that the improper use of force by the officer was a proximate result of lack of training and/or supervision to a degree that constitutes "gross neglect" or "deliberate indifference" of the supervisor and/or the employing agency to the plaintiff's rights. Indeed, liability might be imposed on a supervisor in his individual capacity for his own culpable action or inaction in the training, supervision, or control of his subordinates.[28] Under the theory of negligent retention, a supervisor and/or agency might also be liable for "indifference" to the retention of an employee who is known to be or should have been known to be unfit for the job.[29] In such cases, the history of the officer's training, both formal and informal, which might protect the supervisor and the department from liability arising under the "deliberate indifference" test, should be gathered and retained in the investigation file.

Employers and supervisors also may incur liability if they deprive an employee of some federally guaranteed due process right. An officer can now go to the federal courts and seek monetary damages and/or injunctive relief against an employer and a supervisor at any stage of disciplinary proceedings when it is determined that such a right has been denied him. Courts have held employers liable for damages for denying an employee the right to notice and hearing to clear his name from stigma arising from public disclosure of the discharge, even when he holds his job at the pleasure of his employer.[30]

Coroner's Transcripts

Should a death result from police action and a coroner's inquest is to be held to determine the cause of death, the investigating supervisor should make a formal request for a transcript of the proceedings. When it is received, it should be placed in the investigation file of the incident. Provisions for interested parties to obtain such information are ordinarily made in the laws of various states. These transcripts of sworn testimony have frequently been of considerable value to the officer involved and his employer in defending themselves against concocted or changed testimony in a wrongful-death action, which is sometimes filed even though the homicide has been previously ruled to be justifiable.

---

[28] *Owens v. Haas*, 601 F.2d 1242 (2d Cir. 1979). See also *Lelte v. City of Providence*, 463 F. Supp. 585 (D. R.I. 1978); *Popow v. City of Margate*, 476 F. Supp. 1237 (D. N.J. 1978). For an illustration of the extent to which liability for training may be extended, see *Sager v. City of Woodland Park*, 543 F. Supp. 282 (D. Col. 1982); *Monell v. New York City Department of Social Services*, 436 U.S. 658 (1978); *City of Oklahoma City v. Tuttle*, 105 S. Ct. 2427 (1985); *Still v. San Francisco*, 154 Cal. Rptr. 559 (1908); *Robinson v. Smith*, 211 Cal. App. 2d 473 (1962); *Clay v. Conlee*, 815 F. 2d 1164 (8th Cir. 1987).

[29] Kären M. Hess and Christine Hess Orthmann, *Management and Supervision in Law Enforcement* (Clifton Park, N.Y.: Delmar, 2012), p. 507.

[30] See Chapter 9 for a discussion of an employee's property and liberty interest in his position. See also Chapter 11 for a discussion of the civil liability of employers for denying an employee's due process right.

SUMMARY

Every supervisor should attempt to further the aims of his organization through the constructive process of positive discipline, which seeks to develop in the individual members of the force the same objectives as those of the organization. Negative discipline involving punishment should be reserved for the persons who fail to abide by the rules of the organization and cannot be corrected through the process of positive discipline.

When punishment is required to correct the nonconformist, not only must it be administered swiftly and certainly but it also must be fair, impartial, and reasonably consistent. To be most effective, punishment must fit both the offense and the individual on whom it is imposed. If it is so severe that it engenders only bitterness and resentment in the recipient, it will not be an effective deterrent for him, nor will it provide training for others, since it may be considered a form of revenge by the organization. On the other hand, excessively lenient punishment may indicate that the organization considers the deviant act inconsequential.

The supervisor can best carry out his disciplinary function if he engages in self-discipline and sets an example for his subordinates. If he follows one standard and demands that they abide by a more rigid one, they will eventually exert some form of upward discipline against him. This may take the form of work slowdowns, absences, and other forms of subtle resistance to his leadership efforts. Soon his authority will be undermined, and he will lose much of his effectiveness.

Morale, esprit de corps, and discipline are interdependent—each affects the others. If the level of discipline in the organization is low, morale and esprit de corps are likely to be poor, and standards of the organization will deteriorate. The effective maintenance of these standards is largely dependent on a forthright policy of investigating every complaint of misconduct against employees, except those too trivial to dignify by formal investigation or those solely against the established procedures of the agency.

Supervisors are often reluctant to pursue an investigation because they fear that if an employee is separated from the service, upon appeal, it will be the supervisor who is on trial, not the employee. Supervisors will often tolerate the substandard employee rather than risk this eventuality.

The objectives of a complaint investigation policy should be the protection of the organization from criticism that it will not punish derelict employees, the protection of the public interest, and the protection of the employee from unjust accusation.

A new dimension has been added to the importance of such investigations in recent years with the enactment of legislation and the changing philosophy of the courts that have made the public agency civilly liable for the acts of its employees occurring within the scope of their employment. The supervisor not only must preserve the integrity of his investigation but also must protect his organization from unjust claims. He needs to consider any evidence that might be used against his department in a civil action in addition to that which might reveal the truth or falsity of the accusation against the employee.

REVIEW

Questions

1. What are the two forms of discipline? Discuss the characteristics of each.

2. What are the requisites of punishment? Which of these is the greatest deterrent to future misbehavior of a like nature? Discuss your reasons.

3. Distinguish between a "mistake of the head" and a "mistake of the heart." How should these mistakes affect corrective action?

4. How can subordinates exert upward discipline against a superior?

5. What are some means you can use as a supervisor to ensure that negative disciplinary actions are also training for others?

6. What is morale?

7. What is esprit de corps?

8. Discuss how discipline, morale, and esprit de corps are interrelated.

9. What are some indicators of the level of morale in an organization?

10. Discuss some of the adverse effects that often result when an employee is reinstated after he appeals his dismissal.

11. Should the supervisor make an inquiry into every complaint of personnel misconduct of subordinates? Justify your answer.

12. What are the three major objectives that a personnel investigation policy should cover?

13. Explain the doctrine of sovereign immunity. What other name is this doctrine known by?

14. What is the "empty pockets" principle?

15. What liability does a city have for the acts of its employees?

16. What personal liability might a supervisor have for criminal misdeeds by a subordinate on duty?

Exercises

1. Your superior has assigned you to look into the operations of a unit under his command to determine what the reason might be for an excessive number of complaints against personnel in the unit. Prepare a plan of procedure you would follow in your inquiry. Justify your method of procedure.

2. Your superior believes the morale in his unit is extremely poor. He asks you to verify or disprove his suspicion. How would you proceed to do so?

3. Write a policy statement covering personnel complaint investigations.

4. Prepare a procedural order for the handling and disposition of personnel complaints and investigations.

11

Personnel Complaint Investigation Procedures and Techniques

Chapter Objectives

This chapter will enable you:

- To become acquainted with some of the policies and practices of discipline systems
- To gain an appreciation of the objectives of an adequate complaint investigation policy
- To be able to develop a better understanding of procedural due process requirements

Professional handling of personnel complaints is imperative. "If the police are to maintain the respect and support of the public, they must deal openly and forcefully with misconduct within their own ranks whenever it occurs."[1] The procedures and techniques involved in conducting a personnel complaint investigation and preparing disciplinary action will vary somewhat depending on the origin and nature of the complaint. The supervisor will be limited in his procedural approach by rules and regulations of his organization, but his techniques of investigation will ordinarily be limited only by his imagination and ability.

Case Preparation

The general procedures for handling minor infractions observed by the supervisor in the course of his activities will involve a discussion of the incident with the concerned employee, an on-the-spot warning or admonishment given when appropriate, and a record made of the incident for future reference. Then a follow-up should be made to determine the effect of the warning.

The procedure that will be followed by the supervisor in initiating appropriate action in response to a more serious complaint from within or from outside the department will follow a general pattern. First, the exact nature of the alleged misconduct must be ascertained from the complainant. Broad generalizations, such as "I am being harassed by the police," do not state a cause for investigation unless the complainant can specify the exact nature of the harassment. Second, an inquiry must be initiated for

---

[1] Gary W. Cordner and Kathryn E. Scarborough, *Police Administration*, 7th ed. (New Providence, N.J.: LexisNexis Group, 2010), p. 91.

the purpose of determining the merit of the complaint (and the degree of culpability of the accused officer if investigation supports the allegation). Third, conclusions must be drawn from the facts collected and recommendations made concerning the disposition of the case. Corrective action may be indicated, or the case may be closed if the evidence does not reasonably support the allegation. Fourth, if corrective action is decided upon, it must be administered. Fifth, the supervisor should follow up to ascertain the effect of any disciplinary action, especially if it is negative.

Sources of Complaints

The following discussion will consider first those investigations initiated as the result of complaints by supervisors who have observed infractions or complaints based on information received from inside the organization that an employee has committed a breach of conduct. Second, complaints of others from outside the organization will be discussed. The first type may be called the internal complaint; the latter is designated the external complaint. Also covered are anonymous complaints.

Internal Complaints

Internal complaints are those emanating from within the organization. They include those made by report auditors who find deficiencies or irregularities in reports; jailors, who report on improper conduct of employees in the treatment of arrestees or prisoners; and supervisors, who observe misconduct and initiate disciplinary action.

External Complaints

External complaints are those that come from persons outside the organization. These may be classified as primary complaints—those received directly from alleged victims of police action or debtors—and secondary complaints or second-party complaints—those from persons who are not themselves victims but who complain on behalf of others. Such complaints may be made by attorneys, elected officials, representatives of organized groups, parents, or others whose attention has been directed to possible deviant behavior through observation or who act as the spokesman for others in complaining of such behavior.

Anonymous Complaints

The National Advisory Commission on Criminal Justice Standards and Goals recommends all complaints be permanently recorded.[2] From this standard flows another type of complaint that comes from an unidentified source: the anonymous complaint. This could be an internal or external complaint. A police agency serious about professionalism and the public trust must take anonymous complaints as seriously as those brought forward by a known complainant; in fact, anonymous complaints have the potential to be even more serious when you consider that the complainant probably has serious fears about identifying himself.

---

[2] International Associations of Chiefs of Police, *Model Policy—Investigation of Employee Misconduct* (Alexandria, Va.: July 2001).

Non–Job-Related Misconduct

Courts have held that some conduct that in the past was an unquestioned breach of good order and discipline is no longer actionable by the employer. Unbecoming conduct and certain officer regulations, for example, have been held by some courts to be unconstitutionally vague.[3] Recent decisions, primarily in the federal courts, have accorded employees far broader First Amendment rights than have ever existed in the areas of freedom of expression, association, speech, participation in politics, sexual activity, and privacy. Some conduct in these protected areas is now generally held by the courts to be none of the employer's concern unless it could be shown that the acts substantially affected or interfered with the employee's job. These factors should be considered by the supervisor in conducting an investigation based on allegations of misconduct that might or might not be job connected. He should check his inquiry to determine if the balancing test has been met (discussed later in this chapter).

Of vital importance is whether the employee's conduct involved a *proper* departmental interest. The U.S. Supreme Court held in *City of North Muskegon v. Briggs* that the government would have to prove the agency's reputation was actually damaged by the employee's adulterous off-duty conduct in order to sustain discipline.[4] Under present law, a determination of this interest is sometimes very troublesome to the supervisor, especially in connection with conduct involving bad debts, cohabitation, off-duty drinking, posts on websites, public criticism of the organization or its managers, and the like.

Observed Infractions

The extent of the action taken in a given case will be determined by the nature of the infraction. Many minor deviations involving the employee whose work is somewhat substandard, who has drifted into bad habits, who has committed a minor breach of regulations, or who has otherwise engaged in unacceptable conduct can be disposed of at the time they are observed by the supervisor issuing a warning or an admonishment. Such reproof should obviously be given only when the act of the employee does not require immediate and more severe disciplinary action.

Discuss in Private

In every such instance of an observed breach of discipline, the supervisor should call the matter to the attention of the employee promptly and in private. Rarely can a castigation in the presence of fellow employees or the public be justified; on occasion, however, this may become essential in order to stop a continuing breach of conduct.

Sometimes, the supervisor will learn that a misunderstanding of rules and regulations has been the cause of a minor dereliction, and if so, he should clarify the matter to prevent a recurrence. The supervisor should assure himself that the subordinate understands specifically what the nature of his act is and what is expected of him in the future. This can be accomplished by having him "play back" what *he* understands is

---

[3] *Bence v. Brier*, 501 F.2d 1185 (7th Cir. 1974).

[4] *City of North Muskegon v. Briggs*, 473 U.S. 909 (1985).

expected of him. This procedure will ensure that the subordinate cannot later claim as a defense that he misunderstood instructions should the incident recur.

Record Results

Except in very minor cases, a record of the circumstances of every incident and the action taken should be made where a breach of discipline requires punitive action by the supervisor. Such records may vary from a brief notation in the supervisor's activity log to an incident report for an infraction requiring only an on-the-spot warning or admonition to a full detailed report for a more serious dereliction requiring review by higher authority and possible punitive action of a more formal nature.[5] Such records will provide documentation in the event of a recurrence of such unacceptable conduct.

The recording of the incident without calling the act to the offending employee's attention or otherwise confronting him with it is indefensible, since, in essence, such a procedure involves a charge being made against the employee without giving him an opportunity to respond. He will be resentful when he ultimately learns that a written record of his act has been placed in his file without his having been apprised of the matter. A secondary but nonetheless important side effect that should be avoided is a general weakening of supervision when such covert practices are permitted. Certainly, such conduct by the supervisor would bring into question his moral integrity.

Some supervisors tend to avoid making a negative incident report when they are required either to discuss it with the involved subordinate or to allow him to see it before it is filed. Conversely, such supervisors are often prone to overdo these reports when they involve commendatory incidents. Although failures to make these reports when called for are an evasion of responsibility, they nevertheless based on a natural psychological reaction to do those things that produce a pleasant experience and to avoid those activities that are unpleasant. This psychological truism explains such occurrences but does not excuse them. Employees need to be told of deficient performance, or they will be unaware of it and unable to correct it.[6] Supervisors should be expected to face the problems they encounter forthrightly but judiciously at all times and to take whatever corrective action may be indicated.

Follow Up

In order to determine if the initial discussion was successful, the supervisor should discreetly make a follow-up inquiry, which may consist of a casual conversation with the offending subordinate, observations to determine if improvement has taken place, or whatever additional action may be necessary. A follow-up discussion with

---

[5] An incident report may be used as a formal record of a minor censurable act (or a meritorious act deserving formal recognition) when a full detailed report is not indicated, such as in cases of minor mishandling of equipment, tardiness, improper uniform, and the like, which the supervisor considers actionable. These report forms should be simple and easy to make, or they will not be used to full effect. Commonly, these reports will be held for a prescribed period, depending on the agency's policy, and will then be destroyed.

[6] Childress Consulting, *4-Square Human Development System: A Comprehensive Process for Human Behavior and Performance Development* (Tucson, Ariz.: Wheatmark, 2007), p. 35.

the subordinate may be necessary if no improvement has occurred. Such an interview should involve discussion, clarification of the misunderstandings that may have contributed to the incident, understanding of what is expected, suggestions for improvement, playback, warning when indicated, recording of results, and perhaps referral to higher authority with a recommendation for punitive action when circumstances dictate.

Even if improvement has taken place, a follow-up meeting is in order. Such feedback not only helps the individual officer stay on track but also helps to motivate him. Unfortunately, this sort of feedback is often neglected, despite its power to keep the organization humming.[7]

Every supervisor should be aware that the selection and training of a police officer to a point where he has become a productive employee are costly and draw heavily on the resources of the force. Therefore, the supervisor must make every effort to prevent the eventual loss of an officer when he could be saved by dealing with his minor deficiencies intelligently, purposefully, and positively before they are beyond correction. For example, the police supervisor serves neither his own best interests nor those of his organization or of his subordinates if he tolerates or "blinks at" an incident (however minor) involving drinking on duty (except, of course, in those few assignments requiring such activity on occasion). It has been an unfortunate experience in many forces that such conduct all too often becomes so excessive as to require the termination of an employee who represents a considerable investment to the organization and who might otherwise have been of considerable value to it rather than an embarrassment that could have been avoided by proper treatment of the problem when it was small. It is not suggested that the supervisor become a martinet in his adherence to rules and regulations; however, he should not overlook conduct that requires corrective action merely to foster his own popularity.

Complaint Types

Primary Complaints

Supervisors taking complaints against police personnel should listen courteously and attentively and should avoid any body language, facial expressions, or statements indicating disbelief. When the complaint is patently false, a different approach may be indicated.

Occasionally, the complaint, while made in good faith, is based on misinformation or misunderstanding. The supervisor should then make the necessary explanations or provide the information needed to clarify the issue. Often this is all that is necessary to satisfy the complainant, but when it is not, the matter should be processed in accordance with departmental practices.

Supervisors should avoid acting as arbiters when complaints involving the validity of police action are received with no allegation of misconduct. Adjudication of such matters as traffic citations and arrests is within the province of the court or jury hearing the facts, and "curbstone justice" in such instances can lead only to eventual accusations of "ticket fixing" or "quashing" a case if you know the right people. Such complaints should

---

[7] Paul M. Whisenand, *Supervising Police Personnel: The Fifteen Responsibilities,* 7th ed. (Upper Saddle River, N.J.: Pearson Prentice Hall, 2010).

be referred as gracefully as possible to the courts for adjudication. Where police action appears to have been patently unjust or improper, however, the supervisor should follow established procedures to determine precisely what happened. In certain situations an apology by the supervisor is appropriate. So many times the focus of the complaint is on verbal discourtesy. If you investigate and sustain this complaint, a simple apology by the supervisor and an acknowledgement that the officer will be counseled is often what the complainant is looking for. If misconduct exists on the part of a subordinate, appropriate corrective action should be initiated as indicated.

Anonymous Complaints

Complaints coming from unidentified sources should be treated with the greatest caution and discretion because of the great impact they may have on the morale of employees involved. Each such complaint should be considered on its own merit. Unfortunately, no rule of thumb can dictate whether an investigation should or should not be initiated in such cases; however, no agency can afford the risks of rejecting a complaint for lack of merit solely because it comes from an anonymous source. Experienced supervisors will recall that some of the most serious and bizarre police personnel incidents have been brought to light by anonymous information.

Complaints from Intoxicated Persons

Occasionally, complaints against police personnel are made by intoxicated persons who have been arrested by the police; less frequent are those complaints from intoxicated victims of crime. Such complaints will tax the judgment of the supervisor, since many prove to be totally without merit and are made by the arrestee in an attempt to evade further criminal action; however, the complaint should not be discredited merely because it is made by an intoxicated person who is the subject of police action. The supervisor must exercise the greatest caution and discretion in treating complaints made under these circumstances.

When a complaint involves the loss of personal property and is made under conditions giving the supervisor reasonable cause to believe that it has some merit, immediate steps must be taken to determine whether such loss occurred. If so, make sure how to protect not only the interests of the complainant but also the integrity of the police agency and, above all, that of the accused officer should the investigation reveal that he has been subjected to an unjust accusation or a hint of wrongdoing. Under such circumstances, the supervisor should promptly examine the police premises in which the arrestee was detained and the police vehicle in which he was transported. It has been the experience of many supervisors that property is frequently concealed on police premises or in vehicles by arrestees who later complain that their property was stolen by the arresting officer. The motives behind such complaints are obvious. Supervisors, jailors, searching officers, and booking officers are, therefore, sometimes prone to discredit such allegations—sometimes at considerable risk because of the occasional meritorious complaint. If the property is found, the circumstances may nullify the complaint; if the property is not found, further search might be indicated. Should this delicate decision become necessary, the admonishments discussed later in this chapter should be considered. When a series of similar complaints has been received, supervisors should be especially alert for a pattern of conduct that may be indicated.

Persons making complaints while intoxicated should always be reinterviewed when they are sober. It has been found that, at this time, they will often temper their original complaint, change it, or withdraw it completely when sober reflection indicates to them its injustice. For example, sobriety often enables them to recollect what happened to property they thought was taken by arresting officers.

Second-Party Complaints

Complaints received from second parties on behalf of an alleged victim of police action should not be rejected merely because they are not made directly by the person claiming he has been aggrieved. Bona fide complaints from whatever source should set the wheels of investigation in motion to determine all the facts in the matter.

When accusations have been brought to the attention of the department by second parties such as ministers, attorneys, or parents, the investigator should insist on interviewing the complainant personally to obtain his firsthand version of the incident. During this interview, he should not commit his organization to a particular course of action regarding the investigation, the disposition of the complaint, or the assignment of penalties, nor should he indicate directly or by implication his impression regarding the merits of the accusation, the culpability of the accused officer, the history of past complaints against him, or his proclivities to commit the type of act alleged. Facts uncovered during the investigation may cause the supervisor to regret his editorializing and may cause considerable embarrassment not only to himself but also to his superiors if their judgment, based on mature consideration of the facts, does not coincide with his own premature commitments.

The supervisor should be alert for expressions of the complainant indicating his possible motives for complaining. These may provide valuable clues that will often assist in the investigation. For example, it is not unusual for a person who has been arrested to complain that the arresting officer relieved him of his money. He may find this accusation, however unjust, a more convenient explanation for the loss of his paycheck than the fact that he lost his money in a bar, in a gambling game, to a prostitute, or in some other activity equally difficult to justify to his spouse.

In serious cases, initial (and sometimes follow-up) statements from parties and witnesses should be tape-recorded; after transcription, these should be made part of the investigation file. They may be of great importance, especially in civil cases that may not come to trial for several years.

A check of records should be made, and the interview report should indicate if the complainant has had previous encounters with the police, the reasons (if they are known), the nature of the charges against him (if any were made in the previous incident), and similar complaints of misconduct against the arresting officer in these other police contacts. This information may help in assessing the complainant's credibility—or lack of it—and in determining the merit of his allegations.

Recording of Complaints

Oral complaints should be translated into writing as soon as practicable after they are received, when the facts are usually most readily available. Occasionally, a verbatim record or tape recording of the accusation may be indicated because of its nature; usually, however, a carefully made record of the substance of the complaint will serve as an adequate basis for the investigation. The policy of the organization will dictate whether a crime report must be made when a complaint alleges a criminal act.

In recording complaints against police personnel, the supervisor should avoid including as part of the report his subjective observations. He should, however, record objective evidence that comes to his attention, such as the existence of conflicts in the complaint, intoxication of the complainant, the existence of particular motives in the making of the accusation, and other evidence that might be useful in the investigation and subsequent proceedings.[8]

Complaint Investigation

The techniques of investigating personnel complaints will not vary substantially from those employed in other investigations. A few cautionary admonitions should be recited at this point, however, since ordinarily no criminal act is involved—the vast majority of complaints against personnel involve noncriminal misconduct only. One study found that serious misconduct (excessive force or corruption) comprised a very small portion of these complaints and that most complaints against officers were about attitude, verbal abuse, discourtesy, ethnic slurs, and the like.[9] Furthermore, experience reveals that more than half the complaints received from all sources, from both inside and outside the department, cannot be supported by investigation or are conclusively found to be without merit. Finally, an unusual amount of discretion must be exercised by the supervisor conducting a personnel investigation because his approach will have a vital effect on the morale of the force.

The protections given an employee by due process provisions in the law and in collective bargaining agreements must be meticulously observed by the investigating supervisor, not only for morale purposes but also for compliance with such legal restraints imposed on him. Rules granting procedural due process rights may provide for notifying the employee of such rights. It should be assumed that these requirements would be hollow if he were not given the corollary protection of exercising those rights, so the supervisor should acquaint himself with the rules in his area to determine how they apply to administrative matters, criminal investigations, or both.

Avoidance of Premature Conclusions

The investigating supervisor should avoid drawing a conclusion regarding the merits of the complaint until all evidence has been collected. He should exercise the greatest of care to avoid unnecessary discussion of the merits of the accusation with subordinates before the case is concluded, since his statements are apt to be misconstrued. If he appears defensive toward the accused subordinate prematurely, he subjects himself

---

[8] In some states, such as California, it is a misdemeanor to knowingly file a false complaint against a peace officer (see California Penal Code, Section 148.6). Whether or not the application of such a statute constitutes an abridgment of a citizen's right to petition his government for redress of a grievance under the First Amendment of the U.S. Constitution has not been uniformly settled by appellate courts throughout the nation.

[9] A. E. Wagner and S. H. Decker, "Evaluating Complaints against the Police," in *Critical Issues in Policing: Contemporary Readings,* 3rd ed., ed. R. G. Dunham and G. P. Alpert (Prospect Heights, Ill.: Waveland Press, 1997).

to the criticism of superiors, and rightly so. If he hastens to a conclusion concerning the employee's guilt before learning all the facts, he risks seriously impairing employee morale by his attitude.

Although the supervisor may tend to be influenced in his investigation by his personal feelings, he should approach the inquiry as objectively as possible. If he is reluctant to collect facts adverse to his subordinate's interest, his organization suffers, since effective corrective action will become impossible. If he fails to make a complete and proper investigation or makes none at all, the incident may never be resolved because evidence that might clear the accused officer will not be uncovered. The officer may live under a cloud of suspicion, doubt, and uncertainty thereafter because the supervisor did not do his job.

Prevention of Additional Harm

In some instances involving allegations of serious misconduct supported by evidence that points to the incontrovertible conclusion of guilt of the accused employee, the supervisor must take steps to prevent the matter from becoming worse. Protective custody of the employee involved or his actual confinement may be indicated in instances of felonious conduct. In less serious cases in which the errant employee cannot be continued on duty, the supervisor may find it desirable to send him home with instructions to report back at a later specified time. Should the breach of conduct involve intoxication of the type that does not indicate more severe action at the time than relieving the employee from duty, he should be taken home by a supervisory officer rather than by a colleague. Often, a secure place is available at the station where an intoxicated employee can be isolated until he becomes sober, should that course of action be appropriate.

In some cases where department rules permit, an alternative procedure is available to the supervisor in preventing further aggravation. He might assign the employee to leave with pay, subject to call until the matter is resolved. Since the employee is still on the payroll and is considered to be on duty in this case, necessary control can be maintained over him without exposing him to further hazards that might only subject the organization and the employee to more embarrassment during the period in which the matter is being resolved. In other cases, he might be relieved from duty until completion of the investigation, which will permit a disposition of the case.

Arrest and Booking of an Employee

Physical arrest and formal booking of an accused officer should be made only after the chief officer of the organization has been apprised fully of the circumstances in the matter. It is he who must answer inquiries of other city officials or the press, so he must be kept informed of such important happenings in his department.

Serious misconduct of a peace officer involving felonious crimes such as bribery, morals offenses, or theft will invariably result in considerable adverse publicity for the entire force, yet the bad effects will be minimized in the eyes of the public if the organization demonstrates its willingness to police itself by uncovering such employee breaches and by dealing vigorously with them. Less serious offenses (though technically low-grade misdemeanors, such as traffic infractions and intoxication), in some instances can be disposed of administratively within the organization. Such infractions should rarely be handled by an on-the-spot arrest. In many jurisdictions, whenever a criminal offense appears to have been committed by an employee, the department investigates the case and the findings are routinely submitted to the local prosecutor to decide whether or not there will be a criminal prosecution. Such a course of action is not **adverse** to the public interest, since administrative punishment within the law enforcement organization has traditionally been far more severe than criminal penalties.

In cases where a police employee of another agency is involved, his own department should be promptly informed of the circumstances. At times, it is desirable to turn the investigation over to them, especially when the conduct involves a serious breach of a department rule but is not a crime.

Promptness of Investigation

After receiving the basic complaint intake information, a preliminary review should be made of all available evidence, including documents, statements, photographs, and any departmental records that could confirm or refute the allegations at hand.[10] Delays in beginning a complaint investigation and failures to pursue it diligently to a conclusion can only hamper an inquiry. Witnesses often disappear or forget details with the passing of time, stories may be concocted, or evidence sometimes disappears, with the result that the findings become progressively unreliable. It should be stressed again that investigations of cases that are not clearly resolved usually serve no useful purpose either for the accused employee or for the organization; to the contrary, the case often creates a doubt as to whether or not the employee was culpable of the act alleged.

Collection of Negative Information

Investigating supervisors sometimes fail to record information from persons who were in a position to observe what happened in the incident under investigation but who say that they saw or heard nothing. Such negative evidence usually has little probative value but may be exceedingly important in refuting the testimony of such persons who may appear several years later as witnesses in a civil trial and testify that they witnessed the entire occurrence. Taped statements are especially useful in refuting such testimony.

Personnel Record Check

Personnel records of the accused employee should be carefully scrutinized for evidence that he has previously been the subject of similar complaints. The existence of similar accusations may point to the need for a closer examination of the officer's conduct. Valuable clues to the employee's pattern of behavior may be revealed by a series of similar complaints.

When the allegations involve failures in performance, personnel evaluation reports should be analyzed for evidence that the officer has been previously warned or admonished concerning his performance. Considerable difficulty would be encountered in bringing a successful action against an employee for general unfitness or substandard performance if his supervisors had rated his performance satisfactory in their periodic service ratings.

---

[10] Kenneth J. Peak, Larry K. Gaines, and Ronald W. Glensor, *Police Supervision and Management in an Era of Community Policing*, 3rd ed. (Upper Saddle River, N.J.: Pearson Prentice Hall, 2010), p. 257.

Time sheets, attendance records, and daily performance logs may reveal evidence of false statements regarding duty activities. Accomplishment reports may indicate substandard performance in relation to established norms but should be viewed with caution, since quantitative records are seldom (in themselves) true indicators of the employee's worth.

Interview of the Accused Employee

At some time during the investigation, the investigating supervisor must decide when the accused employee is to be interviewed. There are no hard-and-fast rules governing this decision, and each case must be decided on its own merits. At times, the interview should be conducted at the very beginning of the inquiry. This procedure might be indicated where the accusation is minor or where the accused person has certain information that is needed before the inquiry can be continued. For example, if an allegation is made that an officer misappropriated certain property he had taken from a suspect, the accused employee might easily be able to explain what happened to it. But an interview with the employee in connection with a serious dereliction under investigation generally should not be conducted until the full accusation has been recorded and as many facts as practicable concerning it have been collected and reviewed by the investigating supervisor. Departmental policy and the nature of the complaint will usually dictate whether a written, stenographic, or taped statement should be taken of the interview and whether the investigatory procedures to be followed should be explained to the concerned employee.

Investigating supervisors must proceed cautiously in cases in which there is potential for criminal charges against an officer. Officers may be ordered to give statements and/or write reports under threat of dismissal for refusing to follow such orders. However, the U.S. Supreme Court has ruled in *Garrity v. New Jersey* that under such orders, the statements may not be used against the officer in a criminal trial due to the *Miranda* rights against self-incrimination.[11] It is imperative that investigators consult with the jurisdiction's prosecuting attorney's office when an officer may face criminal charges.

The supervisor should scrupulously avoid the tendency to draw a conclusion or discuss the merits of the case with uninvolved personnel before the investigation is completed (as previously discussed). His function is to obtain facts, not to give out information. At this stage of the inquiry, every effort must be made to avoid disparaging the employee with his family and fellow workers by interviewing him, making necessary searches, or otherwise conducting inquiries in others' presence.

The investigating supervisor should approach this contact with the accused employee as an interview, but he may find it necessary to complete it as an interrogation, depending on the nature of the accusation. It is imperative that the interview with the accused employee be approached in a matter-of-fact manner, giving him full opportunity to explain his side. No apology need be given for the action taken, since disciplinary investigations are an important and necessary part of the supervisor's responsibility to his

---

[11] *Garrity v. New Jersey*, 385 U.S. 493 (1967).

organization. His manner, however, should reflect an objective, unbiased attitude, with no indication that a preconceived conclusion has been reached.

Should a dereliction under investigation indicate that separation from service is desirable, the supervisor should avoid coercing the employee to resign in lieu of disciplinary action, since such action might result in reversal by the courts and a reinstatement of the employee. Allowing an employee to resign in lieu of disciplinary action is largely a matter of organizational policy. Voluntary resignations are desirable at times because they are generally more final than forced separations from service, as the latter must often withstand court action to bring about reinstatement along with the risk that the employer will be required to pay the back salary due the employee.

Should the employee be permitted to resign in lieu of administrative punishment, the supervisor should refrain from promising or implying that the resignation will bring immunity from any further action, either civil or criminal. The supervisor is rarely in a position to offer such immunity. Likewise, statements made as ultimatums should be avoided. The supervisor may not be in a position to take the action indicated by his ultimatum because of legal limitations prohibiting coercion, duress, or undue influence or because of a disinclination by his superior to take a particular course of action merely because it was thought by the supervisor to be appropriate.

Legal Counsel

The investigating supervisor should follow meticulously the statutory and case law in his jurisdiction and past practices in his organization as to whether to grant an accused employee's request for legal counsel before or during the fact-finding interview. A procedural rule granting an employee under disciplinary investigation certain rights must also be carefully adhered to, since even a minor misapplication of such a safeguard might result in an embarrassing and expensive reversal on appeal.[12]

The right to consultation prior to questioning delays the proceedings and implies a right to counsel during the questioning. Unless required, counsel should not generally be permitted during this stage of the inquiry. If counsel is permitted by the supervisor even though it is not required, a claim may be made in a later inquiry that such procedure is a general practice and that the denial of counsel at that particular inquiry was arbitrary and unfair. Several cases in federal courts have held that employees have no right to legal representation during such interviews and that absent some statutory provision or other mandate granting them particular rights, employees could be forced to answer questions concerning performance of their duty.[13] Refusal could expose them to loss of their job. If, however, the investigation becomes accusatory (that is, the focus is on the employee as a suspect in a criminal case), then the employee is protected the same

---

[12] *Kelly v. City of Fresno*, 205 Cal. Rptr. 416 (1984); *Lybarger v. City of Los Angeles*, 221 Cal. Rptr. 529 (Cal. 1985).

[13] *Boulware v. Battaglia*, 478 F.2d 139 (1973); *Mobil Oil Corporation v. National Labor Relations Board*, 482 F.2d 842 (1973); *National Labor Relations Board v. Quality Manufacturing Co.*, 481 F.2d 1018 (1973); *Texaco Inc., Houston Producing Div. v. National Labor Relations Board*, 408 F.2d 142, 168 (1969).

as any other person under the self-incrimination protection of the Fifth Amendment of the U.S. Constitution.[14] Likewise, if the questioning focuses on matters the officer himself reasonably fears are likely to result in punitive action, he would be entitled at his request to a representative of his choice who may be present at all times during the interrogation. The representative should not, however, be allowed to interfere unduly with the questioning process but should be permitted to make additions or clarifications and to render assistance.

Written Statements

The nature of the investigation will dictate whether formal verbatim statements should be taken from the accused concerning his version of the incident, whether a memorandum report from him will suffice, or whether a summary report by the interviewer is all that is indicated. Supervisors are prone to require the accused to make an employee's report too frequently—such reports seldom give a complete account of what happened, and rarely do they satisfy the requirements of the investigation, especially when the accused is expected to make admissions against his own interests. Invariably, inaccuracies or omissions require reinterviewing him. It is often said that "you can tell the truth without convicting yourself." This philosophy implies that the truth can be rigidly adhered to by telling only part of the story and conveniently omitting the incriminating part. It is the supervisor's responsibility to arrive at the truth of the matter, and he must do so by whatever proper means present themselves. Generally, he can accomplish the most by directly asking the questions he expects answered.

Requiring the accused to make a written report of the incident presents a further danger. The accused is often unwittingly made the subject of rumor that can (and usually does) start with the typing and distribution of the report. Such an event should be avoided whenever possible because of the adverse effects rumors and gossip concerning matters of this nature have on morale. Handwritten reports without routine distribution will, of course, eliminate some of these problems. In those cases where they are obtained, they should contain a specific unequivocal answer to each and every allegation by the complainant because unless such a response is made to every issue in the accusation, the investigation is not complete.

As an investigative tool, written statements can be very helpful. According to statement analysis expert Sapir, guilty persons subconsciously reflect the truth in written statements, especially statements that are handwritten. The way the statement begins and the use of personal pronouns, grammatical errors, and specific phrases provide vital clues, as do the relative lengths of the introduction, main body, and conclusion.[15] State laws and local contractual agreements can affect when the supervisor may order a written statement, so he should consult with the department's legal advisor when in doubt. However, there is clear evidence that written statements can do much to resolve the question of an officer's guilt.

---

[14] *NLRB v. Weingarten, Inc.*, 420 U.S. 251 (1975); *Leftowitz v. Turley*, 414 U.S. 70 (1973); *Lybarger v. City of Los Angeles*, 221 Cal. Rptr. 529 (1985); *Kelly v. City of Fresno*, 205 Cal. Rptr. 416 (1984).

[15] Avinoam Sapir, "Scientific Content Analysis," http://www.lsiscan.com.

Avoidance of Face-to-Face Encounters

Despite the dramatic success of fictional investigators in face-to-face confrontations, experienced supervisors have found that only on the rarest of occasions would a situation arise in which it would be advisable to bring the complainant and the accused employee together in a face-to-face encounter. Seldom will anything beneficial to the investigation be accomplished by this procedure, but it could well make a bad situation worse. Claims and counterclaims, if not downright violence, can easily be precipitated in such volatile situations involving the accused and his accuser. If the case is serious enough to require a show-up for identification purposes, the supervisor can easily make the necessary arrangements without risking the possible complications that might result from a confrontation of the parties.

Pictures of employees might suffice for the purpose of identification if such is necessary. The guidelines set forth by the courts should be followed in this process to ensure fairness and impartiality to all parties involved.[16] Several photographs should be selected, showing individuals with dress, features, pose, and complexion similar to those of the accused. The person making the identification should not be influenced or open to suggestion in his attempt to select the right photograph, nor would he be given reason to conclude or guess that the photographs shown him include the picture of the person to be identified. The ultimate purpose of this procedure must be kept in mind—to arrive at the truth.

If an apology is demanded by the complainant for an act allegedly involving misconduct of an officer, the supervisor should not allow the apology to settle the matter even if it is forthcoming. To do so would establish a dangerous precedent. Other personnel would soon come to believe that all they need to do to escape punishment for their misdeeds is to apologize.

Searches

One of the most distasteful of the supervisor's investigative responsibilities, but on occasion a most necessary one, is the making of a search that might involve an officer's person, his private vehicle, his locker and effects, or his home. The need for a search might be indicated in conjunction with an investigation of a complaint such as one alleging that an employee misappropriated property. The task becomes especially onerous for the investigator and equally distressing for the employee when the allegation is made by an intoxicated arrestee. However, when the decision has been made by the supervisor to follow this course of action, he should proceed with the search with the utmost tact and discretion; whenever possible, it should be made with the employee's consent. Searches of his personal property without his consent are limited by the many rules of law that have

---

[16] See *Simmons v. United States*, 35 U.S.L.W. 4227 (1968), for additional guidelines in making identifications by photographs. Although the procedures suggested by the U.S. Supreme Court are ideal in criminal cases, they are not required in all cases. Such procedures might even be impractical at times. Generally, however, they may be applied with good effect in administrative proceedings. The main objective would be to lessen the risk of misidentification. Neither the manner used in displaying photographs nor the pictures themselves may be "unfairly suggestive." See also *Biehunik v. Filicetta*, 441 F.2d 228 (2d Cir. 1971), *cert. denied*, 403 U.S. 932 (1971).

evolved under the Fourth Amendment. These rules are applicable to administrative disciplinary proceedings, as well as criminal trials, and should be adhered to meticulously by the supervisor.[17]

Some courts have held that searches of departmental property, such as lockers, police vehicles, and desks, generally may be conducted without a warrant.[18] Rulings in some states, however, may depart from the general rule because past practices in an organization have led employees to believe that they may expect privacy in the use of such equipment or facility. Under such circumstances, the employee may be protected from warrantless searches and inspections of this type of department property. If it is the employer's intent not to grant an employee a reasonable expectation of privacy in such assigned property, that intent should be clearly indicated by practice or in a policy statement. Therefore, the supervisor should be fully aware of the search-and-seizure rules in his particular jurisdiction so that he may avoid the exclusion of evidence that has been seized in violation of the employee's reasonable expectation of privacy or other Fourth Amendment rights. The department's legal advisor or representative of the prosecutor's office may always be contacted for guidance and direction.

Whenever practicable, searches should be made in private. The matter can be disposed of with a minimum of resentment if the subordinate is convinced of the need for such steps to protect him from future aspersions resulting from a failure on the part of the investigator to follow what might appear to be a necessary investigative procedure. A forthright approach by the supervisor will tend to reduce the adverse effects on morale often accompanying such incidents.

Whenever practicable, a search of the vehicle or effects of the accused should be made in his presence. Should a search of his residence become necessary because of the nature of the complaint and evidence, steps should be taken to make it in the absence of other members of the employee's family to avert the implications and the irreparable harm to family relations that might result from the mere fact that a search had been found necessary.

Regardless of what evidence is revealed, such searches often will result in a total loss of an employee as a productive member of the organization. If incriminating evidence is found, the employee may be lost to the service through termination, or if he is severely punished, he will (in all probability) lose much of his organizational zeal. If the search is nonproductive, it will often cause irreparable harm to his morale, which is often in direct proportion to the selling job done by the supervisor. In any case, it is incumbent on the supervisor to take whatever investigative steps are indicated within the framework of the law.

Lineups

An employee may be ordered to participate in a lineup to be identified by a complainant and may be disciplined for refusing, but the lineup must not be unfairly suggestive.[19] The order to submit to this investigative procedure should be made in writing if the employee refuses (as discussed later in this chapter). It is increasingly becoming standard procedure,

---

[17] *McPherson v. New York City Housing Authority*, 365 N.Y.S.2d 862 (1975).

[18] *Peo v. Tidwell*, 266 N.E.2d 787 (1971). See also *United States v. Katz*, 389 U.S. 347 (1968).

[19] *Biehunik v. Felicetta*, 441 F.2d 228 (1971); *Stoval v. Denno*, 385 U.S. 293 (1967).

however, to use photographic lineups consistent with local law and court decisions, which avoids many potential administrative pitfalls that can evolve from the physical lineup technique.

Investigative Aids

The investigator should not overlook the many aids at his disposal in making a complete inquiry into the circumstances of a personnel complaint. A tool of great value in some investigations is the in-car camera system. By seeing and hearing what actually happened, the investigator has direct evidence at his disposal. The video alone may prove or disprove the allegation. Additionally, information obtained from department computers and vehicle GPS devices may provide helpful data to investigators. Social media sites such as Facebook and YouTube are readily available information sources as well.

Ordinarily, the courts will permit far greater latitude in the collection and admissibility of evidence in administrative proceedings than in criminal cases. Supervisors should, therefore, familiarize themselves with the rules of evidence applicable to such procedures, especially those permitting the use of hearsay evidence and the results of polygraph examinations to determine the truth or falsity of accusations against personnel.

In those localities where it is legally permissible or legal under certain circumstances, a polygraph examination might be of value to the inquiry, but its limitations should not be forgotten. It is not infallible and is not yet considered an absolute indicator of guilt or innocence regardless of the qualifications of the examiner. Use of this device on an officer should be reserved for the most serious complaints and should be carefully controlled by the policy of the organization. Approval of its use should be reserved to the highest officer of the department or his delegate because of the adverse impact it might have on morale if used indiscriminately in personnel investigations. The supervisor should remember that this device is merely an aid to his investigation, not a crutch for him to rely on, and does not take the place of a thorough investigation. Nevertheless, it may be a useful supplement to it.

Even in those states where the use of a polygraph is legal under all or limited circumstances, courts have given only qualified approval of its use in personnel investigations:

> While lie detector tests do not as yet have enough reliability to justify the admission of expert testimony based on their results,... it does not follow that such tests are completely without value. It is well recognized that polygraph tests are commonly used by law enforcement agencies in the investigation and detection of crime.... Such tests can serve to guide police investigators in their hypothesis.[20]

If local laws allow, an unwilling officer accused of misconduct can properly be ordered to submit to such an examination by the chief administrative officer.

In many states, the courts will support the right of a public organization to protect itself from unscrupulous employees. Although the provisions of the Fifth Amendment

---

[20] *Frazer v. Civil Service Board of the City of Oakland, et al.*, 170 Cal. App. 2d 333 (1959). See also *Roux v. New Orleans*, 233 So. 2d 905 (1969), and *Chambliss v. Board of Fire and Police Commissioners*, 312 N.E.2d 842 (1974).

to the U.S. Constitution protect the employee from being required to answer questions that may tend to incriminate him for a criminal offense, the amendment does not give him a constitutional right to his employment. It does, however, protect him from being forced to answer questions not related "narrowly and directly" to his duties or the investigation being conducted.[21] Obviously, when the employee's statements are to be used against him in a criminal prosecution, he should be given his *Miranda* rights.[22] If he is not, his statements generally will be excluded at the trial, with few exceptions. If an employee answers a question in response to a direct order, his statements will be admissible against him in an administrative hearing, but if he is threatened with the loss of his job if he does not waive his privilege against self-incrimination and answer the question, the coercion makes any of his incriminating answers involuntary and inadmissible in a criminal proceeding.[23]

In some instances, an employee's refusal to submit to a scientific test that would aid the organization in the investigation of a criminal offense could make him subject to discharge. In those cases, such an order should be given in writing whenever possible if an employee refuses to comply with an oral directive. It has long been the law that any reasonable and lawful order to an employee is enforceable administratively, and the courts have been reluctant to interfere if arbitrariness or capriciousness is not shown or if there has been no breach of procedural requirements such as might be contained in a police officer's "Bill of Rights" or in a contractual agreement. Refusal of such an order by an employee would properly be considered misconduct for which he could be punished. Because of the varying laws affecting this subject, it is again emphasized that the supervisor should become thoroughly familiar with the relevant statutory or case law in his jurisdiction and act accordingly. Procedural guidance may always be requested from the personnel or legal department.

Physical Tests

Blood, urine, and breath tests are often helpful to prove or disprove intoxication when this condition is an issue. Objective symptoms of intoxication are not always sufficient to provide conclusive proof of this physical state. Constitutional law is very supportive of drug and alcohol testing for public employees. In *O'Connor v. Ortega*, the U.S. Supreme Court held that government's compelling need for "supervision, control, and the efficient operation of the workplace" was sufficient to justify testing workers for drug or alcohol use based on reasonable suspicion, a lower standard than probable cause (required in most other cases).[24] Police officers, as public employees, are held to a higher standard due to their sensitive positions and may be ordered to submit to tests. When an accused employee is requested to submit to such test or tests, they should be administered in private (by a supervisor if possible) to avoid embarrassing him unnecessarily or causing rumors unjustifiably.

---

[21] *Gardner v. Broderick*, 393 U.S. 273 (1968); *Furutani v. Ewigleben*, 297 F. Supp. 1163 (1969); *Spevak v. Klein*, 385 U.S. 511 (1967).

[22] *Miranda v. Arizona*, 384 U.S. 436 (1966).

[23] *Garrity v. New Jersey*, 385 U.S. 493 (1967); *Varela v. Commissioners*, 383 P.2d 62 (1962).

[24] *O'Connor v. Ortega*, 480 U.S. 709, 107 S. Ct. 1492, 94 L. Ed. 2d 714 (1987).

Other scientific devices, tests, and equipment should be utilized when investigative procedures indicate their need. The law governing the seizure and use of nontestimonial evidence in connection with a personnel investigation is generally the same as that relating to criminal investigations.[25]

Investigative techniques common to other police investigations generally should be employed to enable the person conducting the inquiry to arrive at the truth of the matter; however, when these techniques are used, it is stressed that the investigator must abide carefully by the employee's constitutional safeguards and by local rules or contractual provisions that may be more restrictive than the law in protecting employee rights. Utmost tact and diplomacy must be exercised in this sensitive area of complaint investigations, since they ordinarily involve noncriminal misconduct.

Procedural Due Process Requirements

In Chapter 9, procedural due process was discussed as it related to a tenured employee's rights when he is terminated or if any employee's property or liberty interest in his position was affected by the employer's action. Courts will reverse on appeal, and the employer may be civilly liable, if the employee is arbitrarily deprived of any such rights that have been accorded him.[26] The safest course of action to avoid such liability and reversal in serious disciplinary cases where termination is likely would be to adhere to the minimum requirements of procedural due process described in *Morrissey:*[27]

1. Written notice served on him of the specific charges against him
2. Disclosure of evidence to be used against him
3. Opportunity to be heard in person and to present witnesses and evidence in his behalf
4. Right to confront and cross-examine adverse witnesses (unless the hearing officer specifically finds good cause for not allowing confrontation)
5. Hearing before a "neutral and detached" body
6. Written statement by this body as to the evidence relied on and the reasons for their actions

An employer intruding on a protected due process right not only will probably suffer a reversal of the case but is now exposed to damages involving reinstatement, with back pay and benefits, damages, and costs of litigation. The burden is on the employer in such cases to show that the conduct involved substantially affected or interfered with the officer's job.[28]

---

[25] *Schmerber v. California*, 384 U.S. 757 (1966); *Krolick v. Lawrey*, 308 N.Y.S.2d 879 (1970).

[26] *Cleveland Board of Education v. Loudermill, et al.*, 105 S. Ct. 1487 (1985).

[27] *Morrissey v. Brewer*, 92 S. Ct. 2593 (1972). See also *Board of Regents v. Roth*, 408 U.S. 564 (1972).

[28] Emory A. Plett, Jr., "Civil Liability for Improper Discipline—Recent Developments," *The Police Chief*, 40, No. 3 (March 1984), 52–55.

Charges and Specifications

When investigation supports the complaint, written specifications of the charges on which a penalty or hearing is to be based should be served on the employee. A certification of the service should be made a part of the case file.

A preferred procedure in drafting charges against the employee for misconduct is to prepare them in terms of specific violations described in rules and regulations as unbecoming conduct. Ordinarily, the courts will not uphold a broad, vague charge of unbecoming conduct only.[29] This is not specific enough to put the employee on notice of exactly what he must defend himself against.

Balancing Test

With these liability problems in mind, the supervisor should take certain precautions that will help him avoid the possibility of costly and time-consuming litigation arising from procedural errors in connection with disciplinary action taken against an employee. Among some questions to ask are these: Did the employee have prior knowledge of the disciplinary consequences of his act? Was a rule violated relating to the proper interests of the organization? Was it factually established that there was a substantive violation of a rule? Was the charged act justified? Was the investigation fair and objective? Did it reveal substantial proof of the offense? Were the charges justly drawn without discrimination? Was the penalty reasonable?

Protective Rules for Employees

In addition to adhering to the minimum due process requirements of the *Morrissey* case and the balancing test, supervisors should become thoroughly familiar with state laws, local ordinances and rules, collective bargaining agreements, and court holdings that grant rights to officers in disciplinary investigations so that procedural errors and the attendant liabilities previously discussed may be avoided. Such employee rights may vary greatly from place to place, but it appears reasonable to assume that they will become more rather than less restrictive on employers in the near future.

Reporting Procedures

Basic to all police reports but of special importance to complaint investigation reports are the requisites of accuracy and completeness. All allegations of misconduct made by the complainant must be answered. Each report should contain a brief account of the complaint, the details of the investigation of each and every accusation, and the findings.

Investigative Report

The report of the investigation should ideally contain a heading, a statement of the complaint, a summary of the investigation, details of the investigation, conclusions and recommendations (when requested by higher authority or required by rules and regulations), and addenda.

---

[29] *Bence v. Breier*, 419 U.S. 1121 (1975); *Perea v. Falis*, 114 Cal. Rptr. 808 (1974).

The heading of the report should follow the established format. It should ordinarily contain the details that identify the reporting supervisor, the person to whom the report is directed, the date and time of the report, and other details that may be required.

The complaint (sometimes referred to as the subject) should contain a brief statement of the accusation and the names of the accuser and the accused. The who, what, where, when, and how (and sometimes why) should be recapitulated in this section of the report to provide those who review it a brief description of the subject matter. A typical complaint section of a report would contain the following information:

> *Complaint.* Winthrop J. Spinning alleges in a letter to the department that he suffered a twisted shoulder as the result of unnecessary force used on him when he was arrested for being intoxicated by Officer James S. Jones, #23, on [date] at [place].

The summary of investigation section should contain a concise account of the material findings of the inquiry and give the reviewer a complete but brief résumé of all the evidence obtained that is germane to the complaint. Extreme care should be exercised in preparing such summary statements to avoid misleading those who wish to familiarize themselves with the circumstances surrounding the incident without studying the details of the investigation. Busy administrators often find it necessary to rely on summary statements of occurrences to keep abreast of current happenings so that they may keep their superiors informed and deal intelligently with news-gathering services, complainants, and other interested parties. In effect, the summary is an overview of all relevant evidence obtained, whether tending to prove or disprove every allegation of the complaint.

Unless requested by his superior to give his opinions, the investigating supervisor should refrain from editorializing in his report, since to do so would usurp the function of higher reviewing authority, which ordinarily reserves the right to draw ultimate conclusions from the facts presented. This should not deter the investigator from giving his opinion regarding the credibility of or conflicts in the evidence if doing so will aid others in reaching a fairer and more accurate conclusion. If possible, he should support his opinions by explaining why he believed the witnesses were not credible or the evidence conflicting. These comments are of value to the reviewer, especially in complex investigations. The data assembled should be reported in a factual manner so that an intelligent, informed, reasonable, just conclusion can be drawn.

The investigation section of the report should contain a detailed account of the inquiry to which the reviewer might refer for particulars beyond those contained in the summary of investigation section. This section should report the substance of verbatim transcripts of witnesses' statements, those of the accused, and those of the complainant. These substantive statements must be carefully prepared to preserve the integrity of the total report.

In the conclusions section of the report, the investigator should report the conclusions he has drawn from the inquiry—but only after he has been requested to do so by a superior or if he is required to do so by departmental rules. The responsibility for drawing conclusions at times places an extremely difficult burden on him. Little difficulty will be encountered in those cases wherein the evidence unequivocally points to the innocence or guilt of the accused employee; however, where the evidence conflicts and the complaint can be neither sustained nor disproved, the supervisor is often hard put to arrive at an objective conclusion because of his personal involvement in the investigation. Ordinarily, he will not be required to draw a formal conclusion from the investigation for his superiors, since the jury function is their prerogative.

Recommendations, when required by departmental procedures or requested by superiors, should be placed in a section similarly titled. The investigator's familiarity with both the case and the accused employee may enable him to render invaluable aid in evaluating the merits of the case for his superiors; however, this section is normally omitted from the report, since ultimate disposition of the case is usually reserved for superiors.

Where an agency has adopted a schedule of suggested corrective actions for typical derelictions, it may be used as a guide by supervisors if they are directed to recommend corrective action for personnel who have committed a breach of conduct. They should be mindful, however, that the penalty to be imposed not only should fit the dereliction but also should fit the individual. For similar infractions, a penalty that might demoralize one employee may be insufficient and ineffectual for another. The supervisor is usually in the best position to evaluate this. He must balance the organization's need for consistency in punishment, against other factors in order to promote fundamental fairness in discipline.[30]

In recommending punishment, the supervisor must consider the totality of circumstances surrounding the commission of the act. The motive and intent with which it was committed will necessarily influence his judgment. Deliberate violations of established standards of conduct or offenses involving moral turpitude will usually require a far more severe punishment than offenses resulting from ignorance or carelessness. The latter can usually be resolved by application of positive disciplinary measures. Obviously, the employee's past record should be carefully reviewed in connection with penalty recommendations to determine if he is a recidivist.

The addenda section of the report should include such supporting data as verbatim transcripts of statements, arrest reports, crimes, evidence or property reports, booking information, exemplars, and descriptions of physical evidence.

Pagination and Cross-References

For ease in referring to the component parts of the investigation report, each page should be numbered. After summary statements, cross-references to the page or pages from which the summary was taken should be included in parentheses. Such references are invaluable in conserving the time of busy administrators who must review such reports but who wish to refer to additional detail from place to place.

Avoidance of Offensive Terminology

Terms such as *suspect* used in referring to the accused employee or the complainant who happens to be the subject of a criminal matter should be avoided in personnel investigation reports. Neither should the complainant be referred to as *the arrestee* if such references can be avoided. These titles will often be offensive to the accused employee, the complainant, the public, or a jury and may result in criticism that the investigation has been unjustifiably slanted in favor of the officer should they appear in press accounts. Proper names are more descriptive and should be used in lieu of terms that might be considered derogatory.

---

[30] Janice Langan-Fox, Cary L. Cooper, and Richard J. Klimoski, *Research Companion to the Dysfunctional Workplace: Management Challenges and Symptoms* (Northampton, Mass.: Edward Elgar Publishing, 2007), p. 297.

Classification of Complaint Investigations

The following simple but effective classification has been found highly useful in classifying cases after investigation has been completed so that they will reflect the findings in the matter when filed in personnel files.[31] When the facts obtained support the complaint, the case is classified as "sustained." When the evidence indicates that the alleged act did in fact occur but was legal, proper, and necessary, the case is classified as "exonerated." For example, in an incident wherein the complainant alleges that excessive force was used on him by an officer in making an arrest but investigation reveals that the force was made necessary by the complainant's resistance and was not excessive under the circumstances, the classification "exonerated" is placed on the case to indicate that there was no evidence of improper conduct on the accused officer's part.

The "unfounded" classification is used to indicate that the alleged act did not in fact occur and that the complaint was false. Those cases that cannot be resolved by investigation, either because sufficient evidence is not available or because there are material conflicts in the evidence, are resolved without further disposition or action and are classified as "not sustained." Should investigation reveal that the employee was guilty of misconduct not part of the original complaint, the case might be classified as "misconduct not based on the complaint."

The internal affairs policy of the Knoxville, Kentucky, Police Department adds a sixth, important disposition of internal affairs investigations: "exonerated—policy failure." If the complaint investigation concludes that the allegation is true but that the employee's actions were consistent with departmental policy, the complaint will be classified as "exonerated—policy failure."

Discipline and the News Media

The supervisor conducting a personnel investigation is often confronted by members of the news media pursuing a lead related to the matter under inquiry. Obviously, a premature release of details of the investigation before it has been completed would be improper and might jeopardize the entire inquiry; however, deceit will be resented and may result in the publication of a news story based on inaccurate information gleaned from unreliable sources and adverse to the interests of the department. Usually, reporters will appreciate a frank explanation of why a release cannot be made at the time and an assurance that it will be made when the case has been completed. This procedure presupposes that there exists within the department a policy of full cooperation with the news media and that news releases, when made, will emanate from an authorized source.

In those jurisdictions, however, in which privacy laws restrict disclosure of disciplinary actions against peace officers, members of the news media must be informed of the prevailing laws. It will then, of course, become their prerogative to publish the facts developed from other sources if they so decide.

---

[31] Los Angeles Police Department, *The Department Manual*, 3/820.20; Daryl E. Gates, with Diane K. Shah, *Chief: My Life in the LAPD* (New York: Bantam Books, 1992), p. 204.

Disposition of Complaints

Notification to the Complainant

In the interests of good public relations, the complainant should be notified of the disposition made in the matter when the investigation has been completed and the case resolved. Even though the complaint has been sustained by the investigation, the communication should state only in general terms that appropriate action has been taken to prevent a recurrence of the act without indicating the specific penalty imposed on the employee. As was mentioned above with reference to members of the news media, it is important to note that the law in some jurisdictions expressly forbids further disclosure.

When the investigation reveals that the complaint was unfounded in fact or that the officer should be exonerated because the act on which the complaint was based was legal and proper and was made necessary by the failure of the complainant to cooperate, he should be forthrightly apprised of such conclusion and the general reasons therefor.

Notification to the Accused Employee

In addition to the notice given the complainant that final disposition has been made in the incident, the accused should be promptly informed of the conclusions drawn from the investigation and the action to be taken (if any). Some agencies communicate this information on a simple form established for the purpose. In addition, a copy of the communication to the complainant can be sent to the employee with good effect when the case is classified as unfounded or when he is exonerated of the charges—this procedure will do much to relieve his anxiety.

Rarely will the employee be exposed to a more harrowing and emotionally upsetting experience than when he is the subject of an investigation of a personnel complaint alleging a serious dereliction. Therefore, it is of utmost importance to his morale, and indeed that of the entire organization, that he be informed at the earliest possible time when the matter has been finally resolved.

Imposition of a Penalty

When a penalty is to be imposed, it should be administered promptly to have the greatest effect and should not be used as a threatening device but as a constructive tool of supervision. It will usually be accepted by employees if they have confidence in its reasonableness and necessity, but if it is used as a club, it will often result in resentment and downright resistance to supervision.

To delay administering a penalty when one has been imposed merely because it is a disagreeable supervisory task is inexcusable. This does not mean, however, that the execution of a nominal penalty cannot be delayed somewhat, at times, on the mutual agreement of the employee and the department. For example, a short suspension might best be executed when the deployment demands of the shift require the least personnel or when a delay in executing a suspension will avert the imposition of an unreasonable hardship on the employee.

Disciplinary Failures

A certain portion of all disciplinary actions fail because supervisors do not know how to make personnel investigations, and the answer to this problem is training. Other disciplinary actions fail to accomplish their objectives not because of the insufficiency of the evidence but as a direct result of the failures of the investigator to fulfill his responsibilities. He avoids doing what has to be done in fulfilling his obligation to maintain departmental disciplinary standards, either because of his overprotectiveness or defensive attitude toward his subordinates or because of his disinclination to do anything that might hurt one of them, even one whose actions have brought discredit to other members of the profession. His failures are often the result of his fear of disapproval from those with whom he works. On occasion, he will fail to investigate complaints completely (if at all). His delays in making prompt inquiry into personnel breaches often result in the destruction or disappearance of evidence that might otherwise have been collected, the cooling of witnesses, or the downright concoction of stories that will prevent any possible resolution of the matter.

Fortunately, such failures are not common, but when they do occur, the supervisor responsible does a grave disservice to his organization by contributing to a general lowering of its prestige and the public's confidence in it, not to mention the disservice he does to his hardworking, dedicated subordinates who subscribe fully to the organizational standards of conduct and are proud of their professional stature. Furthermore, his well-intended protectiveness might harm rather than help the accused employee who is innocent of any wrongdoing but is merely in need of someone to collect the evidence to prove his innocence unequivocally so that the matter will not be the subject of further doubt.

SUMMARY

Once the exact nature of a personnel complaint is ascertained, the supervisor must initiate an inquiry to determine the facts surrounding the case. Conclusions must then be drawn from all the evidence secured and corrective action taken when indicated or the case closed without punitive action when the facts absolve the accused person.

The supervisor investigating a complaint against his subordinate must pursue every channel of investigation available to him in seeking the truth. He must remain objective in his approach and avoid drawing a conclusion of innocence or guilt before the facts are known. Traditional investigative procedures generally should be followed; however, since ordinarily the complaint involves an allegation of noncriminal conduct, it is imperative that the employee and the complainant be treated with compassion to prevent (insofar as possible) shattering the morale of the employee or destroying the confidence of the complainant in the integrity of the force.

Promptness of investigation is essential to prevent loss, destruction, or contamination of evidence and to minimize the adverse effects of long, drawn-out inquiries of this nature on employee morale. When the case has been resolved, both the complainant and the accused employee should be promptly notified of the conclusion reached. If punishment is to be imposed on the employee, generally the amount or degree should not be specified in the communication to the complainant notifying him of the disposition of the case. Likewise, if investigation reveals that the accusation is without merit, this fact should be brought forthrightly to his attention.

The taking of disciplinary action against subordinates imposes on supervisors the obligation to use discipline forthrightly and impersonally. It should be a constructive tool of supervision rather than a threatening device used to secure compliance with departmental standards of conduct.

REVIEW

Questions

1. What are internal complaints? Give examples.

2. Where do primary and secondary complaints originate? Give examples of each.

3. Discuss anonymous complaints and how you would handle them.

4. How would you handle a complaint from an intoxicated person?

5. If a complaint was made against one of your employees, why should his personnel record be checked as part of the investigation?

6. Why should face-to-face encounters be prevented between the accused employee and his accuser?

7. What are the general procedures a supervisor should follow when he discovers a minor infraction on the part of a subordinate? A serious complaint?

8. If you received a complaint concerning a serious incident involving one of your subordinates but the complainant was not able to identify him, what means of identifying him would you use? What precautions would you take if the incident involved a criminal offense?

9. If a search of a subordinate's person, locker, private vehicle, or residence is indicated, how would you accomplish each search? Discuss the general procedures you would follow.

10. Generally, what are the sections of a typical personnel investigation report, and what information should each contain?

11. What are some of the common failures of supervisors in making personnel complaint investigations?

Exercises

Assume that you are a field supervisor. You observe or your attention is called to the following incidents involving personnel under your direct supervision. Explain how you would handle each in a manner that would not be in conflict with legal and administrative rules.

1. Over a period of time, you have noted that one particular officer has been slow in responding to calls between 2 A.M. and 5 A.M. His explanations have not satisfied you, but you do not have evidence to dispute them. You suspect that he is sleeping on the job.

2. While you are conducting roll call, an officer arrives late. Upon entering, he creates a disturbance and then interferes with the proceedings by whispering to other officers.

3. Your vice officers have received several complaints that an illegal gambling game is taking place in the back room of a bar. They investigate and arrest several persons for illegal gambling; one of them is your subordinate officer, who is off duty. The vice officers call you to the scene and ask your advice. What would you advise? Would you handle the incident differently if the officer was on duty at the time? Explain. How would you handle the incident differently if the officer involved were assigned to another unit of your department? What would you do if he were a member of a neighboring force?

4. While checking your officers at the end of a watch, you observe one of them take a box of groceries from the police vehicle and transfer it to his own.

5. For some time, you have been hearing rumors that some of your subordinates have been frequenting a bar and drinking illegally after closing hours. You check the bar one-half hour after closing time and find two of your officers drinking there. One is intoxicated; they are both off duty but are in uniform.

6. You follow up on a call and find one of your subordinates involved in a minor traffic accident. He is not in uniform. You observe that he has been drinking but do not conclude that he is under the influence of alcohol. The other party to the accident maintains that the officer is intoxicated. How would you proceed? How would you handle the matter if the officer were intoxicated? Explain.

7. You receive a call from a collection agency that one of your subordinates has failed to pay a bill for medical services after repeated requests from the physician. The officer assures you that the matter will be taken care of promptly. Two weeks later, the collection agency notifies you that the officer has not contacted them to make arrangements to pay the debt. Would your disposition in this case be different if, upon the first interview with the officer, he claimed the charge was excessive and therefore in dispute? Explain.

8. You follow up on a call in which one of your subordinate officers has arrested an intoxicated person. The arrestee, a pedestrian, is well dressed, is intelligent, and appears to be a responsible citizen when sober. He tells you that not more than five minutes before your arrival, the officer stopped him and asked for identification, which he produced from his wallet. He alleges that the officer took his wallet and examined it and that when it was returned to him, a twenty-dollar bill was missing. He says that when he complained, he was placed under arrest.

9. One of your subordinates, whom you consider a very promising young officer, tells you that he is planning to quit because of pressure he is receiving from his spouse and family. He believes he can be more successful in some other endeavor, although he likes police work. He indicates that his spouse is opposed to the job because of the bad working conditions, irregular hours, low pay and prestige, and hazards of police work.

10. You receive information from a person who declines to identify himself that one of your subordinates arrives home nearly every morning at about the time the informant arises. According to the informant, the officer frequently unloads cartons or packages from his car and carries them into the house. This observation usually takes place about 8:00 A.M. The officer identified is assigned to the 11:30 P.M. to 7:30 A.M. watch. The informant thinks that the property may be stolen because he has seen it carried into the house and garage so regularly.

11. You receive a complaint from the parents of a young attractive woman that one of your subordinates made offensive, sexually suggestive remarks to her when he stopped her for a minor traffic violation. The officer's personnel file contains one unsustained complaint of a similar nature. Explain what you would do.

12

Personnel Evaluation Systems and Performance Rating Standards

Chapter Objectives

This chapter will enable you:

- To gain an appreciation of the objectives of a personnel evaluation system
- To become familiar with some of the reasons why evaluation systems fail
- To become acquainted with the methods of gathering rating data and the criteria on which such data should be based
- To become acquainted with personnel rating standards and uses
- To gain an understanding of the common rating errors and some methods of avoiding them

Organizations are judged by their records of achievement. The military establishment is judged by its ability to win battles, the industrial enterprise by its capacity for making profit for stockholders, the law enforcement agency by its ability to suppress unlawful activity. In each of these activities, the factor that determines whether there is to be victory or defeat, profit or loss, order or disorder is the personnel who constitute the organization. In order for those responsible for planning programs and directing the many projects of the enterprise to accomplish their mission most efficiently, they must be able to utilize effectively the skills and abilities of their most costly and important resource—personnel. To do this, the capabilities of employees must be known and a means must be provided to assess their level of performance in comparison with what is desired.

Studies have revealed that the evaluation or appraisal of employees is one of the most important parts of the management process. The fact that a major share of employee grievances has involved challenges of personnel evaluations reinforces this conclusion.[1]

---

[1] Donald C. Mosley and Paul H Pietri, *Supervisory Management: The Art of Inspiring, Empowering and Developing People*, 7th ed. (Mason, Ohio: Thomson Higher Education, 2008), p. 441.

Objectives of Evaluation Systems

Service ratings, personnel evaluations, employee appraisals, merit ratings, or whatever the method is called will provide one tool for measuring employee capabilities and giving management an inventory of them. Such evaluation systems also provide a means for supervisors to record systematically at specified intervals their opinions regarding the performance of subordinates. They establish a basis for rewarding or penalizing personnel and for explaining to them why they are or are not progressing satisfactorily. Evaluations based on sound, objective data are unparalleled as a foundation on which the supervisor can help a substandard employee develop a program to improve his performance. Properly executed, such a system will also be a valuable tool in the placement and promotion of personnel, the administration of merit pay or salary increases, disciplinary proceedings, and similar matters.

In addition, these evaluation systems provide supervisors with a means for measuring those abstract traits of their subordinates that cannot be easily measured otherwise. Absences, tardiness, production, and accomplishments can be easily measured directly, but this is not so with such traits as loyalty, ability to get along with others, and temperamental stability.

Every supervisor worthy of the name engages constantly in the process of comparatively rating subordinates, whether there is a formal or informal rating system or none at all. In small agencies, an informal rating system may serve management well because everyone knows everyone else. In larger organizations, however, it has been found that in the interests of efficient management, a more formalized system is necessary so that an individual employee's progress may become a matter of record. This system gives management a tool for comparing that employee's performance with that of others in similar assignments in various parts of the organization.

No system of measuring the qualities of a human being is perfect because personal bias and subjectivity cannot be entirely eliminated from the appraisals. However, the process should always have the purpose of seeing how actual employee performance compares to the ideal or standard it is intended to measure.[2]

In those agencies where no evaluation system has been adopted, each supervisor is left to his own devices to evaluate his personnel comparatively. More often than not, such ratings become highly subjective and are of little value in providing management with an accurate and unbiased source of information concerning employee skills. Furthermore, management is deprived of a ready means of determining what has been done, what is being done, and what needs to be done.

A Case for Evaluation Systems

Personnel rating systems are inherently unstable because the instruments are subjective. As the result of this characteristic, workers demand frequent changes and are seldom satisfied when the changes are made; thus begins the cycle of change to meet the need for measuring the comparative worth of people. Deficient as some of these systems

---

[2] *Ibid.*

are, they comprise a universally accepted method for appraising personnel for a variety of reasons and can be very useful to management if proper attention is given to their preparation.

Evaluation systems have been established in some organizations because of legal requirements; in others, enlightened administrators have adopted a system as a means of improving employee morale by giving employees recognition in proportion to the excellence of their performance. Since the desire for recognition is one of the basic human drives, not surprisingly it often has been found that the effectiveness of the working force is dependent (at least in part) on the recognition it receives from management for its efforts. The personnel evaluation system should serve as a means of providing at least a degree of the recognition employees desire.

Rating reports carefully made and judiciously used serve as valuable aids to the organization in the maintenance of reasonable performance standards and in the administration of a progressive training, placement, promotion, executive development, and salary program based on merit. If these reports are made and filed without further reference to them, however, they serve no useful purpose other than that they have focused the supervisor's attention on the specific characteristics of the employee. There can be no denial of the cost of administering these programs—it is considerable—but management must weigh the costs in terms of the results achieved from such a system.

Impartial administration of an evaluation system should make it obvious to personnel that at least an effort is being made by management to eliminate snap judgments and favoritism in the personnel relations program and that an attempt is being made in good faith to reward the most faithful producers by objectively giving credit where it is due. The extent to which this is done will determine, in large part, the degree of employee confidence in the whole process.

As an administrative tool, the data obtainable from personnel evaluations are useful in a progressive personnel management program. Personnel evaluations are valuable devices for determining if employees should be granted tenure or if they are entitled to earn or retain longevity or merit pay. The converse is also true: They are instruments that can be useful as one basis for determining if employees should lose merit pay, and industrial concerns often utilize evaluation reports to determine the order in which to lay off personnel or reemploy them. In recent years, however, union agreements and the courts have reduced the prerogatives of the employer to hire and fire according to relative employee worth rather than seniority.

As clinical instruments, rating reports not only are valuable in giving employees credit for superior performance but also afford a basis for calling attention to inadequate performance. Properly prepared, they cannot be equaled when used as a basis for constructive employee counseling. They provide an excellent means of establishing production and accomplishment standards within the organizational unit and may be effectively used to support disciplinary actions and reveal training needs. Additionally, they provide clues to the detection and weeding out of personnel who are unfit for the job and thus help to avoid liability arising from the doctrine of negligent retention (discussed in Chapter 10).

Properly administered personnel evaluation programs can be useful to administrators in research activities, such as the refinement and validation of personnel relations techniques. These systems are helpful in evaluating the selection process, since they provide some clues to the correlation between job success and the testing program.

Evaluation reports also are useful in assessing with some accuracy the effectiveness of a training program at the operating level. They often provide data on the degree of police efficiency as it is influenced by the presence or absence of a good field training program.

When rating reports are utilized as one basis for promotion, ratings over a period of years by many supervisors will tend to be a highly accurate appraisal of the employee's worth—far more accurate generally than an appraisal by an oral examining board that observes the candidate in a relatively short interview and then can assess only a limited number of characteristics desirable in a leader. These reports should thus afford a fertile source of information concerning a candidate's suitability for promotion based on his past performance and many individual supervisory appraisals. The importance of evaluating employees for promotability and salary increases, in addition to evaluating them on their productivity and institutional value, is obvious.

Causes of Evaluation System Failures

Evaluation systems fail for many reasons. Some of the most prominent causes are described in the following sections.

Indifference

Regardless of the sophistication of the rating procedures or the importance of the program, an evaluation system will be successful only if the raters or those rated really want it to succeed. Indifference of supervisors to the need for accuracy in rating can damage the effectiveness of the system, as can the failure of the administrators of the organization to support the program actively, since their passivity will discourage the raters below and cause them to lose interest in the program. When the system fails because of the disinclination of management to make it work, morale of the better employees inevitably suffers first because they lose a source of recognition for their efforts. Placement procedures soon become shoddy and unscientific based on internal politics, personal biases, or favoritism rather than worth.

Employee Pressures

Even the persons rated may thwart an evaluation system by sheer pressure, especially when the level of their performance as reflected by ratings forms a basis for their pay. Employee groups sometimes are solicited to bring formal organized pressure to bear on management when merit pay is withdrawn—unjustifiably, in the eyes of the employee affected—on the basis of performance rating reports. If it appears that the employee's welfare must be protected, often the employee group will vigorously press management to justify its action.

Individual employees can also bring a kind of pressure to bear on the entire system. When they view their rating reports and see their defects being made a matter of formal record, they often become hostile and resentful. The marginal employee is usually the most vociferous and may attempt to embarrass his superiors by accusing them of prejudice.

Those supervisors who really believe in the program and honestly want it to work soon become discouraged when the brunt of employee pressures disproportionately falls on their shoulders. Unfortunately, some of them soon lose their zeal for honest evaluation, with the result that their ratings become riddled with inaccuracies and consequently are useless as management tools. Experience has shown that some supervisors will go so far as to change unjustifiably their rating reports on an employee if his complaints are loud enough.

Failure to Train Raters

Systems devised to provide a means of assessing employees will ordinarily not survive (or if they do, will be relatively noneffectual) unless training is provided for those who are to do the rating. Raters must be given an understanding of the objectives a properly administered evaluation program should meet and be made aware of the means of avoiding the common errors that cause inaccuracies in ratings and reduce their value.

The common errors that too often creep into personnel evaluations are the most noticeable and troublesome deficiencies in any rating program. They can be reduced considerably by training the raters to become more objective and more sophisticated in their rating methods.[3] Training raters is the key to the successful administration of a rating system and is its most usual source of weakness.

When standards of measurement of employees are not consistently applied from unit to unit or when difficulties are encountered in attempting to compare ratings from several divisions of the organization, the deficiencies can usually be traced to the lack of training or a failure on the part of management to clearly define rating traits. These deficiencies are perhaps the greatest source of complaints about administration of the system.[4]

Another cause of failure in rating programs results from the neglect of management to give raters an opportunity to learn rating procedures under supervision. Rating failures can be reduced through regular conferences among supervisors wherein rating problems and solutions are discussed, proposals for modifications in procedures or methods are presented and considered, and common agreements are reached concerning rating standards that should prevail in the organization. Without this training, it is highly probable that the system will collapse because of its cost inefficiency and uselessness.

Rating Abuses

A rating system is bound to fall into disrepute if personnel rated come to lose confidence in it because it has been abused by management. Ratings should be utilized only as they were intended; once the purposes for which they were adopted have been announced, their use should be confined to those purposes. They are most commonly used in promotional examinations, as a basis for assignment, or for merit pay raises. A broadening of this use may be necessary from time to time, but such changes should be mutually agreeable to management and employees because a breach of faith with them may cause the whole system to be subtly sabotaged.

---

[3] Richard L. Daft and Dorothy Marcic, *Understand Management*, 6th ed. (Mason, Ohio: South-Western, 2009), p. 340.

[4] Richard C. Grote, *The Performance Appraisal Question and Answer Book: A Survival Guide for Managers* (New York: American Management Association, 2002).

Slipshod Procedures

Rating reports often affect a person's entire career; therefore, those made carelessly may have serious consequences. Slipshod, inaccurate methods affect every person in the organization because each one rates or is rated. In some cases, an individual may rate others and be rated himself. Even nonsupervisory personnel have to rate other personnel on occasion. For example, the patrol officer acting as a training officer to orient the new recruit in field procedures invariably must perform the important task of rating the new employee. Peer rating is often practiced in training situations, and these ratings are usually given great credibility because they are apt to reveal traits not often observed by supervisors. Therefore, careful instructions must be given to the raters to prevent subjectivity as much as possible. Ratings made perfunctorily by raters who have evaded their responsibility lose most of their value and become costly administrative trivia. In any event, they are probably not worth the time invested in preparing them, and sooner or later the entire system will fail.

Rating Shortcuts

A personnel evaluation system worthy of the cost should not be compromised by shortcut methods. Experience has shown that abridged versions of rating scales devised to economize on time at the expense of accuracy have been responsible for a high percentage of failures.

Gathering and Recording of Performance Data

The competence of the rater, the effort he expends in observing and recording evidence of the behavior of his subordinates, his judgment in weighing and evaluating this evidence, and his fairness in applying it to the service rating procedure directly reflect the type of training he has received, the degree of his attitudinal conditioning, and the climate established for the system by management. The first-line supervisor, usually a sergeant in the police service, is the key figure in any rating system, since his job involves the productivity of the officers under his command. If he accomplishes his objectives as a leader and discharges his responsibility to his organization, he must continuously collect and record evidence reflecting the quality of service being rendered by his subordinates so that he may periodically evaluate them. If he is required to rate them, he will be forced to learn more about them and about the job they are performing. He must know at least generally how the work should be done and how every person in the particular unit over which he exercises supervisory control is doing it. This knowledge is gained by keeping abreast of technical developments in the field of law enforcement and allied professions, by inspecting results of operations, and by following up on his observations.

Recording Methods

The method of accumulating evidence about his subordinates' performance may be established as a matter of practice and policy. The techniques used by supervisors may vary according to their individual needs. Some agencies have adopted an incident report form to be used to record commendable or censurable performance of a minor or routine nature. These reports should be retained during the rating period, as they form a substantial basis for performance evaluations. They should then be placed in the employee's personnel folder or destroyed. Some supervisors prefer to record observations in a separate file for future reference; others record incidents in the supervisor's log and later transfer these notations to a file or a control card kept for each officer. Whatever system is used to record such incidents, the evidence is helpful in making periodic rating reports more objective. In recording censurable incidents, the right of the person rated to be informed of matters placed in his personnel file must be meticulously observed by the supervisor.

The memory of the supervisor alone will not store the multitude of observations he makes each day on his subordinates. If he relies on recollections alone, his ratings are likely to be based on broad impressions rather than on specific objective data. The larger the span of control of the supervisor and the more frequent the changes in the supervisory staff, the greater is the need for written documentation of a subordinate's performance.

Critical Incident Technique

The critical incident technique involves the collection of objective data about an employee's performance, which can be used as a basis for more effective performance ratings. Critical incidents indicating superior or unsatisfactory performance are reported as they are observed and can be used as an objective standard for ratings about which raters can agree. The use of in-car video clips can complement the written documentation. Vague or abstract trait ratings that often reflect personal bias can thus be minimized. Such data dealing with specifics rather than abstractions are also valuable as a basis for counseling employees about their performance.[5]

Rating Traits

Rating forms will usually list from four to twelve traits or characteristics that must be considered by the rater. Not more than twelve traits relevant to the job performed should ordinarily be used for best results.[6] Figure 12–1 shows a typical rating report form.

Rating traits and abilities can be grouped into broad categories such as personal characteristics. Evaluation reports for probationary officers of all ranks should be made at least once per month during the probationary period to give the broadest picture of the employee. These should be carefully considered as one of the criteria for giving probationary officers tenure.

The supervisory officers' rating form should be constructed to focus the rater's attention on the many traits and characteristics required for a supervisory position. This is consistent with Oettmeier and Wycoff's advice that there should be separate forms for different assignments.[7] Just as a probationary officer's evaluation form must differ from a supervisor's form, a detective should be evaluated on different criteria from a staff officer. Space should be provided for evidence justifying extremely high or low ratings and for

---

[5] Diane Arthur, *Managing Human Resources in Small and Mid Sized Companies*, 2nd ed. (New York: American Management Association, 2005).

[6] McMillan J. D. and H. W. Doyel, "Performance Appraisal: Match the Tool to the Task," *Personnel*, 57, No. 4 (July–August 1980), 12–13.

[7] T. N. Oettmeier and M. A. Wycoff, "Police Performance in the Nineties: Practitioner Perspectives," in *Managing Police Organizations*, ed. G. W. Cordner and D. J. Kenny (Cincinnati, Ohio: Anderson, 1996).

CMB ID # _____

Employee _____ Title _____

Department _____   O Classified   O Unclassified

Anniversary Date (MM/DD/YY) _____

Evaluator _____ Title _____

Number of Months with Supervisor _____

Period Covered (MM/DD/YY) _____ To _____

Date Review discussed with Employee (MM/DD/YY) _____

┌─ Review Type ───
│ O Annual   O Follow Up   O Completion of Probation   O Change of Supervisor   O Other

Is Employee eligible for a Merit Increase?   O Yes   O No or N.A.   **If yes**   O Approved   O Not Approved

Department Head Signature / Date _____

Step I: Establishing Expectations

I acknowledge that I have discussed the Performance Factors with the Employee. _____

Supervisor's Initials / Date

I acknowledge that my Supervisor has discussed the Performance Factors with me. _____

Employee's Initials / Date

Step II: Mid-term Feedback

Employee's performance discussed at Mid-term Feedback session.

Supervisor's Initials / Date _____

Employee's Initials / Date _____

Step III: Completion of Review

Department Director/ACM/CM Signature / Date: _____

Evaluator's Supervisor Signature / Date: _____

Evaluator Signature / Date: _____

I received this Review and discussed it with my Supervisor. (On signing this Review, I acknowledge having discussed it with the Evaluator and having received a copy. I may not necessarily agree with the conclusions.)

Employee Signature / Date: _____

Step IV: Appeal Process

Appeals must be made within ten calendar days and are only for ratings below 5 or overall below 50.

_____ **Classified**   _____ **Unclassified**

☐ I wish to Appeal   ☐ I do not wish to appeal   ☐ I cannot decide at this time whether or not to appeal, however, I have been advised of the above requirements.

Employee Signature / Date _____

PMP revised 12-10-02

Figure 12–1

Typical Performance Appraisal Evaluation Report.   Source: *City of Miami Beach, Florida.*

City Wide Performance Factors

Performance Factors are to be completed and initialed by both the employee and the supervisor at the beginning of the evaluation period.

Score Definition								
Significantly Exceeds Expectations 10–9	Exceeds Expectations 8	Meets Expectations 7–5	Needs Improvement 4–3	Unsatisfactory 2–1				
Select the factors most appropriate to level and scope of the employee's position.					W	S	Total	Mid-term Feedback on Target Yes / No
CUSTOMER SERVICE	Provides effective, efficient service to external/ internal customers and represents the City in a positive manner.				10			
TEAMWORK	Develops rapport with people at all levels. Establishes and maintains cooperative relation- ship and deals with others in a factual manner. Encourages continual team improvement.				10			
PRODUCTIVITY	Produces quality work in a timely manner.				10			
JOB KNOWLEDGE	Possesses knowledge required to accomplish job duties. Understands job via experience, education, training or observation. Strives to learn and adapt to changes and new methods.				9			
COMMUNICATIONS	Communicates clearly (written or oral). Keeps supervisor informed.				9			
DEPENDABILITY	Reliability in the job; includes meeting deadlines.				9			
ATTENDANCE	(S/L, Tardies, AWOL, LWOP) Number of sick hours / incidents used [ ].				9			
SAFETY	Complies with rules of safety on the job.				9			
PROBLEM SOLVING	Identifies key issues and analyzes appropriate alternatives.				9			
DECISION MAKING	Uses good judgment when developing and evaluating alternatives.				9			
INNOVATION	Offers creative suggestions, develops new & unique approaches to service.				9			
TIME MANAGEMENT	Uses available time efficiently and displays appropriate sense of urgency.				9			
DIVERSITY LEADERSHIP	Supports hiring, promoting and maintaining a diverse workforce							
TEAM BUILDING	Encourages internal and cross functional teamwork. Emphasizes cooperation among employees.				10			
EMPOWERING	Provides information, training & authority. Empowers employees to make decisions.				10			

Left margin labels: SUPERVISOR MANAGER& EXECUTIVE FACTORS | ADMINISTRATIVE FACTORS | EMPLOYEE FACTORS

Score Definition				
Significantly Exceeds Expectations 10–9	Exceeds Expectations 8	Meets Expectations 7–5	Needs Improvement 4–3	Unsatisfactory 2–1

	Select the factors most appropriate to level and scope of the employee's position		W	S	Total	Mid-term Feedback on Target Yes / No
SUPERVISOR, MANAGER & EXECUTIVE FACTORS	MANAGEMENT OF INNOVATION	Creates a climate where employees are comfortable expressing ideas.	10			
	EMPLOYEE DEVELOPMENT	Provides employees with accurate and timely feedback. Works with employees to establish development plans for professional growth.	10			
	COACHING / COUNSELING	Supports and assists employees with action plans for problem performance.	10			
	APPRAISING	Evaluates employee's performance and discusses in a constructive way. Number of employee evaluations completed this period [ ] due [ ].	10			
	PLANNING/ ORGANIZING	Plans ahead, schedules work, sets realistic goals, and anticipates and prepares for assignments. Sets logical priorities.	9			
	MANAGEMENT OF SAFETY	Promotes good safety habits. Trains & ensures employees use safety procedures.	9			
	PERSUASIVENESS	Conveys ideas in a convincing way & gains support from others. Communicates clearly in writing and orally.	9			
	ECONOMIC MANAGEMENT	Develops realistic forecasts & budgets. Effectively utilizes resources. Meets forecast & budget objectives. Is responsive to business conditions.	9			
	STRATEGIC MANAGEMENT	Makes decisions & operates with attention to long range strategic direction.	9			
	PROFESSIONAL/ TECHNICAL EXPERTISE	Has a clear understanding of current practices, materials, concepts and knowledge of relevant fields.	10			
		Totals:		0	0	
					0	

City Wide Overall Score:	0

Overall Score

Significantly Exceeds Expectations 100–90	Exceeds Expectations 89.9–80	Meets Expectations 79.9–50	Needs Improvement 49.9–30	Unsatisfactory 29.9–1

Figure 12–1
(*Continued*)

Individual Performance Factors

Performance Factors are to be completed and initialed by both the employee and the supervisor at the beginning of the evaluation period.

Score Definition

Significantly Exceeds Expectations 10–9	Exceeds Expectations 8	Meets Expectations 7–5	Needs Improvement 4–3	Unsatisfactory 2–1

Employee's Individual Performance Factors: Key expectations, goals, projects, responsibilities	Weight	Score	Total	Mid-term Feedback on Target Yes/No
1. Conduct random and directed patrol, to prevent crime and respond to a wide spectrum of public safety issues.	10			
2. Properly arrest individuals who engage in any violation of a criminal law or ordinance and to oversee their custody, up to and including their transportation to the appropriate facility.	10			
3. Enforce traffic laws and investigate traffic accidents.	10			
4. Properly complete reports In a timely manner.	10			
5. Conduct thorough investigations at crime scenes to include gathering, preserving and correlating of evidence as well as the identification and transportation of victims, witnesses, complainants and suspects.	10			
6. Establish a positive working relationship with fellow employees, supervisors and other departmental units.	10			
7. Utilize proper patrol tactics and work effectively in emergency situations with minimum supervision.	10			
8. Attend all required court appearances, profiles and depositions (properly prepared).	10			
9. Maintain all city issue equipment in proper working condition and maintain a professional appearance at all times.	10			
10. Interact with citizens to identify and solve community problems.	10			
11. Provide quality customer service by exhibiting the highest level of professionalism when interacting with the community.	10			
12. Maintain a proper working knowledge of the Department's rules and regulations, policies and standard operating procedures, commensurate with CALEA accreditation standards.	10			
(OFFICER)				
Totals:	120	0	0	

Individual Overall Score:	0

Overall Score

Significantly Exceeds Expectations 100–90	Exceeds Expectations 89.9–80	Meets Expectations 79.9–50	Needs Improvement 49.9–30	Unsatisfactory 29.9–1

Figure 12–2

Police Officer Performance Evaluation Form.

Individual Performance Factors

Performance Factors are to be completed and initialed by both the employee and the supervisor at the beginning of the evaluation period.

Score Definition

Significantly Exceeds Expectations 10–9	Exceeds Expectations 8	Meets Expectations 7–5	Needs Improvement 4–3	Unsatisfactory 2–1

Employee's Individual Performance Factors: Key expectations, goals, projects, responsibilities	Weight	Score	Total	Mid-term Feedback on Target Yes/No
1. To fairly and thoroughly complete a subordinate's Performance Evaluation Report and foster a work environment that will facilitate improvement in a subordinate's performance, to Include the recognition of superior performance.	10			
2. To direct and coordinate personnel in response to major incidents. Supervisors will also ensure proper procedures are utilized in forming perimeters, vehicle pursuits, crime scene preservation and coordinating with other Units/Divisions of the Department.	10			
3. To continuously monitor all aspects of a subordinate's performance for compliance with departmental policies, initiating corrective action and/or discipline of the Department.	10			
4. To monitor and supervisee assignments and activity in the supervisor's district and coordinate with other supervisors for the delivery of quality police services throughout the City.	10			
5. To review crime analysis reports, offense reports, and all other pertinent sources of information and disseminate relevant tasks, assignments, and details at daily roll calls.	9			
6. Provide conflict resolution to shift level, interdivisional and department concerns.	10			
7. Remain available at all times for his subordinates to create an atmosphere of guidance and learning.	10			
8. To conduct shift level investigations and recommend discipline when appropriate.	9			
9. To monitor available training opportunities in order to enhance subordinate's proficiency.	10			
10. To foster an atmosphere of teamwork in order to promote the Department's/City's community policing and customer service initiatives.	10			
11. Maintain a current working knowledge of the Department's CALEA accreditation SOP requirements.	10			
(SERGEANT)				
Totals:	108	0	0	

Individual Overall Score:	0

Overall Score

Significantly Exceeds Expectations 100–90	Exceeds Expectations 89.9–80	Meets Expectations 79.9–50	Needs Improvement 49.9–30	Unsatisfactory 29.9–1

Figure 12–3
Police Sergeant Performance Evaluation Form.

Individual Performance Factors

Performance Factors are to be completed and initialed by both the employee and the supervisor at the beginning of the evaluation period.

Score Definition

Significantly Exceeds Expectations 10–9	Exceeds Expectations 8	Meets Expectations 7–5	Needs Improvement 4–3	Unsatisfactory 2–1

Employee's Individual Performance Factors: Key expectations, goals, projects, responsibilities	Weight	Score	Total	Mid-term Feedback on Target Yes/No
1. To thoroughly and aggressively investigate all assigned cases. To follow all available leads and to maintain the highest clearance rate possible.	10			
2. To interact in a professional manner with all individuals whom we have contact with while presenting a positive image for the Miami Beach Police Department.	10			
3. To conduct criminal investigations in a manner consistent with progressive investigative techniques. To abide by the Mission Statement of the Miami Beach Police Department and observe all legal rules and procedures while conducting criminal investigations in an ethical manner.	10			
4. To provide weekly updates to Sergeants of crime trends in your district or assignment.	10			
5. To identify community based organizations in your district or assignment and provide them with pertinent information.	10			
6. To recognize crime trends and forward these patterns to Crime Analysis.	10			
7. To conduct proactive investigations when crime analysis dictates the need for this action.	10			
8. To ensure that each employee supports the spirit of teamwork both within the Unit and the Department.	10			
9. To ensure that each employee provides quality customer service to citizens and fellow employees.	10			
10. Follows/adheres to the SOP in reference to Court Policy	10			
Totals:	100	0	0	

DETECTIVE

Individual Overall Score:	0

Overall Score

Significantly Exceeds Expectations 100–90	Exceeds Expectations 89.9–80	Meets Expectations 79.9–50	Needs Improvement 49.9–30	Unsatisfactory 29.9–1

Figure 12–4
Police Detective Performance Evaluation Form.

specific comments by the rater relative to characteristics of the person rated not covered elsewhere on the report.

Rating traits and abilities can be grouped into broad categories such as personal characteristics (traits needed for the job), ability (adequate performance of the duties of the position), performance (quality and quantity of work), and suitability for promotion (acceptable to superior work). Additional or fewer categories may be used depending on the purpose to be served by the rating report.

The traits selected for rating purposes should be examined critically to ensure that they are as specific as possible, that the traits to be measured can be relatively easily observed and uniformly evaluated by all raters, that the traits describe actual characteristics required by the job, that they are common to the largest possible number of employees, and that they are selected so as not to overlap with others, which would tend to defeat the purpose of the rating.[8]

Many other traits can be added to the following list of possibilities for traits that can be rated. Undoubtedly the list should be considerably more detailed for probationary personnel than for tenured officers. The most important criteria for job success should be selected and evaluated carefully to prevent granting tenure to unsuitable personnel. Here are a few subcategories of rating factors:

Personal Characteristics	Ability
Honesty	Stability
Character	Initiative
Attitude	Job knowledge
Appearance	Judgment
Persistence	Common sense
Imagination	
Loyalty	

Performance	Suitability for Promotion
Quality of work	Leadership ability
Quantity of work	Administrative ability
Accuracy	Job knowledge
Attention to duty	Communication skills
Perseverance	Interpersonal skills
Efficiency	Ability to plan
Supervision required	Acceptance of responsibility
Ability to resolve complaints from public	Ability to organize
Handling of specific job duties (patrol, traffic, investigations, reports)	Decision-making ability
Performance under stress	Command presence
Effectiveness	Disciplinary function

---

[8] Michael James Jucius, *Personnel Management*, 8th ed. (Homewood, Ill.: R. D. Irwin, 1975), p. 280.

Performance Standards

The first-line supervisor plays a prime part in setting standards of performance for his subordinates. If he exacts anything less than full and honest performance from them, he is negligent in his own duty. They must be thoroughly indoctrinated in what he expects from them; in turn, they have the right to know what they may expect from him. Indeed, one of the most significant organizational factors contributing to poor performance is the failure of the supervisor to clearly communicate the expected standard of performance to subordinates.[9] They must recognize that he is responsible for the manner in which the police function is performed by them in the area in which they operate and should also be made to understand what he expects from them by virtue of their particular assignment. Subordinate personnel too often do not know (other than in very abstract terms) what their supervisors expect simply because they have not been told or because the scope of their responsibilities has not been delineated.

Every supervisor in the patrol service, for example, must make it clear by every means at his disposal that officers are theoretically accountable for most crime in their assigned area or beat, for selective enforcement of the law to reduce the incidence of traffic accidents resulting from accident-producing violations, for an acceptable level of service for those in need of it, and for other police activities calculated to reduce crime when patterns begin to appear. The supervisor must let his subordinates know that in addition to the rating basis noted above, they will be rated on the manner in which they observe and report police incidents and conditions requiring correction, such as inadequate street lighting, which might be corrected to reduce crime; engineering changes, which might be needed to reduce traffic accidents; or exposed hazards, which might be better controlled to reduce the incidence of juvenile delinquency.

In letting his subordinates know what he expects of them, the supervisor will be performing a training function and will give them a basis for understanding what standards will be used to measure and evaluate their effectiveness. They will then recognize what should be done, how they are expected to do it, and what degree of competency is expected of them. Regardless of their assignment, they are entitled to know this, and when they do, certain standards will emerge based on their relative productivity, both qualitative and quantitative. These then can be used as goals toward which the employee can strive when he is told where he stands in comparison with other employees doing the same job with the same established norms.

Rating Criteria

Some criteria that have been found to be useful by supervisors as a basis for rating the performance of personnel are listed in this section. Obviously, evidence must be collected that demonstrates the employee's value to the organization. Some of this evidence will

---

[9] Steve M. Jex, *Organizational Psychology: A Scientist-Practitioner Approach* (New York: John Wiley & Sons, 2002), p. 150.

be accumulated for specific periods (usually monthly) in accomplishment reports. This evidence must be interpreted with great care, however, since such data usually measure quantitative production only and do not equate it with the quality of the work done. Because this is a shortcoming and because such data do not lend themselves to the measurement of the more abstract traits important in the police officer's job, arithmetic accomplishment reports reflecting quantity only are perhaps one of the least useful devices in the evaluation of personnel.

Some of the following criteria may not be applicable in all personnel appraisals because of the particular assignment of the employee, but all of them are easily adaptable for most field assignments and can be easily evaluated through the process of inspections. Effective supervisors often gain much valuable information about their subordinates by occasionally riding with them on patrol, and watching in-car videos where their capabilities can be measured through firsthand observation.

Patrol and Traffic Personnel

The following criteria are useful for evaluating officers assigned to patrol or traffic control:

1. Are officers keeping themselves informed of what is happening on their beat or in their area? Are they making use of crime and traffic data or police incident summaries to gain an awareness of crime, developing traffic accident patterns, and/or exposed hazard areas?

2. Are officers familiar with crime, delinquency, and traffic trends in their area of responsibility?

3. Are officers familiar with patrol techniques, and are they performing their patrol functions effectively?

4. Are reports complete and accurate? How many errors are observed in their reports?

5. What is the quality of traffic enforcement citations issued? Are traffic citations reasonably related to accident-producing violations on a selective basis? Do citation books, turned in for inspection and filing when completed, reveal quality enforcement effort? Do errors or erasures appear on file copies?

6. Are preliminary investigations made carefully? How do officers preserve evidence?

7. Do activity logs reflect a high proportion of quality arrests based on observation? Do the officers' repressive patrol activities appear to be adequate? Do these activities involve adequate random inspections of business and residential premises and places exposed to criminal attacks, vehicle checks, and so forth?

8. What is the quality of field interviews with pedestrians and motorists, juveniles and adults, as reflected by field contact reports?

9. What type of image do the police officers project in their personal and public lives?

10. How do the officers handle assigned calls? Do the follow-up inquiries and observations by the supervisor reveal that they lack enthusiasm, self-assurance, confidence, ability, or interest in handling called-for services?

11. Does their court performance reflect poise, fairness, and preparation?

12. How do the subordinates care for their personal equipment and that of the organization?

13. Do the employees' medical records reflect a favorable attitude toward the job, or does their medical history reveal an inordinate use of sick time? Do sick patterns reflect evidence of malingering?

14. How do the employees relate to other members of the organization (fellow workers and superiors) and the public?
15. Do the employees observe the usual safety precautions in their work?
16. Does the organization receive an unusual number of complaints about the officers' performance or conduct?
17. Do officers strongly support their superiors and the organization, or are they passive, antagonistic, or hostile?
18. What is the growth potential or promotability of officers?
19. Is the overall quantity of their work acceptable?
20. How do they react under stress?
21. How do they carry out directives?
22. What is their overall worth to the organization in comparison with others doing similar work?
23. Does the officer learn neighborhood problems, solve problems, and use community resources effectively?
24. Does the officer attend and participate in community meetings and identify and formulate plans of action to solve problems?

Investigative Personnel

Some criteria that may apply in addition to those listed for patrol and traffic officers are as follows:

1. Are follow-up calls made promptly in the interests of good investigative procedures and public relations?
2. Are the officers thorough and systematic in their investigative activities?
3. What percentage of their assigned cases is cleared by investigations? What percent is cleared by arrest resulting from investigations? Are clearance rates bona fide, that is, are they cleared by arrest or by investigative activity, or are there an excessive number cleared improperly by weak and inadequate modus operandi factors?
4. Do they have an unusual backlog of cases that have not had preliminary follow-up calls made?
5. Do progress reports reflect satisfactory progress on their assigned cases, or does it appear that investigators are directing their efforts primarily toward the investigation of those cases that are newsworthy or that may earn them some special recognition?
6. Do the officers enjoy a high conviction rate on cases they have investigated? Do records reveal that an unusual number of their cases that have been submitted to the prosecutor for complaint are rejected because of improper or inadequate case investigation or preparation?
7. How effectively do they deal with juveniles who have been involved in police incidents?
8. Do they keep complete and accurate records of their investigative activities?
9. Do the investigators work well with a minimum of supervision?
10. Do the investigators' court performances indicate thorough investigation and case preparation?
11. Do they work well with colleagues? Are they good team workers?

Staff and Auxiliary Personnel

Additional criteria useful as a basis for rating personnel assigned to staff and auxiliary activities are listed below:

1. Do the employees complete their assigned projects promptly, thoroughly, and objectively?
2. Do they practice the principles of delegated staff work, or do they require an inordinate amount of direction?
3. Do their reports meet accepted standards for staff writings?
4. Do their relations with operating personnel reflect a clear understanding of their organizational function as advisor rather than director?

Rating Standards

Rating systems are inherently subjective, since they involve a personal audit by one person of another's conduct or performance. Many of the personal traits supervisors are called on to evaluate cannot be measured by precise tests. One of the inherently difficult problems in the police service is that of fairly comparing persons assigned to widely different tasks. For example, extreme difficulties are encountered trying to compare the performance of the detective with that of the jailor or the performance of the patrol officer with that of the staff officer when all are of equal classification on the pay scale.

Most supervisors recognize that many of the observations they make of their subordinates cannot be completely objective. Yet if these observations are systematically made and recorded for the prime purpose of eliminating bias, which is likely to occur if ratings are based on inadequate evidence, they will provide an excellent basis for trait evaluation involved in personnel rating systems. The biggest problem seems to be the selection of a rating method that will yield the most reliable results within large groups where functions vary widely. Some of these methods of rating employees will be discussed in this chapter.

Employee Ranking

Many of the earlier systems, such as those of the military, used the technique of ranking all employees in a particular group according to their relative overall value to the organization. This method of "ranking" or "scaling" ratings is still widely used and ranks employees from highest to lowest in the unit or on the basis of most valuable to least valuable. For example, if a unit contains twenty persons performing similar functions, each would be rated on his relative position within the group. The most valuable employee would be ranked number 1 of 20, and the least valuable would be ranked number 20 of 20 in terms of overall value to the organization.

This method is simple and easy to administer but has the disadvantage of lacking common standards of measurement, especially when employees from widely different assignments must be compared. Furthermore, the employee ranked highest in a large unselected group might be of less value to the organization than the employee ranked lowest in a unit where employees are carefully selected. When this method of ranking employees is used, the supervisor is forced to make meticulous appraisals of his subordinates or risk the danger of hurting morale and being accused of arbitrariness or favoritism. Rarely will his judgments be in accord with the individual opinions of many of those evaluated, who are often prone to overrate themselves in comparison with others.

Representative Employee Standard

Accuracy may be improved when the rater compares each employee with others who have been selected as having the greatest value to the organization, those who are in the middle group having average value, and with those who are considered as having the least value. The rater is thus able to rank employees by comparing them with other representative employees whom he has selected through personal knowledge as having the greatest, average, or least value to the organization. Standards are thus established that can be used effectively as criteria for ratings in smaller organizations where the varying capabilities of employees are generally known and usually agreed on by raters. In large organizations, raters are limited by their own past experiences in the selection of representative employees, so a larger number of selected employees will be used as the standard of comparison, with the consequent lessening of the uniformity initially intended.

Additional standards may be selected that will tend to increase rating flexibility and accuracy. For example, accuracy can be increased if additional employees are selected who are representative not only of the outstanding, average, and unsatisfactory groups of employees but of intermediate groups as well. These groups may include above average (but not outstanding) and below average (but not unsatisfactory).

Ideal Employee Standard

Instead of using selected employees who are representative of certain groups of personnel with varying values to the organization, ideal employee descriptions may be developed to avoid the necessity for changing criteria when the selected employees leave the unit or the organization or their performance becomes such that they can no longer be used as a pattern for ratings. The rater is instructed to decide in his own mind the attributes, professional qualities, and performance of the *ideal* employee performing a similar function to that of the employee to be rated and make the rating in comparison with this standard.

Whatever criteria are used, however, it is of utmost importance that all raters apply them uniformly or the system will not yield reliable results. Precise guidelines developed by the organization for raters will contribute materially to the achievement of this uniformity.

Numerical Standard

When quantity of production is most important to an organization, descriptive standards may be used to advantage in measuring accomplishments. These are often expressed numerically; however, such measurements are difficult to apply to the many abstract traits that are important in police work.

In a purely arithmetic method, the rater gives a numerical grade to each trait on the rating form according to the degree to which the employee possesses it.[10] Predetermined weights are established by the organization for various traits. The numerical grade given

---

[10] A grade may be expressed in percentages, on a scale of 1 to 5 or 1 to 10, or on some other scale selected by the organization as a guideline representing various degrees of the employee's proficiency or the extent to which he possesses a trait.

Table 12–1
TRAIT RATING BY ARITHMETIC STANDARD METHOD

Personnel Rating Report

Trait	Numerical Rating	× Trait Weight =	Value Points
Initiative	5	2	10
Dependability	4	3	12
Judgment	4	4	16
Total Value Points			38

Numerical Rating Scale

1	2	3	4	5
Unsatisfactory (improvement needed, etc.)	Fair (satisfactory but below average, etc.)	Average	Very Good (above average, etc.)	Outstanding (excellent, superior, etc.)

each trait by the rater multiplied by the weight assigned that trait equals its value points; by totaling value points, the organization is able to rank each employee arithmetically according to his overall value[11] (see Figure 12–1). This weighting adds the element of subjectivity to the rating, since weights assigned to traits are estimates of the value of each in comparison with others.

Table 12–1 depicts a typical trait scale and the simple method of deriving value points for the various traits being assessed, which are used in arriving at total value points for the employee. The arithmetic rating scale for use as a guide in determining total value points assigns numerical values to each trait or performance factor and gives each a weight, as illustrated in Table 12–1, which increases the flexibility of the report. These guides may be provided on a separate form or may be preprinted on the rating instrument.

Forced-Choice Standard

Once traits are selected that are considered to be the most important indicators of quality of performance, several options can be provided from which the rater must select the one that most closely describes the performance of the person being rated. The options can be given a numerical value to indicate the subject's overall rating, or the options may be classified in broad terms such as poor, fair, good, very good, excellent, or other descriptors indicative of the rater's assessment of each trait. Figure 12–5 is an example of a forced-choice standard where raters decide whether the employee's performance in each rating category either exceeds expectations, meets expectations, needs improvement, or is unacceptable. Figure 12–6 is a list and definition of additional competencies that may be measured.

---

[11] James R. Morrow, Allen W. Jackson, James G. Disch, and Dale Mood, *Measurement and Evaluation in Human Performance*, 4th ed. (Champaign, Ill.: Human Kinetics, 2011), p. 296.

CITY OF ANAHEIM PERFORMANCE PREVIEW/REVIEW FORM: INDIVIDUAL CONTRIBUTOR

An Individual Contributor is responsible for his/her own performance and value added contribution.

Employee name: Click here to enter text.

Evaluation Period (Note start and end date): Click here to enter text.

Department: Click here to enter text.   **Unit/Program:** Click here to enter text.

FOUR CORE COMPETENCIES	COMPETENCY DEFINITION
Achieves Results	Delivers on objectives; meets deadlines; produces high volume and quality outcomes; ensures that techniques optimize speed, quality and consistency in work products; knows what needs to be done and does it without being told; does not confuse effort with accomplishment; work attire meets departmental dress code standards; uses equipment as intended and in accordance with City procedures and policies.
FOUR CORE COMPETENCIES	COMPETENCY DEFINITION
Interpersonal Skills	Ability to develop and sustain effective working relationships; tailors their approach and behavioral style when communicating; establishes rapport and has the ability to relate well to all levels in the organization; approachable; treats others with sensitivity, respect, fairness, and consistency.
FOUR CORE COMPETENCIES	COMPETENCY DEFINITION
Responsive Customer Service	Shows interest and understands the needs, expectations, and circumstances of internal and external customers and responds accordingly. Takes personal responsibility for addressing external/internal problems in a professional manner.
FOUR CORE COMPETENCIES	COMPETENCY DEFINITION
Technical Proficiency	Understands and masters the skills, requirements, concepts, principles and technologies of a discipline; well versed in the most current information, theories, techniques, practices, and procedures of the field; has a solid developmental record and on the job acquisition of knowledge and skills of the occupation; uses knowledge, judgment, tools, equipment, information and other resources relevant to job.

BEHAVIORAL RATING SCALE FOR CORE COMPETENCY				
Directions:	Unacceptable	Needs Improvement	Meets Expectations	Exceeds Expectations
In this row, check the box that best describes the level in which the employee demonstrates this competency.	Not able or willing to perform or demonstrate the essential elements of the competency.	Inconsistent demonstration of the competency.	Performs all essential elements of the competency effectively.	Performs all essential elements of the competency significantly above the criteria required of a Valued Contributor; mastery of this competency has a vital impact to others and the organization.
	☐	☐	☐	☐
Under the rating box selected, provide two work-related examples to support the behavioral rating.				

Figure 12–5

Performance Preview/Review Form. Source: City of Anaheim, California.

ADDITIONAL COMPETENCIES	COMPETENCY DEFINITION
Public Safety: COP/PS— Community Oriented Policing and Problem Solving	*PS: COP/PS—Recognizes the community is our customer; understands/addresses needs; indentifies leaders/partners; builds strong relationships; flexible/responds to situations/ people; provides meaningful suggestions /collaborates to resolve problems*

ADDITIONAL COMPETENCIES	COMPETENCY DEFINITION
Public Safety: PF— Physical Fitness	*PS: PF—Demonstrates reasonable recovery from physical stress/exertion; maintains a level of fitness to adequately perform all of the functions and duties of assigned job.*

ADDITIONAL COMPETENCIES	COMPETENCY DEFINITION
Click here to select a Competency	Click here to select a Definition.
	Click here to customize definition.

BEHAVIORAL RATING SCALE FOR SELECTED COMPETENCY				
Directions:	Unacceptable	Needs Improvement	Meets Expectations	Exceeds Expectations
In this row, check the box that best describes the level in which the employee demonstrates this competency.	Not able or willing to perform or demonstrate the essential elements of the competency. ☐	Inconsistent demonstration of the competency. ☐	Performs all essential elements of the competency effectively. ☐	Performs all essential elements of the competency significantly above the criteria required of a Valued Contributor; mastery of this competency has a vital impact to others and the organization. ☐
Under the rating box selected, provide two work-related examples to support the behavioral rating.				

<u>NOTE</u>: To rate additional competencies, Click on the table above to highlight; then Copy (ctrl C); place the curser where you want to insert the new table; and then Paste (ctrl V). A new table with the additional competencies will appear; use the Competency and Definition drop-down menus as before.

Figure 12–5
(*Continued*)

STRENGTHS:

Everyone has strengths. If applicable, in the drop down menu, you may select up to three additional strengths the employee demonstrates. Next to the competency provide an example.

If identified strength(s) were already rated in the "Four Core" sections of this form, selecting additional strengths from the drop down menu may not be necessary; please note previously identified strength from above.

Click here to select a Competency
Click here to enter text.

Click here to select a Competency
Click here to enter text.

Click here to select a Competency
Click here to enter text.

OPPORTUNITIES TO IMPROVE:

Everyone has areas in which they can improve; select up to three competencies in which the employee can improve. Next to the competency, describe the expectations to be achieved.

If identified opportunities to improve(s) were already rated in the "Four Core" sections of this form, selecting additional areas to improve from the drop down menu may not be necessary; please note previously identified areas to improve from above.

Click here to select a Competency
Click here to enter text.

Click here to select a Competency
Click here to enter text.

Click here to select a Competency
Click here to enter text.

LEADERSHIP:

In the City of Anaheim, anyone can be a leader regardless of his/her role. Further, an Individual Contributor is considered a leader when he/she consistently demonstrates any of the "Leadership Competencies" listed in the drop down menu below or when he/she receives a "Distinguished Contributor" rating in any of the Competencies.

In the drop down menu, select up to three Leadership Competencies or select "Refer to the Distinguished Contributor Rating Above". *Next to the Competency, provide an example.*

Click here to choose a Competency.
Click here to enter text.

Click here to choose a Competency.
Click here to enter text.

Click here to choose a Competency.
Click here to enter text.

Figure 12–5
(*Continued*)

PROFESSIONAL DEVELOPMENT PLAN:

A Development Plan is designed to address and correct poor performance, hone and strengthen existing skills, and to expose employees to learning opportunities, which build capabilities. *This may include on-the-job training, reading books, attending seminars, and new projects and responsibilities.*

Click here to enter text.

EMPLOYEE COMMENTS:

Optional—in this section the employee provides his/her own perspective on the competency ratings.

Click here to enter text.

	DEFINITION	
Attendance (If applicable)	The practice of regularly going to work as scheduled.	
Paid Leave Hours Used/Percent Used:	☐ Meets Established Attendance Standard	☐ Does not meet Established Attendance Standard
	Comments:	

Overall Rating:

Unacceptable	Needs Improvement	Meets Expectations	Exceeds Expectations
☐	☐	☐	☐

Employee Signature:		Date:
Supervisor/Manager Signature:		Date:
Supervisor/Manager Signature:		Date:
Supervisor/Manager Signature:		Date:

NOTE: This *Performance Evaluation Form* is used in conjunction with the *City of Anaheim Objectives and Planning Worksheet*. The worksheet will help employees and supervisors/managers collaboratively plan at the beginning of an evaluation period and identify future projects, goals, and objectives to be achieved **(what they will do)**. As the City's priorities change, projects can be added or deferred as needed.

While the *Planning Worksheet* can be used for all levels and roles within the City of Anaheim, this *Performance Evaluation* Forms is customized with the unique roles of **Individual Contributors** in mind. It is used to identify the competencies needed to accomplish the work **(how they will do it)** and provides feedback/documentation at the end of an evaluation period. Both forms are essential to effective performance management.

Figure 12–5
(*Continued*)

City of Anaheim Competency Definitions by Roles

Competency	Definition—Individual Contributor
Additional Competencies:	
Budget Savvy	Is aware of basic budget principles related to the City's budget; if needed, can access information related to the budget; demonstrates sound decision making and is conscientious regarding managing ones time, expenditures, and resources.
City Knowledge	Understands the internal environment of the organization; Citywide knowledge of mission, goals, resources, key contacts, services provided, and City leaders.
Continuous Learning	Seeks and uses feedback on how to improve performance; anticipates future needs of the organization and pursues related learning; has a career plan and development objectives.
Communication Skills	Presents verbal and non-verbal information clearly and in an organized manner; gets ideas across; paraphrases to ensure understanding; communicates effectively with all levels of the organization and community.
Critical Thinking/Problem Solving	Analytically/logically evaluates information, issues/problems; identifies/understands root causes/underlying issues; detects flaws, inconsistencies/illogical conclusions; recognizes compelling arguments on the basis of solid data/assumptions/logic.
Decision Making	Considers alternatives/anticipates consequences; separates fact from opinion; demonstrates self-confidence/discipline to transition from analysis to action; decisions are in alignment with Department/City policies/procedures.
Functions with Ambiguity	Performs with limited information; navigates with unclear direction; able to identify, extract, and utilize resources to accomplish a goal.
Learning and Watching Trends	Stays current on new developments and trends; scans the environment and identifies needs; is aware of internal and external factors that impact the workplace; keeps up with technology, techniques, methods, and new practices within field or industry.
Leverages Technology	Proficient with equipment and computer applications used on the job; learns new versions and how to use new features and functions; finds ways to apply technology to increase speed, quality, and/or create new capabilities.
Project Management	Ensures projects are on time, on budget and on specifications; defines project purpose, scope, and criteria for success; establishes milestones and timelines; achieves project deliverables and efficiently manages resources.
Resiliency	Takes setbacks and criticism in stride and moves forward; rebounds quickly and positively after confronted with negative news or results; responds well to adversity.
Safety	Does not have on-the-job, work-related accidents; demonstrates a high degree of awareness of the job at hand and the work environment; implements proactive techniques that improve safety of self and others; adheres to City, Department, and Cal-OSHA safety rules and regulations; documents and reports unsafe conditions; provides good stewardship on the care and operation of equipment; anticipates, pre-plans, researches, and takes action to mitigate when dealing with potentially dangerous situations; If applicable: Wears appropriate/required clothing to ensure safe working conditions; Actively demonstrates proficiency in tactics and control techniques; maintenance of weapons and equipment.

Figure 12–6
City of Anaheim Competency Definitions.   Source: City of Anaheim, California.

	Abbreviated definition: No accidents; obeys rules/regulations; reports unsafe conditions; provides care/op. of equip; anticipates/researches/takes action to mitigate dangerous situations; If applicable: Demonstrates proficiency in tactics/control tech; maint of weapons/equip.
Self Management	Functions with minimal oversight; appropriately prioritizes time and effectively performs tasks; manages personal time and work schedule; independently prioritizes tasks and adjusts priorities as situations change.
Values Diversity	Respects others regardless of differences in interests, perspectives, background, and organizational level.
Public Safety: Community Oriented Policing and Problem Solving	Recognizes the community is our customer; understands/addresses community needs; identifies community leaders/partners; takes action to build strong relationships in the community; is flexible/responds appropriately to varying situations/people; provides meaningful suggestions /works collaboratively by assisting community members to resolve problems; awareness of how City services directly/indirectly support/impact the community. Abbreviated definition: Recognizes the comm. is our customer; understands/addresses needs; indentifies leaders/partners; builds strong relationships; flexible/responds to situations/people; provide meaningful suggestions/collaborates to resolve problems.
Public Safety: Physical Fitness	Demonstrates reasonable recovery from physical stress/exertion; maintains a level of fitness to adequately perform all of the functions and duties of assigned job.
Leadership: Creativity/ Innovation	Sees old problems in a new light and comes up with novel, resourceful, and/or imaginative approaches to problems or opportunities.
Leadership: Initiative	Finds ways to handle the situation and takes action without the need to be prompted and prodded; before asking for direction, develops a set of alternatives and identifies pros/cons for each solution.
Leadership: Leading the Way	Regardless of role or formal position inspires trust, clarifies purpose, rallies people, identifies resources and utilizes an effective process to achieve a common goal.
Leadership: Passion	A person who displays pride, ownership, commitment, and "buy-in" to their daily work.
Leadership: Risk Taking	Accepts and implements solutions to problems that are outside the "norm"; recognizes that there can be more than one path to the same goal/outcome.
Leadership: Role Model	Leading by example; wears suitable attire and presents ones-self as a positive representative of the City in what one does, says, and commands positive attention from others.
Leadership: Servant Leadership	Not to proud to do what it takes to get the job done regardless of role; understands that each individual is responsible to serve and lead from every position.

Figure 12–6
(Continued)

In this standard of rating, the rater must select only one choice for each trait evaluated. Only one trait should be considered at a time to avoid an unconscious bias that often creeps into trait ratings when several traits are considered together, and the rater should disregard any general impression he has of the person being rated to avoid undue influences on the independent ratings of traits. The rating should be a true report of how the person rated performs his work in each category rated, not a personal analysis of that person.

Highest or lowest ratings for the various traits should not be based on only one favorable or unfavorable talent or event. If extreme ratings are given, they should be supported by objective evidence that is more than just one person's subjective opinion. The making of these extreme ratings should not be avoided merely because of this requirement, for to do so would result in commission of the error of central tendency (discussed later) and would tend to discredit the entire rating. When justified, such ratings will provide the rater with an opportunity to give credit when it is due for meritorious service or to take action necessary to improve the performance of an employee rated at the lowest end.

Rater Characteristics

The best supervisors are usually the best raters because they are more diligent in carrying out their rating responsibilities than are the poorer supervisors and are less likely to commit the error of leniency by overrating the poor performers. Liberal ratings are the easiest course for weaker supervisors, who are prone to overrate subordinates because this permits them to evade their responsibility of correcting deficient employees. The better supervisors are generally more discriminating and more objective than are their less effective colleagues.

Lenient supervisors who rate all their subordinates alike are covertly disrespected. The outstanding employee is penalized, while the marginal one is rewarded simply because the rating officer did not have the personal interest, or perhaps the ability, to prepare a thorough, accurate service rating report based on the objective evidence he has gathered (if he has bothered to gather any). The preparation of these reports is directly dependent on his ability to observe and record evidence of the type of performance of his subordinates; his judgment, patience, and understanding in dealing with them; and his ability to lead, maintain discipline and morale, and to otherwise control them. These same abilities are involved in all his supervisory activities and are in direct proportion to his proficiency as a supervisory officer. If his rating attitude is one of leniency, morale problems will inevitably result. The industrious, dedicated officer will ask why he should continue to extend himself when he gets little or no more credit for his efforts than the lazy officer who rarely works diligently.

In addition, employees tend to believe that most supervisors are influenced by personal relationships—either good or bad—more than they are by performance, and lenient raters lend support to this belief. Strict but fair raters are usually approved by almost all subordinates, or, at least if they are honest with themselves, subordinates will realize that this type of rater is doing the best job he knows how to do with the tools or evidence at hand. The unfair rater will rarely (if ever) receive the approbation of his subordinates.

Every supervisor should realize that he is evaluated informally by his subordinates on the basis of how his personnel evaluation duties and responsibilities are performed. It is no wonder that so much importance is attached to employee ratings! The economic life of the employee is directly affected by the evaluations he receives from his superiors—promotions and related salary increments, merit pay, longevity pay, tenure, seniority rights, and other job benefits are often directly involved. When ratings used as management tools are improperly or carelessly made, irreparable harm is often done to the employee's career. If employees demand nothing else, they will insist on fair and impartial treatment from their superiors; in turn, if the supervisor gives his subordinates little else, he owes them this.

Certain broad characteristics are usually found in supervisors who excel in rating their subordinates. These supervisors:

- can distinguish facts from feelings or impressions.
- are able to weigh the performance of their subordinates against a consistent standard, which they accomplish by establishing norms of conduct and performance as a point of departure for rating personnel.
- base their ratings on objective data whenever possible, without allowing subjective emotions, individual likes and dislikes, or biases to influence them.
- are careful to avoid committing the error of rating on the basis of vague general impressions and, instead, make every effort to rate on the basis of personal individual traits.
- are systematic and thorough in recording accurate data relating to their observations of employees throughout the rating period.

Unfortunately, some raters allow personal idiosyncrasies to influence them in their appraisal of subordinates. Strong, often unreasonable, likes and dislikes sometimes cloud their vision and result in these supervisors seeing only good in some officers and only bad in others. Adequate records of observations can help dissipate such prejudice and favoritism.

The more confidence subordinates have in the objectivity of the rating system, the less likely they will be to complain, to offset poor ratings by playing politics, or to develop a defensive attitude. The most effective raters are those whose temperament and personality are well balanced. It is not necessary that they be intellectually superior to all of their subordinates to be effective. From an organizational standpoint, individual raters' accuracy and system integrity can be improved by higher review. Gaines and colleagues found that raters were more consistent and reliable when they knew a manager would review their ratings.[12]

Common Rating Errors

Invariably, when ratings fail to accomplish their true purpose, it is found that the fault lies not in the form used but in the rater. When either the report is prepared merely to fulfill a policy or legal requirement or the activity adds just another burden to his already overworked position, he has become indifferent to or unconcerned with the probable results of carelessly prepared reports and completes them in the easiest way possible. Even the simplest forms can achieve a very beneficial effect if care is given to their preparation. A thoughtful simple narration of the rater's appraisal of a subordinate sometimes is more

---

[12] Larry K. Gaines, John L. Worrall, Mittie D. Southerland, and John Angell, *Police Administration*, 3rd ed. (New York: McGraw-Hill, 2012), p. 313.

meaningful than complicated formulas that attempt to equate the various personal traits by a series of checkmarks in boxes. The quality of personnel evaluations, then, is largely a matter of attitude—the attitude of the rater.

It is for this reason that the training of the raters is the most important requisite in the administration of a successful evaluation system. Yet, even with training, some errors creep into the rating process. The following section discusses some of the most common ones.

Leniency

The error of leniency is by far the most common of all errors in the rating of personnel.[13] It occurs when the rater marks an inordinately large number of the rating reports in the highest one or two categories, such as very good and excellent, or excellent and outstanding, depending on the particular terminology used in the report form. Occasionally, such forms include a percentage figure denoting the percentile within which the rate is marked in comparison with other persons rated. The lenient rater will mark an excessive number of his subordinates in the upper 20 percent or upper 10 percent and fewer in the lower ranges.

This tendency to overrate has many obvious dangers, foremost of which is the damaging effect it has on the morale of the truly outstanding workers. They will soon begin to wonder if it really pays to work diligently when less proficient employees receive the same ratings anyway.

The marked tendency to rate high results is called a skewed curve, with an excessive number of personnel rated in the upper range. Such a tendency is a perfectly human one but should be avoided to preserve the integrity of the rating system. Often the rater who commits this error will start overrating his subordinates because of his intense desire to be popular and to be liked by them. He will lower ratings only when he is offended by an overt act committed by the person rated.

The error of leniency is contagious and has a tendency to spread rapidly from one supervisor to another who feels compelled to overrate his subordinates so that they may compete favorably with others who have been rated too high by an overly lenient supervisor. "The effects are to force ratings so drastically high that they are useless as management tools and to create unrealistic employee confidence when improvement in performance is really needed and quite possible."[14]

A supervisor may tend to overrate deficient subordinates for many other reasons besides the desire to be popular. He may do so if he is forced to confront them about their deficiencies or if he feels that he might be challenged about the low ratings and forced to justify them; he also might overrate employees merely because he likes them and wishes to protect them.

The better supervisor will not allow these personal considerations to color his judgment. He will rely on his ability to convince the employee that the rating was fair and point him in the right direction to correct his deficiencies.

[13] Frank J. Landy and Jeffrey M. Conte, *Work in the 21st Century* (Hoboken, N.J.: Wiley-Blackwell, 2009), p. 257.
[14] *Ibid.*

Personal Bias

Raters often tend to rate higher than is justified those persons they know well and like as well as those who subscribe to the same opinions as the supervisor. Those who are not liked or who are not compatible with the supervisor's own particular philosophies are likely to be rated lower than is justified.

This tendency toward bias in ratings should be guarded against because it destroys their validity. Such bias can be reduced if the rater tests his rating by asking himself if it was influenced by the fact that the employee is like (or unlike) himself. If it was, then the rater must reappraise the facts on which he based the rating.

Supervisors must likewise consciously guard against overrating subordinates merely because they have been selected by him or are working in his particular unit. True, ratings of individuals selected for a specialized unit because of their special abilities may be generally somewhat higher than ratings of a large randomly selected group where the distribution of ratings follows a normal bell-shaped curve, but when 80 or 90 percent of the personnel in a certain group are rated in the top category or very near the top, the effect is that there is no normal curve of distribution of ratings showing differences in performance. Thus, all ratings are open to question and are often considered unreliable.

The conclusion of a superior that "all my employees are good because they work for me" or "if he works for me, he must be good" is absurd. Such philosophy applied to a rating program usually results in other supervisors becoming reluctant to penalize their own subordinates by attempting to make honest, objective ratings when they know others are not using objective standards. This attitude also tends to penalize the best employees because it reduces the spread in the ratings and thus fails to discriminate adequately between the best and worst performers. Some supervisors feel that this may ingratiate them with their subordinates, but the best employees (as previously indicated) will resent having to "carry" the worst ones, and they will resent the failure of their superior to give honest credit where it is due.

Central Tendency

All too often, raters will group their ratings near the center of the rating scale, with few ratings at the bottom or top. This tendency to avoid the extremes on the rating scales usually results from a policy requiring justification for extreme ratings. Again, outstanding employees are penalized by being unjustifiably rated lower than they should be, while those personnel who should be rated at the lowest part of the scale are rewarded by the lazy supervisor who either is indifferent to the effects of his neglect or is disinclined to take the trouble to collect sufficient data to justify high or low ratings.

Undoubtedly, as in other cases of overrating employees, some raters consciously or unconsciously make this error to escape the responsibility for the unpleasant task of confronting the deficient employee about his poor performance and taking steps to see that he improves it. In either case, the organization suffers, as do the better employees. This error of central tendency is especially common when no system has been devised by the individual rater or the organization to gather adequate, specific, and objective information that could be used to defend or justify a high or low rating.

Halo Effect

The tendency of raters to rate in terms of a very general impression rather than on the basis of specific traits is commonly referred to as the halo effect.[15] It occurs when the rater thinks in terms of the "good" or the "poor" officer and groups all the ratings for an individual at the high or low end of the scale. This often happens when the rater has been unduly influenced by the error of related traits or the error of overweighting incidents, both of which are discussed in the following paragraphs.

Related Traits

Sometimes referred to as logical error or association error, the error of related traits is committed when the rater gives similar ratings to traits that seem to be similar. For example, this rating error is made in reports when the rater assumes that if a person has good judgment, he must also have good presence of mind; if he is attentive to duty, he must have a high degree of initiative; if his physical health is good, his mental health must also be good; if he is dependable, he must also be cooperative; or if he makes errors, he must be fatigued.

Each trait must be considered by itself by the rater. If he associates several traits, he is apt subconsciously to allow one to influence another similar one and thus reduce the accuracy of his ratings.

Overweighting or Recency

The tendency of raters to be unduly influenced by an occurrence, either good or bad, involving the person rated near the end of the rating period is known as overweighting. This rating error often occurs when one or more outstanding occurrences near the end of the rating period are out of proportion to the average performance during the entire period. This is an application of the principle of recency wherein those things most recently perceived will be remembered best. Ratings influenced by such events are less reliable and may be inordinately high or low depending on the nature of the occurrence and its effect on the rater. Such ratings are often influenced by factors much like those resulting from the halo effect, especially if the rater has not diligently kept himself informed about the standard performance of his subordinates.

Subjectivity

The error of personal bias is often confused with the error of subjectivity, but close examination of the two will reveal subtle differences. The error of subjectivity occurs when the rater is unduly influenced by one or two characteristics that have special appeal to him. The cooperative or pleasant officer, for example, is sometimes rated much higher because of these traits than his overall performance justifies.

The rater must constantly be alert to the possibility that he may harm morale if he fails to utilize the objective data available to him and bases his ratings on subjective

---

[15] Tim Hindle, *Guide to Management Ideas and Gurus* (London: The Economist Newspaper, 2008), p. 97.

influences and idiosyncrasies, which will have the tendency to distort his appraisals. It must be recognized, however, that human traits cannot be measured with mathematical precision. The rater must consider the ratee's progress, his accomplishments (both qualitative and quantitative), and the probabilities of his future patterns of performance being generally similar to what they have been in the past. Any projection of such performance patterns must be founded on what has been learned of the individual's previous behavior.

For example, the rate at which a person produces is only one factor to consider in rating him. If the rater is appraising a person and attempting to predict his suitability for promotion to a position wherein the activities and responsibilities are quite dissimilar to those of his present rank, all those traits that contribute to competency in the new position, such as attitude, initiative, and leadership ability, must be considered. At best, a series of educated guesses would be involved in such projections, but these are perfectly acceptable if carefully made because workers who are good performers and who possess those basic characteristics desirable in a leader can be trained to be good supervisors.

Validity and Reliability of Ratings

Raters must be given a deep appreciation of the great need to make evaluation reports valid and reliable indicators of performance if they are to have maximum value as tools of supervision. If ratings do not reflect with reasonable accuracy the relative competency of personnel—their capabilities and their value to the organization—the effort and expense involved in making them are largely wasted.

Appraising personnel obviously involves not only a measuring device but also the judgment of the person making the rating. If the measuring device is sound, similar results will be attained by any rater using it. In judgment, the results that an informed and qualified person obtains supposedly will be the same as those reached by any other person who has the same qualifications as the rater. Judgment is, therefore, as objective as is measurement when the same information and expertise are used.[16] This presupposes that the way the information is used is the same. Validity deals with the measuring device; reliability deals more with the judgment of the rater in collecting, interpreting, and applying the information to the rating. Therefore, it logically follows that a rating system is only as valid as the measuring instrument used and the judgment, ability, and integrity of the rater in applying the information available to it.

Validity

A valid report is one that is an accurate measurement of the ability it purports to measure. Valid reports actually reflect the officer's value to the organization in terms of specific traits that are related to his work, such as amiability, industry, attention to duty, and cooperativeness. If the report is truly valid, it will not measure something it is not

---

[16] Peter F. Drucker, *Managing in Turbulent Times* (Boston: Harvard Business Review, 2002), pp. 131–32.

supposed to measure. If the form requires that certain traits or characteristics be measured that have little bearing on the traits and abilities required for a particular job, the validity of the rating form as a measure of the individual's competency is lowered, and if trivia are emphasized, the form's value is further reduced.

Obviously, in modern police agencies that are involved in highly complex activities of varied types, it would be impractical (if not almost impossible) to gear a separate rating form to each assigned job; it is necessary that at least the core traits and abilities necessary for the police job be included in the rating form if it is used for all nonsupervisory personnel. In some organizations, a rating report is especially constructed for evaluating supervisory or management personnel because skills and traits necessary for these positions differ somewhat from those required for personnel performing nonsupervisory tasks.

The rater must exercise care to avoid weighting all traits and abilities equally, since the job being performed by the person rated may not require the same abilities—or at least the same amount of a particular ability—that another job may require. For example, a police laboratory assignment may not require the same administrative ability as a supervisory assignment. Unbalanced emphasis on a particular trait being assessed will reduce the validity of the rating.

Reliability

A rating report is said to be reliable if it measures consistently and reasonably accurately (even if not perfectly) each time it is used. If several persons using the same information rate an individual substantially the same, their ratings would be a reliable measure of the employee's abilities; however, raters rarely have the same abilities to observe, collect, and report evidence regarding the performance of subordinates with the same degree of accuracy and objectivity. Therefore, training must focus the rater's attention on means of bettering the collection and use of data. The ideal rating, of course, is one in which the results are not unduly influenced by subjectivity or chance but are based on sound objective evidence.

Evaluation Period

Evaluations should be prepared from evidence collected during a particular rating period. Ratings for an established period should not be contaminated by observations carried over from some other period. Generally, an employee should not be forced to live forever with a poor rating occasioned by an unpleasant incident in the past.

Supervisors are sometimes concerned that a single rating report that covers an excessive length of time might involve too great an adverse impact on the employee rated, especially when such reports are an important basis for merit pay increases, promotion, or placement. When this occurs, appraisals become overly lenient. Such concerns can be reduced by the averaging of more frequent ratings, which would have the effect of reducing the impact of any single report. Management must decide whether the value of the added reports would offset the substantial costs of preparing them.

Rating Methods

The method selected for rating personnel depends in part on the individual needs of the organization and the preference of the raters. Each method has its merits and shortcomings.

There is general agreement that whatever method is selected, when ratings are made under supervision so that instructions are understood and some controls are exercised over them by a superior familiar with the performance of those rated, the quality of the evaluations improves.

Composite Ratings

Some supervisors prefer to rate their subordinates individually, with the superior officer of the unit making a composite rating from the several individual appraisals, usually by a process of averaging the ratings. Occasionally, the ratings of the various supervisors will be identified on one composite report by use of numbers or symbols keyed to the names of the raters, which are listed on the form. The shortcomings of this method are readily apparent. Extreme ratings will tend to be in agreement, while midrange ratings will often be in conflict. In addition, all individual raters often do not have access to the same evidence; some who have had limited opportunity to make observations of a particular subordinate will, of necessity, base their ratings on general impressions rather than on specific, factual, observed evidence. Before the more abstract personal traits of individuals can be accurately measured, many observations must be made.

Group Ratings

In the police service, a common practice followed is to make group ratings of individual employees in a conference of supervisory officers. Some research has shown that use of multiple raters is a safeguard that prevents rater bias.[17] For example, all first-line supervisors who have supervised the officer rated over the rating period rate him by conferring. By pooling observations, discussing factual evidence, and preparing a group rating with which the raters agree, the tendency to overweight the evaluation is reduced, individual biases are tempered, and a rating norm can be established by the group for more accurate results. The disadvantage of this method is that a biased (but articulate) supervisor may unduly prejudice the other raters in favor of or against the person being rated.

Group conference ratings should always include the names of the participants on the report form. Theoretically, raters who are properly trained in the procedure of personnel appraisals will always make reasonably accurate ratings; however, this rarely occurs, and as a result, superiors and examining boards reviewing such reports are often inclined to "rate the rater" before they attempt to assess the rating itself.

---

[17] Manuel London, *How People Evaluate Others in Organizations* (Mahwah, N.J.: Lawrence Erlbaum Associates, 2001), p. 171.

Individual Trait Ratings

It is recommended by many who are experienced in the merit rating process that raters be encouraged to rate each employee on one characteristic at a time rather than to rate each employee completely before rating another. It is argued that the halo effect is increased when only one employee is considered at a time until his rating is completed because of the good or bad influence one trait has on another, whereas if only one trait is considered at a time for all employees being rated, a more desirable norm can be achieved. The logic of this contention is sound. The supervisor may, however, find it difficult at times to rate separate items separately, and some may have to be considered together because of the effect each has on the other.

For example, in the police service, quantitative production reflected by the number of traffic citations issued or the number of arrests made will be definitely affected by the quality of the traffic citations or arrests. The officer issuing numerous "apple orchard" citations should not receive greater quantitative credit than that given the officer who writes considerably fewer violations but of a much higher selective enforcement quality. The same applies to quantitative and qualitative arrests as well as to many other police activities.

Discussion of Rating with Employee

Perhaps one of the greatest uses to which personnel evaluations can be put is their discussion with the person rated.[18] The supervisor is provided an opportunity to commend or thank his subordinates formally for their high level of performance during the rating period, or in the case of marginal or substandard employees, he can help them when improvement is indicated. If carefully made, the rating report provides a medium for showing the employee how he is measuring up to standards or how he may be falling short of them in his performance. Unfortunately, this critical feedback is often neglected or mishandled in many police agencies.[19]

Some supervisors believe that discussion of ratings with personnel accomplishes little and only leads to controversy; however, the training value of such discussions is readily apparent, and undoubtedly the benefits outweigh the liabilities if the discussions are conducted in a constructive manner. Unfortunately, it must be stipulated that some interviews do not accomplish what was intended because if they are conducted for the purpose of informing the substandard employee of his weaknesses, they are inherently threatening not only to the supervisor, who is expected to be constructively critical of his subordinate, but also to the subordinate, who is on the receiving end of the criticism. This threat is an obstacle to effective communications between the two and, over a period of time, causes a lessening of such face-to-face contacts and a weakening of the whole system.

---

[18] See Chapter 6 for further discussion of the progress interview.

[19] Paul M. Whisenand and R. Fred Ferguson, *The Managing of Police Organizations*, 7th ed. (Upper Saddle River, N.J.: Pearson Prentice Hall, 2008), p. 92.

Interview

The interview with the employee calls for a degree of tact and forthrightness if it is to have maximum effect. Rating officers invariably have little difficulty in interviewing the high producer, but difficulty is usually encountered in approaching the marginal or substandard employee. Often supervisors find this an onerous and unpleasant task, easier to avoid than face, but if the interview is approached objectively, it will be a constructive training device.

At the conclusion of the interview, a substandard employee should be asked to recap his understanding of what was agreed on and what is expected of him in the future. Such playback will eliminate any real or feigned misunderstandings that may be claimed later.

Acknowledgment of Rating

Although the person rated cannot be forced to sign his rating report, a signature space should be provided on the form, and he should be encouraged to sign it. This ensures that he has been informed of its content. Some agencies require the employee to sign the rating in order to validate and document the process; a disclaimer, such as "Signature indicates awareness of the contents and does not imply agreement," can protect the employee's rights while facilitating the rating process.[20]

Follow-Up

Arrangements should be made in the supervisor's schedule for follow-up observations that will provide clues to the effectiveness of the interview. These observations will often assist him in determining the usefulness of the plan the employee has been helped to make and if the specific objectives set for the employee have been realized. It should be made clear to him that help will be readily forthcoming if needed, and he should also be informed that future discussions regarding his performance will be held. If present weaknesses are to be corrected, a specific date might well be set for follow-up discussions. The interview and follow-up contacts should be conducted on a friendly, helpful, positive basis.

Written Notification of Rating

Some superior officers utilize the written notice procedure to inform the employee of his overall rating. This technique is effective as a method of commendation but has serious limitations if utilized to replace the face-to-face interview with the employee whose work needs improvement. This procedure does not afford a suitable medium for full discussion and goal setting, which are desirable and which can be accomplished in the face-to-face interview.

---

[20] Woodbridge Township (New Jersey) Police Department, *Employee Evaluation Form* (Woodbridge, N.J., 2005).

Summary

Personnel evaluation systems are a valuable tool for giving employees recognition for their efforts, for revealing operational deficiencies that might be corrected by training, for uncovering weaknesses in selection procedures, for placing and promoting personnel, for establishing a basis for merit pay, and for providing an inventory of the capabilities of the manpower of an organization.

The basic objectives for which the system was adopted in the first place must continuously be kept in mind by those who are responsible for its success if they are to make it a useful and effective management tool. The system must be used as it was intended; abuses will be considered a breach of faith by the employees and may become a cause for them to bring pressures to bear that will thwart the objectives of the program.

Of perhaps the greatest importance to an evaluation system is the training of the persons who are to do the rating. The rater's competence in carrying out the objectives of the program reflects the type of training and attitudinal conditioning he has received. The training should be directed toward giving him a fuller appreciation of the need for judging subordinates in objective terms from a viewpoint of the service rendered rather than from a personal standpoint of likes and dislikes. The rater should be made aware of the means at his disposal to collect evidence that can be used as a factual basis for evaluations. A rating philosophy should be impressed on him so that he will see the purpose and value of ratings; such indoctrination will give him an understanding of the program that may lessen the tendency for him to consider this periodic task as routine drudgery. The positive aspects should be stressed rather than the negative ones, which emphasize why the system is bad and cannot be made much better.

Once traits have been selected and the rater has been made aware of the shades of meaning of the rating terminology, he can apply rating criteria to performance standards. He will thus be able to assess the employees according to their relative value to the organization.

One of the biggest problems in performance evaluations is the selection of a rating method that will yield reliable results. Employees may be ranked, they may be rated on the basis of a comparison with selected employees or a comparison with the ideal employee, or they may be rated on a numerical basis. Whatever standards the supervisor is expected to use as guides in interpreting the performance norms of his subordinates should be clearly defined. He should be made conscious of the difference between ability and performance. Procedures should be standardized so that all raters perform their tasks uniformly.

The performance standards that emerge from an effective rating system will give employees an understanding about what is expected from them. These standards will serve as goals toward which they can strive, especially when they know where they stand in comparison with other employees.

The supervisor responsible for rating his subordinates must be fully aware of the common errors that creep into ratings so that he may avoid inaccuracies that penalize the better performers and tend to discredit the entire system. The error of leniency will cause his appraisals to be inordinately generous, while personal bias will tend to destroy their usefulness as accurate measures of the level of an employee's performance. When almost all ratings are grouped near the center of the scale because of the reluctance of the rater to defend extremely high or low ratings, the error of central tendency penalizes the best and rewards the poorest employees. The halo effect will also reduce rating accuracy, as will the error of related traits wherein the rater unconsciously allows one trait to influence another merely because both seem to be similar. Overweighting or recency as well as subjectivity of ratings will also adversely affect the report's value as a management tool.

Whether the composite, group, or individual trait rating method is followed, the rating process should be supervised so that the raters will apply a common standard in their ratings because such supervision will improve their quality. The value of the reports will also be enhanced if they are accurate indicators of the ability they purport to measure and if they measure consistently and reasonably accurately each time they are used, since they will then be statistically valid and reliable instruments.

Upon completion of periodic evaluations, the ratings should be used as bases for discussing with each employee his performance, whether commendable, acceptable, or unsatisfactory. Substandard performance can often be corrected by planning a course of action for him, motivating him to improve his performance, and following up to ensure that he is making acceptable progress.

REVIEW

Questions

1. Discuss the uses that can be made of the data obtainable from an effective service rating system.

2. List and discuss the causes for service rating system failures.

3. Discuss some of the methods for gathering and recording employee performance data that can be used as a basis for personnel evaluations.

4. What are the main categories into which traits and abilities of employees should be grouped for rating purposes?

5. List several of the most important subcategories under each of the main groupings in the preceding question.

6. Discuss the rating criteria that the supervisor may utilize in appraising patrol and traffic personnel, investigative personnel, and staff and auxiliary personnel.

7. Discuss the rating standards and methods commonly used in rating systems to compare employees.

8. What broad characteristics are usually found in supervisors who excel in rating subordinates?

9. List seven common rating errors, and discuss how each is committed.

10. Distinguish between validity and reliability in rating reports.

11. What are the most common rating methods? Discuss the advantages and disadvantages of each.

Exercises

1. Develop a rating form for the evaluation of probationary officers.

2. Prepare a rating form for the evaluation of all personnel other than supervisors.

3. Prepare a rating form for supervisory personnel. Include instructions for its use.

4. Assume that you have rated your subordinates on a scale of 1 to 10 for their traits, abilities, performance, and value to the organization. A rating of 10 represents the outstanding employee, while a rating of less than 5 represents the deficient one who needs to improve.

You are to interview a concerned employee, whom you have rated as indicated below, for the purpose of informing him of his deficiencies and assisting him to establish a program for self-improvement. Make any assumptions reasonably required for the interview.

Quality of work	4
Quantity of work	6
Knowledge of job	7
Initiative	3
Loyalty	5
Cooperation with fellow employees	5
Diplomacy and tact in dealing with public	4
Personal habits	4
Emotional stability	5
Overall value to department	4

13

Tactical Deployment of Field Forces

Chapter Objectives

This chapter will enable you:

- To gain an understanding of the procedures and techniques of supervising personnel in the tactical control of unusual incidents
- To become familiar with the logistical requirements in the control of unusual incidents
- To become aware of basic tactics of controlling unusual incidents

The allocation of field personnel according to the normal needs for their services by time of day, day of week, and area involves the simple matter of both computations and judgments based on experience. Such usual deployment criteria must be abandoned at times to meet the tactical needs of the moment under unusual conditions associated with such occurrences as major disasters, barricaded persons, bomb threats, civil disorders, labor disturbances, and searches for lost persons. Detailed guidance on developing procedures for all such incidents can be found in Chapter 46 of the fifth edition of *Unusual Occurrences, Standards for Law Enforcement Agencies*, published by the Commission for Accreditation of Law Enforcement Agencies (CALEA).

Supervisory Responsibilities in Unusual Occurrences

Patrol units almost invariably are the first to respond to the scene of an unusual occurrence and are responsible for taking whatever police action may be indicated. In almost all such cases, they must look to the field supervisor for guidance during those first few critical minutes when it is his responsibility to initiate control operations. He may not delay action in the expectation that he will soon be relieved of responsibility by higher authority; rather, his actions should be predicated on the assumption that he will not be relieved and that it will be incumbent on him alone to make decisions.

Any miscalculations he makes may cause irreparable harm. For example, failure to evacuate residents from an area endangered by a potential disaster resulting from a major fire, a rupture in a dam, or escaping chemicals or dangerous gas from a broken container or line might result in untold loss of life, with consequent civil liability. The accuracy of his evaluations of the field intelligence conveyed to him by field units, the correctness of his appraisal of the occurrence, and the effectiveness of his initial actions in deploying and directing the efforts of control personnel will largely determine the success of the police mission in containing the effects of the incident.

In incidents such as civil disorders where force is reasonably necessary, its sufficiency and decisive application are largely a supervisory responsibility. A delay in applying appropriate control measures may cause a relatively minor incident to escalate into one of major proportions.

Basic Procedures for Unusual Occurrences

One general framework for handling unusual occurrences of any kind is the Now, Scene, Future (NSF) model.[1] In the Now phase, the supervisor gives initial orders while heading to the scene, gets an assessment from the first responding officers, evaluates the scene for hazards, determines the need for additional assistance, and so on. In the Scene phase, the supervisor takes control and directs the response—he sets up perimeters, assigns responders to handle specific tasks, keeps higher command advised, and so on. In the Future phase, the supervisor conducts debriefings and then evaluates all reports to determine the need for commendations, discipline, training, policy changes, and so on.

Every supervisor should become familiar with the basic procedures applicable to the procurement and use of personnel, equipment, and facilities common to the policing of most unusual occurrences. Although practices may vary somewhat from place to place because of differences in reciprocity, mutual aid agreements, or policy considerations, usually these will not substantially affect the immediate action the supervisor must take to initiate control measures. The application of usual standard operating procedures will ordinarily require some deviations from normal operations to the extent that personnel, equipment, and facilities must be redistributed to meet the needs of the unusual condition. The principal objective should be to deploy available personnel and equipment rapidly in the initial stages to prevent escalation of the incident or aggravation of the circumstances.

In implementing control activities initially at the scene of an unusual occurrence, the supervisor may perform or cause to be performed several very important tasks almost simultaneously. The sequence he will follow and the extent of his activities will depend largely on how well he organizes, systematizes, and delegates; how complex a police operation is required to control the incident and its effects; how many personnel he has immediately available and how proficient they are; and what equipment, supplies, facilities, and other support are available to him. He should also assess and communicate to a higher authority whatever other resources might be required in the immediate future if the occurrence becomes more acute.

Although some of the following basic operating procedures may not apply to all situations, many of them will be found useful in most unusual incidents. They are recommended as guidelines to keep the supervisor from overlooking, in a stressful situation, some important procedures that may help him avoid later criticism.

---

[1] Jeffry Bernstein, *Field Supervision for Chicago PD Management and Supervision Guide* (Fort Lauderdale, Fla.: Bernstein & Associates, 2006), Section 2, pp. 7–9.

Communication of Field Intelligence

One of the supervisor's first tasks at the scene of an unusual incident should be to quickly evaluate the occurrence and then communicate to his headquarters the field intelligence available so that plans can be started for the dissemination of necessary control material and equipment and the deployment of required personnel. Wherever applicable, the following information should be transmitted as it becomes available:

1. *Nature of the incident.* This might include fire, flood, civil disorder, or barricaded suspect.
2. *Type and size of the incident.* Data should include the extent of the disturbance and the size of any crowd in a civil disorder, whether military or civil aircraft is involved in a plane crash, what type of fire is involved and what its likely progress will be, or similar relevant information.
3. *Location of the incident and type of area and property involved.* The location could be a residential area, brushy hillside, business district, bank building, school, or manufacturing firm.
4. *Potential effect of the incident on persons or property.* Possibilities include danger from noxious substances or fire, disruption of specified utilities, water damage, looting or destruction of specified property by hostile and destructive persons, as well as direction of movement, direction of wind, and other applicable predictors that might have bearing on the control of a fire or the use of gas to control a crowd.
5. *Unusual circumstances present.* An unruly crowd, barricaded streets, a sniper armed with sidearm or rifle, explosives, or broken waterlines could be involved.
6. *Need for evacuation.* Evacuation might be ordered for a broken dam endangering a specified area, a fire approaching a specified residential area, a poisonous or explosive gas blowing toward a school, persons being endangered by rifle fire, or the progress of toxic spills endangering people.
7. *Antilooting measures required.* These are based on need for evacuation.
8. *Need for outside or traffic perimeter.* Areas and sites where an outside perimeter should be established to control pedestrian and vehicular traffic into or out of the area and locations that should be manned or barricaded would be assessed.
9. *Need for inside perimeter boundaries to be established at immediate scene.*
10. *Personnel needs.* Officers might be required for patrol of inner and outer perimeters, control duties, searches, evacuations, or rescues. Special weapons teams, hostage negotiators, or other specialists should be requested as needed.
11. *Command post location and location of staging area for personnel and emergency support.*
12. *Emergency equipment and personnel needed and routes available for their use into and out of the area.*
13. *Equipment, supplies, and facilities needed.* Portable communications, radios, bullhorns, loudspeakers, flares, armor, gas equipment, gas masks, rope, barricades, floodlights, lanterns, rifle-equipped marksmen, and so on, might be required.
14. *Number of persons injured or dead.*
15. *Ambulances or hospital facilities needed.*

16. *Other.* Additional needs might include search dogs; helicopters or aircraft for surveillance; ammunition; food and drink for control personnel; blankets; maps; special investigative equipment, such as a photographic booth for pictures of arrested persons and arresting officers for future identification in court; or other special equipment, such as bomb disposal gear, tow trucks, or torches.

The more field intelligence that is made available to headquarters personnel, the better they will be able to make good control plans and provide for the operational needs of personnel at the scene. In fact, without adequate field intelligence, support operations will probably be greatly impaired.

Establishment of a Command Post

When a command post is needed, the supervisor should carefully select a suitable site. It should be easily identifiable on maps available to operating personnel and should permit radio communications without dead spots. It should be near the affected area but not exposed to attack or gunfire, fire, floodwaters, noxious gases, or other hazards. It should be located upwind from the affected area, if practicable, in those situations in which the use of tear gas might be necessary or if smoke or harmful gases may disrupt command post operations. If possible, it should be positioned near a power supply where electricity is available (if needed) to operate floodlights and mobile command post equipment. To prevent clogging of radio frequencies with the long messages often required and to provide continuous communications with headquarters, telephones should be used and kept available; portable equipment works well under these conditions.

The command post's location should provide a staging area for personnel and their equipment as they arrive. The supervisor should also consider the accessibility of routes to and from the scene for emergency equipment such as fire trucks and ambulances. Routes should be selected that are not unnecessarily exposed to man-made or natural dangers and that can be protected from persons who might attempt to ambush control or support personnel as they approach or leave the scene.

The command post might be the supervisor's vehicle, a van driven by the supervisor, another mobile radio unit, an office or building, the police station, or any place that provides an immediate base of operations with communications equipment, water, restrooms, and other facilities. An officer or helicopter should be directed to scout the area for an alternative site if the location initially selected proves to be unsatisfactory.

A formal command post may be necessary later should the incident require a major police effort. Care should be exercised, however, to avoid unnecessarily moving it as this may cause confusion and disruption of operations. The first choice is not necessarily the best; if another location is substantially better suited for the operation, a change in location should be undertaken. Command posts established for scheduled events will ordinarily pose no problems to the field supervisor because they are staffed and operated according to established plans.

Incident Command System (ICS)

The incident command system (ICS) is the command and control system for unusual occurrences that require coordinated multiagency or multijurisdictional responses, a modular system capable of expanding or contracting to the appropriate size for any crisis. This system provides a common language for all responding agencies and is a comprehensive

NYPD Mobile Command Post at Ground Zero. New York, NY.

model for all aspects of response to large-scale emergencies. (Go to www.fema.gov for more information.) Any properly trained officer may initiate ICS and serve as incident commander until relieved by a supervisor or other higher authority.

In his presidential directive in 2003, President Bush mandated the creation of a National Incident Management System (NIMS) (Homeland Security directive, February 2003). This directive ordered the Secretary of the Department of Homeland Security (DHS) to develop a national response plan that would treat crisis management and consequence management as a single integrated function; it also required adoption of the NIMS standards by all state, tribal, and local organizations as a condition of receiving federal grants. "This system will provide a consistent nationwide approach for federal, state, local and tribal governments to work effectively and efficiently together to prepare for, prevent, respond to, and recover from domestic incidents, regardless of cause, size or complexity."[2]

The NIMS includes and expands on the ICS. Developed by the Federal Emergency Management Agency (FEMA), ICS training is being conducted for emergency services agencies across the nation, including police, fire services, first aid providers, and others.

Reconnaissance

As they become available, one or more vehicle patrol units or foot patrol officers should be assigned to reconnoiter the affected area and its perimeter as might be necessary for the purpose of securing current field intelligence. Helicopters are of immense value for this

[2] Tom Ridge, Secretary of the Department of Homeland Security, *National Incident Management System*, memo, March 1, 2004.

purpose in some situations. When new information is obtained, it should be promptly relayed to headquarters.

Logistics Aide and Press Relations Officer

When the supervisor assumes responsibility for directing police action to control an unusual occurrence, one of his first acts should be to appoint aides to assist him in performing the many tasks he cannot perform personally and to free him to concentrate on directing the operation. Many of these functions must be accomplished simultaneously at the beginning of the operation: Communications must be established and maintained with headquarters, the command post must be activated, supporting facilities must be set up, and security measures must be taken. An aide should be responsible for keeping a chronological log of control measures taken in all but the simplest of incidents and should include the details of the operation from its inception. Names, unit numbers, and assignments of personnel should be recorded as they arrive at the staging area as well as a list made of the department equipment they bring. They should then be assigned to units with designated leaders, and available equipment assigned as needed.

Officers should be briefed (by the supervisor when necessary), informed of their specific duties and responsibilities, and dispatched to their assigned posts. They should be instructed to remain there until relieved.

Supplies must be requested and distributed as needed. The area affected by the incident and the positions of control personnel and equipment should be plotted on a map to provide a ready overview of the entire operation. This map should be part of each supervisor's field kit and be of small scale, ideally not larger than one inch per mile. A plastic overlay sheet and colored grease pencils should be available for plotting

Boston Police Officer speaks to media.

data. Such maps can be easily improvised by the individual supervisor and mounted on hinged plywood, like a checkerboard is mounted on its backing, if they are not provided by his department. They can be stored in the trunk of his vehicle or in a special map kit. Portable computers and tablets may be used as well.

A well-selected public relations officer can be of great value in maintaining good media relations by collecting information and coordinating current news releases. He is also in an excellent position to secure media assistance in deterring onlookers from entering the area. Because of his position, he can do much to prevent unrestrained media coverage that sometimes disrupts police negotiations, alerts terrorists to the tactics being used by the police, or otherwise causes unnecessary confusion at the scene.

Operational Guidelines for Unusual Occurrences

The foregoing discussion offers broad operational guidelines for the supervisor who is responsible for directing the police activities required to control an unscheduled unusual incident for which a specific operating plan has not been established. Obviously, the nature of the occurrence will dictate which procedures are applicable in a given situation.

Some tactics that have been tried and found effective in handling specific types of unusual occurrences are discussed in the following pages. Basic procedures will be referred to briefly as a reminder to the supervisor of the essential parts of the operational procedures that he must set in motion. He should become thoroughly familiar with local policies and procedures that may require him to perform certain functions in addition to those described.

Usually, organizational rules will designate whether the uniformed field supervisor or a supervisor of investigators, who may be present, is in charge of the operation. Sometimes both may believe they have this responsibility. For example, if a barricaded suspect is involved, they will reason that organizational rules give both uniformed personnel and detectives the responsibility for apprehending criminals. In such cases, it is imperative that they decide at the outset who should assume charge to prevent the confusion and conflicts that invariably result when there is no unity of command.

Barricaded Persons

A potentially dangerous person may take refuge in a building or other structure to escape arrest, or he may be discovered in a building while committing a crime and barricade himself with the hope of later escape. A direct assault on him usually should be avoided, especially when he can be neutralized and apprehended by the use of special weapons without creating unnecessary danger to police personnel or other innocent persons in the area.

Hostages

The suspect may capture a hostage, hoping to increase his bargaining power with the police. The presence of an innocent victim in the barricaded premises complicates the matter because his safety must be considered, but the basic problem of taking the suspect into custody remains substantially the same.

When the criminal has seized a hostage, he will usually demand that officers withdraw or provide him a means of escaping without interference. The period when the initial seizure occurs is the most critical because of the emotional tensions that are present—it is then that the danger of injury or death to the hostage is greatest. If a short hesitation in police activity occurs at this time, conditions at the scene are likely to stabilize and the immediate initial danger to the hostage will be reduced.

Time operates to the advantage of the police in such cases. Any delaying tactics will enable them to prepare effective plans for dealing with the suspect. Delay may provide them with an opportunity to seize the individual in an unguarded moment, give the victim an opportunity to escape, or enable the police to gain more time through negotiations, as discussed in later paragraphs.

Although there are no hard-and-fast rules applicable to such cases, the supervisor in charge at the scene must decide whether to accede to the demands or refuse to do so. Ordinarily, a general practice followed by the police in such instances is that no deals will be made. It has been shown all over the world that such arrangements encourage others to make the same demands.

The supervisor must judge each case on its own merits. He must weigh the danger to the hostage's life against the possibility that the suspect is bluffing. The supervisor should recognize that if he allows the hostage to be taken from the presence of the police, the police lose any advantage they may have and will no longer be able to provide any protection, whereas their mere presence may deter the criminal from harming the hostage. If they refuse to bargain with the criminal, he will be forced to continue to hold the hostage, to release him, to bargain for an opportunity to escape by himself, or to harm the hostage and risk capture or death.

Refusal to allow the suspect to take the hostage from the scene probably will not increase the danger to the hostage. Assurances that the hostage will not be harmed if he is taken away by the suspect cannot be relied on. If the suspect is permitted to remove the hostage because of unusual circumstances, the route of escape should be under surveillance by ground and air units. Should an attractive opportunity present itself to gain the initiative, these units should take advantage of it quickly and decisively.

Direction of Assault

Any attempt to rush a suspect who holds a hostage without careful planning and preparation might result in at least two deaths—an officer's and the hostage's. Any such attempt should be resorted to only after all other reasonable means to rescue the hostage or secure his release and the surrender of the suspect have been exhausted. The supervisor should make it clear to all personnel that he reserves the right to decide how and when organized force is to be used to achieve this objective.

If he enforces such directions, unity of command will be maintained. Personnel will be forced to act in harmony with each other rather than as independent agents. To permit each officer involved to decide such matters individually would only create unnecessary danger to themselves and others and cause considerable confusion. Generally, direct assault tactics have been proved to be the least effective course of action, especially when modern armor, gas equipment, concussion devices, and other weapons are available.

Operating Procedures in Hostage and Barricaded Suspect Cases

As soon as a determination is made that a suspect has taken a hostage and barricaded himself in a structure, the supervisor should set into operation a tactical plan to neutralize and arrest the suspect and to rescue or secure the release of the hostage unharmed.

Preliminary Operations

The supervisor should perform the following tasks or designate an aide to perform them (the sequence in which they are carried out may vary according to the circumstances):

1. *Secure premises.* When it is first learned that a suspect has barricaded himself in a structure, officers should be posted at the front and rear of the premises and in other locations as needed to prevent his escape. Nothing is more embarrassing to the supervisor than putting a major police operation into effect only to discover that the suspect has been allowed to escape because the premises were not properly secured.

2. *Set up command post.* Locate command operations in a safe strategic area upwind from the scene to avoid contamination of the area if gas is used.

3. *Attend to injured persons.* Give aid to, interview, and remove anyone who has been injured.

4. *Set up communications.* Notify headquarters of the situation as previously discussed.

5. *Add personnel support.* Acquire necessary personnel for cordoning off the area and for operations at the scene. Only personnel reasonably needed at the scene of operations should be requested because too many may cause danger to each other by crossfire. Special teams, including trained negotiators, snipers, and their observers, should be summoned when necessary through headquarters from local sources or nearby agencies. When marksmen arrive, they should be thoroughly briefed, specifically instructed in the duties of their assignment, and positioned to meet current needs.

6. *Obtain special equipment.* Request gas grenades and cartridges, masks, body armor, high-powered rifles and marksmen, portable communications equipment, loudspeakers for communicating with the suspect, portable lights and generators at night, helicopter patrol, materials suitable for cordoning off area to keep out curiosity seekers and uninvolved persons, ambulance, and fire equipment as needed.

7. *Set up the staging area.* Locate a staging area where officers and equipment are to report upwind from the scene of the incident.

8. *Identify officers as they report.* Assign officers to positions where they can secure escape routes without exposing themselves to each other's crossfire; assign other personnel as needed to cordon off the area around the perimeter.

9. *Perform evacuation.* Persons in the area who may be endangered by sidearm, rifle, or shotgun fire or other police control measures should be removed to a safe location. Provisions should be made to protect their property if it is left exposed to theft or damage during their absence.

10. *Obtain field intelligence.* Collate intelligence from police and civilians who can provide information regarding the suspect, his victim, and his precise location. Information should be obtained concerning the types of weapons he may have access

to, the type of crimes he has committed, his purpose in barricading himself or seiz-ing a hostage, his mental and physical condition, his attitudes concerning police and society, and a complete physical description. Such a description should be dissemi-nated to control personnel so that they may avoid shooting or unnecessarily taking other action against a person who is unidentified. A detailed description of the hos-tage should also be given to control personnel so that they will not mistake him for the suspect. Additional information on the suspect's true intentions may be obtained from social media sites such as Facebook, blogs, and website postings.[3]

11. *Communicate with the barricaded person.* Establish communications with the suspect by telephone if one is available (the number can be obtained from the telephone company based on the address). If a telephone is not accessible, communications might be established by a loudspeaker. A portable battery-operated bullhorn is ideal for this purpose. Additionally, a cell phone may be sent in if circumstances permit.

General Considerations

Several alternatives are available to the supervisor at a scene where hostages are involved. Each situation is different; therefore, each alternative must be carefully evaluated in terms of its potential for a successful resolution of the problem with a minimum of danger to the hostage, the police, and the public.

The preferred procedure—negotiation—will buy time, which operates to the advantage of the police. It gives them an opportunity to develop alternative plans of action should negotiations fail, it permits greater opportunity for the suspect to make a mistake that can be exploited, and it often increases the suspect's affinity for the hostage. In some hostage situations, cases have been reported where the hostages have sympathized and empathized with their hostage takers. This positive feeling of the hostage toward the hostage taker is sometimes called the Stockholm syndrome.[4] A characteristic of this syndrome is the captors also develop positive feelings toward the hostages. When it occurs, the likelihood that the suspect will take the hostage's life is reduced. Time may also give the hostage an opportunity to escape.

Skillful use of negotiation procedures has much potential for success. Negotiation activities should be supervised by a person specially trained for that purpose, but if no one is available, the supervisor should talk with the suspect, preferably by telephone. This type of communication generally tends to calm the suspect and be more effective than use of the natural voice or communication by amplifier or bullhorn.

The supervisor should be extremely cautious in allowing unskilled persons to communicate with the suspect because of the ever-present danger that the dialogue might unintentionally aggravate the suspect's hostility and unnecessarily endanger the hostage. Furthermore, there have been occurrences where unskilled negotiators have themselves been taken as hostages.

---

[3] Jeffry Bernstein, *Situational Management Training Guide for New Jersey Police Commanders* (Fort Lauderdale, Fla.: Bernstein & Associates, 2013).

[4] W. Ronald Olin and David G. Born, "A Behavioral Approach to Hostage Situations," *FBI Law Enforcement Bulletin,* 52, No. 1 (January 1983), 19–24; Thomas Strentz, *Psychological Aspects of Crisis Negotiation* (Boca Raton, Fla.: CRC Press, 2012), p. 281.

Conversations with the suspect should always be carried out in positive terms (as discussed in the following sections on rational and emotionally troubled suspects). Patience and a calm demeanor are essential because they tend to have a calming effect on the suspect. A negative, hostile, or antagonistic manner might only aggravate the delicate balance that exists between the hostage holder and the police and should be avoided.

The negotiator should proceed on the premise that every issue is negotiable except that he must not agree to provide the suspect with offensive weapons or instruments, as these will only increase his capacity for violence. The negotiator should adopt the position that he does not have authority to make final agreements with the suspect but must clear these with higher authority. Such techniques will buy further time. Every effort should be made to maintain constant communications with the suspect to focus his attention on negotiations and to divert his attention from the hostage.

Suitably equipped snipers and an observer for each should be strategically posted as soon as a hostage situation develops, and both should be thoroughly briefed about their duties. If negotiations break down, it may become necessary to use them to neutralize the suspect should he become careless. This tactic may pose a danger to the hostage or other innocent persons and must be used with caution and restraint in controlling the activities of the suspect. Assault combined with the use of chemical agents (as discussed later) should usually be reserved as a last resort if other means fail to produce results.[5]

Rational Suspect

If evidence indicates the suspect is rational, an attempt should be made to point out the futility of his actions. A logical appeal in which he is informed that he is surrounded and cannot escape and that he will not be hurt if he gives himself up might be effective in inducing the suspect to surrender. Such an appeal may have greater influence if it is made by a member of his family, a relative, a close friend, or his minister. Ordinarily, any of them should be allowed to converse with the individual, but they should not be permitted to negotiate binding agreements without clearing these with the supervisor in charge of the operation, nor should they be allowed to enter the barricaded premises because they, too, might be taken hostage.

Emotionally Troubled Suspect

If the reason for the suspect's resistance is not obviously to escape arrest for a crime but appears to be based on a real or imagined grievance of an emotionally troubled person, an attempt should be made to determine the cause of the grievance. It may be trivial, but to him it may be sufficient to cause him to destroy himself and his hostage. He should be given assurance that everything possible will be done to help him.

A calm, patient attitude should be reflected in all conversations with him. These should be directed toward convincing him that he should give himself up and, at the same time, should be used to stall for time. He should be encouraged to talk—time often has a settling influence on such a person and may provide the police an opportunity to gain the initiative or give the hostage an opportunity to escape.

---

[5] Nathan F. Iannone, *Principles of Police Patrol* (New York: McGraw-Hill, 1975), pp. 253–56; Gene L. Scaramella, William P. McCarney, and Steve M Cox, *Introduction to Policing* (Thousand Oaks, Calif.: Sage Publications, 2011), p. 141.

Atlantic City SWAT
Team in action.

Whether the barricaded person is a rational suspect wanted for a crime or an emotionally troubled, irrational individual with a grievance sufficient to cause him to kill, every effort should be made to persuade him to surrender voluntarily. If he refuses, force may become necessary to take him into custody and rescue the hostage.

Assault Tactics

In those cases where the acts and threats of the suspect indicate that he realizes he cannot escape and that his intent may be to harm a hostage, positive direct action may be required. The use of tear gas and smoke, concussion, or other devices to cover a direct assault on his barricaded position by personnel in body armor, shields, and masks should be considered. To wait longer might unnecessarily endanger the hostage. The decision the supervisor must make should be based on his evaluation of whether the hostage would be jeopardized more by the force necessary to rescue him than by the suspect.

When a decision is made to force entry into the suspect's position, plans previously formulated should be put into operation. Depending on the type of structure to be entered, an entry team consisting of three to five officers should be dressed in protective armor and masks and be equipped with a pry bar, sledgehammer or battering ram, gas gun, gas cartridges and grenades, smoke grenades, and concussion devices.

A cover team of at least two officers should be selected and equipped with gas masks and other protective clothing. They and the officers of the entry team should be thoroughly briefed by the supervisor in the tactics to be used in the operation—precision in executing the established plan is vital to success.

The personnel of both teams should agree on the safest route to approach the premises. Other officers, including expert marksmen equipped with rifles and scopes and their observers, should be strategically positioned to cover the advance of the approach team and to prevent the suspect leaving with the hostage.

A marker board or computer is useful in illustrating the plan of attack that officers involved must thoroughly understand. It may be used to depict the arrangement of rooms, hallways, and other interior features of the premises to be entered.

Diversionary tactics such as talking over the speaker system or bullhorn, making loud noises on the side of the premises opposite the approach route, or calling the suspect and occupying him may sufficiently divert his attention to allow the approach team to take their positions without being observed. Smoke might also be used to cover this operation if adequate concealment is not otherwise available. When the approach team is in position to cover windows, doors, and other apertures through which the suspect might fire on the officers, members of the entry team should make their advance to a position where entry is to be effected.

On a prearranged signal, the suspect's attention should be diverted away from the point at which gas is to be thrown or fired into the premises. This will permit detonation of the gas cartridge before it can be covered, kicked, thrown away, or otherwise neutralized by the suspect. In one instance, a suspect was able to scoop several gas projectiles into a kitchen exhaust system, which effectively drew the gas out of the room in which he was barricaded, and it was only after electricity to the exhaust system was shut off that the suspect was overcome by gas fired into the room and forced to surrender.

The gas should ordinarily be fired or thrown directly into the room where the suspect is believed to be. This will force him to take action to protect himself from it and will tend to divert his attention from the hostage. Such a technique will also prevent him from shutting a door and sealing off the room he occupies.

Grenades and projectiles that dispel dust are preferred to those that dispel gas by combustion, which cause considerable heat and often ignite curtains, upholstery, and other inflammable materials with which they come in contact. They also subject the hostage to another hazard—fire.

Simultaneously with the gas attack, the entry team officers should force entry into the premises. One officer should quickly assume a prone position in front of the place of entry, covering it with his shotgun at the ready position as the other members enter. The first should make a sudden entry, proceed to the right or left as previously agreed on, flatten himself against the wall, and give protection to the others as they enter on signal and assume the positions agreed on.

As each room is secured, officers should proceed to other rooms until the suspect is located, neutralized, and captured. Other officers should be assigned by the supervisor as they are needed to secure an area after it has been searched to prevent the suspect from moving back into it after the search. The success of the mission will depend largely on the swiftness and precision with which the operation is carried out.

Response to the Active Shooter

The mass murders at Columbine High School in April 1999 and at Virginia Tech in 2007 illustrated the need for new assault tactics by police. Standard tactics for barricaded suspect situations previously called for containment and negotiations, but when subjects are actively killing people, new tactics call for an immediate response. In their course "Rapid Deployment to High-Risk Incidents," the International Association of Chiefs of Police (IACP) trains officers in the rapid deployment system. (Go to www.iacptraining. org for more information.) This system calls for the first responding officers to enter the structure and attempt to neutralize, or contain, the active shooter until a special weapons team can arrive. Since patrol officers are the first to arrive, supervisors must be trained in this technique and be prepared to lead an assault team to minimize casualties.

Search for Other Suspects

Even though one suspect is apprehended, the officers should not assume that there are no others on the premises. The remainder of the building should be searched for other suspects with the same care as was used in apprehending the first one.

Arrest of Suspect

At times, the suspect will voluntarily leave his position to surrender after gas has been employed against him. Should this happen, he should be directed to drop his weapons, hold his hands high above his head with fingers spread, and move from the immediate scene toward the officers. The supervisor should admonish the officers not to leave their cover positions to approach the suspect but to require him to approach them. From their positions, they can cover him while he is being secured and searched.

Officers from the California Highway Patrol, Los Angeles Police Department, Los Angeles School Police, and Cal State Northridge Police Department take part in an active shooter drill on a school campus.
(© ZUMA Press/ Newscom)

Civil Disorder: Minor Unlawful Assemblies

Civil disorder may take several forms. It may take the form of small assemblages bent on disrupting the public peace by demonstrating or by committing acts of vandalism, looting, or violence against persons or property, or it may involve mass civil unrest characterized by riotous mob action.

Relatively small disturbances by a limited number of persons usually can be dealt with effectively by a small force of well-trained officers under the competent leadership of a field supervisor; a large riotous mob may require a major police effort involving hundreds of peace officers. In either event, the role of the supervisor is rather well defined by the basic admonition that a leader should not commit his forces until they are of sufficient strength to perform their mission with a reasonable expectation of success.

When a supervisor responds to a disturbance where a small group of persons has spontaneously assembled for an apparently unlawful purpose, he should evaluate the occurrence from a strategic location to determine what force may be needed to control the incident. He should establish communications with headquarters to notify his superiors of the nature of the incident, the number of persons involved, and their probable intent. Sufficient personnel to handle the matter should be requested, along with any special teams available, to report to a specified staging location near the scene. Equipment that might be needed should be requested, and supporting reserve personnel should be alerted to stand by in the event they are needed.

As personnel respond to the staging area, they should be directed to park their vehicles in a position least exposed to harm from the crowd and to lock shotguns in their racks and special equipment in the cars' trunks. Officer personnel should be assigned to guard this equipment. When sufficient officers have arrived to handle the crowd, the supervisor should form them into an appropriate squad formation with himself as squad leader; if more than one squad is to be employed, he should designate a leader for the second squad. These formations should then take action to disperse the persons unlawfully assembled.

The supervisor should direct the squads that are to be committed to advance in close formation on an assemblage that is fighting or engaging in other unlawful acts. Squad members should be commanded to carry their batons in a port arms position. Often such a display of force will cause dispersal without the necessity of making arrests.

When the laws of the jurisdiction require the police to give a dispersal order to the persons unlawfully assembled, the supervisor should give that order from a position near the group. It should be given loudly and clearly (with a mechanical device if necessary) to refute any later claim that the announcement could not be heard by those assembled. To avert such claims, an officer should be stationed at the furthermost border of the crowd to signal that the dispersal order was audible. After a reasonable time has elapsed, the supervisor should move his personnel forward to disperse the group into a predetermined escape route that has been left open to them.

Should arrests be indicated, the supervisor should concentrate the force of his squad formations on the leaders of the group. When they have been arrested and moved quickly to the rear, the probability that the disturbance will continue is greatly reduced. When a group loses its leader, the members often will lose their desire to resist further and will disperse on their own volition. At times, however, arrest of the real agitator who is not the group leader has more effect than the arrest of the leader. The objective of an agitator is often to gain crowd support, cause a confrontation between the group and the police, and then leave before he can be arrested. Often such an agitator can be followed and arrested away from the crowd to avoid precipitating further mob violence.

Once dispersal has been effected, officers should be directed to prevent small residual groups from forming. If such groups do form, they should be dispersed promptly unless arrests of the participants are indicated.

If persons have been arrested, they should be processed by officers best able to testify against them. Photographs of arresting officers and their prisoners, fingerprints, and the like are valuable evidence that may help in making proper identification of defendants later in court. Other officers not involved in arrests and not needed for further control measures should be instructed to return to their former assignments.

When the incident is under control, the supervisor should communicate this fact to his headquarters. He may find it desirable to supervise the booking of prisoners and the preparation of routine reports.

A summary report of the incident should be made for future reference. Such reports are useful not only in court but also for training in critique sessions that should follow such occurrences.

Civil Disorder: Major Disturbances

A major police effort that is likely to be required in the control of an extensive civil disturbance will usually be directed by high-ranking police officials after the initial occurrence. However, during the critical initial period when units assigned to routine field duties first respond to the scene of the disturbance, the field supervisor bears the brunt of the responsibility for directing their activities.

What might start as an ordinary occurrence may turn swiftly into a widespread riot if improperly handled. Even a so-called routine incident may abruptly erupt into one of major proportions. The 2006 San Bernardino punk riot is an example of how a minor arrest expanded into a widespread riot marked by violence and destruction.[6] Likewise, the extensive riots accompanied by arson, looting, mass destruction of property, and assaults in Los Angeles and throughout the country in 1992 following an unpopular jury decision involving the use of force by police officers bear stark testament to the extreme importance of proper on-the-scene supervisory judgments at the inception of these incidents.

Students of civil disturbance control and police administrators desiring to improve their abilities to direct control measures of such serious incidents more effectively should study the reports of major disturbances in the recent past and the techniques used by police to control them. This will provide insight into the reasons why errors occurred and some means for avoiding them.

Analysis of many civil disorders has shown that the availability of good field intelligence, the accuracy of the evaluation of the initial incident, the effectiveness of the operational plan selected to deal with it, the speed with which personnel responded, and

---

[6] A. Hunsicker, *Behind the Shield: Anti-Riot Operations Guide* (Boca Raton, Fla.: Universal Publishers, 2011), p. 69.

the decisiveness of their actions determined whether the incident remained a relatively minor one or developed into one of major proportions.[7] Responsibility for collating and assessing facts and for implementing the first course of action rests on the field supervisor in charge at the time. The effectiveness of his initial action may well determine how much more serious the matter will become.

Basic tactical and operational procedures similar to those applicable to minor unlawful assemblies generally can be employed with good effect in major disorders. The very nature of major disturbances, however, will usually require more sophisticated planning and far more personnel in carrying out control operations. The following factors should be considered by the supervisor in such occurrences.

Communications

Communications should be established with headquarters to transmit information regarding the nature and extent of the incident and the mood of the rioters. Details should be given describing the area involved; what acts, such as looting, rock throwing, arson, or other serious offenses, are being committed; the type of weapons being used; and the existence of snipers or other special conditions revealed by initial observations, reconnaissance units, or observation posts. Logistical support should be requested (as previously described). A command post should be established upwind of the scene of operation if possible to avoid gas contamination, should such devices be necessary. An aide should be assigned to start an operational log and assist with coordinating personnel, equipment, and supplies as they arrive if it appears that the operation may last for an extended period. The command post location and that of the staging area should be indicated so that officers responding may wait there in reserve or otherwise be assigned as they arrive. Access routes to this area should be specified if the situation requires; sometimes, special efforts must be made to keep these routes open for emergency services.

Field Tactics

Field tactics and standard operating procedures that have been adopted or are normally utilized in civil disorder control may have to be modified to some extent to meet the needs of a particular situation. Supervisory personnel should be thoroughly indoctrinated in these practices and should, as an integral part of their training function, acquaint their subordinates with the techniques and procedures that have been found to be most effective in such incidents.

If the supervisor decides that his force is not sufficient to commit immediately, he should wait until he has adequate personnel to overwhelm the riotous elements. This strategy of striking swiftly with adequate force to ensure success should be the basic concept of civil disorder control.[8] He should, however, avoid any appearance of weakness because it might have an adverse effect on the morale of his subordinates. If sufficient

---

[7] Arnold Sagalyn, *The Riot Commission: Recommendations for Law and Order in Confrontation—Violence and the Police,* eds. C. R. Hormachea and Marion Hormachea (Boston: Holbrook Press, 1971), p. 160.

[8] Los Angeles Police Department, *Tactical Manual* (Los Angeles, Calif., February 1979), Section D 001.01.

personnel have responded, he may conclude from his appraisal of field intelligence and his assessment of the problem, the area, and his logistical support that quick, decisive action should be taken immediately before the gathering becomes a riotous mob beyond what available personnel can handle.

The supervisor must make the decision concerning such matters. A limited number of well-trained officers acting in unison can ordinarily handle adequately a much larger group of hostile rioters, but it would be foolhardy to commit a grossly outnumbered force of officers to confront such a group.

Personnel available for the striking force should be assigned to squads or other duty as needed and be thoroughly briefed regarding their mission, the type of crowd and its direction of movement, weapons being used, specific tactics to be used, the direction of dispersal, and other such matters of concern to control personnel. Squad members should be told that they must confine themselves to their primary mission of dispersing the crowd or making arrests of its leaders, as the case may be, rather than becoming involved in secondary skirmishes that may jeopardize the entire mission.

If a dispersal order is required, it should be given as previously described. A standard squad formation might then be employed effectively in dispersing the group. No particular formation is suitable for all situations. The supervisor should select the one that may be most effective depending on his specific mission, the nature and structure of the riotous group, and the type of area involved.

Every effort should be made to avoid provoking the crowd into attacking control personnel. The supervisor should direct his squad in such a manner that the crowd may escape rather than be forced into a position where it must attack the police because no escape route is available. The supervisor should plan his operation so that the members of the hostile group will be forced to disperse into an open area where they can do little damage or into one where the crowd can be broken into small segments and dealt with separately as necessary. Sparsely settled areas, districts with few buildings, and many escape routes can be used effectively for this purpose. However, the supervisor should alert his subordinates to be cautious that hostile elements do not disperse into buildings only to reform and attack the control force from the rear.

Care should be used that members of the crowd are dispersed away from residential or business districts foreign to them and forced to move toward the area in which they live, whenever practicable. They are unlikely to attack neighbors, destroy property, and loot the immediate area of their residences. Obviously these admonishments will not apply where, as often is the case, rioters have moved into an area from elsewhere for the specific purpose of provoking widespread civil disorder.

If sufficient control personnel are present, the supervisor may employ the tactic of dividing them into two or more squads and attacking the crowd from two directions simultaneously. If he follows this strategy, he must fully consider the dangers of dividing his force to a point where neither group is sufficiently strong to achieve its objective and each has been so weakened by the division as to be vulnerable and unable to defend itself successfully if attacked. This division of force may not be practicable if chemical agents can be used more effectively in bringing about dispersal.

A pincer movement, in which the crowd is attacked from the front and both flanks, may force it to escape to the rear, and a flanking maneuver, in which the crowd is attacked from the front and from one flank, will usually force the group to disperse to the opposite flank. An attack from the rear and front of the crowd may force dispersal to the flanks but may permit hostile units to regroup and attack the police from the rear; the bottling effect may force the crowd to fight because there is no other acceptable option left to them.

Use of Force

Only that amount of force should be exerted in dispersing the group or making arrests that will enable the control personnel to achieve their objectives. The use of force beyond that which is reasonably necessary must not be condoned. It will only inflame the crowd and may result in violent reactions; in addition, the use of excessive force is illegal and may subject the individual officer involved and his entire organization to unnecessary criticism or to criminal or civil liability.

Arrests

When arrests become necessary, they should be made quickly with whatever force is reasonably necessary and equated, as far as possible, with the resistance involved. Arrests of persons refusing to disperse or committing other serious violations should be made quickly when that course of action appears necessary. Police action in making arrests is usually most productive when it is directed toward leaders of the group. Persons arrested should be removed immediately from the scene for identification and processing, which will also tend to reduce chances of added violence by the crowd trying to rescue the suspects in custody.

Use of Chemical Agents

Chemical devices and other special weapons should be employed in dispersing hostile groups when such use is indicated. Local policies and procedures will ordinarily dictate how and when such measures should be put into effect. In making a decision about whether chemical agents should be used, the supervisor should evaluate what the wind conditions are; the direction in which the crowd is to be moved; the type of area the members of the group might disperse into; how the dispersal will expose innocent residents and businesses to vandalism, destruction, and danger; and what effects the chemicals might have on merchandise, supplies, materials, and property of innocent persons in the affected area.

Hostile Sniper Fire

Snipers, rock throwers, and other persons dangerous to the control force invariably operate from concealment behind buildings or at the rear of the crowd where they cannot be seen by control personnel. Protection against them may be provided by one or more officers assigned to observation posts in positions high above the affected area. They should be equipped with radios and cell phones so that they can communicate with the field supervisor concerning the numbers, identities, and positions of such individuals. In some cases, observation post personnel should be equipped with rifles and scopes to provide control officers with an additional measure of protection from snipers. The observers can also provide the supervisor with valuable information regarding the most appropriate approach or strategy he can use to counter the tactics of the rioters, what overall strategy the crowd is following, what weapons are in evidence, and the location of snipers and other hazards.

Limited Withdrawal

The supervisor should withdraw his forces when the odds are overwhelmingly against the police and the danger of encirclement or flank attack by the mob makes his position untenable. When a new defensible position has been reached, he should hold it until sufficient reserves arrive to permit the police to carry out their mission with reasonable assurance of success.

Withdrawal should not be ordered under the theory that the mere presence of the police at such occurrences is inflammatory and tends to generate hostility and violence. Although some subscribe to this theory, there has been ample experience to controvert it.

The strategy of establishing a control around the perimeter of the affected area and withdrawing police from the interior has been tested and generally has failed. Analysis of numerous reports of serious civil disobedience reveals that when the police fail to carry out their responsibility for maintaining peace and order, chaos—not control—is the likely result. Law enforcement designed to control such occurrences should be extended to any place where it is required when there are reasonably adequate personnel for doing so. There should be no sanctuary for lawbreakers.

Follow-Up Action

Follow-up action ordinarily will be necessary to prevent reformation of small groups that break off from the main body of the mob. When dispersal has been accomplished, sufficient control personnel should be directed to remain in the affected area to prevent new outbreaks and looting, which often accompany rioting. Such control should be maintained long enough to allow a general cooling of the situation.

Mobile follow-up units can be used as an effective deterrent for this purpose. Units manned by four officers can usually disperse small isolated groups that reform to harass the police, to loot, or to damage property, and teams of officers on foot may perform the same task in highly urbanized areas. Specially trained tactical teams can render valuable assistance if they are available.

Labor Disputes

Disorders that arise from minor labor disputes ordinarily can be controlled by minimal police action. When a major strike is called that directly or indirectly affects a large segment of persons in an industry, however, considerable violence often results. Life and property are jeopardized, and violent breaches of the peace might occur. Although it is not a police responsibility to settle economic disputes between labor and management, it is an obligation of law enforcement to take action when the public peace and order are threatened.

Large-scale labor conflicts, unlike civil disorders, do not occur spontaneously. Usually, the police have sufficient forewarning to make whatever plans are necessary to cope with the problem. Normally, the field supervisor must assume a major role in implementing such plans.

The brand of law enforcement at the scene of a strike has considerable impact on both labor and management segments. If the police act in unison, with confidence in their ability to cope with any problem that might arise, those involved might have second thoughts about conduct that might result in their arrest.

Strikes are a legitimate exercise of the right to protest, which must be protected as long as this right does not degenerate into violence. When it does and unlawful acts occur, the police must act, but their action must be impartial. When they are partial to one side or the other, police will be accused of either strikebreaking or siding with the strikers; in either case, their conduct might provoke violence. Their mission is to protect the rights of both parties and the public.

Maintenance of Impersonal Attitude

The supervisor should admonish his subordinates assigned to strike duty that they must not allow themselves to become personally involved in the labor dispute. They must avoid overreacting when they are subjected to taunts, insults, and derision. If they become emotionally involved, their reactions may be exploited against them not only by the strikers but also by the media and in the courts.

Avoidance of Fraternizing

Fraternization with either the strikers or management, acceptance of gratuities from either, or any other act that might be interpreted as partiality must be avoided. The supervisor should even caution his subordinates to avoid using management parking lots, telephones, and restrooms for the same reason.

Display of Weapons

Officer personnel at the scene should be cautioned against displaying their weapons unnecessarily. Special weapons should never be displayed in a threatening manner because doing so might unnecessarily provoke violent reactions.

Meeting with Labor and Management Representatives

One of the supervisor's first acts at the scene of a labor dispute should be to arrange a meeting with the picket captain and a representative of management to discuss ground rules that both parties should be expected to follow if this has not been done previously. He should emphasize that his is a neutral position but that he must insist the strike be conducted lawfully. He should make it clear that damaging property; blocking sidewalks, streets, entrances, and exits; interfering with lawful business and the rights of uninvolved employees and the public; or provoking incidents by either side in the dispute cannot and will not be tolerated. Usually, such meetings will be welcomed by both sides and can be extremely productive as a means of maintaining the peace.

Control Tactics

The tactics used to control disorders arising from a strike should generally follow the same patterns as those used in the control of other civil disturbances. Slight modifications may be required to handle situations in which the acts of pickets become illegal. For example, pickets may urge prospective patrons of a business establishment not to patronize it, but they may not use force or coercion to do so; when coercion is used, violence is likely to follow.

Picket lines deployed to unlawfully block entrances and exits to businesses being struck must be broken by coordinated action of the control personnel. The pickets should be clearly warned against such illegal action. They should be requested to allow patrons and vehicles of employees or of persons delivering merchandise to the business to pass. If they fail or refuse to do so, the supervisor should direct his subordinates to effect an opening in the line. Pickets should be permitted to resume their line of march on the picket line once this has been accomplished. To avoid giving the impression that they are encouraging or forcing persons in vehicles to enter the premises through picket lines, officers should not use the customary hand signals in directing vehicular traffic at picket lines, but should merely open the lines when necessary to permit ingress or egress of persons or vehicles.

Officers should be instructed to face the pickets at this time and thus prevent their sidearms and batons from being taken. In addition, this places them in a more favorable position to observe the action of the pickets.

The force used to breach picket lines should be firm but temperate. Acts that can be construed as harsh or officious will only incite resistance, which is contagious.

Strike Scene Arrests

Force sufficient to accomplish arrests should be reasonable at all times. The police should not hesitate to arrest when violations justify that course of action because vacillation may be construed as weakness and may encourage those involved to commit other acts that will eventually weaken police authority at the scene.

The blocking of exits to keep persons inside buildings against their will may constitute false imprisonment or involve a breach of fire ordinances. Appropriate action to open such passageways should be taken in such instances, or the arrest of offenders might be justified as a means of removing them from entrances or exits. Should they passively resist by lying on the ground or going limp, such acts might constitute resistance to arrest and would justify their removal on stretchers.

The supervisor should direct his personnel to disregard minor acts that might best be handled by the picket captain. Drinking and littering are technical offenses, but making arrests for such minor violations would distract the police from their primary mission. The supervisor should maintain such a relationship with the picket captain that he will cooperate in dealing with incipient troublemakers. Should an officer be assaulted, however, other officers should quickly give him assistance in making an arrest. Evidence of the crime should be seized, and the assailant should be quietly and promptly removed from the scene to a place where he can be identified, photographed, and processed.

Arrests for destruction of property should be made as in other cases. For example, if can openers, bolts, screwdrivers, ice picks, suspicious keys, or other objects are concealed in the hands of pickets and used to maliciously damage vehicles as they pass, officers observing the acts should seize the evidence and arrest the offenders. If such acts are overlooked, others will feel they can break the law with impunity, which will only increase the police problem.

Disaster Control

The field supervisor is occasionally confronted with an occurrence of a disaster. It may directly or indirectly cause great destruction of property, loss of lives, and injuries. Such incidents may result from acts of nature or man. Floods, fires, earthquakes, explosions, aircraft crashes, broken chemical or gas lines or containers, toxic chemical spills, and the like can threaten the welfare and safety of vast numbers of persons. Although the police can do little to prevent these incidents, once they occur, law enforcement forces must assume a major role in controlling and reducing the aftereffects of the disaster. Sometimes, these aftereffects are as destructive as the initial occurrence.

The field supervisor's effectiveness in directing control efforts during the period immediately following a disaster will have a vital bearing on the success of the entire police operation. An error in selecting an evacuation route from an endangered area might result in utter confusion and chaos, or persons fleeing from an approaching fire might be trapped on roads cluttered with sightseers because perimeter control measures were neglected. Emergency rescue equipment might be deprived of access to the scene of an incident, such as a train wreck or aircraft crash, because access and exit routes were improperly selected and controlled. Once such locations are released by the media, the area usually becomes chaotic because of sightseers unless effective control measures are quickly established.

Basic Operational Procedures

Field intelligence must be collected and transmitted to headquarters. A command post must be established, perimeter control must be initiated, reconnaissance units should be deployed, available support personnel should be assigned, and a disaster control plan should be put into operation. Other basic control procedures should be implemented as quickly as possible. Routine notifications and logistical matters should be assigned to an aide so that the supervisor may be relieved from the responsibility of handling details, which will enable him to concentrate on establishing control plans, making decisions, and directing the activities of control personnel.

Evacuation

Ordinarily, the decision to evacuate an area threatened by fire, flood, poisonous gas, or some other major occurrence should be the responsibility of a superior officer of the highest position available because of the liability that might result from an ill-conceived act. Should the police fail to take action that might reasonably be expected to ensure the safety of the public, considerable criticism and possibly civil liability may result; likewise, they would undoubtedly suffer criticism if residents incurred injuries or if their property were damaged or stolen because they abandoned it when they were warned or forced to do so by police acting beyond their authority. Any decision concerning evacuation must, therefore, be made judiciously.

As the field supervisor may have to assume this tremendous responsibility for a considerable period after such an incident, his decision must be based on the field intelligence he has received, an accurate assessment of this information, and an appraisal of the alternative courses of action available. He must give consideration to the consequences of each decision based on the presence or absence of imminent peril to the public. If he decides that evacuation warnings should be given, persons affected cannot justly complain if they refuse to heed the warnings.

Rescue

Police units should be directed by the supervisor to confine their activities to their assigned missions. The responsibility for normal rescue operations can best be carried out by other elements of the control force specially equipped and trained to perform such functions. Emergency rescue and aid in exceptional cases must, however, be treated according to the needs of each situation.

Chemical, Biological, or Radiological Attack

With the ongoing war on terror, all law enforcement agencies should be prepared for a chemical, biological, or radiological attack. In order to prepare for such an event, most law enforcement agencies have trained their personnel. Early identification of an attack involving chemical, biological, or radiological agents is critical because the health and welfare of first responders and those affected by the attack depend in part on the initial assessment. Chemicals, biological agents, and radiological materials are extremely dangerous. Some indicators of a chemical, biological, or radiological attack follow.

Indicators of a Chemical Attack

The following list contains possible indications of a chemical attack:

- Large volume of calls reporting sick or injured persons with no known reason
- Numerous persons reporting similar illness (signs or symptoms)
- Numerous calls from the same general geographic area or from a large gathering of people (such as a sporting event) reporting unusual illness
- Symptoms indicative of chemical agent exposure (drooling; tearing; shortness of breath; difficulty breathing; irritation of the eyes, nose, throat, and/or skin; redness or itching of skin)
- Report of an explosion with little or no structural damage
- Reports of unexplained liquids (droplets, oily substances)
- Reports of unusual odors (such as mowed grass, garlic, bitter almonds)
- Reports of a release of a spray (hissing sounds, presence of a mist or vapor)
- Suspicious devices or packages (spray devices, damp or wet packages or bags, explosive device with little explosive damage)
- Unexplained dead wildlife or animals
- Discarded masks, gloves, gowns

On-Scene Indicators

These may be found at the scene of a chemical attack:

- Multiple casualties with similar signs or symptoms
- Multiple casualties with no visible injuries other than being sick (no trauma injuries)
- Widely dispersed casualties indicating a possible aerial dispersal of an agent
- Unusual or unexplained liquid in the area
- Unusual odors (such as mowed grass, garlic, bitter almonds)
- Immediate loss of contact with officers already on the scene (such as those performing security or traffic control at large gatherings like sporting events)
- Officers reporting signs or symptoms associated with chemical agent exposure
- Distress calls indicating medical problems as opposed to physical attack

Officers without personal protective equipment are too close to the suspected agent if they can observe pools or droplets of liquid; officers who can smell the odor of a potential chemical agent should immediately evacuate the area and don protective clothing.[9]

---

[9] U.S. Army Soldier and Biological Chemical Command's Improved Response Program for Department of Justice, "Law Enforcement Officers' Guide for Responding to Chemical Terrorist Incidents" (January 2003), http://www.dola.state.co.us/dem/publications/leofficersguide.pdf.

Indicators of a Biological Attack

The following may indicate a biological attack:[10]

- Reports of an explosion that causes little damage or of devices that disperse a mist or powder, with no immediate effects
- Reports or observations of unscheduled spraying (time or location inconsistent with normal pesticide spraying)
- Abandoned spraying equipment or discarded protective suits, biohazard bags, and laboratory equipment (incubator, fermenter, or container with biological label), as these are indicators that may identify the use or development of biological agents
- Presence of unusual swarms of biting insects (They may be used as a mechanism for dissemination.)
- Observation of unusual numbers of sick or dying animals, often of different species (Most biological agents are capable of infecting a wide range of hosts, and sometimes animals are more susceptible, so some animals may be affected before humans.)
- Unexplained outbreak of respiratory or flu-like illness

Indicators of a Radiological Attack

The following lists some possible signs of a radiological attack:[11]

- Unusual numbers of sick or dying people or animals (As a first responder, strong consideration should be given to calling local hospitals to see if additional casualties with similar symptoms have been observed. Casualties may occur hours to days or weeks after an incident has occurred; the time required before symptoms are observed is dependent on the radioactive material used and the dose received. Additional symptoms include skin reddening and, in severe cases, vomiting.)
- Unusual metal debris (such as unexplained bomb- or munitions-like material)
- Radiation symbols (Containers may display a radiation symbol.)
- Heat-emitting material (that is, material that seems to emit heat without any sign of an external heating source)
- Glowing material or particles (If the material is strongly radioactive, then it may emit a radioluminescence.)
- Placards associated with radiological incidents
- Radiation detected on the scene by Geiger counters or other equipment
- Written or verbal threats

Immediate identification of a radiological attack is difficult. Radiation can't be detected by the senses, and symptoms of radiological exposure may not be present for hours or days.

---

[10] Homeland Defense Business Unit, Edgewood Chemical Biological Center, U.S. Army Research, Development, and Engineering Command, "Biological Incident Operations: A Guide for Law Enforcement" (September 2004), http://www.edgewood.army.mil/hld/dl/ecbc_le_bio_guide.pdf.

[11] Director of Central Intelligence, Interagency Intelligence Committee on Terrorism, Community Counterterrorism Board, "Chemical/Biological/Radiological Incident Handbook" (1998), http://fas.org/irp/threat/cbw.

Response Actions

First responding units are considered critical because the initial proper identification and/or assessment of the incident will determine the proscribed response inherent in the respective policy and procedure manual in place by the law enforcement agency involved in the incident. When responding to a terrorist incident, the initial assessment is crucial. Is the crime scene "hot"? Is there potential for risk to those arriving at the scene from snipers, undetonated or undiscovered explosives, or biological, chemical, or radioactive agents exposed at the scene? These are only a few of the questions that need to be answered properly if potential loss of life or risk of injuries is to be prevented or diminished.

The first responding supervisor also has critical decisions to make. What level of further assistance is requested? When does the supervisor or command-level personnel at the scene activate the incident command system? Who needs to be notified at the higher levels? What other local, state, or federal agencies need to be contacted per protocol or based on need to reduce risks of potential serious injury or loss of life? These are the critical concerns and issues that a first responding supervisor at the scene will encounter during a critical incident.

Training and experience can be great tools to prepare the responding officer to meet the challenge successfully. However, no two critical incidents are alike, so a checklist of action steps to take in the event of a critical incident assignment can be a very useful tool to ensure that all necessary steps are taken in accordance with established policies and procedures.

Any scene considered to be a critical incident may be addressed by the supervisor using the NSF model. Once the supervisor is made aware of the incident, Now actions are appropriate and may be initiated while at headquarters or en route to the scene. Scene actions are initiated when the supervisor arrives as well as when he is en route; Future actions may be initiated once the critical incident is over or when the supervisor has left the scene. Supervisors responding to the scene of a chemical, biological, or radiological incident will find the checklist in Figure 13–1 to be extremely helpful.

The Critical Incident Response Checklist in Figure 13–1 is a guide for supervisors who may respond to a chemical, biological, or radiological attack. The first responding supervisor will have a lot to do. After the initial assessment, action will need to be taken, with officer safety a key concern.

Most officers are trained to assess a situation and react quickly. In a chemical, biological, or radiological incident, officers cannot rush in because if they do, there may be mass casualties. The supervisor will need to monitor the situation carefully to ensure officers are always acting with safety in mind. The arriving police units cannot do everything; they must operate within their level of training and protective equipment. A key element to successful response to a chemical, biological, or radiological incident is the rapid identification of the hazard and immediate control over all responding units.[12]

In a chemical, biological, or radiological incident, someone needs to take charge quickly. That will usually be the supervisor. Individual police department plans and procedures will dictate required actions. The NSF checklist is a frame of reference for the supervisor to use and works for any critical incident. Once the incident is dispatched, the supervisor initiates Now actions and then Scene and eventually Future actions.

---

[12] Paul M. Maniscalco and Hank Christen, *Terrorism Response: Field Guide for Law Enforcement* (Upper Saddle River, N.J.: Prentice Hall, 2002).

Critical Incident Response Checklist

The following steps should be considered by the supervisor upon receiving notice of a chemical, biological, or radiological incident.

Now Actions

1. ☐ Ensure first responding officers assess situation and threat level from a safe distance upwind and uphill of incident area.

    ☐ Weapons _____

    ☐ Chemicals _____

    ☐ Biological agents _____

    ☐ Explosives _____

    ☐ Radiological dispersal devices _____

    ☐ Suspects, victims, witnesses _____

2. ☐ Assume command. Direct, guide, and control responding subordinates.

3. ☐ Detail subordinates to the scene during initial response to assist in removing people from harm's way.

4. ☐ Advise units to be aware of secondary devices.

5. ☐ Ensure following responders are given updated information.

6. ☐ Direct personnel entering hot zone to use full personal protection equipment.

7. ☐ Establish initial perimeters (starting big).

8. ☐ Ensure information regarding suspects is transmitted.

9. ☐ Ensure notification of emergency response agencies (fire, EMS, bomb squad, Haz-Mat, med evac, public health, FEMA).

10. ☐ Ensure that area hospitals are alerted.

11. ☐ Notify next in command.

12. ☐ Request updates on survivors, injuries, and fatalities and status of situation.

Figure 13–1

Critical Incident Response Checklist.

Source: The compilation of the NSF action steps related to a chemical, biological, or radiological incident was developed from a variety of sources: Jeff Bernstein, *Situational Management Training Manual for Miami Police Sergeant & Lieutenant* (Fort Lauderdale, Fla.: Bernstein & Associates, 2003); Jeff Bernstein, *Management Training Manual for Chicago Police Sergeant & Lieutenant* (Fort Lauderdale, Fla.: Bernstein & Associates, 2006); Paul M. Maniscalco and Hank Christen, *Terrorism Response: Field Guide for Law Enforcement* (Upper Saddle River, N.J.: Prentice Hall, 2002); U.S. Army Soldier and Biological Chemical Command's Improved Response Program for Department of Justice, "Law Enforcement Officers' Guide for Responding to Chemical Terrorist Incidents" (January 2003), http://www.dola.state.co.us/dem/. publications/leofficersguide.pdf, accessed May 18, 2011; Homeland Defense Business Unit, Edgewood Chemical Biological Center, U.S. Army Research, Development, and Engineering Command, "Biological Incident Operations: A Guide for Law Enforcement" (September 2004), http://www.edgewood.army.mil/hld/dl/ecbc_le_bio_guide.pdf, accessed May 18, 2011.

On-Scene Actions

1. ☐ Assume command, and designate who is in charge of special details.

2. ☐ Establish communications between police and other responders.

3. ☐ If crime has occurred, ensure that scene is properly preserved and protected. Restrict access.

4. ☐ Ensure safety perimeter (inner and outer) has been established and modify as needed.

5. ☐ Ensure crowd and traffic control is established.

6. ☐ Stabilize the incident.

7. ☐ Establish command post and personnel staging area (safe area) upwind, uphill, and upstream if chemical attack has occurred.

8. ☐ Coordinate with fire department (evacuation versus shelter in place).

9. ☐ Consider that subject or subjects may still be at the scene or in the area.

10. ☐ Assist fire department in establishing decontamination corridor and triage area apart from the contaminated scene.

11. ☐ Assist fire department with security of initial isolation zone and decontamination area as needed.

12. ☐ Ensure adequate equipment for traffic control, disorderly crowds, personal protective equipment.

13. ☐ Monitor personnel for compliance with personal protective equipment.

14. ☐ Ensure that detectives respond and that witnesses are separated and interviewed prior to departing.

15. ☐ Ensure notification of other government agencies (DHS, public works, FBI, DEP, OSHA, prosecutor's office).

16. ☐ Ensure tactical contingency plan is in place to deal with other issues such as wind direction changes and crowd control.

17. ☐ Request assistance from neighboring agencies (local, county, state) if necessary.

18. ☐ Plan out safe evacuation and escape routes.

19. ☐ Ensure that public information officer is notified.

    ☐ Designate temporary media relations officer.

    ☐ Assign and establish a media staging area in a safe location away from command post.

    ☐ Ensure periodic media updates with regard to public safety.

20. ☐ Ensure victim assistance.

    ☐ Preserve victims' personal effects and property.

    ☐ Notify next of kin in accordance with policy.

    ☐ Notify Red Cross (shelter, clothing, food), as required, as well as other social services.

21. ☐ Provide updates to next in command.

22. ☐ Reassign nonessential personnel, and ensure service and proper coverage for nonaffected areas.

Figure 13–1
(Continued)

23. ☐ Conduct periodic meetings, with liaison, as required.

24. ☐ Ensure personnel have the following:

      ☐ Relief   ☐ Food   ☐ Medical supplies

      ☐ Rest periods   ☐ Water   ☐ Shelter

25. ☐ Ensure personnel and equipment are decontaminated after leaving the contaminated area.

Future Actions

1. ☐ Review and approve all reports.

2. ☐ Ensure notification of incoming shift commander.

3. ☐ Provide long-term security over the immediate incident site.

4. ☐ Debrief all personnel, and review and critique incident.

5. ☐ Request and/or ensure department training based on the above (as needed).

6. ☐ Ensure appropriate counseling after critical incident.

7. ☐ Follow up regarding assistance for survivors, victims, and families as required (counseling, victim assistance).

8. ☐ Commend and/or reprimand personnel, as necessary.

9. ☐ Ensure updates are provided to personnel at roll calls.

10. ☐ Document incident, and submit findings and recommendations to superiors.

Figure 13–1
(*Continued*)

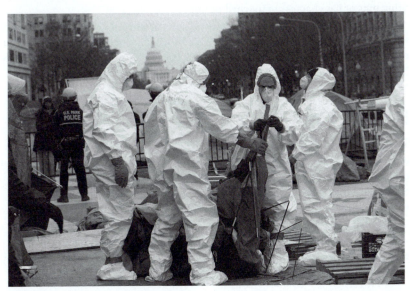

U.S. park police officers in protective hazmat suits clear the belongings of protesters from the Occupy DC protest movement at the Occupy DC encampment at Freedom Plaza in Washington.
(© REUTERS/Jose Luis Magaua)

Aircraft Crashes

When an aircraft crashes in a densely populated area or under circumstances that may jeopardize the public safety, responsibility for initiating control operations will fall on the field supervisor. It is he who is most immediately available to coordinate the activities of field units that respond. His primary duty will involve directing their efforts in rendering aid to seriously injured persons, making appropriate notifications to headquarters, requesting necessary support, minimizing the danger to bystanders or victims, and protecting persons and property against looting. Where immediate rescue efforts are needed, these should be given prompt attention. Establishing traffic control at the immediate scene and at the perimeter and providing assistance to rescue or fire control units are secondary responsibilities.

Precautions in Rendering Aid

The supervisor should caution his subordinates that great care should be exercised in moving injured persons. If they cannot walk and are in danger of further injury by fire, explosion, or chemicals, immediate steps should be taken for their removal to a safe location. Ambulance or medical personnel at the scene should perform this task whenever possible because injuries worse than those initially suffered might result if victims are improperly moved.

Security of Military Aircraft

The supervisor should post personnel in strategic positions where they can safely keep unauthorized persons from approaching military aircraft. Most of these are equipped with explosive charges that eject canopies and seats. Serious injuries may result if mechanical firing pins or gas charges are touched or improperly operated.

Spectators should be discouraged from taking pictures of such aircraft unless authorized military personnel request their services.[13] Those taking pictures should be identified and their names transmitted to military representatives. News cameramen should not be prevented from taking pictures, as control of their release is the responsibility of the military.

Bomb Threats

When a supervisor responds to a call in which a bomb threat has been made, he should immediately notify his headquarters by telephone of the circumstances and request personnel and bomb specialists to help handle the matter. The radio should not be used, as radio waves might detonate the bomb. If fire equipment is summoned, he should request that it be driven quietly to the scene without the use of sirens. Experience has shown that the more commotion a bomb threat call causes, the greater is the likelihood that the call will be repeated. Many of these calls are false, and it is likely that most are made by persons who derive some satisfaction from the noise, the commotion, and the concern they cause.

---

[13] U.S. Code, Title 18, Sec. 791.

If a threat is made against a business establishment, a public building such as a school, an office complex or warehouse, or private property such as a commercial aircraft that a hidden bomb is to be exploded, the person in charge of the premises is responsible for making the decision whether occupants should be evacuated. He will invariably look to the supervisor for advice; when this occurs, the supervisor should discuss the matter in private with him to avoid starting a rumor or alarming others unnecessarily.

A conservative approach should be followed if it becomes obvious that advice should be given. It is far better to advise evacuating persons who might be endangered, even though later evidence proves such action was unnecessary, than to advise against evacuation when that course of action should have been taken. The safety of innocent persons should be the supervisor's first concern.

The decision will ordinarily be based on the facts surrounding each incident. The supervisor should carefully evaluate the possible motives for destroying property—evidence of recent labor troubles involving the firm, the type of operations involved, and previous trouble with disgruntled employees—before he considers giving advice. Schools often experience many such threats from students desiring a recess or holiday. Most schools give credence to all such calls until a search proves them groundless, but pragmatic school administrators will require students to make up the time involved in the search. Such action has proved to be an effective deterrent to other false calls.

Evacuation Procedures

The supervisor should assign personnel to aid in the orderly evacuation of the premises once that course of action is decided on. The distance occupants should be moved will depend on the circumstances surrounding each case, the type of premises, and the existence and type of structures that may give protection in the immediate area against a bomb explosion.

Standard fire drill procedures in which lights are shut off and doors and windows are closed should be avoided. Shutting off lights may trigger an explosion; shutting windows and doors may cause unnecessary property damage from the blast effect, should an explosion take place.

The supervisor should dispatch officers to notify persons in surrounding buildings of the potential danger. Doors and windows should be opened there for the reasons previously discussed. Occupants should be instructed to remain in the building but go to a position farthest from the side where the explosion might affect them, and they should be advised to stay away from windows and places where they might be injured by flying glass or debris.

The supervisor should advise the person in charge of the premises to be evacuated about the danger of theft so that guards may be posted to keep unauthorized persons out while the building is being searched. Persons making the search should be directed to leave the premises enough in advance of the time the bomb is to be exploded, if such information is known, to ensure their safety. They should not be permitted to reenter until it is reasonably safe to do so after the indicated time of detonation.

Traffic outside the building should be diverted if it might be exposed to an explosion. Gas and other utilities such as propane should be turned off if they might aggravate the effects of the explosion.

Search of Premises

Whenever there exists a reasonable likelihood that a bomb or other device will be detonated in a structure, the supervisor should direct that a search be made. A search warrant is not required because the usual limitations on the scope of searches of this type do not apply due to the urgency of the matter.

An explosive device can be concealed in a building so that it is almost impossible to locate it without a very careful search. The supervisor should recognize the extreme danger a hidden and triggered explosive poses to searching personnel and should summon bomb specialists to the scene if they are available for the search or for consultation. Officers should then be directed to conduct the search as quickly and thoroughly as circumstances permit. A minimum of search personnel should be used, depending on the time available and the type of premises to be searched.

Mirrors and screwdriver sets should be obtained if possible and distributed to those making the search to aid them in looking on the undersides of furniture and equipment and behind wall plates and receptacle covers. K-9 units might be of value if dogs trained to sniff explosives are available because their use for this purpose will speed up the search substantially.

The supervisor should request some responsible person to assign employees most familiar with the premises to assist search personnel by pointing out to them objects foreign to the building. All persons engaged in the search should be cautioned against touching or moving anything that might trigger an explosion and should be instructed to look in every conceivable place that might conceal a bomb. They should be especially alert for foreign packages or objects or those items that appear to have been left behind by someone; objects that are out of their usual places should also be suspect. Any of these may conceal an explosive device.

If no bomb or explosive is found, the supervisor should inform the person in charge of the building, but he should avoid suggesting that the building is safe for occupancy. To do so might unnecessarily involve considerable liability for his department in the event persons reoccupy the building in reliance on his statement and are injured or killed from the explosion of a bomb that was not found.

Bomb Precautions

When a bomb is located, the supervisor should summon experienced bomb disposal personnel to remove or neutralize it. He should not attempt to move such a device, nor should he permit inexperienced personnel to do so. The supervisor should ensure an orderly evacuation of the premises as well as establish a safety perimeter around the affected area. Officers should be instructed to be aware of possible secondary explosive devices. Additionally, supervisors should direct officers and civilians to take advantage of available cover such as terrain, buildings, or other solid safe objects. The National

Officers use a video camera on a pole to inspect the results of a controlled blast in one of the rooms of the apartment of movie theatre gunman James Holmes in Aurora, Colorado. Officials used a controlled explosion to neutralize the bombs in the booby-trapped apartment.
(BOB PEARSON/EPA/NEWSCOM)

Counterterrorism Center (NCTC) has provided guidelines for evacuation distances (see Figure 13–2).

When it is essential to neutralize the bomb where it is found, it should be sandbagged to deflect the blast and reduce the danger from fragmentation and should then be detonated in place. Such action should be taken only with the full approval of a person authorized to permit such action; preferably, his permission should be obtained in writing to protect the supervisor and his agency from liability for damage from the blast.

Major Fires

The police frequently are in a position to initiate control measures at the scene of a fire before fire personnel arrive. One of the first acts of the supervisor when he arrives should be to ensure that appropriate notifications have been made to the fire department. Information transmitted should include the type and size of the fire, type of property and area involved (or soon to be involved), wind direction, endangered structures and facilities, public utilities exposed to the blaze, and emergency routes to the scene.

Available personnel should be assigned to the immediate vicinity and to perimeter posts to control vehicular and pedestrian traffic that might interfere with firefighting

This table is for general emergency planning only. A given building's vulnerability to explosions depends on its construction and composition. The data in these tables may not accurately reflect these variables. Some risk will remain for any persons closer than the Outdoor Evacuation Distance.

Threat Description		Explosives Capacity[1] (TNT Equivalent)	Mandatory Evacuation Distance[2]	Preferred Evacuation Distance[3]
	Pipe Bomb	5 LBS/ 2.3 KG	70 FT/ 21 M	1,200 FT/ 366 M
	Suicide Vest	20 LBS/ 9.2 KG	110 FT/ 34 M	1,750 FT/ 518 M
	Briefcase/ Suitcase Bomb	50 LBS/ 23 KG	150 FT/ 46 M	1,850 FT/ 564 M
	Sedan	500 LBS/ 227 KG	320 FT/ 98 M	1,900 FT/ 580 M
	SUV/Van	1,000 LBS/ 454 KG	400 FT/ 122 M	2,400 FT/ 732 M
	Small Delivery Truck	4,000 LBS/ 1,814 KG	640 FT/ 195 M	3,800 FT/ 1,159 M
	Container/ Water Truck	10,000 LBS/ 4,536 KG	860 FT/ 263 M	5,100 FT/ 1555 M
	Semi-Trailer	60,000 LBS/ 27,216 KG	1,570 FT/ 479 M	9,300 FT/ 2,835 M

Preferred Evacuation Distance

Preferred area (beyond this line) for evacuation of people in buildings and mandatory for people outdoors.

Shelter-in-Place Zone

All personnel in this area should seek shelter immediately inside a building away from windows and exterior walls. Avoid having anyone outside—including those evacuating—in this area.[4]

Mandatory Evacuation Distance

All personnel must evacuate (both inside of buildings and out).

Figure 13–2
Bomb Threat Stand-Off Distances.
Source: National Counterterrorism Center (NCTC) website, http://www.nctc.gov/site/technical/bomb_threat.html, accessed May 18, 2011.

efforts. This is the primary responsibility of the police, with other police units being assigned as needed when they arrive.

The supervisor should consult with the commander of the firefighting units, who generally has overall command at the scene, to determine how the police might assist fire personnel. Should extensive police control measures be required, the supervisor should establish his command post near that of the fire department to facilitate maximum coordination, and the police staging area should be located nearby so that personnel can be briefed and assigned to specific posts as they arrive. Usually, the assignments of personnel to traffic perimeter posts some distance from the scene can best be made by radio, not only to save time in setting up traffic controls but also to reduce the confusion and traffic at the scene.

Evacuation of Fire Area

Should it become necessary to evacuate an area endangered by a fire, especially when it occurs in a brushy area and threatens a residential or recreational area, residents and others affected must be notified of the peril. Patrol units should be assigned to specific areas for this purpose, as the police usually must assume responsibility for such warnings. As each assignment is made, it should be logged and plotted on a map overlay to reduce the possibility that some persons might be overlooked.

Officers should be directed to use sirens, horns, loudspeakers, and all other means available in making these notifications and instructed to make personal contacts in those areas where residents live some distance off main roads and might not hear warnings from the street. Sufficient personnel should be assigned to this very important task to permit them to give timely warnings to all persons who might be affected. The supervisor should keep in mind that only a limited number of notifications can be given in sparsely settled areas where residents live a considerable distance off the highways. This seems to be an obvious consideration, but at times when a person is under stress, he tends to overlook the obvious.

Directing dispatchers to utilize reverse 911 notifications for evacuations can be a very effective tool. Some government agencies also have established a wireless emergency alert system whereby citizens can be made aware of impending danger. In addition, FEMA has launched a broad alert network that can send public safety warnings from the president and participating state and local governments. Lastly, units should be cautioned to be alert for radio broadcasts describing the progress of the fire so that they can clear the area safely.

The police fulfill their obligation to protect lives when they inform persons endangered by an approaching fire of the perils they face and help them leave the area. Should they refuse, it would be ill-advised to force them to do so; however, in unusual cases where persons are mentally incompetent and incapable of providing for their own safety, another course of action may be required. Aged, very young, handicapped, or sick persons may require special help in escaping a fire.

Antilooting Patrols

In the aftermath of widespread fires, many sightseers and thieves are attracted to the burned zone. Sightseers can ordinarily be turned back at the traffic perimeter. Thieves, however, are a special problem because they can often penetrate the inner exposed area for the specific purpose of looting property that has been left unprotected.

Antilooting patrols should be assigned to specific beats in the burned zone to protect such property. Personnel in these units should be instructed to check persons who have no legitimate reason for being in the area, and direct them to leave if legal authority prohibits their presence in the emergency zone. They should be checked for possession of property apparently stolen and be handled accordingly. All contacts with persons encountered should be recorded for future reference—information and evidence are often obtained from these contacts that are of value to investigators in determining how the fire started or who was responsible for it.

Area Searches

When a wide area search is called for to locate a missing or wanted person and numerous officers are required, its effectiveness will be directly dependent on how systematically it is conducted and how well it is coordinated. Operations of this type are somewhat unique in that specific plans cannot ordinarily be made beforehand; the supervisor must, therefore, develop them according to the needs of each situation. But even the best plans will not produce the desired results if they are not carried out under adequate direction and control and are not well coordinated.

Missing Children

In many law enforcement agencies, situations involving lost children are considered so important that supervisors are specifically made responsible for directing searches for them. The extent of the effort devoted to such incidents ordinarily is dependent on the age of the child and the circumstances. The younger the child is, the greater the need for locating him promptly. If a crime appears to be involved in the disappearance, its nature and the evidence available will usually dictate whether a localized or a broad search of the area is necessary.

In deciding how extensive an operation should be put into effect, the supervisor should consider several factors: the age and sex of the child, the type of area involved and the attractive hazards in it, the circumstances surrounding his disappearance, the child's previous history of running away, his normal areas of play, his mental and physical condition, his fear of punishment (whether he has recently been scolded or punished), and the circumstances under which he was last seen, as well as any other facts that might provide clues as to what happened to him or where he might be found. Persons who might shed light on the child's whereabouts should be interviewed (playmates usually provide the best information). Parents should be asked to notify the police immediately if the child returns home.

Should the evidence indicate that the disappearance involves a criminal act, the appropriate investigators should be notified immediately so that an investigation may be initiated. If a kidnapping is suspected, the parents should be requested to consult the police before they take any action if they are contacted by the kidnapper.

Broadcasting Procedures

As in all cases of lost children, a full description of the child and the general circumstances of the case should be communicated to all units in the area. Information concerning the child's interests, play habits, and circumstances surrounding his disappearance should be included to alert other police elements of the matter. An AMBER alert may be requested if the child meets the criteria.

Initial Search

Frequently, the child will be found in the immediate area from which he disappeared despite assurances of the parents that they have made a complete search. Parents are prone to look in only the most obvious places and often fail to search carefully. Even though parents insist that they have already made a search, a careful inspection of the inside and outside of the premises should be made. Children have been found asleep in unmade beds, in large chairs surrounded by their toys and dolls, behind furniture, and in other places where a careful search might have revealed their presence.

Every place that might offer concealment should be inspected. Containers, tanks, chests, and the like should be carefully examined inside and outside the house. Even though hasps are closed on large containers, they should be searched. Occasionally, a child will lock a playmate inside a container and then panic and fail to tell of the incident because he fears punishment. Vehicle interiors as well as vehicle trunks should be checked carefully.

Operating Procedures for Widespread Search

Should an initial search fail to reveal the child's whereabouts, a widespread operation may be suggested and basic procedures should be followed. The supervisor should establish his command post near the center of operations (usually his vehicle will suffice for this purpose). He should request sufficient personnel to conduct a systematic search, depending on the time of day, the weather, and other circumstances. As they arrive, they should be briefed and assigned specific tasks and areas, with instructions to return to the command post and report their findings when they complete their assignments. Data should be logged and search areas plotted on an overlay map to provide a ready reference of what is being done and to eliminate duplication of search efforts.

Units should be assigned to check playgrounds, recreational areas, and hazards that attract children. Other personnel should be directed to follow up leads that may be provided by playmates and other persons.

Search Teams

When persons other than officers volunteer their help in the search, they should be assigned to teams under the direction of an officer, with each team being given a specific area to search. Ordinarily, teams should consist of four officers or a combination of officers and volunteers.

Residential Search Patterns

Teams should be instructed to start their search of a residential area from the end of the block nearest the scene and work outward. Two persons should search the area on one side of the street while the other two should check the opposite side. They should inspect side and back yards, vacant lots, alleys, sheds and outbuildings, containers, garages, abandoned refrigerators and freezers and those in use outdoors, large boxes, chests, and every other conceivable place of concealment or hazard.

The more attractive hazards, such as swimming pools, excavations, ditches, wells, cisterns, creeks, storm drains, lumber piles, and unsealed boxcars, should receive first attention. Children have been found in these places after they have fallen in or entered and been unable to get out. Residents of houses in the search area, especially children, should be questioned for information when they are first contacted regarding the search.

When the assigned area has been carefully checked, members of the team should meet at the end of the block to compare notes on their findings. Additionally, they should transmit their findings to the command post. They should then move on and search the next block assigned.

The supervisor will ordinarily be responsible for determining how extensive the search should be. Usually it will be continued until the child has been found or there is strong evidence that he is no longer in the area.

Open-Area Search

When a child disappears in a sparsely settled, bushy, woody, or open area, the supervisor might utilize helicopters, aircraft, or mounted teams to good advantage if they are available. Sometimes dogs may be used effectively even though considerable time has elapsed since the disappearance; the sooner they are put into service, however, the more effective they will be. They may follow false leads if the area has been contaminated by many persons walking through it.

Officers and volunteers available for the search should be organized into search lines in rough terrain. They should be instructed to walk from three to ten yards apart, depending on the nature of the ground to be covered. Lines should be kept relatively straight to avoid loss of contact between persons, and lines should be halted periodically to permit all searchers to proceed at about the same speed. This will permit a more thorough search.

Areas completely searched should be plotted on the supervisor's map to show what terrain has been checked. The search party should then be moved to another area to continue the operation. As with other searches, the supervisor is responsible for deciding when the search is to be terminated or providing information that will permit his superiors to make that decision.

Wanted Persons

When a wanted person flees from the police into a residential or business district, sufficient units should be deployed to seal off his escape as quickly as possible and pin him down while a systematic search is made. Disorganized police efforts may result in gaps in search patterns, and the suspect will almost certainly exploit them to make good his escape.

On-Scene Procedures

Upon his arrival at the scene where the suspect was last seen, the supervisor should assume command of available personnel, organize them into search teams, and direct their activities to cover the widest possible area in a methodical manner. He should ascertain that a complete description of the suspect and the specific area into which he fled has been broadcast to units in the vicinity. Any information on weapons possessed by the subject should also be put out.

Other units should be assigned strategic fixed and mobile posts around the perimeter to prevent the suspect's escape should he elude the police in the interior search. These assignments may be made by radio to ensure the most immediate coverage and prevent confusion at the scene. Units needed for the search should be instructed to report to a specific location for their assignments; the number required depends on the type of area that needs to be searched, the time the suspect has had to leave the initial contact spot, and the means he may have used. Car-to-car communications can be used effectively to brief responding units as the need arises.

Search Strategies

Once the area has been tightly sealed off and the suspect immobilized, two strategies are available to guide the search. The choice depends on the characteristics of the neighborhood, the number of personnel available for the search, the extent of the search, and the type of crime involved, as well as the time that has elapsed since the crime was committed.

One strategy is an inward search from the perimeter of the area. In a small, compact residential area, appropriately armed personnel should be directed to search inward from the perimeter in teams of three or more officers. Each team should be assigned a specific quadrant to search. If blocks of residences are to be searched, two teams should be assigned. Quadrants should be numbered so that search patterns may be complete.

Two members of one (odd-numbered) team should search all conceivable hiding places in and around the houses on one side of the street, and the third member of that team should observe the street that faces the houses being searched. Simultaneously, a second (even-numbered) team should search the houses on the other side of the street; the third member of the second team should search the alley between two rows of residences, as illustrated in Figure 13–3.

Teams should maintain contact with each other by portable radios (if possible), or they may communicate by voice and signals. They should proceed at about the same speed in their search to reduce the likelihood that the suspect can double back and conceal himself in an area already searched. Officers should be cautioned to cover each other and to avoid crossfire between themselves and members of other teams in the vicinity. Fixed observation posts should be established at the perimeter of the search area and supplemented by mobile patrol units, helicopters, and foot patrols.

Officers should inform residents of the search and request permission to inspect yards, outbuildings, or houses when it is essential. Searching personnel should be alert for evidence that the suspect is concealed on the premises and the householder is being forced to mislead them about his presence.

The strategy of searching inward from the perimeter has the disadvantage of cornering the suspect, forcing him to resist if he refuses to surrender. The danger of crossfire, always present, may be greater when personnel converge at the center of the search area and are forced into a gunfight with a suspect.

The second strategy available is to search outward from the center of operations toward a guarded perimeter. If the suspect is moving ahead of the searchers, he will be forced into the hands of personnel guarding the perimeter.

Figure 13–3
*Residential Block
Search Pattern.*

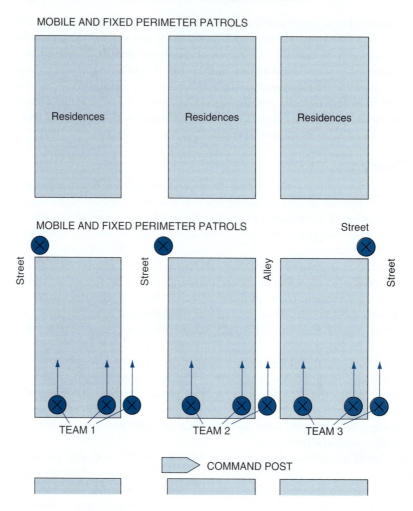

Business District Searches

In assigning teams to search a business district, the supervisor should consider the possibility that the suspect might try to take a taxi, bus, or streetcar from the scene. Street patrols should be alerted to this possibility. Other teams should be assigned to inspect nearby bars, restrooms, restaurants, lobbies, markets, stores, and other places where the suspect might remain inconspicuous.

Building Searches

In many cases, criminals are discovered in a building during their commission of a crime. The procedures applicable to those types of searches described previously for barricaded suspects would generally be useful. Escape routes should be sealed off, and the suspect should be encouraged to surrender. If he refuses, forced entry into the premises may be necessary if the use of chemical or smoke agents is not desirable.

In many cases, the criminal will remain quiet and refuse to respond to the police demands that he give himself up. The only means of determining if he has remained in the building is to search it. The use of chemical and smoke agents is ordinarily not indicated for this type of case, but the need for great caution is always present.

Should reasonable cause exist to believe that a felony suspect or one considered to be a high risk is in the building, the supervisor should select two teams of officers, a search team and a cover team. These teams should be appropriately armed and protected and then briefed on plans and objectives to act in complete unison. Tactics similar to those employed by the U.S. Army in conducting a search should be adapted to the needs of the particular case.[14] The search team should enter the building under protection of the cover team in a manner similar to that previously described for barricaded persons cases but adapted to the needs of the moment. The number of persons permitted to make entry should be carefully controlled by the supervisor. As few personnel as necessary should conduct the search, depending on the size of the premises to be searched and the characteristics of the interior. All avenues of escape from the building should be secured by the cover team, and the cover team should render whatever assistance is necessary to the search team, such as guarding areas already searched.

All possible places of concealment must be searched systematically by the search team until the entire building has been inspected. In multistory structures, the search should begin at the top of the building whenever practicable and proceed downward systematically, if search personnel can start the search there without unnecessary risk. The suspect must either remain hidden, where he can be located and arrested, or be forced downward, where he may be apprehended by the cover team. If he is forced upward by a search that starts in the basement of a structure, he may become more dangerous when he is cornered at the top of the building with no place to go, or he may escape over the roofs of other adjoining buildings.

As each portion of the building is searched, personnel should be assigned to secure that area or keep it under observation to prevent the suspect from moving into it. The search team should then proceed to check the next room or portion of the building until the building has been completely searched.

Department of Homeland Security Initiatives

The Homeland Security Advisory System is designed to guide police protective measures when information specific to a particular sector or geographic region is received. It combines threat information with vulnerability assessments and provides communications to public safety officials and the public. The system utilizes advisories and bulletins:

- *Homeland security threat advisories.*   Advisories contain actionable information about an incident involving or a threat targeting critical national networks, infrastructures, or assets. They could, for example, relay newly developed procedures that, when implemented, would significantly improve security or protection; they could also suggest a change in readiness posture, protective actions, or response. This

---

[14] *US Department of the Army FM 3-19.15* (Washington, D.C.: Headquarters, Department of the Army, April 2005), pp. 4/3–22.

category includes products formerly named alerts, advisories, and sector notifications. Advisories are targeted to federal, state, and local governments; private-sector organizations; and international partners.

- *Homeland security information bulletins.* Bulletins communicate information of interest to the nation's critical infrastructures that does not meet the timeliness, specificity, or significance thresholds of warning messages. Such information may include statistical reports, periodic summaries, incident response or reporting guidelines, common vulnerabilities and patches, and configuration standards or tools. It also may include preliminary requests for information. Bulletins are targeted to federal, state, and local governments; private-sector organizations; and international partners.

Advisories, information bulletins, and threat levels all have significance in regard to how law enforcement agencies respond. Supervisors need to provide guidance and direction during these times. Employees should be directed to be alert and vigilant to suspicious activities that suggest the presence of a potential terrorist threat.

Interagency cooperation presents new opportunities and challenges for police supervisors. Counterterrorism task forces operate in every state. Information is shared more freely among agencies at all levels of law enforcement and emergency response.

Local police departments are always first to respond to terrorist incidents. When they receive warnings, they must be prepared to initiate action on their own. Field supervision is a critical part of an effective threat response. When police receive information of a threat of a *specific* type or for a *specific* target, supervisors should consider these actions:

1. Advise all staff of specifics of the threats (include up-line notifications).
2. Notify high-risk and/or target site security staff (if applicable). Include up-line notifications, such as chief and deputy chief.
3. Assess the threat and/or target.
4. Share all relevant data and descriptive information about possible suspects and potential targets with personnel.
5. Consider increasing uniform patrol presence (high-visibility patrols in and around potential target sites).
6. Assign/order frequent inspections of high-risk and/or specific target areas.
7. Order additional staff or hold shifts over, as needed.
8. Locate contingency plans, or develop a site/incident plan.
9. Request input from employees (such as intelligence obtained via informants or employee observations).
10. Give assignments based on standard operating procedures.
11. Monitor employees assigned to specific activities.
12. Deploy specialized capabilities (K-9 unit, SWAT team, bomb squad, Marine unit surveillance) as needed.
13. Issue appropriate equipment, including shotguns, binoculars, radiation detectors, and hazmat suits.
14. Notify or put on alert status the Office of Emergency Management, neighboring agencies, fire departments, emergency medical personnel, and hazmat teams.
15. Maintain contact with advising agency for updates or additional information.
16. Provide updates to all employees and target site security personnel.
17. Document all action steps taken.

When there is a *nonspecific* threat, consider these actions:

1. Advise all staff of threats (include up-line notifications).
2. Review and evaluate high-value targets in the jurisdiction (refineries, chemical factories, major transportation hubs, large shopping malls).
3. Notify high-risk and/or target site security staff (if applicable). Include up-line notifications, such as chief and deputy chief.
4. Develop contingency plans.
5. Give assignments based on standard operating procedures.
6. Consider increasing uniform patrol presence (high-visibility patrols in and around potential target sites).
7. Assign/order frequent inspections of high-risk and/or specific target areas.
8. Monitor employees assigned to specific activities.
9. Issue equipment as appropriate.
10. Put specialized units on alert or standby status.
11. Notify the Office of Emergency Management, neighboring agencies, fire departments, emergency medical personnel, and hazmat teams.
12. Provide updates to all employees and target site security personnel.
13. Document all action steps taken.

These actions by the supervisor will assist employees in doing their jobs during these difficult times.

SUMMARY

During the first few critical minutes at the scene of an unusual occurrence such as a disaster, a major disturbance, a barricaded subject, or some other important incident where a number of police personnel are engaged in carrying out control measures, the field supervisor is responsible for directing and coordinating their efforts. He may not delay action in the expectation that he will be relieved of his responsibility by higher authority; rather, he must plan and set into motion an operation designed to minimize the effects of the incident.

Ordinarily, normal police practices, modified to meet the needs of the moment, will be adequate to cope with most unusual incidents. The supervisor's main responsibility is to distribute his forces in the initial period to prevent escalation of the occurrence and control its effects.

Many standard operating procedures are common to such unusual incidents. Field intelligence must be collated and communicated to headquarters so that necessary logistical support may be provided. A command post and staging area should be established in a strategic location near the center of operations, and directions for the operation will emanate from this post. A staging area nearby should be provided to accommodate personnel, their equipment, and the supplies needed to carry out the police mission. Ordinarily, such areas should be on the upwind side if the use of gas is contemplated.

Reconnaissance units may be required to provide current information that will enable the supervisor to meet changing conditions. Added intelligence might be provided by personnel assigned to observation posts; sometimes, they should be armed with rifles and scopes to protect control personnel from snipers.

Many of the initial tasks required by the initiation of a major police operation must be performed simultaneously. The supervisor should assign an aide to execute some of these to relieve himself of many details so that he can devote his attention to planning and directing the operation.

At times, a criminal will barricade himself in a building, hoping to evade arrest, or he may take and hold a hostage in hopes of bargaining for his freedom. The suspect may be rational or irrational.

Once the police seal off any escape route, the supervisor must decide what other action is justified under the circumstances. Usually, the police posture is that no deals will be made with criminals, yet each incident must be decided on its own merit.

In these types of cases, time usually operates to the advantage of the police. Any tactics that will delay a showdown should be used—talk is a most effective means of gaining time. Often, the suspect can be persuaded that he has nothing to gain by resisting further and may then release the hostage unharmed and give himself up.

Occasionally, he will refuse to surrender. When circumstances indicate that the hostage's life is in imminent danger and the decision is made to use force to rescue him and arrest the suspect, a cover team and an entry team should carry out a predetermined plan to force entry simultaneously with a gas assault on the suspect. When body armor and smoke and gas devices are properly used in such operations by trained personnel, danger can be minimized.

Civil disorders of all types constitute a special burden to law enforcement. Often, when these disturbances are minor, they can be handled satisfactorily with a small group of well-trained officers acting in unison under competent direction. When a supervisor assumes command in a situation of this type, he should carry out the basic procedures of advising his headquarters of the circumstances and summoning sufficient personnel and equipment to cope with the incident. When they arrive, they should be formed into squads, which should be directed to disperse the group after an appropriate dispersal order is given (as may be required by law). Once dispersal has been achieved, sufficient personnel should be deployed to prevent reformation of groups that may cause further disorder.

Major civil disorders require more widespread control measures. The decisiveness of police action carried out with sufficient force at the outset of an occurrence will have a direct effect on how serious it may become. The field supervisor is usually charged with the implementation of initial control measures. Basic procedures used to handle minor disturbances may require some modifications to adapt them to the large-scale operations often needed to control a violent disorder. The supervisor should commit his forces only when they are sufficiently strong to overwhelm the rioters swiftly and decisively, a fundamental concept in civil disorder control.

A basic squad formation most appropriate for dispersing that type of crowd should be selected. Squad members should be briefed on the strategy for dispersal and arrests, and cautioned to avoid secondary skirmishes that might jeopardize their primary mission of restoring peace and order.

The supervisor should plan his operation to disperse rioters away from residential or business districts foreign to them; rather, they should be dispersed toward their own neighborhoods, if practicable, because they will be unlikely to damage property and harm persons there. The use of chemical agents may be necessary but should be avoided if dispersal can be effected reasonably safely through other means. Follow-up measures should be taken to prevent reformation of groups that are likely to cause further disturbances, to loot, and to destroy property.

The supervisor should avoid withdrawing his control force under the theory that their presence will only inflame the riotous groups into further violence. Experience has shown that withdrawals made under this rationale have not resulted in the restoration of order but have produced only chaos and further violence.

Disputes between labor and management groups often flare into violence and pose additional problems to the police. While it is not their responsibility to adjudicate such economic disputes, police have the obligation of taking action when necessary to restore peace and preserve good order. In doing so, they must maintain a strictly impartial role. Police personnel must avoid becoming emotionally involved in the issues and must refrain from fraternizing with either the labor or management segments; they should not accept gratuities or use parking lots, telephones, or restrooms of either party.

When he becomes responsible for police operations at the scene of a strike, the supervisor should consult with labor and management representatives to reach agreements about the conduct of participants. They should be informed of the types of acts the police cannot and will not tolerate. The police must then take action when they observe illegal acts.

In carrying out his role in disaster control operations, the supervisor has as his primary function to obtain and transmit field intelligence to headquarters so that relief and control plans might be implemented without unnecessary delay. Evacuation procedures should be carried out when the effects of the occurrence are likely to endanger people in an affected area.

Ordinarily, the police are not responsible for rescue operations; that is the responsibility of other segments of government. The primary mission of the police is the control of traffic at the interior and perimeters, the provision of field intelligence on which control plans can be formulated, and the protection of life and property from unlawful acts of others.

Incidents involving bomb threats can be handled by the application of many of the same basic procedures applied in the case of other unusual occurrences. The decision to evacuate a threatened building is the responsibility of the person in charge, although the advice of the supervisor is invariably solicited. He should assign personnel to assist in evacuation if such action is needed. Search teams then should be assigned to search for the bomb systematically, and if an explosive device is located, experts should be summoned to neutralize it.

Area searches to locate a lost child should be conducted systematically to avoid gaps in the search pattern. The immediate area from which the child disappeared should be searched first despite assurances by parents that they have already looked there. Many lost children are located in the immediate area of their homes, but when they cannot be found there, the search should be extended throughout the neighborhood and should continue until the child is located or until circumstances indicate that the search be terminated.

REVIEW

Questions

1. What is normally the principal objective in deploying personnel during the initial stages of an unusual occurrence?

2. What factors will affect the supervisor's ability to perform or cause to be performed the many tasks needed during the initial stages of an unusual occurrence?

3. What factors should be considered in the establishment of a field command post?

4. What approach should be used with a rational barricaded suspect holding a hostage? An emotionally troubled suspect?

5. When officers respond to an active shooter situation, why might immediate entry into the location be necessary?

6. If chemical agents are to be used against a high-risk barricaded suspect in a business establishment, how should the gas be introduced into the building?

7. Why is a powdered chemical agent preferred over gas agents?

8. Why should a suspect be required to approach officers when he leaves his barricaded position to surrender?

9. What follow-up action should be taken after a mob has been dispersed?

10. What is the basic strategy of civil disorder control?

11. What are the primary police responsibilities in a major disaster?

12. What are some of the indicators of a radiological incident?

13. What are the Now actions that a supervisor should take when responding to a terrorist attack involving chemicals or biological weapons?

14. What are the biggest dangers at the scene of a military aircraft crash?

15. Why should the radio not be used at the scene of a bomb threat?

16. What equipment should personnel use in searching a building for a bomb?

17. What types of objects should search personnel look for in searching a building for a bomb?

18. If a bomb is not found in a building after a careful search, what should the supervisor tell the person in charge?

19. What are the primary police duties at the scene of a major fire?

20. Why should a multistory building search be conducted from the top down?

Exercises

1. Give an example of how a supervisor's miscalculations during the first few minutes of an unusual occurrence might cause irreparable harm.

2. Enumerate and discuss the standard operating procedures that the supervisor should follow in most unusual occurrences.

3. Explain how the passage of time usually operates to the advantage of the police when a barricaded suspect is holding a hostage.

4. Explain the procedures that should be followed by the supervisor and the tactics that should be used if a barricaded suspect is holding a hostage in a large market.

5. Explain the procedures that should be followed in dispersing a small disorderly crowd.

6. Describe the factors a supervisor should consider in deciding whether gas should be used against a riotous mob.

7. Explain what a supervisor should do when he first assumes command at a major strike scene.

8. Describe the instructions a supervisor should give his personnel regarding their conduct at the scene of a strike.

9. Enumerate and describe the most common offenses committed by pickets and by the management sector at a strike scene.

10. Explain the procedures that should be followed in evacuating an office building because of a bomb threat.

11. During a bomb threat, what resources may be requested to assist in the search?

12. Explain the procedures that should be followed if a bomb must be blown up in place.

13. Explain what factors should be considered in deciding whether a widespread search should be made for a missing child.

14. Describe how a search for a small child lost in a brushy area should be organized and conducted. How should one be conducted in a residential area?

15. Discuss how a search should be organized and conducted for a high-risk suspect in a dense residential district and in a business area. Discuss the two strategies that might be employed and their advantages and disadvantages.

16. Discuss how a single-story commercial building should be searched. How should a multi-story department store be searched? Assume that the suspect is dangerous in both cases.

Index

A

Accuracy, in written communications, 115
Acknowledgment of rating, 277
Active listening, in interviews, 129–130
Active shooters, response to, 294
Adler, Alfred, 147, 158
Administrative functions, 14–17
Advice giving, interviews and, 131–132
Affection for others, as leadership trait, 44
Aggression, as reaction to frustration, 153–155
Aircraft crashes, 310
Alcohol dependence (problem drinking), 164–172
  counseling for, 172–176
  deteriorating job performance and, 172
  development and symptoms of, 166–169
  indirect solicitation for help with, 171
  job-related, 171–172
  off-the-job, 170–171
  referral to professional help, 176
  treatment of, 169–172
Alcoholism, 168
Alexander, L. S., 60
Ambition, as leadership trait, 44
Anonymous complaints, 217, 221
Antilooting patrols, 315–316
Anxiety, 39, 43, 148–149, 165–167, 171, 178, 184, 186, 188, 238
Application, in the instructional process, 85–86
Area searches, 316
Arrangement, of written communications, 115–116

Arrests
  of employees, 224–225
  in major disturbances, 299
  in strike scenes, 302
  of suspects, in minor unlawful assemblies, 294
Assault tactics, 292–293
Association error, 272
Auer, J. Jeffrey, 103, 114
Autocratic communications, 113
Autocratic leaders, 35
Auxiliary services plans, 15

B

Balancing test, complaint investigation and, 234
Barricaded and hostage suspect cases, 289–294
  assault tactics in, 292–293
  direction of assault, 288
  emotionally troubled suspects and, 291–292
  preliminary operations, 289–290
  rational suspects and, 291
Bass, B. M., 38
Bias
  elimination of, interviews and, 130–131
  rating errors and, 269–270
Blanchard, Kenneth H., 13, 36, 38, 48
Bomb threats, 310–313
Briefs, 120
Brown, James W., 78
Buckley, Joseph P., 134
Bugelski, B. R., 88–89
Building searches, 320–321
Business district searches, 320

C

Caldero, Michael A., 180, 191
Catharsis, 148

Center for Leadership Studies (CLS), 38
Central tendency, performance rating and, 271
Certainty, discipline and, 204
Chemical, biological, or radiological attacks, 304–309
  indicators of, 304–305
  response actions, 306–309
City of Canton, Ohio v. Harris (1989), 70
Civil disorders, 295–300
  major disturbances, 296–300
  minor unlawful assemblies, 295–296
Clarity of expression, 115
Color-coded threat level system, 65
Command post, establishment of a, 284
Command presence and leadership, 39–40
Commands. *See also* Orders (order giving)
  direct, 51
Commendations by leaders, 48
Commission on Accreditation for Law Enforcement Agencies (CALEA), 17, 119
Common sense, leadership and, 41
Communication(s), 101–121.
  See also Language barriers, interpersonal communications and; Written communications
  autocratic, 113
  barriers to effective, 103–108
  characteristics of, 113–114
  complexity of communications channels and, 107
  consistency in, 111–112
  cultural, environmental, and psychological factors in, 102
  democratic, 113–114

Communication(s) (*continued*)
    empathy and, 110
    failure to listen and, 103
    fear of criticism and, 105
    feedback and, 110
    filtering and, 105–106
    free rein, 114
    individual sentiments and
        attitudes and, 106–107
    intentional suppression or
        manipulation of communica-
        tions and, 107
    jumping to conclusions and, 105
    language barriers and, 104
    major disturbances and, 297
    noise and, 104
    objectives of, 109–110
    of orders, 52
    overcoming barriers to effective,
        108–113
    overloading of communications
        channels and, 107–108
    overstructuring of communica-
        tions channels, 108
    "practicing what you preach"
        and, 112
    psychological size and, 104
    status differences and, 103
    as supervisory responsibility, 8
    total setting of, 109–110
    types of communicators, 114
Communications channels
    complexity of, 107–108
    overloading of, 107–108
    overstructuring of, 108
Community policing, leadership
    issues in, 62–65
Community Policing Consortium,
    96
Competence, technical and
    supervisory, 4
Complaint investigation
    procedures and techniques,
        216–240
    anonymous complaints, 217
    arrest and booking of an
        employee, 224–225

balancing test and, 234
case preparation, 216–217
classification of complaint
    investigations, 237
collection of negative informa-
    tion, 225
disposition of complaints, 238
employee rights and, 234
face-to-face encounters, avoid-
    ance of, 229
follow-up inquiries, 219–220
imposition of a penalty, 238
interviewing accused employees,
    226–227
intoxicated persons, complaints
    from, 221–222
investigative aids and, 231–232
investigative reports, 234–236
legal counsel and, 227–228
lineups and, 230
news media and, 237
non-job-related misconduct
    and, 218
notification to the accused
    employee concerning
    disposition, 238
notification to the complainant
    concerning disposition, 238
observed infractions, 218–220
offensive terminology, avoidance
    of, 236
physical tests, 232–233
premature conclusions,
    avoidance of, 223–224
prevention of additional
    harm, 224
primary complaints, 220–221
procedural due process require-
    ments, 233–234
promptness of investigation, 225
recording of complaints,
    222–223
reporting procedures, 234–236
searches and, 229–230
sources of complaints, 217
types of complaints, 220–222
written statements and, 228

Compliments by leaders, 48
Composite ratings, 275
Conclusions
    drawing of, 54–55
    in written communications,
        114–115
Conferences, 91–92
Confidential agreements, 131
Consistency in communicating,
    111–112
Contractual violations and
    grievances, 197
Controllers, supervisory officers
    as, 8
Coordinating, 14, 18–20
COPNET, 96
Coroner's transcripts, 213
Counseling
    for emotionally troubled subor-
        dinates, 178–179
    for problem drinkers, 172–176
Courtesy, as leadership trait, 44–45
Crank, John P., 180, 191
Critical incident technique, evalua-
    tion of employees and, 248
Criticism
    fear of, interpersonal communi-
        cations and, 105
    by leaders, 48
Cross-references, in investigation
    reports, 236

D

Decision making, 54
    as supervisory responsibility, 8
Delegation, 25–28
    failures of, 26–27
    personnel development by,
        27–28
    process of, 27
    of staff projects, 28–29
Democratic communications,
    113–114
Democratic leaders, 35
Demonstrations, 90–91
Department of Homeland Security
    initiatives, 321–323

Deployment of field forces. *See* Tactical deployment of field forces (in unusual incidents)

Depression, 182–183

Deterrence, punishment and, 207–208

Direct commands, 51–52

Directing, 14, 18

Disaster control, 302–303

Disciplinary action interviews, 138–139

Discipline, 200–214. *See also* Complaint investigation procedures and techniques;Punishment
  adverse effects of punishment and, 202
  certainty and, 204
  complaint investigation policy and, 211
  detection of problem employee behavior and, 203–204
  by example, 208
  failures of, 239
  fairness and impartiality and, 205–206
  forms of, 201–202
  interdependency of morale, esprit de corps, and, 209
  leadership and, 40
  negative, 201
  news media and, 237
  positive, 201
  reversals of administrative actions and, 210
  swiftness of punishment and, 205
  unsustained disciplinary actions, results of, 210
  upward, 209

Dispersal orders, 298

Display aids, 94–95

Display of weapons, in labor disputes, 301

Dissatisfaction of employees, 190–198. *See also* Grievances, employee
  due process violations and, 193–195

inept supervisory practices and, 191–192
  management failures and, 192–195
  misunderstandings of policies, rules, and procedures and, 192
  recognition of, 196
  rule enforcement and, 193
  rules of conduct and, 192–193
  supervisory approaches to, 196
  working environment and, 191

Diverse workforce, supervising, 57–59

Division of work, 23–24

Drawing of conclusions, 54–55

Drinking problems. *See* Problem drinking

Drives, 146–147

Due process, procedural, complaint investigation and, 233–234

Due process violations, employee dissatisfaction and, 193–195

Duplicated aids, 95

E

Editing written communications, 120

Effect, principle of, 74–75

Eisenson, Jon, 103, 114

Electronic media devices, 96

Email, effective managing, 117
  processing and organizing, key factors, 117–118

Emotional and personal problems, 176–187
  depression, 182–183
  family discord, 184–186
  management and remediation of, 179–187
  occupational stress and, 179–181
  physiological symptoms of, 177
  psychological symptoms of, 177
  supervisory role and, 177–178
  trauma-producing incidents, 186–187

Empathy, interpersonal communications and, 110

Employee-centered approach, in interviews, 128

Employee standards. *See* Performance rating standards and methods

Employment interviews, 133–135

Empowering environment, 38–39

Enthusiasm, as leadership trait, 44

Escape (escapism), frustrated employees and, 156–157

Ethics, leadership and, 41

Evacuation
  bomb threats and, 310–311
  disaster control and, 302–303
  of fire areas, 315

Evaluation
  of personnel. *See* Personnel evaluation systems
  of results, 140–141

Example setting, 56

Exception principle, 28

Excuses, frustrated employees and, 157–158

External complaints, 217

F

Face-to-face encounters, avoidance of, complaint investigation and, 229

Failures, management, 192

Fairness, discipline and, 205–206

Faith, as leadership trait, 45

Fayol, Henri, 200

Fear, as a negative motivator, 42–43

Feedback, interpersonal communications and, 110

Female employees, 57

Female supervisors, 57–59

Ferguson, R. Fred, 45, 107, 110, 132–133, 195, 208, 276

Field problems, 89

Field tactics, major disturbances and, 297–299

Field trips, 96

Filtering, interpersonal communications and, 105–106
Fires, major, 313–315
Fiscal plans, 16
Fixations
    frustrated employees and, 149–150
    regressive behavior and, 148–149
Follow-up
    complaints and, 219–220
    order giving and, 51
    staff meetings and, 92
Follow-up actions, in major disturbances, 300
Force, use of, in major disturbances, 299
Forced-choice standards, 261
Format of written communications, 116
Four Ds for decision-making model, 118–119
Fourth Amendment, searches and, 229–230
Fraternization, 56
Fraternizing, avoidance of, in labor disputes, 301
Free rein communications, 114
Freeway therapy, 195
Friendliness, as leadership trait, 44
Frustration (frustrated employees), 149–150
    aggression as reaction to, 153–155
    attitude of resignation and, 155
    barriers causing, 151
    escape and, 156–157
    excuses and rationalizations and, 157–158
    fixations and, 159
    nature of, 150–151
    performance and, 151–152
    prevention of, 159–160
    reactions to, 153–159
    regressive reactions and, 158–159
    relief for, 160–161

Fryer, Douglas H., 160
Functional organization, 21–22

G
Gaines, Larry, 15, 62–63, 65, 225, 269
Gender bias, 61–62
Grapevine, 108, 111, 208
Grievance interviews, 137–138
Grievances, employee, 196–197. See also Dissatisfaction of employees
    noncontractual matters, 197
Group discussions, 91
Group ratings, 275
Guest speakers, 89

H
Haar, R. N., 57
Halo effect, performance rating and, 272
Harassment, 61–62
Hayakawa, S. I., 112
Hersey, Paul, 13, 36, 38
Holmes, Oliver Wendell, 211
Homeland Security Advisory System, 321
Hostage and barricaded suspect cases, 289–294
    assault tactics in, 292–293
    direction of assault, 288
    emotionally troubled suspects and, 291–292
    preliminary operations, 289
    rational suspects and, 291
Human relations, leadership and, 46–49

I
Iannone, Marvin D., 201
Ideal employee standard, 260
Impartiality, discipline and, 205–206
Impersonal attitude, in labor disputes, 301
Implied orders, 52
Incident command system (ICS), 284–285

Indifference, evaluation system failure and, 245
Individual trait ratings, 276
Inexperienced employees, orders to, 52
Inferiority complex, 147–148
Instruction, as a supervisory responsibility, 72
Instructional process. See Learning; Training (teaching)
    five steps of teaching, 83–86
    general problems affecting teaching method, 86–87
    job analysis and material selection, 80
    learning by association, 83
    lesson plan, 80–83
    questions and, 93
    teacher ineffectiveness, common causes of, 87
    teaching aids and, 94–96
    teaching sequence, 81–83
Integrity, as leadership trait, 44
Intelligence, as leadership trait, 45
Intensity, principle of, 76
Interest and learning effectiveness, 78
Internal complaints, 217
International Association of Chiefs of Police, 96
International Association of Women Police, 59
Interpersonal communications. See Communication(s)
Interrogations, 124
Interviews, 123–141
    of accused employees, 226–227
    active listening in, 129–130
    advice giving and, 131–132
    attitude of interviewer in, 127–128
    conducting, 126–130
    confidential agreements and, 131
    definition of, 123
    disciplinary action, 138–139
    elimination of bias and, 130–131

employee-centered approach in, 128
evaluation of results of, 140–141
grievance, 137–138
interrogation v. interview, 124
major functions of, 124
opening of, 126–127
performance rating and, 277
personnel, 132–140
preparation for, 124–126
privacy and, 125
problem-solving, 138
progress, 135–137
psychological reactions in, 132
questions in, 127
recording of results of, 140
separation, 139–140
unsuccessful, causes of, 141
Intimidation, as a negative motivator, 42
Intoxicated persons. *See* Problem drinking
complaints from, 221–222
Intoxication, physical tests of, 232–233
Introduction, in the instructional process, 84
Investigation of complaints. *See* Complaint investigation procedures and techniques
Investigative reports, complaint investigation and, 234–236
Irwin, John V., 103, 114

J
James, William, 83
Job dissatisfaction. *See* Dissatisfaction of employees
Job stress, 179–181
Johnson, Spencer, 48
Jumping to conclusions, interpersonal communications and, 105

K
Kappeler, Victor, 65

L
Labor disputes, 300–302
avoidance of fraternizing in, 301
control tactics in, 301
display of weapons in, 301
maintenance of impersonal attitude in, 301
meeting with labor and management representatives in, 301
strike scene arrests in, 302
Language barriers, interpersonal communications and, 104
Language of leaders, 47–48
Leaders (leadership), 33
command presence and, 39–40
commendations and praise by, 48
community policing and, 62–65
conference. *See* Conferences
criticism and reprimands by, 48
definition of, 32
democratic or participatory, 35
development of ability of, 33–34
elements of, 40–41
and empowerment, transformational, 38–39
failure of, symptoms of, 62
free rein or laissez-faire, 36
human relations and, 46–49
language of, 47–48
manner of, 47
personality of, 45–46
selection of a style of, 39
situational, 36–38
as supervisory responsibility, 9
traits of, 44–45
types of, 35–36
Learning. *See* Training (teaching)
adult learner differences, 77
by association, 83
interest and learning effectiveness, 78
rate of, 76, 77
Learning rate, 76, 77
Lectures, as teaching method, 88–89

Legal counsel, complaint investigation and, 227
Leniency, rating errors and, 270
Lesson plan, 80–83
Liability, vicarious, 212–213
Lie detector tests, 231
Line organization, 20–21
Lineups, complaint investigation and, 230–231
Listening, 112
active, in interviews, 129–130
failure to listen, 103
Logistics aide, 286–287
Lost children, 316–318
Lucia, Al, 201

M
MacGregor, J., 38
Mager, Robert F., 80
Magnuson, D, S., 60
Major disturbances, 296–300
Management, supervisors and, 2
Management failures, 192–195
Managing by walking around (MBWA), 133
Manipulation of communications, 107
Manner of leaders, 47
Manuals, 119–120
Marginal employees, supervision of the, 50–51
Miller, Larry S., 7, 136, 211
Misunderstandings of policies, rules, and procedures and, 192
Moderation in supervision, 55
Modesty, as leadership trait, 45
Morale, interdependency of discipline, esprit de corps, and, 209–210
Moral integrity, as leadership trait, 44
Morash, M., 57
More, Harry W., 7, 136, 211
Motivation, learning rate and performance and, 76–78
Motivation of employees, 41–43

Multicultural work environment, 58

Multigenerational workforce, supervising, 60–61

Muscio, B., 127

N

National Counterterrorism Center (NCTC), 312–313

National Incident Management System (NIMS), 285

National Latino Officers Association of America, 59

National Organization of Black Law Enforcement Executives, 59

Needs, 146–147

Negative discipline, 201–202

Negative information, collection of, 225

News media, discipline and, 237

Noise, interpersonal communications and, 104

Noncontractual matters, employee grievances and, 197

Non-job-related employee behavior, supervisory influence on, 195

Non-job-related misconduct, 218

Now, Scene, Future (NSF) model, 282

Numerical standard, for performance rating, 260–261

O

Occupational stress, 179–181

Offensive terminology, avoidance of, in personnel investigation reports, 236

Officer to supervisor, 9–11
    guidelines for, 10–11

Open-area searches, 318

Operational plans, 15

Orders (order giving), 51–53
    direct commands as, 51–52
    following up on, 53
    framed as requests, 52
    implied or suggested, 52

to inexperienced or unreliable employees, 52
    method of communication of, 53
    requests for volunteers and, 53
    verbal, 53
    written, 53, 114–117

Organizational knowledge, 4–5

Organizational structures, 20–23

Organizing, 14, 17

Overhead questions, 93

Overloading of communications channels, 107–108

Overstructuring of communications channels, 108

Oversupervision, 55

Overweighting errors, 272

P

Pagination, of investigation reports, 236

Panel discussions, 91

Participatory leaders, 35–36

Peer counseling programs, 187

Penalties, imposition of, 238

Performance, frustration and, 151–152

Performance rating standards and methods, 242–277
    acknowledgment of rating, 277
    central tendency, 271
    common rating errors, 269–270
    composite ratings, 275
    discussion of rating with employee, 276–277
    evaluation of employees and, 256
    evaluation period and, 274
    follow-up observations, 277
    forced-choice standards, 261–268
    group ratings, 275
    halo effect and, 272
    ideal employee standard, 260
    individual trait ratings, 276
    interview with the employee, 277

methods of rating, 275–276
    numerical standard, 260–261
    overweighting or recency errors, 272
    ranking of employees, 259
    rater characteristics and, 268–269
    related traits errors, 272
    reliability of rating reports, 273
    representative employee, 260
    subjectivity errors, 272
    validity of ratings, 273–274
    written notification of rating, 277

Personal bias, rating errors and, 271

Personality, of leaders, 45

Personal problems. *See* Emotional and personal problems

Personal warmth, as leadership trait, 44

Personnel evaluation systems, 242–277
    critical incident technique and, 248
    employee pressures and failure of, 245–246
    failure to train raters and, 246
    gathering and recording of performance data, 247–248
    objectives of, 243
    performance standards and, 256
    rating abuses and, 246
    rating criteria and, 256–259
    rating shortcuts and, 247
    rating traits and, 248–255
    recording methods and, 247–248
    slipshod procedures and, 247
    usefulness and value of, 243–245

Personnel interviews, 132–140
    employment interviews, 133–135
    informal interviews, 133

Personnel officers, supervisory officers as, 5

Personnel records, checking, 225

Physical energy, as leadership trait, 44
Physical integrity, as leadership trait, 44
Picket lines, in labor disputes, 301–302
Planning, 14–17
    interviews, 124
    staff meetings and, 92
    as supervisory responsibility, 5–9
Planning projects, 29
Plan of action, in written communications, 116
Police Executive Research Forum (PERF), 64, 96
Policies, 16
Policy manuals, 16
Polygraphs, 231
POSDCORB, 14
Positive discipline, 201
Praise by leaders, 48
Pratt, William V., 44
Premature conclusions, avoidance of, 223–224
Presentation, in the instructional process, 85
Press relations officer, 286–287
Primacy, principle of, 76
Primary complaints, 220–221
Privacy, interviews and, 125
Problem drinking, 164–166
    counseling for, 172–176
    deteriorating job performance and, 172
    development and symptoms of, 166–169
    indirect solicitation for help with, 171
    job-related, 171–172
    off-the-job, 170–172
    referral to professional help, 176
    treatment of, 169–172
Problem-solving interviews, 138
Procedural due process, complaint investigation and, 233–234
Progress interviews, 135–140
Projected aids, 95

Psychological aspects of supervision, 145–161
    catharsis, 148
    drives, satisfactions, and needs, 146–147
    fixation and regressive behavior, 148–149
    frustrated employees. See Frustration (frustrated employees)
    inferiority complex, 147–148
Psychological problems. See Emotional and personal problems
Psychological reactions in interviews, 132
Psychological size, interpersonal communications and, 104
Psychology, leadership and, 41
Punishment
    adverse effects of, 202
    consistency of, 206–207
    deterrence for others and, 207–208
    fairness and impartiality and, 205–208
    as a negative motivator, 42
    requisites of, 204
    swiftness of, 205

Q
Questions
    instructional process and, 93
    in interviews, 126–130
    types of, 125–126

R
Ranking of employees, performance rating and, 259
Rating criteria, personnel evaluation systems and, 256–259
Rating standards for employee performance. See Performance rating standards and methods
Rationalizations, frustrated employees and, 157–158
Readiness, principle of, 74
Recency, principle of, 76
Recency errors, 272

Recognition, as motivating force, 42
Recommendations, in written communications, 116
Records, personnel, checking, 225–226
Regression (regressive behavior), 158–159
    frustrated employees and, 158
Reid, John E., 134
Related traits, error of, 272
Relay questions, 93
Repetition, principle of, 75–76
Reporting procedures, complaint investigation and, 234–236
Reprimands by leaders, 48–49
Requests, 52
Rescue, disaster control and, 303
Researching projects, 29
Residential search patterns, 317–318
Resignation, attitude of, 156
Respondeat superior, doctrine of, 212
Reverse questions, 93
Review, in the instructional process, 85
Roethlisberger, Fritz J., 112, 146
Rogers, C. R., 112, 148
Role playing, 89
Rule enforcement, 193
Rules and regulations, 17
Rules of conduct, 192–193

S
Satisfactions, 146–147
Search(es)
    area, 316
    building, 320–321
    business district, 320
    complaint investigation and, 229–230
    for lost children, 316–317
    open-area, 318
    for other suspects, 294
    of premises, bomb threats and, 310

Search(es) (*continued*)
  residential, 317
  strategies for, 319
  for wanted persons, 318–321
Search teams, 317
Second-party complaints, 222
Seiter, R. P., 38–39
Self-appraisal, situational analysis
    and, 43
Separation interviews, 139–140
Sexual harassment, 61–62
Sherman, Mark, 201
Shusta, R. M., 58
Simplicity, in written communica-
    tions, 115
Sincerity, as leadership trait, 44
Situational analysis, self-appraisal
    and, 43–44
Situational leadership, 36–38
Sniper fire, hostile, 299
"Snoopervision," 55
Southern Police Leadership
    Institute, 34
Span of control, 25
Staffing, 17–18
Staff meetings, 92–93
Staff organization, 22–23
Staff projects, delegation of, 28–29
Status differences, interpersonal
    communications and, 103
Stress
  management of, 89–90
  occupational, 179–181
Strike scene arrests, 302
Style of written communications,
    116
Subjectivity, error of, performance
    rating and, 272–273
Subordinates
  keeping informed, 110–111
  knowledge of, 50
Suggested orders, 52
Summary, in written communica-
    tions, 116
Supervisory competence, 4
Supervisory influence on non-job-
    related employee behavior, 195

Supervisory position, definition
    and role of, 2
Supervisory responsibilities, 5–9
Suppression of information, inten-
    tional, 107
Sutherland, Sidney S., 93
Swanson, Charles R., 22, 126
Swiftness of punishment, 205
Symonds, P. M., 148–149

T
Tactical deployment of field
    forces (in unusual incidents),
    281–323
  aircraft crashes and, 310
  arrest of suspect, 294
  assault tactics, 292–293
  barricaded persons and,
    287–288
  basic procedures for unusual
    occurrences, 282
  bomb threats and, 310–313
  chemical, biological, or radio-
    logical attacks and, 304–309
  civil disorders and, 295–296
  command post, establishment
    of a, 284
  communications of field
    intelligence and, 283–284
  Department of Homeland Secu-
    rity initiatives and, 321–323
  direction of assault and, 288
  disaster control, 302–303
  follow-up actions in major
    disturbances, 300
  hostages and, 287–288
  hostile sniper fire and, 299
  incident command system (ICS)
    and, 284–285
  in labor disputes, 300–301
  limited withdrawal of
    forces, 300
  logistics aide and press relations
    officer, 286
  lost children and, 316–318
  major disturbances and,
    296–300

  major fires and, 313–316
  Now, Scene, Future (NSF)
    model, 282
  operational guidelines for
    unusual occurrences, 287
  reconnaissance and, 285–286
  rescue operations, 303
  response to active shooters, 294
  search for other suspects, 294
  supervisory responsibilities in
    unusual occurrences,
    281–282
  use of force, 299
  wanted persons and, 318–321
Tactical plans, 14–15
Taylor, Robert W., 22, 165, 197
Teachers, ineffectiveness of, com-
    mon causes of, 87–88
Teaching. *See* Training (teaching)
Teaching aids, instructional process
    and, 94–96
Teaching sequence, 81–83
Technical competence, 4
Technical skill, as leadership
    trait, 45
Territo, Leonard, 22, 126, 165,
    187, 197
Tests, in the instructional
    process, 86
Thornton, James W. Jr., 78
Three-dimensional aids, 95–96
Trainers, supervisory officers as,
    5–6
Training (teaching), 70–74.
    See also Instructional
    process;Learning; Teachers,
    ineffectiveness of, common
    causes of
  adult learner differences, 77–78
  as a supervisory responsibility,
    72
  causes and effects of, 70
  failure of, 87
  five steps of, 83–86
  general problems affecting
    teaching method, 86–87
  importance of, 70–72

instructor's approach to, 71–72
interest and learning effectiveness, 78
methods of, 88–92
need for, 72–74
patterns of, 78–79
principles of, 74–76
process variables, 76–78
rate of learning, 76–77
remedy for, 70–71
resistance to, 33
Traits, of leaders, 44–45
Transfer treatment, 195
Trauma-producing incidents, 186–187

U
Understanding, communications and, 112–113
Unions, working with, 198
Unity of command, 24–25
Unreliable employees, orders to, 52

Unusual incidents, tactical deployment of field forces in. *See* Tactical deployment of field forces
Upward discipline, 209

V
Validity of ratings, 273–274
Verbal aptitude, as leadership trait, 45
Vicarious liability, 212–213
Vitality, as leadership trait, 44
Volcker Commission, 4
Volunteers, requests for, 53

W
Wanted persons, 318–321
Warmth, personal, as leadership trait, 44
West Point Command and Leadership Program, 34
Whisenand, Paul M., 45, 107, 110, 132–133, 195, 208, 220, 276

Withdrawal of forces, limited, 300
Women employees, 59
Women supervisors, 57
Workshops, 90
Written communications, 114–117
accuracy of, 115
arrangement of, 115–116
briefs, 120
clarity of expression in, 115
editing, 120
e-mail, 116–117
manuals, 119–120
orders, 119–120
simplicity of, 115
style of, 116
summary, conclusions, recommendations, and plan of action in, 116
typical deficiencies in, 121
Written statements, complaint investigation and, 228